C0068 97716

KV-749-996

HAVE YOU YOU READ GEORGE'S PODCAST?

HAVE YOU YOU READ GEORGE'S PODCAST?

H

HODDER &
STOUGHTON

First published in Great Britain in 2022 by Hodder & Stoughton
An Hachette UK company

1

Copyright © George Mpanga 2022

Transcribed material reproduced in association with BBC Sounds.

The right of George Mpanga to be identified as the Author
of the Work has been asserted by him in accordance with
the Copyright, Designs and Patents Act 1988.

A CIP catalogue record for this title is available from the British Library

Hardback ISBN 978 1 529 39579 2
eBook ISBN 978 1 529 39580 8

Typeset in Galano Classic by Hewer Text UK Ltd, Edinburgh
Printed and bound in Great Britain by Clays Ltd, Elcograf S.p.A.

Hodder & Stoughton policy is to use papers that are natural, renewable
and recyclable products and made from wood grown in sustainable
forests. The logging and manufacturing processes are expected to
conform to the environmental regulations of the country of origin.

Hodder & Stoughton Ltd
Carmelite House
50 Victoria Embankment
London EC4Y 0DZ

www.hodder.co.uk

CONTENTS

Introduction   vii

Chapter One   1
Episode 1: Listen Closer   2
Episode 2: Popcorn   15
Episode 3: Grenfell Special   29
Episode 3.5: Grenfell II   47
Episode 4: It's On Us   78
Episode 5: Press Play   99
Episode 6: The Journey (Part 1)   113
Episode 7: The Journey (Part 2)   142
Episode 8: Sanyu's World   158

Chapter Two   191
Episode 9: Sabrina's Boy   192
Episode 10: A Bedtime Story   210
Episode 11: Writer's Block   229
Episode 12: A Night to REMember   249
Episode 13: A North West Story   274
Episode 14: A Hard Taskmaster   292
Episode 15: Who Am I?   311
Episode 16: Loose Ends   329
Episode 17: The Bag   352
Episode 18: Concurrent Affairs   372

Chapter Three   385
Episode 19: Common Ground   388
Episode 20: Young   406
Episode 21: Flying the Flag   427
Episode 22: Mavado & Vybz   448
Episode 23: Back to the UG   470

Episode 24: The Sixties   491
Episode 25: Who Hurt R&B?   510
Episode 26: Vibrations   527
Episode 27: True Love   550
Episode 28: Songs Make Jobs   567

Acknowledgments   585

INTRODUCTION

Issa Mix

Firstly, thank you for taking the time to read this book. If you're familiar with my work, you'll know me as a spoken word poet – meaning
my words are *heard* more than they're read. If you're not familiar
with my work, here's a disclaimer: *it's never one thing* – always a mix.
For example, this book contains the script of my audio-series, *Have
You Heard George's Podcast?*, but the podcast itself isn't just a
recording of conversations I've had with my friends – it's a mix of
rhymes, stories, music and more. Let me explain why . . .

Songs to Stories

From 2013–2015 I was signed to the world-famous music label,
Island Records. This phase of my career was important because it
reintroduced me to making songs in a studio, like I used to do as a
teenager. Island and I enjoyed some great moments together (like a
sold-out tour and a BRIT Award nomination) but in many ways, we
wanted different things.

Most labels want their artists to be all over the radio, but this
wouldn't work for me. I've never been a chart-topper, and to be fair
that was never my aim. My aim has always been to share a message
with the next generation and this is where I struggled with the radio
game.

My label wanted me to become a popstar without a clear idea of
where the message fit in that picture. In their defence, I can't think of
an artist like me who is all over the radio. For as long as I've been alive,
the most successful songs from young Black men have come from
street culture. As much as I love street music, I've always felt that
over-focusing on it (as an audience) limits our ability to reflect on
how we live. This leads to a vicious cycle: street culture produces
successful music ⟶ street music makes street artists rich ⟶ the
people profiting from street culture aren't motivated to change it ⟶

vulnerable young people buy into street culture ⊡ vulnerable young people become street artists, and the cycle continues.

As a teenager, I committed myself to breaking this cycle. My theory was that the streets could eventually use music to create a financial safety net for young people living in poverty. This could be as simple as community investment in local talent, which would bring financial reward to the whole community if that local talent does well commercially. Sure, not everyone might make it, but it would be an affordable way to strengthen community spirit. That would create a virtuous cycle – the opposite of a vicious cycle. But I couldn't imagine anyone making time to design this system, unless I influenced the generation after me to do it themselves.

For this reason, trying to dominate the radio would be a waste of my time. When I rapped in my teens, I was a good-enough songwriter, but I had always stood out as a storyteller. And there's only so much you can cover in a 3–4-minute song – I needed more space to explain my vision. Fast forward to 2015, I finally sat down with then-president of Island Records, Darcus Beese, as well as chairman of Universal Music UK, David Joseph, and expressed my feeling that we should part ways. To both Darcus and David's credit, they respectfully accepted my position, and have remained supportive ever since. But I still had fans who wanted an album from me, and with my newfound freedom, I intended to deliver a story-driven body of work.

The Netflix Effect

A lot changed when I started prioritising storytelling over songwriting. The first thing I did was watch more TV. The streaming service, Netflix, became my best friend, and I quickly realised that my next body of work should be a series. Like my favourite TV shows, it should have the listener on the edge of their seat, not wanting to miss an episode, campaigning online for another season. Because I had such an elaborate vision to lay out, this concept appealed to me. Shows like *The Wire* and *House of Cards* proved to me that a well-told story could hold someone's attention way longer than a song could. And even though people showed my music a lot of love, I had never experienced that kind of demand before. Most artists haven't. Since

I was now focusing more on stories than songs, this Netflix Effect seemed achievable.

The Disney Effect
Another breakthrough came directly from my childhood. One day I overheard a song from Disney's 1991 animated film, *Beauty and the Beast*, and surprisingly I remembered all the words. For years, I thought it was crazy how musical memory had the power to transport you through time, but for some reason this experience blew my mind. I hadn't watched that movie in ages, and I can't have been older than five when I learned the words. Yet here I was, feeling the emotions of an infant through a song. It occurred to me that Disney music probably had this effect on billions of people, long after they had outgrown the genre. If I could give my listeners this same experience, I could create a world in their hearts that might open them up to new possibilities. This could be how I influence street culture: reimagining our story with the Disney Effect.

A Dead Man's Imagination
Disney and Netflix percolated in my mind for about a year. During that year, I experimented with independent music releases, and they confirmed what I already knew: selling songs put me in a competition that undervalued my talent. After a year of pouring money into my own production, promotion, videos and a whole independent tour, I was exhausted, with not enough to show for my efforts. I started to miss my family and decided to take my nephews on a surprise trip to Disney World, which changed my life.

Having recently rediscovered my respect for Disney movies, I developed a new appreciation for Walt Disney's imagination. What amazed me even more was that the man himself had been dead for over sixty years, yet we were still able to walk through what he saw in his mind. Obviously, there's now a machine in place of the man, and its tentacles are far-reaching. But under the influence of my nephews, I took a childlike view of the whole experience, and cherished the fact that I was standing in a dead man's imagination. This is what I wanted for my audience: to find happiness in a vision that only existed in my head.

We Are The Story

Throughout my transition from songwriting to storytelling, I realised some things. Firstly, I wasn't interested in writing for the sake of writing. I needed a purpose – something I would later thank myself for saying. Secondly, I had to write about what I knew. Client work (like TV ads) taught me how to write really specific poems for really specific audiences, but this took a lot of research. If I wanted the Netflix Effect, i.e. a committed audience, I would need to write a lot, which would take longer if I had to learn new subjects from scratch. So where would my stories come from?

Sanyu

I decided that education was the answer. The best thing I could do was help someone understand something about the world, and I had countless ways of doing that – all related to storytelling. A few months after a Disney World trip, I took my nephews to Uganda for the first time. Here, their influence on me grew even stronger, as all the hours spent listening to their thoughts eventually gave me an idea: what if I created a fun, child-friendly character who only existed to help people learn? Like Mickey Mouse, this character could form the cornerstone of a whole universe. And, like Walt Disney, I could use this character to share a unique view of the world.

It all came together on that Uganda trip during a visit to my mum's old school, Gayaza High School for Girls. Maama asked (told) me to help record an interview with her former schoolteachers, and I agreed. While there, I met a maths teacher named Mr Dungu, who had recently launched a learning programme called 'Farm Camp'. The idea was for students to develop a practical and economic understanding of farming in Ugandan life, over a week-long course. To make this learning feel complete, homework from other classes would relate to the farm – at least, that's what Mr Dungu hoped. His vision was for Gayaza girls to start thinking about the needs of their country as early as possible, so that they would eventually make good leaders. I loved it. I'd had a similar idea for years: using a young person's local economy to explain what they're learning in class – bringing education to life.

This was the day Sanyu was conceived. Over the next few weeks, my mind kept returning to the idea of a young Gayaza girl, narrating her way through life. I could hear her happy little voice explaining everything she'd learned at Farm Camp, talking in an excited, love-able way that made you care. But once we got back to the UK, I felt myself falling into the research trap. I knew nothing about farming, and I wasn't about to learn, just to develop a concept that no one asked for. Still, I believed in the idea, so instead of biting off more than I could chew, I wrote about what I knew: the idea.

In order to guilt-trip myself into working on Sanyu, I wrote her a script from the perspective of a young idea in the fantasy world of George's Mind. It was a two-minute poem asking for the support of George's audience. Writing this actually helped me come to terms with the fact that I was unsure of my next step, and motivated me to take more responsibility for my ideas. It paid off – what followed was a creative outpouring! I quickly wrote more and more of Sanyu's perspective, taking tips from my nephews' favourite shows. Sure, I wasn't any closer to writing about Farm Camp, but I'd found some-thing even better. By using a character to explain my internal process, I was able to write with purpose and confidence. I wouldn't have to do any research, because I was already an expert on my own perspec-tive. This was the final stage of the transition from songwriting to storytelling: I was no longer looking for a story to tell – I had become the story.

Goldmine

By giving a voice to an idea in my head, I unlocked a goldmine of creativity. It was storytelling without limits. The concept was elastic – like animation – meaning it could go in any direction: serious, silly, whatever. More importantly, it could also help a listener understand my process and believe in theirs. Before long, the world around Sanyu started to build itself; it's like different ideas were inspired to step up and be unique, like her. I was relearning to trust my instincts, recording things from parts of my imagination that I had never expressed out loud. If I could bring my audience this far, then I could take them anywhere.

Later that year, the South London rapper, Dave, released a song called 'Question Time', criticising the British government on everything from austerity to arms deals. The song resonated so deeply with so many, and inspired me to talk more plainly about current affairs. I found myself in my element once again, writing longer pieces about the ups and downs of Theresa May's government, as well as the ongoing migrant crisis. This came just before my last adventure with the nephews that year – Christmas in Uganda. Mentally, I was in a great place. I'd achieved my goal of spending more quality time with loved ones, and I had a sense of my next creative step. But when I returned to the UK, I got a reality check in the form of a conversation with my mum, who asked me 'What about the Ends'?

The Ends

My mum's question tapped into the darkest part of my life; many of my friends in the Ends (the Black inner city) were trapped. Some of them ended up in conflict with each other, while others were struggling with the post-traumatic stress of street life, and a new generation was getting locked up. Fathers were separated from their children, the drug trade remained as influential as ever and old tensions flared up unexpectedly. Since my teens, I have detested the helplessness we all feel when we discuss these aspects of our community. But when my mum asked me 'What about the Ends?' I was confronted with that familiar feeling of frustration and shame. I couldn't jump on a plane or throw money at my guilt to fix this one. I had to re-engage with the streets.

Maama's question was reiterated just days later by my friend, Marc, who sat me down one afternoon in Tottenham and patiently explained that 'you've been quiet for too long'. Marc had always respected my move away from the music industry and supported my rebirth. He understood that it took time to reimagine my role in society, and he embraced this long, messy process. But as someone deeply connected to the streets, he couldn't help feeling like I had a responsibility to provide direction for our young people. These early interventions of 2018 triggered a wave of deep, emotional conversations in studios, cars and apartment blocks between me and my counterparts in the streets – Black men who had silently blessed every step of my journey, celebrating my wins as their own, having accepted their place in the system. Sanyu inspired much of these conversations. I would (re)connect with real gangsters and play them rough demos of this high-pitched Ugandan girl who was really me with a faux accent, voicing an idea living in my mind. And they loved it. Guys with heavy problems on their shoulders – they became like children when they heard this world unfold in their ears. It's like the innocence of my nephews was transmitted into them via Sanyu. We talked about storytelling and the need to show young people something new. We got philosophical about how things could be, and I was reawakened to the need for progress.

George's Podcast

After a few months of reconnecting with the streets, I knew it was time to record *Have You Heard George's Podcast?* (*HYHGP*). I'd had the name in mind for a while; I liked that it wasn't tied to a meaning, so I could redefine it every episode. The title was also a marketing thing – I hoped that the podcast would be a big enough talking point someday that people would be embarrassed to admit they hadn't heard it. So, I came up with a plan to record this new content and tour the country with it, in the space of two months (that's why the first episode features a scene 'from my Birmingham show'). I started off with my good friend, Mikey J, the legendary grime and hip-hop producer who was influential in the early careers of East London MCs like Kano, Nasty Crew and East Connection. Mikey helped me record the first episode professionally, but due to scheduling conflicts was unable to do 24/7, back-to-back studio sessions with me – which is what it would take to keep up with the schedule I had planned. That's when I checked in with another friend, named Benbrick.

I wasn't exactly pitching the podcast to Benbrick, we were just at similar points in our lives. I explained to him that I had moved from songwriting to storytelling, and that podcasting was my new medium. I played him the Sanyu demos, like I had been doing for months in the streets, as well as the early recordings from Mikey J's sessions.

Luckily for me, Benbrick had been on his own search for something new. After a successful run as a pop/R&B producer, he had become interested in film scores, so he played me some rough ideas. This was music to my ears, because I wanted the podcast to feel cinematic. Benbrick was so into my vision that he basically started working on it overnight, helping me refine the first two episodes with his own original compositions. Everything he added was perfect. His musical style and mixing abilities elevated the podcast from a cool concept to an out-of-body experience.

Ever since then, Benbrick and I have spent most of our lives developing *HYHGP* in some way, even when we're not recording. It has become our way of explaining ourselves. My poetry tells the story of my community, while Benbrick's soundscape expresses things that can't be put into words. Over the past three years, I have moved from the journalistic style of Chapter 1, through the experimental genre-blending of Chapter 2, to the more factual storytelling of Chapter 3, as I form a clearer understanding of the community. This has allowed me to make use of the one thing that we as Black people struggle to monetise without a university degree, or the support of a big company: our shared experience. Rap music, the streets, migration – all of these things have given us valuable experiences, which no exam paper or application form in my life has ever recognised. Through *HYHGP* I am able to capture that value and show others how to see it in their own lives. We are the story.

CHAPTER ONE

This chapter (or 'series' or 'season') was written without a plan. I started it in March of 2018 and ended up releasing one episode a month. This was a crazy schedule for the amount of work that went in, and I didn't get much attention for it at first. But a small group of listeners got it. They sensed that Benbrick and I were onto some-thing, and showed up every month to follow our creative journey. Much love to you guys! Honourable mentions to my youngest brother, Kenny, who probably connected with it the most out of the whole family. Also, to my guy, Darryl, whose name regularly came up on the 'top listeners' list.

EPISODE 1: Listen Closer

Extra Info:
- My only real aim when I started this episode was to capture what was around me in real-time. This is an idea I got from Rap music, which is built on journalism.
- This episode was inspired by time I spent in my childhood community, St. Raphael's Estate, as well as the nearby estate of Church Road, the North London town of Tottenham and the South London town of Brixton.
- At this point, I didn't know how many episodes there would be, I was just trying out whatever.

Fun Facts:
- To write this episode, I started with the songs. First, I decided what order they should come in, then I figured out the best messages to go with them.
- As soon as we finished this episode, Benbrick and I sent it to the author of the most popular A Level Sociology textbook at the time. I had this vague idea that the podcast could be used to create study material that was more engaging than a massive textbook, so I invited him to listen and have a conversation with us. He wasn't impressed lol.

I kicked off the podcast by challenging myself to write about a local Black artist, and what their work revealed about our lives. My good friend Marc had just recently introduced me to a Tottenham rapper called Dun D, and I took to the brother straight away. He was a mixture of Tottenham pride and Ghanaian humility. Listening to him talk, I heard his awareness of his environment as well as his concern for the next generation. I asked if we could record our conversation, because he was dropping so many gems, and he happily agreed. Not long after meeting Dun, I discovered an upcoming Camden rapper called Ambush. He became famous later that year for his single 'Jumpy', which *Complex* magazine crowned the best song of 2018. But at the time, I just liked his flow and his charisma. Both Dun D and Ambush gave me the inspiration I needed to explain the street element of our community, using music.

[George is dropping his nephews off at school, daydreaming]

George: My name's George the Poet, but right now I'm Uncle George, watching my nephews play with their friends.

I'm 20 years older than these kids, and I'm imagining what the next 20 years will be like for them. Some of them will obviously be dead. Some in jail. Some sitting right here watching their own kids, asking the same questions.

[Page turn]

George: People get uncomfortable when you talk about children like that, like there's a cause-and-effect relationship between the things we say aloud and the way the future pans out. Like these negative prospects are less likely for our children if we don't acknowledge the current reality.

Maybe words really are that powerful. Or maybe that's just a story we tell ourselves to imagine power into existence.

[Page turn]

George: Everything you know is a story; an idea that you've accepted until the day you cross it out and replace it with a better answer. When I was in school there was a planet called Pluto. Turns out there's not. I mean, Pluto's still there, it's just not a planet . . . anymore.

Personally, *I* have no opinion on Pluto because I wasn't there at the time. But when it comes to this beautiful, resilient, overlooked, traumatised community . . . I've got skin in the game, I've got 27 years of experience. So, no matter what stories come up in the papers about our trigger-happy gangland, or our state-dependent single mums . . . I remember everything first-hand.

In fact, we all do. So why is it that we, as a community, have no control over our narrative? Our main storytellers are rappers. But the rappers of today are facing the same struggles NWA did around the time I was born. How? Housing, schools, crime, unemployment . . . is that it? We now provide the fuel for a multi-billion-dollar storytelling industry, and all we have to show for it is new versions of the same story.

[Page turn]

So anyway, I'm watching these kids playing, wondering how many of them will die from stab wounds versus bullet wounds . . . which of them will get sectioned first . . . what kind of drugs they'll be selling in twenty years. How Brexit will affect their exposure to firearms . . . and I've got an idea . . .

We should revisit our story, and instead of retelling it, we should re-write it. I'm not saying 'Let's fabricate history', I'm saying let's learn to interpret what we're going through in a way that makes us stronger.

And leaves us with a better idea of how to manage it.

So, on that cheerful note, welcome to my podcast!

*

SCENE 1: GEORGE'S BIRMINGHAM
SHOW AT EVERYMAN CINEMA

[George the Narrator leads the listener into a dark, elegant cinema screening room. About one hundred and fifty people fill the seats. George the Performer is talking on stage]

George the Performer: Picture a car driving down the road towards you.

George the Narrator: Right now, you're live at my Birmingham show.

George the Performer: The closer it gets, the more excited you get.

George the Narrator: Make sure your phone's off.

George the Performer: Oh, by the way, sorry – quick note about the blindfolds. You can take them off whenever you want, I just feel like it will work better if you start off with it.

[George the Performer notices an audience member not wearing their blindfold]

George the Performer: You're just looking at me like 'nope'.

Audience Member: [Laughing] I can't find it.

George the Performer: That's alright, close your eyes if you can't find it, it's all good. Erm. The car's getting closer towards you, and as it approaches, you hear music, just like a music video. And it's something like this . . .

SCENE 2: GEORGE & DUN D

[Soundtrack: Dun D 'Ooh Wee']

George: So you just got the outside shot but we're in the car now. You're sitting in the back watching me sing my heart out.

SatNav: Head north-west on to Garrett Road then turn right onto Stonenest Street.

George: I'm listening to 'Ooh Wee' by Dun D, a song about hustling Seven days a week and right now that resonates with me

Furthermore, Dun's work's mature – his
Music's so smooth it makes the *trap* sound like a pleasant place to be.
Personally, I don't know how he does it.
Singing about shotting ain't that putting all your business out in
    public?
And all that money in the video looking like a major label album
    budget.
One second this is my bit though.

[George sings along to the pre-chorus]

George: That's my tune.
When I first heard this tune, I just gave a man a spud.
And it's not for the fact that he's saying a bag of crud.
You see with guys that work with drugs they
Might just burst a slug. They might just jerk the plug.
I don't know if that's how it has to be or if that's just the effect of pride.
But what I do know is Dun D's got a mad reflective side.

[George recalls a conversation with Dun D]

Dun D: *So, what is it then? You go through hell on Earth to die to go to heaven, or you go through heaven on Earth, and you die and go to hell – that's basically what's happening.*

George: These are good questions.
And they're particularly relevant to all my hood bredrins.
In a community where there's not much generational wealth and
    there's
Only so many legal ways of elevating yourself.
And they tell you 'Education will help' but you've
Left school with not much to say for yourself.
So now you're hustling white. And you've
been in a couple of fights but you
Scuff with a knife so you've cut up a couple of guys.

But they say God will judge you for what you *decide* to do,
Not what you *try* to do. So, does His mercy still apply to you?

[George returns to the memory of his conversation with Dun D]

Dun D: *So, this is the thing, when we tell the story of the Bible to ourselves, we're the Moses, we're the Davids, we're the Elijahs, we're the Joshuas. You feel me? Now, what happened to the other guys? Everyone puts themselves in that superior place but there's bare man on the side – who's them man there though? 'Cause it's not me, bro. And everyone's gonna tell you that it's not them. So, who's them man? Who decides who gets a mixtape?*

[Back to George driving]

SatNav: Head north-east on Tollington Park.

George: So now I'm driving in silence. Trying to decide how to
Fit these thoughts into a song.
Saying to myself, 'You owe it to the people that supported you this
        long'.
But you know what I've realised? I talk to you lot wrong.

I can't shoehorn this in to a three-minute song with
Two verses and two choruses
Only to be bored at my own performances.
Nah. I need a more potent form for this.
I need to introduce you to the people in my life. The
Ones that are telling me I'm keeping them alive. It's
Like Dun was saying, the other people in the Bible.
'Cause telling your own story is the secret to survival.

If I can make you grieve and cry and celebrate and laugh with me,
        it
Might help you understand the generation after me.
Especially in times like this when better days are hard to see.

Youngers moving mad. Since the
Start of the year it's like a
Hundred youts been stabbed.
But it's better to embrace them in this mayhem than
Cage them 'cause
Once they come out it's like we relegate them partially. It's like
Nines said: these guys wanna blast for their squad,
Do thirty and still gotta answer to God.
Or they beat the case and they can't get a job, can't
Leave the life behind it's like they're part of the mob. I'm
Telling you something crazy is happening. And the
Key to understanding it may be this rapping thing.

[Soundtrack: Ambush 'Kenny Allstar Freestyle']

SCENE 3: RAP & PRISON

George: This is a freestyle from a young rapper called Ambush
Big up Kenny Allstar 'cause I've had this on repeat. It
Sounds like he's just talking badness on the beat, but
Remember this is life experience – madness on the street.
What's he supposed to do? Not expose his truth?
You might not like what he has to say but mandem gotta eat.

[Prison ambience builds up]

George: See, a lot of this music is full of hatred and sin and that's
'Cause it comes straight from the wing.
From the cage, from the bing where guys take the
W/rap 'cause they ain't gonna sing.
Where there ain't much to do other than
Read books and bang weights in the gym.

Listen to what he's saying . . .
This guy just said he sold drugs in jail using phones and drones.

I'm not saying this to expose the bro; obviously he's
Put this out there, which I don't condone, but you
Have to ask yourself, why would he discuss this recklessly?
Let's ask the Justice Secretary.

Justice Secretary: *Spice and other drugs ordered with a Deliveroo-style responsiveness on tiny mobile phones, from prison cells and delivered by drones direct to cell windows.*

[Switch to beach ambience]

George: Alright let's think about this logically.
Obviously, in jail a lot of money gets made off drugs.
Now according to – it's nice out here innit?
According to Ambush, he was able to do this 'cause he
'Paid off guvs'. That's prison officers
(As opposed to prison governors).
See this has been a persistent issue for different governments and they
All talk about how they're gonna make adjustments and it's
No different here – we have the Secretary of State for Justice,
A man called David Gauke.
Sometime in early March he gave a talk in which he said . . .
In fact, I'll just play it to you:

Justice Secretary: *Increasing the numbers of prison officers and deploying them in a more effective way will help create more positive relationships between offenders and prison officers.*
But if we are to bear down on the levels of violence we need to deal with the biggest cause of the violence, which is drugs.

George: See, it's interesting: he recognised the need for more prison officers
But the solution he put forth didn't offer this.
Instead, he took it back to the war on drugs,
Positioning, you know, offenders as morons, thugs.

Justice Secretary: *It is clear that the reason drugs are so prevalent in our prisons is in large part because gangs are fuelling demand, boosting the supply and catching prisoners in a cycle of debt and further criminality, from which they struggle to break free.*

George: So, the number one reason people take drugs in jail is
    because
Money-hungry prisoners force them to.
Not the fact that they're locked in a cage,
And they're struggling with emotions that cause them to.

Justice Secretary: *Gangs enforcing control by using threats and violence towards prisoners, extorting their families, and attempting to corrupt prison staff.*

George: 'Attempting'.
A 2017 report by the Howard League found that a lot of prison
    officers feel like their importance is neglected.
It said they feel undervalued, understaffed, ill-trained,
    ill-equipped,
And generally ignored and ineffective.
So, when you got the Justice Secretary up there
Acting like there's no way these guys could ever be compromised,
Let's just put it all into perspective.

Justice Secretary: *From the conventional to the cunning, by design or device, through fear or intimidation, these criminal gangs will stop at nothing to maintain their access to such a lucrative market.*

George: If the purpose of prison is rehabilitation, you can
Look at his approach and see the limitations. If it
Wasn't for drastic reductions in prison staff
Evidence suggests we'd be heading down a different path.

A recent study by the Runnymede Trust and
Greenwich University's Faculty of Law
Sheds light on potential reasons why a
Prisoner might end up living like a casualty of war.

Despite staff numbers having heavily decreased, the
Prison population has steadily increased. Some
People end up locked in their cell for half a week which is
Peak! No exercise, minimal human contact
So how much drug abuse do you think stems from that?
And statistically, if you're Black, Muslim or mentally ill,
There are more consequences you could potentially feel.

Our prisons need more officers, staff diversity and
Training on cultural awareness,
Unless we care more about punishment than fairness.

SCENE 4: TAKE A DEEPER LOOK

George: Now, there's two ways of listening to rap: you can focus on what's missing, or take a deeper look at what's there.

In the piece I just played you, Ambush talked about a girl getting punched in the face, drug dealers getting robbed of their product and guys getting stabbed up in front of their loved ones. Now, if we focus on what's missing, we could say his words lack compassion, or even humanity. Alternatively, listen closer and you'll notice how he keeps repeating the same line: 'Real life, tryna let man know'.

He warns his audience about the danger of getting 'lost in the bando', i.e. losing your way to the drug game. This implies not only that he's addressing young people like himself, possibly caught up in crime, but also that he promotes aspiration, even in this dark and depraved space.

I can explain that to you, because I'm native to that environment and Ambush reminds me of people I love. So, I'm able to put his words in context and recognise the social value in them.

This kind of critical analysis is a habit that I picked up from studying English Literature. Nothing's ever said without reason; even if it's a lie. So, instead of letting rap music wash over us, resenting or ignoring the experiences these young commentators are sharing with us, let's try and understand where their stories are coming from.

It wasn't hard for me to link Ambush's freestyle with the Justice Secretary's speech – they were released within about a week of each other, and I listened to them both over and over again.

Now, I'm grateful for everyone who's listening to this right now, but I'm addressing my rappers here. If you're really from the hood – especially if you've got a big following – please my guy, push these conversations as far as you can. Did you really sell all those drugs, just to get famous and spend the rest of your life talking about that time you had to sell drugs? Or was it so that you could speak with decision-makers on a higher level and offer insight that they might not have? You trying to make a little money for you and your peoples? Or you trying to stand for something?

Police, Crown Prosecution Service, National Probation Service, National Offender Management Service – who has more expertise in dealing with these people than you? Come on . . .

SCENE 5: CRIMINAL JUSTICE REFORM

[Soundtrack: Jorja Smith 'Blue Lights']

George: See, our community's so immersed in the Criminal Justice System,

But really and truly what do they know . . . about this life?

Think about it.
How many people in the Ministry of Justice have experienced crime?
How many people in the Ministry of Justice have a
Family member doing serious time?
Do they bring that trauma with them into the office?
Or do they come with a whole lot of theory in mind?

How many people in the Ministry of Justice have
Ever confused a gunshot with a firework?
And how many of them are from an environment where
Everyone's shotting and buying work?
Do they know what it's like to flirt with death without
Ever realising how close you're getting? Where
Crime starts off as a means of survival
Then becomes part of the social setting.

Do you think the prison minister has ever spent the night in a cell?
Writing his mail while his cellmate's slicing himself?

See, the perspective I'm describing is so inner city
If you haven't lived through it,
I don't expect you to show sinners pity.

See, if their idea of justice is based only on legal precedent
You have to ask yourself, who *do* these people represent?
It's not the ones most affected, do we need more evidence?
For all of the brothers, fathers, sons,
Sisters, daughters and mums missing in our community
Anything less than criminal justice reform is feeble recompense.

EPISODE 2: Popcorn

Extra Info:
- At this point, my goal was to provide context. We're used to seeing news headlines about the *effects* of street life – a stabbing, or an arrest. I wanted to show my listener the *causes*.
- It was also important for me in these early episodes to use music from the UK, or at least from undiscovered talent who I knew personally. It wasn't until Episode 6 that I branched out and used Ugandan music to tell a Ugandan story, but for the first five episodes of 'HYHGP?' I kept it local.

Fun Facts:
- All the conversations overheard in this episode were recorded in the weeks before release. They are parts of my life that I wouldn't usually share, but they make the podcast so real.
- After finishing this episode, I randomly bumped into Lethal Bizzle, founder of More Fire Crew. I sent it to him and he praised it highly. Legend.

Episodes 1 and 2 were originally one episode, until someone advised me to separate them. That's why Episode 2 starts in the middle of a scene. At that point I was seven years into my poetry career, but I had never shared anything more personal than those first few minutes. I guess I was trying to earn the listener's trust by letting them in. As the podcast was about seeing the value in our experiences, it made sense to include real moments from my life. I would listen back to recorded conversations and write down whatever came to me. This time, it was about what great parents I had, and how so many people around me were unsupported. Reflecting on that led me to revisit the London street music we grew up listening to. The aim was always to use music to explain reality.

Random Guy: Alexa, have you heard George's podcast?

[Alexa powers on]

Alexa: Yes. *Have You Heard George's Podcast?* is the latest project from spoken word artist, George The Poet. I find him attractive.

Random Guy: Wait, what?

Alexa: And his voice has this kind of sensual quality—

Random Guy: Alexa, stop. Let's get back on the . . . come on.

Alexa: Sorry. Since graduating from Cambridge University, George has won critical acclaim both as a recording artist and social commentator.

Random Guy: Nice.

Alexa: Most recently, George performed at the Royal Wedding, which was seen by 1.6 billion people worldwide.

Random Guy: Woah. Didn't even know there were that many people . . .

Alexa: In fact, George is working on Episode 2 of the podcast right now.

Random Guy: Cool, OK . . .

Alexa: Let's take a listen.

SCENE 1: GEORGE'S MUM & NEPHEW

[Enter a room in which George's nephew is crying out of frustration at his building blocks. George's mum is encouraging him to calm down and keep trying]

[Soundtrack: Klashnekoff 'Murda']

George: I'm walking you through an actual memory.
This is my mum talking to my nephew, listen carefully.

George's Mum: *You can't play PlayStation, you can't do anything else until you've built it properly, OK? You can either sit here and cry . . .*

George: In fact, that's the thing.
You see, my parents actually spoke to us,
Even when they were vexed, and it was just a joke to us. Listen.

[George's nephew cries even louder]

George's Mum: *Silika ko! Be quiet!*

George: See, my little nephew's stressing, bless him
Because his Lego fell apart.
But from the way my mum handles it you can tell she's got hella
    heart.
First, she recognises why my little guy's stressing,
Then she tries to make him see the life lesson.

George's Mum: *If you do something properly, it will not break. If you do it in a hurry, talking nonstop, looking at Nicholas's, moving all over the place, you will not build it firmly and it will break. OK? So, what you need to do is challenge yourself to build it firmly so that it doesn't break, OK?*

George: See, in this situation my mum makes a choice.
Instead of just telling my nephew to stop making noise
And allowing him to carry on, pissed off and hopeless, she
Explains the value of persistence and focus.
She's showing him how to manage his emotions,
And she's teaching him ways of using language in the process,
    listen . . .

George's Mum: . . . *do you understand? So, they are not going to defeat you because you have got the super-brain. OK? So, calm down a little bit, think about it, then go back and tackle it.*

George: In everything my mum's saying,
She's balancing correction with positive reinforcement.
And to do this she uses little man's teacher's endorsement.

George's Mum: *You're the one with the brain, do you understand? You don't just have a brain; you've got a super-brain. OK? Everybody says so. Even Miss – what's that Miss in the other class? Ms Silver? Well, the other teacher said as well. Everybody knows you've got a great brain for building things. An absolutely super brain for building things.*

George: See how my mum says he's got a brain for building things?
That's 'cause she observes him when he's playing with children's
    things.
So, whenever he's building things, she notices the
Skills it brings out of him from deep down within.
And that's how she's been with all of us;
Very in tune with our strengths and weaknesses.
My mum believed we could overcome anything and she
Went to great lengths to teach us this.

Now, that kind of sensitive nourishment
Gives a child a sense of encouragement.
It gave me confidence in my own ability that's

Why I didn't let my environment limit me.
'Cause at some point most of us wanna leave the hood
But before you've even formed a plan you've
Absorbed all these norms and values. And
That's why the formative years are a significant period.
But some of my friends? Very different experience . . .

SCENE 2: KIDS WITH A STREET UPBRINGING

[Enter a smoke-filled room with adults talking about street life in the presence of kids]

George: Some of my friends were more exposed than me. In
My opinion, more exposed than kids are supposed to be.
Every time I come around there's mandem in the yard
Talking street life, gambling with cards.
Now, as a kid coming up in that kind of space, you
Learn the world in relation to that time and place.

Outside the yard you see fiends getting badded up,
Just across the hall, you see your big cousins bagging up.

[Women in another room also having adult conversations]

George: You go to the kitchen, the fridge is empty.
Instead of cooking you something someone hits you with a twenty.

[An adult gives a child some money]

George: So you leave the yard any time you want and
Go to the nearest place you can buy food from.
Obviously, it's gonna be low quality food and
I can't believe your life, but I don't wanna be rude so I
Go along with you 'cause you're my dude. Plus, you
Just got more money than I've seen in a month.

I can't get that kind of P from my mum. But
True we're young so it's a reason to stunt, so we
Go shopping for all the sweets that you want.
Bearing in mind, now, we're walking through the ghetto—

Wait hold on, this crackhead's talking to a kettle!

But you don't seem fazed 'cause you're on the road for days so
I follow your lead, I put on a poker face.
Get to the shop now and what do we see?
Two hood chicks and an alcoholic . . . having an
Argument but I can't make out the topic.

[Inaudible argument in the background]

George: No one seems to care that two kids walked in, so they
carry on anyhow, broke and lost fam.
You just grab your sweets and ask me what I want. Then
Hand over the twenty-pound note to bossman.
See, even though your home life is hectic it's
Given you steady nerves, so I respect it. You
Teach me things my parents aren't equipped to, so
Coming up in Harlesden with you evolves my perspective.

The downside is you've got too much independence. Your
Family don't know what you're doing right now. Your
Mum's busy working, your cousins dem are hustling but
Anything could happen to you and I now . . .

Back in the day I used to envy you for that. I could
See it in your body language when we used to chat.
When we wanted peace and quiet, we went to my yard but
When we did badness then we used your flat.

SCENE 3: BROKEN HOMES

George: I never realised your dad was beating up your mum and that's
Why you used to cry when people said 'suck your mum'.

I never realised he was struggling to cope,
Taking flights back and forth to smuggle in the coke.

I never knew that when he went to jail, he
Told the police things he wasn't meant to tell.

I never knew that was a stain on your family name and that's
Part of the reason why your mentality changed. And all the
Crazy relationships your big sister had for the same
Reason you was pissed and sad: you missed your dad. I
Never realised that with him gone that put a
Whole lot of pressure on your mum's income. So she
Works more hours, struggles more than ever
Bare responsibility she juggles altogether. Now you're
Spending more time around your sister's latest boyfriend.
He's a big drug dealer. And he hates the boy dem.
Tells you they don't protect communities, they destroy them.
And true they took your dad away, so you see his point then.
Now he's bringing his mandem to chill in your mum's house.
Always talking money, always bringing his funds out. Your
Sister's in the living room with her female bredrins but
You stay with the mandem 'cause you need male presence.

Yeah, he's a gangster but you're impressed 'cause he's cool. And
Around this time, we're starting secondary school.

[Montage of school drama]

George: Anyway.
That's the bit that you've heard before. And I
Hate repeating it 'cause first of all, for

My community this is personal and it's
Not the case for everybody, furthermore.
But there's another story to be told, one that
Often gets ignored, purely 'cause it's road. For
Every troubled young person out on the streets there's a
Local producer with a mountain of beats. And from the
Things some of these kids see on a daily basis there's
Enough material for an album of heat. Now
As of March 2018 this country had hundreds of thousands of
NEETs – that's
Young people not in education, employment or training.
58% of them aren't looking for work,
Some of them physically can't put in the work
So they're classified as economically inactive.
But honestly from what we see of the economy . . .
Obviously they're active.

SCENE 4: MORE FIRE CREW

[Soundtrack: More Fire Crew 'Oi']

George: Alright, now to all my listeners who don't like this music
Please don't forward this bit, it's lit.
Trust me, this bit is lit.
Where you going? Come, this way, this way . . .

The song's called 'Oi' by three good bredrins,
Ended up becoming a couple of teen hood legends.

So if you're not familiar with this song,
Let me be a tour guide for you, if that's alright with you.
I'll show you what it means to us, that's
all I can do . . . I mean, come on man we're talking about
More Fire Crew.

[Transition to inside George's flat]

George: This music's straight from the gutters of London –
No government funding, no big machines, no business teams just
    kids with
Dreams . . . and the ability to turn nothing to something.

More Fire Crew was a group from East London.
Growing up I heard their tunes at street functions and
Even though we knew nothing about East London,
We loved them.

[Soundtrack: So Solid Crew '21 Seconds']

George: At the time So Solid was flying the flag and them
Man there had it right in the bag.
From the vibe to the swag. They sounded like
Bosses without even trying to brag. And as
Much as I rated that I couldn't relate to that.
More Fire felt a little younger. Like them
Youts that would rob you out of hunger, but they didn't look
Hungry, they looked like they were on the come up!

[Soundtrack: More Fire Crew 'Oi']

George: To this day you can hear this song in clubs
F'ing up the dance. The single peaked at number
7 on the charts.

At the time of recording this, the song's almost twenty years old
And at their time of recording it, the guys were almost twenty years
    old.
So how did these almost-twenty-year-olds create
Something that made them legendary heroes without
Any involvement from big donors?
Coming from a poor community, where drug
Money that should go towards student fees is
Usually stored in jewellery.

At a time where this kind of art was largely regarded as
Little more than coonery if we're talking truthfully.

You gotta remember: the UK was just about acknowledging the
Fact of institutional racism.
Obviously to minorities it wasn't exactly a secret but a
Lot of white people didn't actually believe it
Until the police mishandled Stephen Lawrence's murder in
Court, which led to the Macpherson Report.
That was a public inquiry; the first of its sort to admit that the police . . .
Don't actually give the same service for all.

[Montage of Stephen Lawrence reflections]

George: Bear in mind Stephen Lawrence got mad media coverage so the
Government's further support didn't serve much purpose at all but you know.
That's another story for another day. My
Point is in a lot of ways we're trapped in the system.
But because we've adapted to England
Many of us feel like we're unable to run away.
So the least we could do is give a little space for the greeziest youth to
Speak their truth when releasing this music.
'Cause they represent the streets with this music.

[Soundtrack: More Fire Crew 'Oi']

George: This music is the result of all the tension and the pressure.
The result of multiple detentions a semester.
Value in our community is something we ain't used to seeing so these
Youts are preeing an adventure for the treasure.

[More Fire Crew Live performance of 'Oi']

SCENE 5: THE LIBERAL NEIGHBOUR

[George answers a knock on the front door]

Neighbour: Hi George, sorry to knock so late. I was listening to your podcast – massive fan – I absolutely adored the piece you did on the More Fire Crew. Quick question though.

George: Sure.

Neighbour: If you don't mind.

George: No, go ahead.

Neighbour: Do you not think it's slightly unfair to characterise white people as a sort of homogenous group that was universally oblivious to institutional racism prior to the Macpherson Report? Not least given that (being the 'majority ethnic group') it's not something we would have experienced first-hand? And don't you think it's slightly disingenuous to suggest all minority ethnic people had that shared understanding of racism? I was just wondering . . .

[George closes the door without answering]

Friend: Who was that? She looked cool. What did she want?

George: Bro, it's one of the new neighbours. She helps me out sometimes, I've done her a few favours. She's cool but I wasn't feeling the conversation we just had, I'm not gonna lie. Did you hear it?

Friend: Well, what did she say?

George: Alright, let me ask you this as a member of the white community.

Friend: Yeah.

George: You heard my More Fire Crew thing, innit?

Friend: Of course.

George: Did you feel like that was in any way accusatory towards the white community in a way that was unbalanced? Or do you feel like it was even about—

Friend: Ehhh, it's its own thing. You know, it's cool.

George: Bro, she's all telling me I'm mischaracterising white people as being oblivious and insensitive with regards to racism.

Friend: Right. She's a fan, though?

George: She might be a fan, that's not the point, cuz. I'm saying it's—

Friend: I don't get it.

George: I'm saying it's a bit inappropriate. Do you understand? She's come to my door, talking to me about a piece that I've made about an experience relevant to my community to give the — like, she wasn't thinking about no Stephen Lawrence before—

Friend: Come on . . .

George: What do you mean 'Come on' fam? She was knocking on my door – yes or no?

Friend: Yeah, of course. But . . .

George: Alright, so I'm saying what makes her feel en—

Friend: You gotta think of everyone. I mean if she's a fan, she's the one kind of . . . buying the records.

George: Mmm.

Friend: Right?

George: Want something to eat, bro? I haven't got much, just a bit of fruit and . . . popcorn. Popcorn cool?

Friend: Yeah man, thank you. Put it in the microwave. Power 9?

[George puts popcorn in the microwave]

George: You know, about that thing, she did seem cool, George. You know? Like, what she's saying, she's thinking about her perspective . . .

SCENE 6: POPCORN

[George stares absent-mindedly at the popcorn in the microwave]

George: This is what it's like when we talk about racism.
My mind's disengaged but you can't tell 'cause my face isn't.
We just go round and round in circles like the popcorn in the microwave.
Like the next generation about to jump on the Lyca wave.

I feel you, popcorn. I know what it's like to be stuck in a box.
Surrounded by corn like you're bucking your ops,
Feeling nothing but heat.
That's what it was like coming up on my street.
Course you blow up. That's bound to happen when you're forced to grow up.
You feel the heat, so you get it popping 'cause there is no second option.
And before you blew up, no one used to feel you too tough
They thought you're too . . . tough.
Just like those rappers that start off street and scruffy.

Then you go pop, people think you're sweet and fluffy.

And hear the joke: after everything you've been through,
They take you in as a light snack,
You know like that?
Not even a proper meal.
Like all of the pain in the community suddenly disappeared 'cause a
Couple of rappers got a deal.

But popcorn, let's be honest.
What do you actually contribute?
I mean I know what you've gone through, I know that was long for you.
But what do you really bring to the table?
A bit of starch, bit of carbohydrate.
Popcorn you lack substance and it's hard to hide it.

And that's where you and I differ.
'Cause substance is something this music doesn't lack.
It shouldn't be viewed as just a snack.
This music's like sociological journalism.
But the producers' and the consumers' concerns are different,
Imagine its potential if we stop pushing this historical determinism
     and
Force the world to learn to listen.

The problem is if you don't wanna act like everything's sweet
They label you salty.
And that's why labels are faulty.
I dunno, g.

Yo, popcorn's ready.

28

EPISODE 3: Grenfell Special

Extra Info:

- Miss B is an important character because she shows how people can be taken for granted because of their status. From the first scene, it is clear that she's very clever, and has a gift for making Maths relevant to her students. But all she gets is disrespect from the class and bad vibes from the Deputy Head.
- Savannah's speech at the end symbolises the regret we all feel when we lose someone who we didn't show enough appreciation to.

Fun Facts:

- The first song of this episode, 'Touch' by Chika Dole, fell into my lap when I randomly met Chika one day. I needed to replace my laptop, which had been stolen, so I went to the store, and she was the assistant who helped me. She told me she'd travelled from Norway to work on her music career and gave me her SoundCloud. I checked it out later that day and decided on the spot that I'd use it in my next podcast episode. It became one of my favourite moments of 'HYHGP?'. So out of a lost laptop, we got a classic moment! Even more proof that every experience matters.
- The rowdy classmates are voiced by my brothers, Freddie and Michael.
- My youngest brother, Kenny, and my friend Kalil helped me work out the maths for Miss B's script.

I didn't want to write this episode, but I had to. The Grenfell tragedy was such a powerful example of institutional violence, it took me a whole year to put it into words. I don't necessarily speak for those who were most directly affected, but I speak for those of us who feel for them, and wish there was more we could do. In the run up to the first anniversary of the fire, a voice in my head was pushing me to write something. My starting point was the idea that I could have easily been visiting someone in a building like that on a night like that. This is why the climax comes when I ask Miss B for her address. Thinking about the residents gave me an opportunity to write a story involving teachers, students and families. People regularly tell me it's their favourite episode, and I think I understand why. As listeners we crave emotional connection, and as humans we're weirdly fascinated with darkness. But I'm very cautious about over-celebrating this episode. It was more like a love letter to the Grenfell community – my way of saying 'I see you, and I believe you are more than a headline.'

Scene 1: Maths Class

Savannah: Miss, probability trees ain't relevant to my life plan.

Classmate 1: About life plan. You're just trying to marry a rich white man.

[Class laughs]

Savannah: Actually, I'm gonna employ myself, then retire when I'm thirty and enjoy my wealth.

Miss B: OK everyone eyes on the board now.

Classmate 1: How you gonna retire when you're thirty, b?

Savannah: I'll let you know when I'm hiring. You can work for me.

Classmate 2: Come on, Savannah!

[Class laughs]

Savannah: I'm gonna set up a laundry business. It's gonna wash the mandem's clothes and their dough.

Miss B: Savannah, enough!

Savannah: But Miss I'm just saying I got plans to be wealthy and I don't see how this lesson's gonna actually help me.

Miss B: So let me get this straight, Savannah: your whole plan is to launder dirty money for a road man—

Savannah: Nah, not for 'a' road man – for the whole gang.

[Class laughs]

Miss B: Yet you don't think you need to pay attention in maths though . . .

Savannah: Miss, this is probability that's— no! Just no.

[Class laughs]

Miss B: So, you plan to run a business handling cash without a basic understanding of maths?

Savannah: But Miss, my business is about helping guys stop doing crime and start doing positivity. What's that got to do with probability?

Classmate 1: Nah, nah, listen to her, Miss . . .

Miss B: Savannah, if you let me teach the lesson—

Savannah: Miss d'you know what it is? Everyone's got their lane. D'you know what I'm saying? Like, I hustle I don't need no class but obviously you teach so it will look bad on you if we don't pass.

Miss B: Savannah I'm not having this conversation with you—

Savannah: OK, I get it. Maths is like ideas and theories and that, but my business, yeah this is for real. I'm not being funny but business isn't your field.

Classmate 2: Ooo . . . Miss are you gonna have that?

Miss B: Savannah, where's your pen?

Savannah: I forgot my pen, Miss.

Miss B: Can someone lend Savannah a pen please?

[Classmates offer Savannah a pen]

Miss B: Write down what I'm about to say. See, Savannah, given that 50% of new companies in London cease to function past the first three years – write this down –

Savannah: I'm writing, Miss.

Miss B: Cease to function past the first three years, to me the importance of this work seems clear. And you said you want to retire by thirty?

Savannah: Yeah.

Miss B: Well annual growth of 20% in the first three years only happens to 6.6% of start-ups in the city, actually. And given that you plan to retire by thirty, your company will have to grow pretty rapidly. In fact you'll need a turnover of at least a million pounds a year, is that sounding fair? You hearing me loud and clear?

Savannah: Yeah that's me, come on.

Miss B: OK so less than 3— [classmates bickering] – write this down. Less than 3%— [more bickering]. Less than 3% of new businesses do those kinds of numbers. And many of them rely on private funders. Now, I can tell you this 'cause you guys are grown: companies owned by Africans – like you, Savannah – are four times more likely than ones owned by white people to be denied a loan.

Classmate 1: That's dread.

Miss B: But when you're self-employed, obviously, you ride alone. So it's up to you to decide if you're down for the ride or not. But to answer your question, Savannah: what's probability got to do with your business? Actually quite a lot. The three biggest [Savannah begins to argue] – listen. The three biggest challenges to Africans and women who have businesses are access to finances, choosing to move into saturated markets and straight up mismanagement. So, if all your money is coming from gangbangers and crooks, and you're running a laundry service as bad as it looks, you're gonna need a lot of maths skills to balance the books. And I've already mentioned the strain on business that mismanagement puts. So, you're gonna need qualified staff but your business partners aren't on the right path. Let's say for every year they spend in the streets their chances of ending deceased or with a sentence at least have gone up by half. So, what's the probability your business will last? Given that you're taking on such a difficult task in which a criminal past is a prominent feature?

Savannah: Miss, if I was smart enough to answer that question I'd do more with my life than becoming a teacher.

[Classroom erupts]

Miss B: Savannah, get out.

Scene 2: George's Place

[Miss B is chilling with her love interest, George, who has just listened to her story about the incident with Savannah earlier that day]

[Soundtrack: Chika Dole 'Touch']

George: She said what?! And what did you say?

Miss B: I just told her to get out. I hate doing that. It's like giving up. It's a bit neglectful but obviously she was disrespectful.

George: That was mad disrespectful. You gotta draw the line before you get drawn out. Look – it's still on your mind all now.

Miss B: I think she felt like I was raining on her parade 'cause I was hitting her with all these statistics.

George: Yeah, but she needs to be more realistic. How you gonna be in a maths class talking about washing money for trap stars? These kids listen to two-two rap bars, they get gassed fast.

Miss B: Obviously, I don't wanna have those conversations with any fifteen-year-old but if I shut them down, they're gonna disengage. It's like sometimes I feel like fifteen's not such a distant age but this generation's on a different page. And if I don't talk to them about the roads then someone else will 'cause its fascinating, I know how these girls feel.

George: The good thing is you speak their language, babe. So, you can control the conversation and take it back to their studies, even when they're acting bare cruddy.

Miss B: Sorry, I don't mean to laugh . . .

George: What's funny?

Miss B: You should tell that to my senior staff.

George: Oh, swear down. Are they on a different page?

[Miss B gets a call from Shaun, the father of her daughter]

Miss B: Ugh it's Nevaeh's dad. One second. Hello?

Shaun: Yo. What you doing?

Miss B: Nothing. What's up?

Shaun: What you mean 'Nothing'? You must be doing something.

Miss B: Is there something I can help with, specifically?

Shaun: Yeah, I can't take Nevaeh tomorrow so you're gonna have to take her.

Miss B: Come again? Shaun, can I ask you something? When we make these arrangements do you think I do it for your entertainment?

[Miss B takes the call to another room. George receives a voice note on WhatsApp from Layla, a work friend]

Layla: Oi stranger, long time no see – how come we never link? Anyway, I heard you're performing at a conference I'm at tomorrow. We should get a drink. Let me know.

[Miss B hangs up and returns to the room]

Miss B: Sorry about that.

George: It's cool, B.

Miss B: No one told me life was this hard.

George: You seem tense, would you like a massage?

Miss B: You think you're slick.

George: Nah, you think I'm slick.

Miss B: No comment.

George: Alright, wait there.

[George leaves and returns with massage oil]

George: What you saying? Neck, shoulders, lower back?

Miss B: Neck is more than enough, thank you.

George: No problem with that...

[George gives Miss B a neck massage]

Miss B: George, can I tell you something?

George: What's that, B?

Miss B: Some days I feel like I ruined my life by having a baby . . . but if I had to live life without my daughter I'd be like a fish out of water. And I can't bear the thought of leaving her in this world with a father who can't support her.
Mmm. Feels good.

George: You like that, yeah?

Miss B: But 'cause I had her crazy young . . . even people at work treat me like I'm just another baby mum. And them kids try to show me up nonstop. I don't know why, you know me I'm on job.

George: Yeah, they're learning something, thanks to you. Probably 'cause they all fancy you.

Miss B: Erm . . . I thought they're learning 'cause I'm good at what I do.

George: Nah – yeah – obviously, not like—

Miss B: I'm just teasing you. But I do think sometimes people don't see the value in me. I mean, look at you and me. Be real with me. You don't want me you just like to chill with me. And I'm not saying that for sympathy, it's kinda the same thing for me. But I think I feel like that just 'cause I think you feel like that. With me you don't act all lively and excited. You don't even come to my flat despite being invited. I bet you don't even know what floor I live on. Right or wrong?

You just pull up outside and honk. What? All of a sudden you're a silent monk?

George: What am I supposed to say? What do you want me to say? For real?

Miss B: Well, I am gonna have my daughter after all, so I should probably get an early night.

George: Alright, I'll drop you in a second—

Miss B: Nah, I'll get a cab, thanks, I'm fine. *I'm fine.*

George: Fine.

Scene 3: Deputy Head's Office

[Mr Brown, the Deputy Head, is finishing a call in his office as Miss B knocks]

Mr Brown: . . . I would be actually pursuing this at a higher level, but it just stands that I— Yep, come in. I will be leveraging the access I have. So thanks for your assistance, I'll be awaiting your call.

[Miss B sits down. Mr Brown hangs up.]

Mr Brown: Hello there, sorry about that, terribly rude of me. Just had some bother with the train line. See, every day I get the same train at the same time, pretty early: 6.30. Now, this morning I was actually late in because the train I jumped on changed destination . . . mid-journey. And look, yeah, these things happen, right, you take it up with the service provider, which I did, firmly. 'Cause actually, technically, I didn't sign up to take two trains. I signed up for one. So OK, call me anal, for sure, but, you know, that's the guy I've become. I mean look; I value consistency, and I'd hope that is reflected in the ship I like to run. So, I do like for my staff to sing from the same hymn sheet. You know, ultimately, our differences are only skin deep. See, when you took this job, you committed to upholding certain values. And by that standard, what you stand accused of having said yesterday places you directly in breach. Now, you are a talent. That much is apparent. And hey, a role in senior leadership for you certainly is within reach. But that would require a unanimous feeling that we are, pretty much as I said, singing from the same hymn sheet. Now, I do accept the point that some of the more challenging students may warrant a situational change of tact, but you know, that doesn't actually change the fact that as a school our name should remain intact. And, look, if it turns out you are more interested in helping these young people sort of sharpen their *street smarts* then actually this might not be the place for that. Perhaps you'd be afforded more leeway in a pupil referral unit. But the problem we have in a school like this is if you pay undue attention to the troublesome ones, you can disturb more students. And I appreciate you're using your personal prudence but with the limited time you have you need to choose between work or nuisance. I mean, here's the deal: parents entrust us with their children for seven hours a day so that we can turn them into functional members of society. Not criminal masterminds. And in the typical class environment that's difficult half the time, to say the least. But actually, any deviation from that contract makes us no better than the train that changes destination after passengers board. Which is a misstep we cannot afford. At all. So look, let's draw a line under that one and carry on galloping forth, if—

[Knock at the door]

Assistant: Sorry, Mr Brown, the fire drill is just about to start.

Mr Brown: Ahh yes. Well, I'm actually going to have to take this one, I'm afraid. So, thanks for your time. And remember – galloping forth!

[Miss B leaves the office]

Scene 4: Final hours

[Miss B gets in the car and plays a voice note from Shaun]

Shaun:
Yo change of plan. I can take Nevaeh tonight. So, whatever you planned to do later tonight you can go do that. And next week I'll bring the yout back.

[Miss B is quiet for a bit then sends a voice note in reply]

Miss B: So you *can* take Nevaeh tonight . . . yet you're saying it like . . . I didn't just cancel my plans. Like you couldn't have just taken her to Anne's or her gran's.

Shaun, our daughter needs us to be civil with each other. If she sensed this tension even a little bit she'd suffer. OK, we're not doing great right now but we've done worse. And we only got better by remembering that she comes first.

Changing Nevaeh's schedule in the middle of the week without any warning is not putting her first. Imagine how she feels, it's off-putting for her. And it's frustrating for me having to talk about something this simple. I don't think of myself as a single mum: I'm her mum, and I'm single but it's like you . . .

Can you please make sure she does ten minutes of reading before she sleeps? The book's in her bag. And please keep an eye on what she's watching online, I don't want her obsessing over her looks or her swag.

I know you think I'm saying this 'cause I just like to moan and cuss and over-fuss. But, Shaun, all I mean is . . . our child needs consistency from both of us.

[Miss B sends the voice note and sits there, reflecting, before sending another voice note – this time to George]

Miss B: Hi Georgie Porgie. I don't really like communicating by walkie talkie so if you're free later . . . turns out I won't have Nevaeh, which everyone knew was gonna happen, but yeah man I'm deya. Gonna do some marking and some lesson planning with a glass of wine to pass the time. So, if you're local your ass is mine.

[Soundtrack: Abi Ocia – Running]

[George backstage at his performance. He receives Miss B's message but has no time to listen to it because he's about to go on stage]

Venue Sound Guy: George we're ready for you backstage.

George: Coming now.

[Miss B in her car]

Miss B: Oh my God, if you heard how the deputy head spoke to me today you won't believe it, mate. It's too much to tell, I'll tell you when— *if* you come later.

[Cut to George performing]

George: Pierre Bourdieu said all reality is a construct. We exist in relation to our social ties. So you'll never understand me without considering where I'm from . . . and the local guys.

[Cut to Miss B back in her flat]

Miss B: And for the record I'm over yesterday. To be honest I think your joke about my kids fancying me was poorly timed, but I know that's just you and your horny mind.

[Miss B hesitates before sending then decides not to. Back to George performing]

George: We exist in relation to other guys and girls. So, I had to move to a better reality, from one where everybody tries and fails.

[Back to Miss B in the flat, pouring the glass of wine]

Miss B: So yeah, if you're up for a little vibe, little bants, that invitation to mine still stands. Not 'cause you're hella important; just 'cause you're better than boredom.

[Back to George on stage]

George: See, if we forget how outcast the voice of an outcast is they'll never be heard, every word is noiseless, without answers. See, there are no choices without chances. Thank you.

[Applause]

George: Thank you!

[Cut to the bar, after the performance]

Layla: Not gonna lie, I'm a little hater sometimes but your performance was so entertaining, that poem's amazing! It's like no one in the audience blinks.

George: Thank you. Would you like to order some drinks?

[Back to Miss B in her flat]

Miss B: By the way, do you actually know what floor I live on? You better do . . . 'cause I'm not telling you. Anyway, I'm kinda tipsy (sips tea) . . .

[Time passes]

Miss B: OK, you're taking too long, let me tell you what the deputy head said. Imagine yeah, he basically said I should find work in a PRU. I'm thinking *do you know how lucky you are that I'm working with you?* He was like 'you might call me anal' I was like 'yeah 'cause you're an ass!'

[Miss B gradually gets more intoxicated]

Miss B: Ahhh my head's spinning, my head is spinning, babe. I wish you were here right now.

[Miss B dozes off as memories swim in and out of focus. Cut to George entering a cab]

Driver: Yes, good evening, brother.

George: Yes, bossman, how you doing?

Driver: Yeah, what is your name?

George: George. Is me.

Driver: Thank you, and where are you going?

George: Going to North West 10, bro.

Driver: Oh OK, OK. Crazy traffic, man it's—

George: Bossman, I'm sorry I'm just about to get on the phone.

Driver: Oh, sorry!

[George starts recording a voice note]

George: Yo, B. I listened to your million voice notes! I'd love to come through, but I'm waved right now. Tell a lie, I don't know what floor you live on. I don't even know the name of your block. And I see your point – that's saying a lot.

I've been thinking about what you said. It's been spinning around in my head. And it's true . . . I'm man who only does what he wants to do. And 'cause of that I'm complacent when it comes to you. Just like your baby father or your kids at school; you give more than you get, and it isn't cool. It must be difficult. In fact, let me give you a call . . .

[George ends voice note and calls. Phone goes straight to voicemail. He then notices the driver taking an unfamiliar route]

George: Yo, bossman where you going? We need the A40, brother.

Driver: Brother, crazy fire that side. All over the news – listen.

Radio: *Coming from West London, the London fire brigade are dealing with a huge fire in a residential tower block in West London. This is Grenfell Tower, a 23- maybe 24-storey block of flats in West Kensington—*

George: Bossman, turn that down for me. Turn it down, boss.

[Driver turns the radio down. George sends Miss B another voice note]

George: Yo B, what's your block called, again? I'm hearing there's a madness in your ends. I can't remember what your block's called. Let me know what block it is, B. Please. Soon as you get this, get back to me . . .

[Cut to the tragedy. Residents screaming, newsreaders reporting]

Scene 5: Savannah's Letter

[Through tears, Savannah reads a heartfelt letter to Miss B at her memorial]

Savannah: It was a trick question, Miss. You said 'What's the chances my business will last?' Because I'm taking on a difficult task and my business partners have a criminal path, like . . . typical path.

I thought you were having a dig and a little laugh like 'Where's this girl going with her criminal staff?' But now I remember, the first thing you said was 'there's a 50% chance *any* new business will last'.

So, um . . . I tried to write it down in a probability tree. So I could properly see what the possibilities be.

Only 3% of the 50% of companies that survive their first three years in the same period of time turn over at least a million pounds a year. But I couldn't work that out when you asked me and think it's down to fear.

If a thousand students started a business now and here, fifteen of us could turn over a million pound annually.

I just felt like it wouldn't be me, so my feelings started spilling out angrily and I'm so sorry for being rude to you, Miss. I am, really.

I thought you were trying to dim my little light because with my little sight I was trying to win my little fight, but you were trying to prepare me for *war*.

And all of the things you said – I get it now; they're *independent variables*. They can happen at the same time. So, while I've got access to an education I might as well pattern that to save time.

The fact I'm a female; the fact I'm African; the fact that half my friends are drug trafficking means it might be harder for me securing a loan, and I might end up going all-in alone. But you know what, Miss?

Even if the chances of me closing the business in the first three years is 90% – which, obviously, I would highly resent – there's still a 10% chance I might make it. It's only right that I take it, Miss it's quite basic. So, thank you, Miss B.

[Story concludes, ambience shifts to a cinema screen with people leaving]

George: So, this is like in the cinema at the end when everyone gets up and brushes the popcorn off their clothes. But you're still sitting there, affected. I want you to picture that screen, pitch black with the words *'Based on a true story'*.

Now it says written and directed by George the Poet.
Produced by Benbrick and George the Poet.

. . . and here's the cast in order of appearance:
Jade Alleyne as Savannah
Michael Mpanga as Classmate One
Freddie Mpanga as Classmate Two
Me as basically everyone else.
Sophia Thakur as Work Friend [Layla]
Benbrick as Mr Brown's Assistant and Venue Sound Guy

Featured Music

Touch – Performed by Chika Dole
Written by Chika Dole and Semi Skimmed
Produced by Semi Skimmed

Running – Performed by Abi Ocia

All other original music produced and composed by Benbrick

Special thanks to Kenny Mpanga, Khalil Rouse, Peter Gregson, Greg Jameson, and Future Studies.

This piece was written in honour of the Grenfell Tower residents and their surrounding community.

EPISODE 3.5 Grenfell II

Extra Info:

- My mind was blown when I found out who Grenfell the man was, and noticed that the tower wasn't even mentioned on his Wikipedia page.
- At times I've reflected on some of the things I said here and cringed not because it's bad, just because it's very transparent. Sharing this much of yourself isn't always easy.

Fun Facts:

- The underwater scene was inspired by an advert I filmed at the time, which put me in a film studio with a massive underwater filming facility. I'd never seen anything like it. Sometimes I write this stuff into the podcast because life goes by so fast - I want to hold onto these moments.
- This is the longest podcast episode. I wanted to walk through my thoughts without thinking about time.

This one was written for the live show that I put together in the same month of writing and recording the previous Grenfell episode. Again with the crazy schedule. I was trying to kill two birds with one stone: pushing my new podcast and giving my fans an *"I'm Back!"* tour. They were two different jobs, with two different thought processes, but for Grenfell's first anniversary, they shared the same purpose. I wanted my audience to really think about the tragedy - not just cry, but *think*. This was definitely too much work, but I think it left my listeners and I better off. If I had a school, I would give the students assignments like this.

Intro

George: Can I tell you a secret?
I can make people see things that aren't in front of their eyes
Which I've only recently come to realise.

I'm not an illusionist, 'cause what I show you is not an illusion.
It's my own moments of clarity amidst a lot of confusion.
Sometimes it's hard to see through the
Confusion but I think I've got a solution.

I haven't always known what to do with my kinda talent.
It's between entertainment and education and I'm
Tryna find the balance. 'Cause I think there's much
More that we can do. And that's my
Main thought when I speak to you.

See, we as humans keep assuming our world will keep improving if
We just keep it moving and keep on reproducing. We
Think we're getting better at understanding each other. But
We don't even respect the land that we cover. We
Carve it up with imaginary lines then we
Passionately fight – this happens every time. And we
Think we're getting better at understanding each other.
Yet everywhere on the planet others randomly suffer.

Now, in my opinion... having been born and raised in the
United Kingdom... looking at the world from the inside of England...
It's like we're all having different conversations. And
'Cause of that we're making conflicting observations.

Some people feel their biggest danger's their neighbours.
Others believe in being gracious to strangers.
Some people feel like as much as they wanna help, they're
Better off covering themselves.

So, for many of us, our best potential life is
Basically finding peace in an existential crisis. But I

Don't think we'd feel that if the information we needed to
Impact our world was available to us like...
Like art and fashion.
But it's hard to fathom a world you can't imagine.

Still... it's a vision that fills my heart with passion. To
Some of you I'm just another artist rapping. But
If my art can change someone's destination,
Would you call that entertainment or education?

I've already initiated this investigation.
Nowadays before I write I do some proper research.
Otherwise, I'm saying what everyone else is saying and I've
Been there, I've done that, I've got the T-shirt. I
Fill my art with actual information,
That way it's more like practical inspiration. The
Listener's a bit more G'd up afterward. And I
Cover everything from street to fatherhood.

This information is specifically curated to
Inspire new belief in my community. The
Writing's as critical as I'd like the youth to be 'cause I'd
Like to introduce the streets to...
New belief. And leave behind the useless beef.

This is for the youts in school I couldn't defend, the
Prisons and the funerals I couldn't attend. If I
want you to learn from my life, I should tell you what I've
Been through before and I shouldn't pretend.

So, here's a snapshot of life on Earth. It's the
Only life I've known, right from birth. But
You can only see this with your eyes closed...
So please put on your blindfolds...

Director: Great, thank you. Cut everybody.

Crew member: End board.

Director: How was that for you, George?

[George goes over the recording with the director and gives more ideas. First scene of Episode 3 starts playing]

Scene 1: Maths Class

[A secondary school maths teacher struggles to keep the attention of her restless class]

Savannah: Miss, probability trees ain't relevant to my life plan.

Classmate 1: About life plan. You're just trying to marry a rich white man.

[Class laughs]

Savannah: Actually, I'm gonna employ myself, then retire when I'm thirty and enjoy my wealth.

Miss B: OK everyone eyes on the board now.

Classmate 1: How you gonna retire when you're thirty, b?

Savannah: I'll let you know when I'm hiring. You can work for me.

Classmate 2: Come on, Savannah!

[Class laughs]
v**Savannah:** I'm gonna set up a laundry business. It's gonna wash the mandem's clothes and their dough.

Miss B: Savannah, enough!

Savannah: But Miss I'm just saying I got plans to be wealthy and I don't see how this lesson's gonna actually help me.

Miss B: So let me get this straight, Savannah: your whole plan is to launder dirty money for a road man—

Savannah: Nah, not for 'a' road man – for the whole gang.

[Class laughs]

Miss B: Yet you don't think you need to pay attention in maths though . . .

Savannah: Miss, this is probability that's— no! Just no.

[Class laughs]

Miss B: So, you plan to run a business handling cash without a basic understanding of maths?

Savannah: But Miss, my business is about helping guys stop doing crime and start doing positivity. What's that got to do with probability?

Classmate 1: Nah, nah, listen to her, Miss . . .

Miss B: Savannah, if you let me teach the lesson—

Savannah: Miss d'you know what it is? Everyone's got their lane. D'you know what I'm saying? Like, I hustle I don't need no class but obviously you teach so it will look bad on you if we don't pass.

Miss B: Savannah I'm not having this conversation with you—

Savannah: OK, I get it. Maths is like ideas and theories and that, but my business, yeah this is for real. I'm not being funny but business isn't your field.

Classmate 2: Ooo . . . Miss are you gonna have that?

Miss B: Savannah, where's your pen?

Savannah: I forgot my pen, Miss.

Miss B: Can someone lend Savannah a pen please?

[Classmates offer Savannah a pen]

Miss B: Write down what I'm about to say. See, Savannah, given that 50% of new companies in London cease to function past the first three years – write this down –

Savannah: I'm writing, Miss.

Miss B: Cease to function past the first three years, to me the importance of this work seems clear. And you said you want to retire by thirty?

Savannah: Yeah.

Miss B: Well annual growth of 20% in the first three years only happens to 6.6% of start-ups in the city, actually. And given that you plan to retire by thirty, your company will have to grow pretty rapidly. In fact you'll need a turnover of at least a million pounds a year, is that sounding fair? You hearing me loud and clear?

Savannah: Yeah that's me, come on.

Miss B: OK so less than 3— [classmates bickering] – write this down. Less than 3%— [more bickering]. Less than 3% of new businesses do those kinds of numbers. And many of them rely on private funders. Now, I can tell you this 'cause you guys are grown: companies owned by Africans – like you, Savannah – are four times more likely than ones owned by white people to be denied a loan.

Classmate 1: That's dread.

Miss B: But when you're self-employed, obviously, you ride alone. So it's up to you to decide if you're down for the ride or not. But to answer your question, Savannah: what's probability got to do with your business? Actually quite a lot. The three biggest [Savannah begins to argue] – listen. The three biggest challenges to Africans and women who have businesses are access to finances, choosing to move into saturated markets and straight up mismanagement. So, if all your money is coming from gangbangers and crooks, and you're running a laundry service as bad as it looks, you're gonna need a lot of maths skills to balance the books. And I've already mentioned the strain on business that mismanagement puts. So, you're gonna need qualified staff but your business partners aren't on the right path. Let's say for every year they spend in the streets their chances of ending deceased or with a sentence at least have gone up by half. So, what's the probability your business will last? Given that you're taking on such a difficult task in which a criminal past is a prominent feature?

Savannah: Miss, if I was smart enough to answer that question I'd do more with my life than becoming a teacher.

Miss B: Savannah, get out.

Analysis 1

[George walking alone in a field at night]

George: Alright, you can open your eyes. I'm
Hoping you guys can see the scope and the size of some of the
Challenges I've mentioned in my opening lines. The
Student was disconnected from the learning system 'cause
That environment and her concerns were different; the
Messages she was receiving weren't consistent.

The priority in life is making as much money as
Soon as possible, as far as she was aware. And

That goal is bigger than a maths class, so she feels it's
Unlikely she'll start achieving it there.
But the aim of the class is she's leaving prepared. So
How did it become so optional to her?
The only way to bridge that gap is for a
Teacher to stop and talk to her.

Now, this exchange faces obstacles at first.
As an adult who's responsible for her, the
Teacher is expected to preach and give perspective that
Realigns the student with the school's ideology.
But the student's coming from a place where the
Ideology is shaped by crime and poverty. Now
Remember what I said about different conversations
Causing conflicting observations? Here's a
Perfect example; the student's contribution could be
Interpreted as worthless or harmful.

'Cause essentially, she's interrupting the class
And potentially she's been corrupting the class with
Discussions of fast money that people around her made
Decent amounts of selling drugs in the past.

[George walks through a door in the middle of the field, entering the
classroom from the previous scene. George walks to the back of that
classroom as he continues to talk]

George: But even though she seems to wanna muck around...
The teacher doesn't shut her down.
Instead, she interrogates this line of thinking:
Does this girl see herself as some kind of kingpin? Or
May she be deflecting and maybe redirecting
Feelings of inadequacy? May she need protecting?

Luckily, the teacher sees this as a chance for
School life and street life to start intersecting.

If the student is shut down for referencing the streets, one of
Two things happens: she either exits or retreats.
And that way she probably ends up in the streets, so in the
Grand scheme of things everything repeats. Now,
Fair enough the subject matter is problematic, but
By taking time and weaving through this pathway
The teacher proves that her effectiveness
Lies in her ability to meet the student halfway.

The teacher is aware of the fact that
In the local area there's people moving Class As. But she's
Less concerned with what she can and what she can't say than
Helping the student, connecting the dots, her only
Question is 'Is the method effective or not?' Now despite the
Student responding rude and despondent
She actually respects it a lot.

When the teacher started engaging with her situation,
For the first time the student just concentrated.
And even though that should be enough to win her over...
Humans are complicated.

This podcast is my chance to explore why, I
Want it on every phone and every other device.
But anyway, let's get back to the story.
Cover your eyes.

[Return to Episode 3]

Scene 2: George's Place

[Miss B is chilling with her love interest, George, who has just listened to her story about the incident with Savannah earlier that day]

[Soundtrack: Chika Dole 'Touch']

George: She said what?! And what did you say?

Miss B: I just told her to get out. I hate doing that. It's like I'm giving up. It's a bit neglectful but obviously she was disrespectful.

George: That was mad disrespectful. You gotta draw the line before you get drawn out. Look – it's still on your mind all now.

Miss B: I think she felt like I was raining on her parade 'cause I was hitting her with all these statistics.

George: Yeah, but she needs to be more realistic. How you gonna be in a maths class talking about washing money for trap stars? These kids listen to two, two rap bars, they get gassed fast.

Miss B: Obviously, I don't wanna have those conversations with any fifteen-year-old but if I shut them down, they're gonna disengage. It's like sometimes I feel like fifteen's not such a distant age but this generation's on a different page. And if I don't talk to them about the roads then someone else will 'cause its fascinating, I know how these girls feel.

George: The good thing is you speak their language, babe. So, you can control the conversation and take it back to their studies, even when they're acting bare cruddy.

Miss B: Sorry, I don't mean to laugh . . .

George: What's funny?

Miss B: You should tell that to my senior staff.

George: Oh, swear down. Are they on a different page?

[Miss B gets a call from Shaun, the father of her daughter]

Miss B: Ugh it's Nevaeh's dad. One second. Hello?

Shaun: Yo. What you doing?

Miss B: Nothing. What's up?

Shaun: What you mean 'Nothing'? You must be doing something.

Miss B: Is there something I can help with, specifically?

Shaun: Yeah, I can't take Nevaeh tomorrow so you're gonna have to take her.

Miss B: Come again? Shaun, can I ask you something? When we make these arrangements do you think I do it for your entertainment?

[Miss B takes the call to another room. George receives a voice note on WhatsApp from Layla, a work friend]

Layla: Oi stranger, long time no see – how come we never link? Anyway, I heard you're performing at a conference I'm at tomorrow. We should get a drink. Let me know.

[Miss B hangs up and returns to the room]

Miss B: Sorry about that.

George: It's cool, B.

Miss B: No one told me life was this hard.

George: You seem tense, Would you like a massage?

Miss B: You think you're slick.

George: Nah, you think I'm slick.

Miss B: No comment.

George: Alright, wait there.

[George leaves and returns with massage oil]

George: What you saying? Neck, shoulders, lower back?

Miss B: Neck is more than enough, thank you.

George: No problem with that...

[George gives Miss B a neck massage]

Miss B: George, can I tell you something? Some days I feel like I ruined my life by having a baby . . . but if I had to live life without my daughter I'd be like a fish out of water. And I can't bear the thought of leaving her in this world with a father who can't support her.

Mmm. Feels good.

George: You like that, yeah?

Miss B: But 'cause I had her crazy young . . . even people at work treat me like I'm just another baby mum. And them kids try to show me up nonstop. I don't know why, you know me I'm on job.

George: Yeah, they're learning something, thanks to you. Probably 'cause they all fancy you.

Miss B: Erm . . . I thought they're learning 'cause I'm good at what I do.

George: Nah – yeah – obviously, not like—

Miss B: I'm just teasing you. But I do think sometimes people don't see the value in me. I mean, look at you and me. Be real with me. You don't want me you just like to chill with me. And I'm not saying that for sympathy, it's kinda the same thing for me. But I think I feel like that just 'cause I think you feel like that. With me you don't act all lively and excited. You don't even come to my flat despite being invited. I bet you don't even know what floor I live on. Right or wrong? You just pull up outside and honk. What? All of a sudden you're a silent monk?

George: What am I supposed to say? What do you want me to say? For real?

Miss B: Well, I am gonna have my daughter after all, so I should probably get an early night.

George: Alright, I'll drop you in a second—

Miss B: Nah, I'll get a cab, thanks, I'm fine. *I'm fine.*

George: Fine..

Analysis 2

[George is in an underwater tank]

George: When I was in school, I studied literature. It
Taught me to analyse the big picture. It
Showed me how to think outside myself, consider
Other perspectives, you know. Switch it up.

But it couldn't teach me to be a man.
To care for a woman as deeply as I can. To
Make a commitment and stick to it. To

Study the book of life and not just flick through it. The
Subject improved my vocabulary.
Didn't teach me nothing about keeping my word.
I could break down anything that was said to me
But I couldn't deep what I heard.

[Cut to two onlookers, watching George's performance on a screen]

Onlooker 1: Why did he wanna film this bit underwater?

Onlooker 2: Er, I think it's a metaphor, or... yeah... something along those lines.

Onlooker 1: That's George.

Onlooker 2: Yeah. Do you mind getting a selfie with me?

Onlooker 1 takes a selfie of the two of them]

Onlooker 2: And one landscape...

[George in the background]

There is no school for relationships. When you're
Young you think it's cool to be chasing chicks, start
Getting attention, you take the piss but
What are you gonna do? It's just the way it is.

Over time you start running out of words.
Running out of nouns. Running out of verbs.
Losing interest. Switching your style.
So, where's all the literature now?

[Cut back to George]

The poets I studied in school years ago... they were

Tryna warn me but I couldn't hear it though. The
Language they were using was putting me off and I was
Sixteen so half the time I couldn't be bothered.

But imagine an education system...
Based on how we relate to each other. So,
Instead of taking words from an ancient verse we
Analyse the things we actually say to each other.
See, we invest a lot of time in escaping each other.

[Alarm goes off in George's underwater tank as it quickly gets flooded
with water]

George: The electrician's bill goes on Netflix and chill. And if
Not that, I'll be in a rave with my brother saving a number when I
Don't know how to behave as a lover.
It's just one of them things I can't wait to discover!

[George goes underwater]

George: And as nice as my bars seem,
I'm still the guy from the last scene.
Maintaining a presence even though I'm not involved.
Blowing hot and cold...

I don't know if there's something wrong with me, but this is
Something that I've had to manage constantly. And
Yeah, I've learned a lot so I'm comfy with it now, but these are
Things we should be talking to our young people about.

[George comes up for air]

George: These kids are exposed to much more than they would have
been before.
I never knew that I could make a woman insecure.

Or maybe I did but I was just hood and immature.
Giving samples when I couldn't give her more.

[George in the shower]

George: Under my education system, we'd
Set aside time every day to listen.
Listen to the voices, decisions and the choices,
Musicians and politicians, the whispers and the noises.
Yeah man.

[Cut to a performance shot]

George: See, with these phones we're beside each other daily...
So connected that we drive each other crazy.
At the same time, we're more alone than ever. But
What you gonna do, ignore your phone forever?
That's why we maintain these unhealthy connections, posting
Selfies, reflections, wealthy projections.
Situation-ships. Shit relationships.
What's the future generation meant to make of this?

The least we could do is capture our experience,
Create that feedback loop and feed that through.
This podcast is how I choose to go about it,
And I want it on every phone and every other device.
For now, though, come we get back to the story.
Cover your eyes.

[Return to Episode 3]

Scene 3: Deputy Head's Office

[Mr Brown, the Deputy Head, is finishing a call in his office as Miss B knocks]

Mr Brown: . . . I would be actually pursuing this at a higher level, but it just stands that I— Yep, come in. I will be leveraging the access I have. So thanks for your assistance, I'll be awaiting your call.

[Miss B sits down. Mr Brown hangs up.]

Mr Brown: Hello there, sorry about that, terribly rude of me. Just had some bother with the train line. See, every day I get the same train at the same time, pretty early: 6.30. Now, this morning I was actually late in because the train I jumped on changed destination . . . mid-journey. And look, yeah, these things happen, right, you take it up with the service provider, which I did, firmly. 'Cause actually, technically, I didn't sign up to take two trains. I signed up for one. So OK, call me anal, for sure, but, you know, that's the guy I've become. I mean look; I value consistency, and I'd hope that is reflected in the ship I like to run. So, I do like for my staff to sing from the same hymn sheet. You know, ultimately, our differences are only skin deep. See, when you took this job, you committed to upholding certain values. And by that standard, what you stand accused of having said yesterday places you directly in breach. Now, you are a talent. That much is apparent. And hey, a role in senior leadership for you certainly is within reach. But that would require a unanimous feeling that we are, pretty much as I said, singing from the same hymn sheet. Now, I do accept the point that some of the more challenging students may warrant a situational change of tact, but you know, that doesn't actually change the fact that as a school our name should remain intact. And, look, if it turns out you are more interested in helping these young people sort of sharpen their *street smarts* then actually this might not be the place for that. Perhaps you'd be afforded more leeway in a pupil referral unit. But the problem we have in a school like this is if you pay undue attention to the troublesome ones, you can disturb more students. And I appreciate you're using your personal prudence but with the limited time you have you need to choose between work or nuisance. I mean, here's the deal: parents entrust us with their children for seven hours a day so that we can turn them into functional members of society. Not criminal masterminds. And in the typical class environment that's difficult half the time, to say the least. But actually, any deviation from that contract makes us no better than the train that changes destination after passengers board. Which is a misstep we cannot afford. At all. So look, let's draw a line under that one and carry on galloping forth, if—

[Knock at the door]

Assistant: Sorry, Mr Brown, the fire drill is just about to start.

Mr Brown: Ahh yes. Well, I'm actually going to have to take this one, I'm afraid. So, thanks for your time. And remember – galloping forth!

[Miss B leaves the office]

Analysis 3

George: Before uni I planned to become a Member of Parliament.
I intended on representing an argument: that
We could change our own prospects with the right
support. But then I realised life is short.

British politics is like a sort of members' club. And
That's not where I saw my life ending up. I
Used to think that if I was incensed enough about the
Spending cuts, the best thing I could do with that emotion was to
Take it to the political space, which is a
difficult place for representing us. It
Took me a while to figure it out at first...
But that's not how power works.

Power's a numbers game. People respond to
Pressure. I'm the same. If I'm
Under strain and it's starting to numb the brain then I'm
Much more likely to succumb to pain. And

That's what gets results when people want a change. They
Organise themselves around an idea,
Build support by leveraging funds and fame,
And when their cause reaches critical mass after they
Fill it up with enough political gas...
No one really wants the blame of
Stunting change that's already underway. And by
then it doesn't matter what the pundits say. In
Industry and culture we see a lot of this, but what
made me acknowledge this was politics.

The reason I didn't wanna become an MP was 'cause I
Felt none of them's free.
The Party gives them their credibility and I
Can't allow a party to ever limit me.
My perspective's quite reflective of my collective's
Respective experience and sensibilities.
But I'm a minority – either by geography or ethnicity.
The political establishment wasn't built around me,
Even though they won't say this explicitly.
So, as I proceed into the higher leagues of this society
I perceive people like me fading into the distance quietly.

Whether that's because of poverty, geography or ethnicity,
Either way, message received. To
Realise this all has been a blessing for me, and now I've
Realigned my thoughts I'm thinking less typically. The
Freedom-fight for more inclusion domestically...
It's not that interesting to me.

I don't even know if I wanna be more included, I'm
Talking my slang and they think I'm talking stupid, I'm
Thinking 'You're deluded.'
Speaking to my people's not an effort for me, I could
Do that as a career indefinitely.
Definitely.

So, the question for me... is 'What
Do I wanna get them to see?' And
Should it be the same message for everybody?
Bearing in mind it's a varied and wide territory.

All I know is from that previous scene,
I need my own space and I need me a team.
It's all well and good me being keen but a
Lot of people see me and scheme because I represent
Change, and the change I may present...
Might come as a danger they resent...
It might change the day-to-day for them, so no
Matter how much they fake and they pretend they have
No intention of relinquishing powers and if they
Feel threatened they'll start extinguishing ours.
That's one thing I've learned from a
Life in England full of English encounters.

There's all these internal ways of making you learn your place,
From a fake smile to a, sort of, turn of phrase.

Believe me, power expresses itself in subtle forms and for
Us, it's just the sound of shutting doors. We
Need our own doors if it's not a sound that we like
Otherwise, this is what it's bound to be like.

A one-size-fits-all education policy
That doesn't at least account for race and poverty...
Can't possibly create equality.

And forcing that conversation in unchanging spaces
To me is not the most effective use of time. It
Limits the prospect of reducing crime. It's
Like a boring way to lose your mind.

The ecosystem of power would be on the
Curriculum every day in my system of education.
That way we could reposition a generation away from
Misplaced persistence and dedication –
Entering professions with the best of intentions
Only to be met with resistance and segregation.
Putting up with tacit addresses from passive-aggressive employers
Who refuse to be transparent. It's a
Waste of opportunity and talent. It's
Better to redirect the energy we inject into
Those structures towards our own needs, so
We can reapply the rewards and proceeds of our
Wasted potential to our basic essentials.

And this podcast is how I choose to go about it, I
Want it on every phone and every other device.
But for now, let's get back to the story...
Cover your eyes.

[Return to Episode 3]

Scene 4: Final Hours

[Miss B gets in the car and plays a voice note from Shaun]

Shaun:
Yo change of plan. I can take Nevaeh tonight. So, whatever you planned to do later tonight you can go do that. And next week I'll bring the yout back.

[Miss B is quiet for a bit then sends a voice note in reply]

Miss B: So you *can* take Nevaeh tonight . . . yet you're saying it like . . . I didn't just cancel my plans. Like you couldn't have just taken her to

Anne's or her gran's.

Shaun, our daughter needs us to be civil with each other. If she sensed this tension even a little bit she'd suffer. OK, we're not doing great right now but we've done worse. And we only got better by remembering that she comes first.

Changing Nevaeh's schedule in the middle of the week without any warning is not putting her first. Imagine how she feels, it's off-putting for her. And it's frustrating for me having to talk about something this simple. I don't think of myself as a single mum: I'm her mum, and I'm single but it's like you . . .

Can you please make sure she does ten minutes of reading before she sleeps? The book's in her bag. And please keep an eye on what she's watching online, I don't want her obsessing over her looks or her swag.

I know you think I'm saying this 'cause I just like to moan and cuss and over-fuss. But, Shaun, all I mean is . . . our child needs consistency from both of us.

[Miss B sends the voice note and sits there, reflecting, before sending another voice note – this time to George]

Miss B: Hi Georgie Porgie. I don't really like communicating by walkie talkie so if you're free later . . . turns out I won't have Nevaeh, which everyone knew was gonna happen, but yeah man I'm deya. Gonna do some marking and some lesson planning with a glass of wine to pass the time. So, if you're local your ass is mine.

[Soundtrack: Abi Ocia – Running]

[George backstage at his performance. He receives Miss B's message but has no time to listen to it because he's about to go on stage]

Venue Sound Guy: George we're ready for you backstage.

George: Coming now.

[Miss B in her car]

Miss B: Oh my God, if you heard how the deputy head spoke to me today you won't believe it, mate. It's too much to tell, I'll tell you when— *if* you come later.

[Cut to George performing]

George: Pierre Bourdieu said all reality is a construct. We exist in relation to our social ties. So you'll never understand me without considering where I'm from . . . and the local guys.

[Cut to Miss B back in her flat]

Miss B: And for the record I'm over yesterday. To be honest I think your joke about my kids fancying me was poorly timed, but I know that's just you and your horny mind.

[Miss B hesitates before sending then decides not to. Back to George performing]

George: We exist in relation to other guys and girls. So, I had to move to a better reality, from one where everybody tries and fails.

[Back to Miss B in the flat, pouring the glass of wine]

Miss B: So yeah, if you're up for a little vibe, little bants, that invitation to mine still stands. Not 'cause you're hella important; just 'cause you're better than boredom.

[Back to George on stage]

George: See, If we forget how outcast the voice of an outcast is they'll never be heard, every word is noiseless, without answers. See, there are no choices without chances. Thank you.

[Applause]

George: Thank you!

[Cut to the bar, after the performance]

Layla: Not gonna lie, I'm a little hater sometimes but your performance was so entertaining, that poem's amazing! It's like no one in the audience blinks.

George: Thank you. Would you like to order some drinks?

[Back to Miss B in her flat]

Miss B: By the way, do you actually know what floor I live on? You better do . . . 'cause I'm not telling you. Anyway, I'm kinda tipsy (sips tea) . . .

[Time passes]

Miss B: OK, you're taking too long, let me tell you what the deputy head said. Imagine yeah, he basically said I should find work in a PRU. I'm thinking *do you know how lucky you are that I'm working with you?* He was like 'you might call me anal' I was like 'yeah 'cause you're an ass!'

[Miss B gradually gets more intoxicated]

Miss B: Ahhh my head's spinning, my head is spinning, babe. I wish you were here right now.

[Miss B dozes off as memories swim in and out of focus. Cut to George entering a cab]

Driver: Yes, good evening, brother.

George: Yes, bossman, how you doing?

Driver: Yeah, what is your name?

George: George. Is me.

Driver: Thank you, and where are you going?

George: Going to North West 10, bro.

Driver: Oh OK, OK. Crazy traffic, man it's—

George: Bossman, I'm sorry I'm just about to get on the phone.

Driver: Oh, sorry!

[George starts recording a voice note]

George: Yo, B. I listened to your million voice notes! I'd love to come through, but I'm waved right now. Tell a lie, I don't know what floor you live on. I don't even know the name of your block. And I see your point – that's saying a lot.

I've been thinking about what you said. It's been spinning around in my head. And it's true . . . I'm man who only does what he wants to do. And 'cause of that I'm complacent when it comes to you. Just Like your baby father or your kids at school; you give more than you get, and it isn't cool. It must be difficult. In fact, let me give you a call . . .

[George ends voice note and calls. Phone goes straight to voicemail.

He then notices the driver taking an unfamiliar route]

George: Yo, bossman where you going? We need the A40, brother.

Driver: Brother, crazy fire that side. All over the news – listen.

Radio: *Coming from West London, the London fire brigade are dealing with a huge fire in a residential tower block in West London. This is Grenfell Tower, a twenty-three- maybe twenty-four-storey block of flats in West Kensington—*

George: Bossman, turn that down for me. Turn it down, boss.

[Driver turns the radio down. George sends Miss B another voice note]

George: Yo B, what's your block called, again? I'm hearing there's a madness in your ends. I can't remember what your block's called. Let me know what block it is, B. Please. Soon as you get this, get back to me . . .

[Cut to the tragedy. Residents screaming, newsreaders reporting]

Analysis 4

George: Once upon a time there lived a boy called Francis.
Francis was born into a wealthy family. His
Grandfather and his great-grandfather were businessmen.
And his dad earned a healthy salary.

Francis bought his way into the army.
Eighteen years old paying it off calmly. And
Over the course of his life he's earning honours
More than a lot of learned scholars. All
Kinds of them awards like the title of a 'Lord' and the
Cross of St Michael and St George. So

Yeah, he was English...
And as you can tell he was fairly distinguished. When he
died he had a road named after him
Seems like he was always on a path to win 'cause of the
Background of the woman who mothered him and the
Man who was actually there to father him.

But what did these people do for a living? What
Business was his great grandfather in? Them man were
Shotting and ting. But their product just happened to be
Copper and tin.
This is in the 1800s by the way, so you just
Know right away. Those guys were paid.

Little Frankie boy's joined the British army in 1859
And it was a career he stuck to. So, to
Anyone who's got a bit of a history mind...
1859, what you think he got up to?

Of course, the Scramble for Africa. When Europe
Decided to come and handle the land for us, then
Turned into vandals and wrapped it up.
Crushing our systems like plastic cups.

Frankie fought in the South, East and North,
Carrying that White Man's Burden, proceeding forth.
See, even though he came from wealth, on the
Battlefield he made a name for himself. And
Because of his achievements in the time he spent alive he was
Remembered when he died in 1925.

He had a building named after him half a century on,
And that name will last potentially long after we've eventually gone.

See, 'Lord Francis Grenfell' is the first name on

Grenfell Tower's Wikipedia page.
But 'Grenfell Tower'... isn't even mentioned on his Wikipedia page.
At the time of writing, the public inquiry
Hadn't even reached its intermediate stage, and how
Long that will take isn't easy to gauge. Yet
After a whole year of coverage, this is a line of
Commentary with which the media didn't really engage.

Grenfell the man helped to colonise the land that a
Lot of these emigrant residents migrated from.
But even though they weren't the murderers and robbers...
This guy's name lives on. Here's some
Context for those who might take this wrong:

Two hundred and twenty-seven bedrooms.
Two hundred and twenty-three evacuees.
Seventy-two recorded deaths.
So what that means is
We can only account for almost one person per bedroom...
On a Tuesday night, in a
Building that could house 600 people
situated in a low-income immigrant community –
In London.

See, unlike Francis, the Grenfell residents
Aren't individual Wikipedia entrants. So the
Only way most of us can remember them...
Is through their specific media mentions. But
Those who lived in the building were in the middle of building; their
Lives, their futures, their relationships, in the
Sixth richest city in the world.
And out of nowhere devastation hits.

A fridge exploded.
How old is your fridge?
This one was purchased seven years prior.

Imagine waking up and all you hear is 'Fire!' Your
Flatmate's telling you to leave the building... and
Now you can hear the screams of children. The
Smoke is so thick you don't make it too far.
Firefighters are begging you to stay where you are. Then you
Get a flashback to all the meetings you had;
About the landlord treating you bad. About the
Power surge from a few years before...
And all the fires that it nearly caused... the
Refurbishment from just the year before... and the
Cladding with the flammable material. The
Council that stopped you from accessing
Conversations they were having with the architects. You were
Knocking and they wouldn't let you past the steps
'Cause they had no plans of sorting it out...
Eddie from the 16th floor...
This is exactly what he was talking about.

The Prime Minister, Theresa May,
Didn't visit the scene for at least a day. And
Even then she preferred keeping it private, no
Media invited, no meeting survivors.
Maybe she was feeling weak, or maybe she
Didn't see the need to speak with cleaners and drivers. We
Have no way of knowing the reason behind this.
But what we can decide is... that
We choose to recognise and respect the lives of
Those who met their unexpected demise.

From the ashes their memories arise and
Provide a guiding light up in the skies. Now, one last time...
Please cover your eyes.

Scene 5: Savannah's Letter

[Through tears, Savannah reads a heartfelt letter to Miss B at her memorial]

Savannah: It was a trick question, Miss. You said 'What's the chances my business will last?' Because I'm taking on a difficult task and my business partners have a criminal path, like . . . typical path.

I thought you were having a dig and a little laugh like 'Where's this girl going with her criminal staff?' But now I remember, the first thing you said was 'there's a 50% chance *any* new business will last'.

So, um . . . I tried to write it down in a probability tree. So I could properly see what the possibilities be.

Only 3% of the 50% of companies that survive their first three years in the same period of time turn over at least a million pounds a year. But I couldn't work that out when you asked me and think it's down to fear.

If a thousand students started a business now and here, fifteen of us could turn over a million pound annually.

I just felt like it wouldn't be me, so my feelings started spilling out angrily and I'm so sorry for being rude to you, Miss. I am, really.

I thought you were trying to dim my little light because with my little sight I was trying to win my little fight, but you were trying to prepare me for *war*.

And all of the things you said – I get it now; they're *independent variables*. They can happen at the same time. So, while I've got access to an education I might as well pattern that to save time.

The fact I'm a female; the fact I'm African; the fact that half my friends are drug trafficking means it might be harder for me securing a loan, and I might end up going all-in alone. But you know what, Miss?

Even if the chances of me closing the business in the first three years is 90% – which, obviously, I would highly resent – there's still a 10% chance I might make it. It's only right that I take it, Miss it's quite basic. So, thank you, Miss B.

George: So, this is like in the cinema at the end when everyone gets up and brushes the popcorn off their clothes. But you're still sitting there, affected. I want you to picture that screen, pitch black with the words *'Based on a true story'*.

Now it says written and directed by George the Poet.

Produced by Benbrick and George the Poet.

. . . and here's the cast in order of appearance:
Jade Alleyne as Savannah
Michael Mpanga as Classmate One
Freddie Mpanga as Classmate Two
Me as basically everyone else.
Sophia Thakur as Work Friend [Layla]

Benbrick as Mr Brown's Assistant and Venue Sound Guy

Featured Music

Touch – Performed by Chika Dole
Written by Chika Dole and Semi Skimmed
Produced by Semi Skimmed

Running – Performed by Abi Ocia

All other original music produced and composed by Benbrick.

Special thanks to Kenny Mpanga, Khalil Rouse, Peter Gregson, Greg Jameson, and Future Studies.

This piece was written in honour of the Grenfell Tower residents and their surrounding community.

EPISODE 4: It's On Us

Extra Info:

- This episode (and every episode before it) was driven by the idea that our experiences are valuable. I tried to prove this point at every stage of Chapter One, which is why I wrote about the police incident; I wanted to show how even negative moments could be used creatively, and I wanted to send support to others going through these things on their own.
- The title of this episode was adapted from the song 'It's On Me', by Mucky. Mucky and I were introduced by my good friend Klash. We spent some time in Brixton and in my area, reflecting on our communities. These conversations always brought me back to the conclusion that we have to change the way we live, and no one will help us more than we can help ourselves.

Fun Facts:

- My friend Deezy, who speaks in Scene 2, was one of the most influential rappers in my hood growing up. He's also one of the first people my brother and I met as kids on the estate.
- My conversation with Jamelia was unexpected. I was in her city and just reached out to see how she was.

This was another one I wish I didn't have to write. Following the Grenfell episode, my initial plan was to introduce my imaginary character, Sanyu. But (un)fortunately I was distracted, after being searched for weapons by riot police outside my parents' home. This incident pulled me back into the long-running struggle between the Black community and the police. At first, I was angry at being treated like a criminal, and disgusted by the way the police spoke to my parents and neighbours. But looking back now, I can see that this incident helped to refocus me. I needed that reminder of what we went through as teenagers, and I'm glad my audience got a glimpse of it. Still, at the end of the day, these are not the social dynamics we want to pass on to our children, and the burden of renegotiating our position in society is on us. Special thank you to all my friends on the voice notes at the start, and to the interviewees, Deezy and Jamelia, who shared heart-breaking personal stories that the world needed to hear.

[George receives messages from friends after a publicised incident with the police. Around 10pm on June 29th, 2018, George was searched for weapons by riot police outside his childhood home. An investigation later found that the police conducted the search unfairly. George described their conduct as disrespectful towards his family and neighbours. This episode opens with voice notes from concerned friends, intercut with the original recording of the incident]

Kareem: [To George] *Yeah, um, just checking to see if you're good after last night. I don't know what I can offer to do, but . . .*

Yasmin: [To George] *Oh my goodness, I've just seen your post and it's shocking. How are you? Are you OK?*

Marc: [To George] *Good morning, bro. What was I gonna say to you? I probably watched your video about thirty times, man.*

Officer: [During the incident] *He's being stopped and detained for a Section 1 search.*

George's Mum: [During the incident] What is a Section 1 search?

Officer: [During the incident] *It's a search for weapons.*

Richard: [To George] *I see them I'm like 'Nah, man. They're picking on the wrong guy, this guy's not involved in nothing stupid like that' . . .*

Yasmin: [To George] *How are you? Are you OK? How are you feeling?*

Kareem: [To George] *Um, yeah . . . I don't wanna just assume George is alright, it's big George . . .*

George's Mum: [During the incident] *Excuse me, sir. I just need to understand, why a Section 1 search?*

Richard: [To George] *I see your mum . . . like, nah that's not right, like, your mum was distressed and stuff like that and I see your dad proper getting upset.*

Richard: [During the incident] What's the grounds?

Officer: [During the incident] *They've told him that, they don't need to tell you . . .*

Marc: *Obviously, you know me, cuz, I'm anti-system, I'm anti-feds, you know like that. But erm, do me a favour, cuzzy . . . don't post with emotion. You taught me that thinking . . .*

Officer: [During the incident] *I've watched you and listened to your demeanour. You're not very cooperative. You clearly don't like police officers.*

George's Mum: [During the incident] *Do you want to be cooperative?*

George's Dad: [During the incident] *You don't like him as well. You don't like him very much.*

Officer: [During the incident] *I've never met him.*

Marc: [To George] *You don't wanna be seen like you're now targeting the police.*

George's Mum: [During the incident] *Do you have to handcuff my son? Does he need to be handcuffed? He's not going to run away.*

George's Dad: [During the incident] *You don't like the look of us.*

Officer: [During the incident] *I've never met him before.*

Marc: [To George] *. . . 'cause remember, it wasn't the police, it was the actions of a few individuals. They are not representative of that* *whole system ... well we know, we know, George but I just don't want you to ... you get me, remember your fanbase and stuff ...*

Richard: [During the incident] *... you're talking about insurance and weapons.*

Officer: [During the incident] *Well we don't know that by looking at him.*

Richard: [During the incident] *OK, but you're talking about insurance and weapons it's two different things you're trying to look into ...*

Officer: [During the incident] *Well, things ring up. When you're dealing with one thing, another thing will come to light.*

Richard: [During the incident] *So, did weapons come up when you put his name through?*

Marc: [To George] *Call a meeting with them, call a meeting with the Met or, like ... go through the proper channels. Yeah? Alright, my brother, you have a wicked day and if you wanna speak at any point, shout me, man. And I hope that it doesn't affect you. I hope you can just use it to inspire you, and if you're gonna address it, please be articulate, bro. Thank you. And I love you, bro.*

George: Hello and welcome to Episode 4 of *Have You Heard George's Podcast?*

[Soundtrack: Mucky 'It's On Me']

SCENE 1: GEORGE GOES TO UGANDA

[Scene opens with George a plane back to Uganda]

George: After that night I just wanted to be left alone.
So, I went to my second home, Uganda,

I wanted to be around some true survivors
Speaking to Uber drivers. Conversations getting deeper than scuba
    divers.
Conscious of the absence of the people that grew beside us, I
Put my earphones in place, turn up the
track till I'm hearing the bass and stare into space.

[Cut to George in a Ugandan cab]

I'm in the Uber listening to Mucky – this one's called 'It's On Me'
And I feel this strongly. I
Gaze into the distance thinking about Black people's engagement
    with the systems of criminal justice and formal education.
Both of them are used as a form of segregation.

My reflection's looking into my world
Thinking 'You should try living in *my* world!' Then he
Narrows his eyes and looks past me . . .
Sees all the people around me.
That's when he sees that their skin's decomposing
Looks behind him and he's instantly frozen.

Old friends become young friends when they're
Older than you but they die at a young age.
Even though you're getting older, their
Youth is immortalised on a front page. Some of them
Follow me around, reminding me that one day I ain't
Gonna be around. And
When that day comes I'm gonna wanna be around 'cause
Currently we're down.

This is not an opinion, it's a statement of fact:
12% of the prison population is Black, when only
3% of the whole population is Black. I'm
Passionate about changing this stat, so I gotta make an impact.

But when you fight to take control and try to break the mould
Despite an aching soul, over time it takes a toll.
I'm not OK. Certain days I ain't got no faith but
Yo, I'm the artist George the Poet.
If I'm not feeling confident, I can't afford to show it.
If police really got to man I can't afford to show it. I'm
Supposed to do that thing when I half talk-and-flow it.
Endorse the moment, I'm forced to own it.
Record a poem. Explore the whole thing.
Grab the curtains and pull them open. What's all this sulking?
You got this whole place to yourself you know,
Like a twelve-year-old Macaulay Culkin.
Nah man, you ain't been depressed.
Stop claiming you're stressed and ignore that little pain in your
    chest.
It's a minor. Look at Anthony, he's a lifer. Does he phone you up and
    cry, cuz?
You'll be alright, cuz.

[Return to Ugandan cab]

Then I notice the music's gone but at the
Same time the news is on. The
Same social media I take for granted, the
Government tried to tax that.
Looking kind of slapdash and now they're facing backlash. I
Hate seeing people have to fight for their freedoms, but at
Least it's not a racial war. And that's a mad
Thing to be grateful for. But I've got friends that have
Only ever been told that they're Black and never
Saw themselves any other way before . . .

SCENE 2: CONVERSATIONS ABOUT TRAUMA

[Recording of a conversation with George's childhood friend, Deezy]

Deezy: ... *what they put in front of me and what knowledge they feed me, but I don't really know wagwan in Africa. That shit's lost, I can't tell you my surname. You know what I'm saying? I can't tell you what tribe or family I'm from. Man's lost. So, when you see kids out here moving like they're lost, why are people surprised that they're lost?*

George: That's my bredrin, Deezy, talking about displacement.
Talking about feeling awkward and out of place in the land you were raised on
And the land where your ancestors came from.
Why's it so lonely being Black when there's bare of us?
How can we be so powerless when we know for a fact that they're scared of us?

Deezy: ... *whatever their title is, I would ask them when they see or hear about another Black person – child – being stabbed, shot, murdered, or imprisoned in these streets I wanna know how it affects them. Not how it makes them feel, because everyone's gonna say 'Oh, it makes me feel sad I don't want this for my country, I don't want this for the situation,' no. How does it affect you? How does it affect your community? How does it affect your family structure? You know what I'm saying? Because I've lost family to the roads, and I watched my living room break down.*

[Recording of a conversation with the singer and TV presenter, Jamelia]

Jamelia: *I remember at thirteen, my brother got stabbed. And that was ... I can categorically say that was the moment that every single one of us lost our innocence. But then, we go back to school*

on Monday morning. Do you know what I mean? There's no counsel-
ling. There's no ... nobody's thinking 'How does that affect these
young Black children? To have a brother literally taken away from
them ...'

George: Imagine. A whole Jamelia.
Sometimes I think nowadays the roads is greezier
But that happened before Drill music and social media.
See, there's a trauma that I can't put into words
But when you hear it from a successful Black woman like her
It makes getting that point a cross so much easier.
It's mad though ... Jamelia.

Jamelia: *This is it. But nobody ... nobody acknowledged these are*
hurt boys. These are damaged boys. These are pressurised boys.
And you know, they don't have a sense of self in the world, because
they're going to school and the school— the teachers don't like
them. The police on the road ... I remember once going bike-riding
with my brothers ... me, I was such a tomboy when I was little ...
going on a bike-ride with my brothers and the police stopped us on
bikes, you know. So just imagine. Stopping us on bikes and asking us
– particularly the boys – 'Where did you get these bikes from? Who
are these bikes' – it was their bikes! And to me that was the begin-
ning of stop and search, so by the time you get to stop and search,
you've got a terrible relationship with the police.

SCENE 3: VICTIM-BLAMING

George: The fact that we actually have the capacity to
Speak out and not just take this passively ...
That makes a lot of people angry.
They can't stand the audacity.

Our story makes lot of eyes roll in irritation.
We're accused of downplaying our role in this equation.

We're told that we're always self-imposing limitations and if our
Attitude was right there would be no discrimination.

We're told it's because our homes are broken and they're failing.
We're told that this is old, and this is draining.
We're told to quit complaining.
Quit complaining?
Why isn't this known as victim-blaming?

It's the same thing.
Victim-blaming is a term for situations in which the main thing
Focused on isn't just the crime, but the victim's actions and
    decisions at the time. There's two sides to every story, but you
    want to hear theirs first before listening to mine, and you know
    why.
Some people can do no wrong,
Others can do no right.

SCENE 4: THE RIOTS

[Soundtrack: Ghetts 'Menace']

[Montage of reporting on the 2011 England Riots]

George: I couldn't rate the riots of 2011, but I was
Praying for Mark Duggan's entry to heaven.
Most of them man there was cowards to me, I'm thinking
'Why don't you lot take this to the powers that be?'
You lot ain't running up on no police stations 'cause
You lot ain't tryna have it out with police.
I wanna see you all maintaining this energy
Once Mark's body is lain in the cemetery when you're
Sitting on remand in a state penitentiary.
Everyone's reaction was different, that was mine I was
Pissed off at the time.
Pissed off that people's hearts were hardened now, pissed

Off that Mark's family were targets now, pissed his
Killers were defo getting pardons now and pissed
Off at how that woman disrespected Darcus Howe about Marcus
　　Dowe.

Reporter: Marcus Dowe, are you shocked by what you've seen there last night?

Darcus Howe: No, not at all.

Reporter 1: You say you're not shocked, does this mean you condone what happened in your community last night?

Darcus Howe: Of course not! There is a young man called Mark Duggan. He has parents, he has brothers, he has sisters, and a police officer blew his head off . . .

SCENE 5: THE SHOOTING OF MARK DUGGAN

George: A man was killed and his
Family was ignored. Just like my family were ignored that night.
No effort was made to present the facts right. And
Despite any attempts to gaslight, we can't pretend that that's right.
Mark was in the back of a taxi.
Apparently, there was a box with a strap in the back seat
Police stopped the car and according to the driver
Mark started running for his life, but
Two shots caught him – one arm, one chest. And now the
Unanswered question is *why were shots fired at an*
Unarmed suspect . . . if a shot wasn't bussed yet?

Initial reports said Mark fired a gun,
Implying this was why he was trying to run.
No word to the family for a day and a half but
That's not the headline once a riot's begun.

One of the officers said they saw Mark
Pull a pistol from his waistband, implying that's the
reason for the fate that he suffered
But he never touched the gun, as it was later discovered.

The officer that said this, furthermore,
Never mentioned it in his first report.
The irony is police always say it may
Harm your defence if you do not mention when
Questioned something you later rely on in court.
I.e. your story looks shaky if you miss out the important bits once
    you've been caught.
Food for thought.

See I'm trying to explain the demonstrations of resistance.
Three of the officers said they saw a colleague
Throw this gun away into the distance.
These statements were later rescinded.
This kind of behaviour explains the widespread
Intergenerational police hatred in England.

An officer was injured, the Independent Police Complaints
    Commission
Released a statement in which (the police later claimed) 'mistakes'
    were written.
Given the sensitivity and the intensity around these
Events it seems that wasn't a great decision. They
Claimed the officer was shot before Mark but that's
Not at all possible, darg.
'Cause here's the illogical part:
The bullet came from a police gun, and
Got stuck in the officer's radio after passing
Through Mark's arm.

That's why the community's looking at you, police . . . and
Asking *you* wagwan.

Turns out there was no evidence the gun was fired.
Makes you lot look like a bunch of liars.
This reflects the disregard and disrespect that
Characterised the London riots.

[Page turn, return to interviews at the scene of the riots]

Interviewee 1: *Basically, this all started 'cause these feds shot my boy innit. And obviously, everyone knew this guy innit...*

Interviewee 2: *We've all got a story to tell about the fucking police, and individual police brutality. You know what, you see when you treat people like animals, they start behaving like animals.*

Reporter 2: *Scenes of chaos and devastation. Sights no one had predicted and which have shocked the country...*

Interviewee 3: *We was all there, they just set the dogs on us. That's it. They told us to go up here and just set the dogs on us. I've been bitten four times by the dogs...*

[Page turn]

Reporter 1: Mr Howe if I can just ask you, you are not a stranger to riots yourself, I understand, are you? You have taken part in them yourself.

Darcus Howe: I have never taken part in a single riot. I've been on demonstrations that ended up in a conflict. And, have some respect for an old West Indian negro and stop accusing me of being a rioter.

SCENE 6: REFLECTIONS FROM UGANDA

[Return to George on his Uganda trip. Locals laughing and chatting in the background]

George: There's a few reasons why I come up with this podcast
Obviously to drop bars. But also, to remind myself that
Poverty is not ours. We're made to think it is.
'Cause pain sells, that's the nature of the biz,
But our brain cells have to change the way we live.
Do you know how hard that is?
That's why art matters.

[Cut to George in a Ugandan bar]

The status quo can be challenged with a credible
    counter-narrative,
I mean . . . without sounding arrogant
I reckon that's what *we* kinda did.
'Cause obviously, man are talented.

We've got careers 'cause we share stories that not
Everybody hears *or* reads, and we're getting loads
Done. Get a load of Dun from Episode 1.
Ambush, Jorja Smith. We're all recording piff and we're
On the map but what if the coordinates shift?

People really think our reality's all a myth these
Times the ends is shipwrecked and we're all adrift.
Obviously, our prominence is a blessing. Best thing to
do is shed light on the problems that we're addressing.
But I've got an issue with this.

'Cause you can get so consumed in this music biz
Writing about this time in which you exist, that you can
Miss the chance to look past the present, and
See what the solution is.

I don't wanna just talk about what's going on
Now, I wanna visualise what can happen next.
So I paint a picture of the future then

Figure out how to get there by taking backwards steps,
So let's walk backwards, you and me.

The destination is the best and latest in specialist education from
    the
Black community. Reason being, given the
acid attacks, shootings, stabbings and that, all the
Recent beefing we've been seeing . . . it
Seems to be in all our interests for us to school our
Kids separately 'cause they can read between the lines and they
See the deep divides between our lives, ethnically.

There's things our schools have yet to teach and
Shout out to Akala 'cause *Natives* is a great read.
Yeah . . . a community-specific schooling system is
something I think we may need.
The aim would be to teach these kids the alphabet . . .
But simultaneously make them see how to get from A to B.
I know I'm saying a lot but stay with me.
There's so many ways to teach.

Like, imagine a poem about a public health issue that's
Important for us to tell the youth.
But it doubles up as a revision guide too. So I
Do my thing on my side and you can listen wide-eyed to my mind
    and let the
vision guide you.

SCENE 7: THE DIABETES ANALOGY

[George demonstrates a form of education that can be used to make curriculum material more relatable]

92

George: Take Diabetes. Diabetes is a lifelong health condition
In which the respiratory system isn't self-sufficient.

The body can't make use of glucose in the blood
Because ultimately it doesn't have the cell's permission.

[Cut to a personified version of Glucose buzzing an intercom for access to a cell, like a delivery man outside an apartment building]

Cell: Hello?

Glucose: Hi, it's er Glucose.

Cell: Glucose who?

Glucose: It's just Glucose.

Cell: [To someone else] Did we order something from Glucose? We didn't order anything from Glucose.

Glucose: No, you don't order, I just deliver when you need energy.

Cell: Excuse me?

Glucose: It's nothing personal. You need the energy, so I'm—

Cell: No, it's alright. Sorry, we're not interested.

Glucose: Yeah, it's just that I got off a long journey through the blood stream to get—

Cell: Bye.

[Cell hangs up]

Glucose: Nice.

[Return to George]

George: Permission is granted through insulin.
If you're a glucose molecule, insulin brings you into the cell
To be used as a fuel for energy.
But with diabetes, your body can't do all this chemistry.

[Return to the intercom scenario. Glucose buzzes again – this time, with Insulin]

Cell: Hello?

Insulin: Hi, darling . . .

Cell: Hi, who's that?

Insulin: It's Insulin at the door.

Cell: Oh hi, Insulin. How are you doing?

Insulin: I'm just here with some Glucose.

Cell: Right . . .

Insulin: He just wants to come up and provide a bit of energy.

Cell: Yeah, sure! Send him up.

Insulin: No worries, he'll be up shortly.

Cell: Thanks, Insulin.

Insulin: [To Glucose] There you go, mate.

Glucose: That's literally what I said.

[Return to George]

George: So, we eat food, and the body breaks it down.
You know when you've finished your dinner and your belly makes a
    sound?
Yeah, that's the food being broken down into glucose.
Glucose then goes around into the bloodstream delivering energy
    to the cells
But generally, cells tend to keep to themselves.

*I know it sounds crazy right now, but trust me I'm going somewhere
    with this.*

They don't just see glucose and soak it up;
It takes a special key to make the cells open up.
Insulin's that key
And your pancreas is the insulin factory.

Boom. In Type 1 Diabetes . . . you know there's two types,
In Type 1 Diabetes, your pancreas doesn't produce insulin
Why? I don't know, scientists have yet to conclude.
But that means your cells can't access the energy that's stored in
    the glucose you get from your food.

[Cut to personified Glucose trying to enter a nightclub called 'The
Cell']

Bouncer: Sorry, mate, guest list only.

Glucose: Hey, it's Glucose. I've got an energy delivery.

Bouncer: Don't care, you're not on the list, mate.

Glucose: Yeah, if you call Insulin—

Bouncer: There is no Insulin around here you cannot get into The
Cell without being on the list. Step to the side, please.

George: In Type 2, the insulin is there but for some reason the cells don't respond to it.
So again, they can't get energy 'cause it's locked in the glucose
Which uses insulin as a conduit.

[Cut to Glucose trying to access another cell, once again with Insulin]

Receptionist: Hi.

Glucose: Hey, it's Glucose. I've got an energy delivery . . .

Receptionist: I can't see a reservation under that name, I'm afraid.

Glucose: Thought you'd say that. I've actually got Mr Insulin with me this time.

Receptionist: OK . . .

Insulin: Yeah, hi. This guy's, er, he's pretty much good for it, just er . . .

Receptionist: Well, Mr Insulin, access to this cell is on an appointment basis only so . . .

Insulin: No, erm—

Receptionist: Regretfully, I can't offer much in the way of help, but all the best on your journeys.

Glucose: Burn!

[Return to George]

George: Diabetes reminds me a lot of the condition of my community.
In fact, every community is like an organism.
You feed it resources to keep it alive,

But if it shows persistent symptoms of sickness . . .
It must not be getting what it needs to survive.

[Cut to recorded conversations with George's friends Marcelline and Reem, who both work with young offenders]

Marcelline: *So many factors contribute to the issues young adults face. Whether it be substance use, mental health, or family relation-ships. These are serious topics, but knife and gun crime are projected to be the only issue . . .*

Reem: *. . . perspective, and that's everything for these young people because it's a systematic . . . or a systemic change that's needed, as opposed to just one-on-one individual support, although that's necessary as well.*

Marcelline: *Well, my experience has shown me that it's not about being a bad person; it's about making bad decisions. You cannot expect people to do better without providing the tools. People cannot be led blindly. I do what I do so I can be that person to provide the tools.*

SCENE 8: MUCKY SAID IT BEST

George: Even though Uganda can soothe me,
I think about the ends and anger consumes me.
One day I'll realise my vision if I'm lucky.
Until then I'm in my feelings, listening to Mucky.
Considering my position in this uckery.

Gotta make sure my work affects education.
Gotta hold it down for the next generation.
Gotta hold it down for the fam.
Gotta make sure this year goes out with a bang.
I know the fans want an album from man.

I'ma work it out if I can. Generate
Jobs for my brothers coming out of the can.
I gotta pray more. I gotta be way more grateful.
That's why this tune's so relatable. I hit up
Mucks and asked him what he made it for.
He explained it all.

Mucky: . . . *a couple of my young bucks got nicked for murder and whatnot. You get me? But I wasn't around at the time because I got nicked myself. And I was in jail at the time when bare these things happened with my other bredrins, you get me? And then near the end of the year now . . . everybody in the ends got nicked for selling food to undercover police and that, you get me? And then after that, my close bredrin died, you get me? His brother died like nine months before, and then he got killed in Jamaica. So it was just bare things and bare little traumas on man's head, so I'm thinking man's gotta make a way or do something better you get me? 'Cause obviously, when I say . . . include the Sierra Leone part in there cah that's the original struggle, you get me? And then to come here and see it in a parallel view, it's mad, you get me? Still be going through a struggle when it's supposed to be a better land, that's why I'm saying it's on me.*

[Soundtrack: Mucky 'It's On Me']

EPISODE 5: Press Play

Extra Info:

- This episode continued my practice of turning day-to-day experiences into podcast content. In this case, it meant reacting to new music from Maleek Berry and writing about meeting Guala.
- This was also the start of the fantasy/sci-fi element of 'HYHGP?'. In this episode I teleported and put myself inside a microwave full of popcorn, just to try different techniques of storytelling. Later in the podcast, I took this to new levels.

Fun Facts:

- Episode 5 was an accident. I was trying to get to an important discussion, which ended up featuring in Episode 6: why I stopped releasing music. But I realised this would make more sense if I explained my current musical surroundings first – i.e. Afrobeats and Drill music. I wanted to show appreciation to these genres, while explaining their role in our collective journey. My plan was to then explore my individual journey through music (hence the title of the next episode).

I wrote the whole of Chapter 1 under serious pressure. Producing these episodes in the middle of a tour, in which I would perform this freshly written, hour-long material, was . . . intense. So, to accelerate my thought process I would just listen to a song and write something in reaction to it. This was like teleporting to a different world, which I did throughout the podcast. Another technique I used throughout this chapter was to listen to recordings of conversations I had had within twenty-four hours of writing. When Dun D (from Episode 1) introduced me to Guala, he and I clicked immediately – I think it's a Tottenham thing, I always catch a vibe in that community. Chilling in the car with him, I listened to his song and his story about migrating from Ecuador. Unexpectedly, it connected to everything I had been thinking about music as a portal to another world. It was beautiful how all the conversations in my life seemed to interrelate at that time. Maybe I was just paying more attention than usual. At the end of Episode 5, I tried to explain how rap music is actually the world that young people in violent areas escape to. This is funny because the music alone is more violent than what others are used to hearing, but less violent than what the artists are used to seeing. I have many, many thoughts on this, which I didn't share on the podcast till Chapter 3. At this stage, my aim was only to present a new way of thinking about music.

SCENE 1: PAST, PRESENT AND FUTURE

George: Do me a favour, imagine yourself listening to my voice,
And everything else fading into the distance as white noise.

Picture yourself right now while you do your thing.
Start zooming into your face through your skin,
Through your flesh through and your bone
To the centre of your dome.
Now picture these words entering your dome.

Picture the picture they're painting on your mind,
One word behind the other like a conga line.
That's what happens when you listen to this podcast or
Any interview, poem, or song of mine.

Right now, you're standing between two mirrors
Looking directly through yourself.
But it gets deeper.

This verse you guys hear was first an idea.
Before it could ever exist on your computer,
It was nothing more than a vision of the future.

And now there's this recording that I've recorded.
Which ain't more than a live performance I
Thought to provide the audience.
I afforded the time to order my mind
And make sure all the rhymes were organised.
Now, these recorded lines are immortalised.

So that same verse I envisioned in my future,
I'm recording it presently.
But by the time it reaches you,
It's gonna be nothing more than a memory.

So, are you listening to the past, present or future?

[Finger snap]

Are you listening at all?
'Cause if not I'm still here.
And if you are . . . then where are you?

Lemme show you. Move back.

[George opens and closes an aircraft door]

SCENE 2: A WORLD OF THOUGHTS

George: Each podcast episode is a world of thoughts
Flying around my brain.
Thoughts that are scared of spiralling down the drain and dying
    without a name.
Thoughts that are all competing for my attention,
They wanna stand out; they ain't trying to sound the same.
'Cause if they sit in my head for too long, I move on.

That's why sometimes I'm thinking bare things, but I don't really say
    nothing.
You . . . you guys have unlimited access to these thoughts
Through a special entrance controlled by the play button.

Hold on. Let me just remember this.

[George enters a code into a security door. The door opens and reveals a dark, futuristic room]

SCENE 3: THE PLAY BUTTON

George: The play button is a teleportation device that allows you to enter another world while physically staying where you are; meaning you can go anywhere, any time without anyone noticing.

[George teleports to inside the microwave from Episode 2, 'Popcorn']

When you push that play button,
You jump into a different perspective.
Maybe that perspective's right under your nose but the
Way it's presented isn't effective.
Or maybe it's a story that nobody's ever told you –
Remember 'Popcorn' from Episode 2?
Right now, you're hearing it from inside the microwave, it's
Heating up, it's popping off, kind of like a rave.

Can you hear that corn popping yeah?
It's hot in there. You're going round in circles and there's
Not a lot of air.

But from the popcorn's perspective is it blossoming or blowing up?
You can't answer 'cause you don't know enough.

[George teleports out of the microwave]

Not matter how much you listen to these sound effects like a
Broken record spinning around the decks, you'll
Never know what it's like inside a microwave
'Cause inside your mind is safe.

Remember, the play button takes you to another world
While you physically stay where you are.
And that's a nice thought but don't take it too far.
The experience is happening inside your head,

But for all I know right now you're lying in bed es-
Caping your own thoughts by taking on mine instead.

My words can put you in your feelings,
But they can't put you in the situation.

So your body will never carry the knowledge of that reality.

You feel me?

You can imagine what the popcorn's been through
But you can't *imagine* what that popcorn's been through.

Regardless, in order to write that poem,
I have to believe I know more than I do.
So, every minute I spend listening back to this podcast . . . I'm
    playing myself.

[George teleports back to futuristic room]

But I don't just play myself, I listen to all sorts. In my
Head there's more decisions and more thoughts and I
Guess, today, what I'm trying my best to say is you can
Take that stress away by pressing play.

[George teleports to Episode 4]

For example, at the start of Episode 4 I'm on a flight to Uganda
Feeling a mix of excitement and anger –
One, for my peoples 'cause I'ma see them again,
Two, 'cause of recent events with police in the ends.
That's why I'm listening to Mucky; it's
Like hearing parts of my life in a banger.

And think about what he said to me . . .

Mucky: *... something better, you get me? And obviously when I ... include the Sierra Leone part in there ... that's the original struggle. And to come here and see it in a parallel view, it's mad you get me. [To] still be going through a struggle when it's supposed to be a better life, that's why I'm saying, 'It's on me'.*

George: Music can support you, like you're on crutches.
Look how many parts of my life that song touches.
And I love what he said about Africa
Sometimes I press play just to fly back to her.

[Soundtrack: Maleek Berry 'Gimme Life']

SCENE 4: GIMME LIFE

[George is at a house party]

George: See, music's an art but it's a science as well, do you get me?
I'm coming back, give me one second.

[George sings along]

George: The serotonin makes you smile, adrenaline makes you wild,
The oxytocin makes you wanna make a child.
This thing's a science.

You're listening to 'Gimme Life', it's a Maleek Berry song.
I don't even wanna speak very long, this
Music's way too smooth but how can
Sound waves physically make you move?

Maleek Berry: *As soon as the song starts, it just makes you feel good, you just wanna move straight away. And as soon as the song drops, as soon as the beat drops, the hook drops, you start dancing ...*

George: From the man himself.
See, music contributes to the planet's health and its wealth.
When you press play, you're opening your mind to someone
You're acting like a loved one, you're making time for someone.
And in return you get experiences you like; it lifts you high . . .
Literally it gives you life.

Maleek Berry: *No matter what people are going through, my music always makes them happy. Even though I've got sad songs too, but it still makes people happy. Obviously 'Gimme Life' is a happy song . . . literally that's the vibe of the song.*

George: Some of you might be thinking
'I can't believe he sounds like a London man,
'Cause he doesn't always make sounds I can understand.'

You need to understand, Maleek's multi-lingual,
So he can alternate between each culture he sings for on
Each single, and you know what smacks it?
My man finds making beats simple.

Now I don't know many second-generation immigrants that
Lived in this city without ever facing ignorance.
But for us, growing up in North West,
You learn to say certain stuff with your chest.
We used to get cussed for our Africanness, and in
Younger generations it's been happening less 'cause we
Learned how to celebrate ourselves
Then we started generating sales.

So when I see the mandem repping like that
I recognise that . . . it gives me life.

[Party atmosphere]

SCENE 5: DEEPER CONVERSATION

[George is catching up with friends in Tottenham, North London]

George: So imagine I'm chilling with Marc.
But I gotta go and check Guala.
He's linked me with Scyph.
And we've bucked up outside Dun's.
But they're not there at the beginning.
It's Figz and Foz just chilling.
I'm laid back in the cruise ship and we
Start playing each other our music.
Them man are too sick.
And I could say the same for a lotta Dun's crew
Two twos Guala comes thru.
He's got a lotta songs too I be telling a man he better be
Dropping some soon.

So it's me, his girl Dii and him just reasoning.
Fifteen minutes in, Dun's breezing in.
And where we're all sharing music so
The conversation becomes a deeper thing, keep listening . . .

[George lowers car window. He's in conversation with Guala, who has just played George his song, 'Guala Gwala']

George: . . . yo it is a good tune, cuzzy . . .

Guala: *You know what's powerful about it yeah . . . I came here when I was eight . . . the transition from coming from a third world country [to] here . . . the language, the weather change, the food, the system, the . . . everything it's a trauma, bruv. It influences us to do certain things and to be a certain way. So we can help those young people to make better choices and not live like . . . like they don't belong here.*

[Soundtrack: Guala 'Guala Gwala']

Guala: I remember when my mum told me. I said to her 'Where exactly are we going, and why?' She said 'Inglaterra', she didn't say 'London'. And when I hear 'Inglaterra' that's 'England' in Spanish, but it sounds so powerful . . .

Where did Mum bring me, bruv? She sat me down yesterday, told me we're leaving to find a better life . . . what's this? And then I come to T . . . yeah man . . . I'm getting shivers.

George: Guala didn't know the English language as a child.
He came here from Ecuador; the transition was wild.
His family landed in Tottenham, Broadwater Farm.
And he says the sudden move abroad brought him harm.

It's a deeper conversation whenever I talk with man.
He reminds me of my friend from primary called Ivan.
Ivan came over from Colombia. Why? No one knew.
But listening to Guala makes me wonder what he was going through.
So many stories to be told,
I use this podcast to get more people involved.
Like Dun was saying . . . the other people in the Bible.
'Cause telling your own story is the secret to survival.

[Dun D & Scyph Voices]

George: Speaking of Dun . . .
When I looked around it was me, him and Scyph
Guala left me thinking about the meaning of life.
Dun & Scyph were talking about Government corruption
Talking over each other 'cause mandem love an interruption.
It's fascinating 'cause everyone's got their own philosophy, on
Every topic from poverty to owning property. I gotta
Wind the window down to take in this moment properly.

108

Shout out to everyone drifting off with me.
See, the play button allows you to close your eyes

And do things that you can't quite do.
It can show a lot of light in the world.
But there's a dark side too. There's
Fear. There's hatred. There's
Trauma. Et cetera. There's a
Generation of young people that all know someone who got
     cheffed up.

The play button can take you there. In a safety
Chair to a place that should make you scared.

Dun D: ... this is what we're doing, we're playing the best chess player, yeah. And this chess player ... that's what he does, he's a professional chess player. Why the fuck are we playing him at chess?

[Soundtrack: 1011 'Next Up?']

Dun D: I'm not playing you at chess that's all you do, that's what you've mastered.

George: That's what he's saying.

Dun D: You have to flip the table. It's got to be war. War. It's war, it's war, it's war-

Scyph: Yeah. That's what I said, virtual currency. See all this Bitcoin and all this—

Dun D: Forget all that, it's war.

Scyph: I know the war, but—

Dun D: It's war, blud.

Scyph: Yeah. Nah, nah it *is* war.

George: That's why ... that's why, like ...

Scyph: That's why people love Drill.

George: That's why people love Drill.

Scyph: Yeah. Because we subconsciously know we are in a war. But we're playing—

Dun D: So, you're saying we're diverting that energy into . . .

Scyph: Yeah, we're acting as if we're not in a war.

SCENE 6: THE DRILL ISSUE

[Montage of news reports on London's Metropolitan Police taking action against UK Drill rappers for their lyrical content]

George: You're listening to the sounds of 1011 –
The first group to get taken off YouTube by the police
Because the crew's too tied to the streets. They got
Nicked with nanks at a video shoot and in
Court the police argued that they were riding for beef.

Newsreader: *Local gang members producing their own Drill music and taunting the other gangs.*

George: You have to understand, someone's gran got disrespected.
Their lawyer says the incidents are disconnected, and even
though that doesn't change the fact things were found,
the sentencing is affected.
She says they were in custody when the politics happened.
So yeah, when they were arrested, they might not have been lacking.
But their objective at the time was shooting a video; it wasn't
    attacking.

Anyway, the mandem went jail, their videos were taken down
And they got banned from music for three years, now
Think about the crime they're accused of; will
Silencing them reduce or increase this?

Here's my thesis: changing the use of the
Music they release is the smoothest way to peace.

Think about it: the music creates a space to address the conflict,
And after a taste of success, no one
Wants to be locked on a cell pacing it, dressed as a convict.
You've . . . you've now got something to lose.
Money coming in every month from your views,
From your perspective, don, from your *views*.

Community Leader: *People make what they see around them. If you see violence and pain and suffering all around you because you live in a deprived neighbourhood, you're gonna make music that is intense, violent and painful.*

George: If you've been following this podcast,
You'll agree that music has a lot of social value.
As artists we influence people, but as
People we don't all plan to.
And we don't all plan to become a global brand too;
In this thing there's no guarantees, no foregone conclusions.
Our position as musicians is at the crossroads of freedom of
Speech and social contribution.

If my music's reality . . . then it presents an opportunity.
You might use it to challenge me to represent for my community.
But if I'm locked up, or I'm silenced,
Then I'm not in the conversation.

You can understand a lot more about the violence if you
Ask the prison population.

Changing the use of the music they release is the smoothest way to peace.
Without the youth how do you engage the streets?
You can't speak how a teenager speaks.
You're not in a madness three days a week.
You can imagine what they're going through,
But you can't *imagine* what they're going through.
And when they're rapping, cuz, they're showing you.

This play button . . . it's no joke.
If we couldn't use it to bring you to our world
A lot of us would go broke.
And when guys go broke in an ends where they sold dope
Then they're back on the roads with no hope.

That play button would be so much more powerful
If it was used to hold us accountable . . .
To the next generation of kids getting kicked out of school.

For all of the MPs, judges and lawyers,
All of the articles published in Reuters,
Efforts of private and public employers,
Stop and search targets, government pointers
Who sees the value in criminal immigrants
Rapping with typical ignorance?
Who thinks they're more than a public annoyance?
Who sees their music as anything other than pointless?

Their audience . . . they love and enjoy it they're
Playing their stuff in the toilet.
This is young people open to influence.
Isn't that the group we're all hoping to influence?
None of these rappers want their fans to go to jail but
Fam, the roads are hell. No one plans to hold an L.
What's a man supposed to tell them when there's gangs involved as well?

These stories should be put into education and training.
'Cause pushing for better days is the main thing.

EPISODE 6: The Journey (Part I)

Extra Info:
- This is the first drama-based episode since 'A Grenfell Story'. All the other episodes are factual, like documentaries, but in order to launch the character of Sanyu, this one required role play.
- This episode helped create a Ugandan audience for 'HYHGP?'.

Fun Facts:
- The Sanyu segments were written months before the rest of the episode. When I played the segment to people around me, no one had a clue what was going on, so I used this episode to break it down more clearly.
- Memorising this within a week for the live show on 20th September was one of the hardest things I've ever done professionally.

When I wrote this episode, I was trying to steer the podcast towards African audiences. This effort was important on a number of levels. Firstly, I believe that a lack of African consciousness lowers the self-esteem of the Black diaspora – i.e. seeing ourselves only through Western eyes isn't good for us. It makes us act weird. Western society doesn't know enough about us to explain our behaviour. So, we use stereotypes and myths to form an idea of Blackness, in the absence of African consciousness. The second reason for my reach towards African audiences is that Africa needs the diaspora as much as we need Africa. Lots of problems on the continent stem from unstable systems: corrupt politicians, dishonest police, unreliable markets. Those of us who live in countries with strong systems can be very useful to our counterparts on the motherland. This is why Sanyu has a Ugandan accent; she is a bridge between me and my Ugandan audience.

Speaking of which, Sanyu's dramatic escape is another very important part of this episode. After being born in my mind almost a year earlier, this idea helped me out of a creative slump. In just her first few weeks of life, she persuaded me to write her a script about the anxiety of being a new idea in a crowded mind. I recorded this script in my voice and turned the pitch up, making it sound like a young girl. Her survival plan worked; I was proud that such a clever idea had come to me, so I played that early recording to my closest friends and they instantly liked Sanyu, encouraging me to develop the idea further. I wrote a few more demos and introduced a character called Travis the Translator. Travis came to me because I realised that an idea had to be understood before it could be expressed. So, in order for me to develop these characters further, I needed to think about them carefully, and listen to their needs. 'Travis' was basically the name I gave to this process. The last demo ended in Sanyu and Travis being captured by the 'Ambition Commission' – a ruthless team in my mind that decides which ideas get attention, and which ones get forgotten. For the next seven months, I didn't write another word of Sanyu's story. In fact, I started playing the demos to my friends in the streets, just to get a different perspective. Street guys loved her, too. Dun D even called me the African Walt Disney. During this time, I started writing and recording the podcast, which was all inspired by those exciting first few months of Sanyu's life. I had never had an idea that pushed me like she did; she unlocked so much potential so quickly. And I think the demos went so well that I was scared to write anything mediocre for her.

Fast-forward to Episode 6, 'The Journey (Part I)'. After sitting in the 'Research & Development' (R&D) section of my mind for half a year, Sanyu was agitated. She had got off to such a good start, making herself stand out as a revolutionary idea, until I decided to put her on the backburner. Now, it looked like her worst fears were coming true. I was halfway into Chapter 1 of *HYHGP*, and I hadn't even mentioned her to my audience. Was she being forgotten? No chance. One morning I woke up around 6 or 7 a.m., and Sanyu's next move came to me in those first few seconds of the day. She was going to insert herself into an episode of the podcast by pulling off a great escape. During those waking seconds, Sanyu made me see that she was in prison, and the only way she could make it out was if I took a leap of faith and

recreated her prison break in the most creative way possible for the
podcast audience. And as usual with Sanyu, telling her own story was
her secret to survival.

   This episode is called 'The Journey' because it is all about the
distance travelled. It starts off with me reflecting on my career,
remembering who I was before poetry, then talking to my friend on
the phone about the tension between popularity and purpose. The
episode ends with some thoughts on Ugandan singer-turned-
politician, Robert 'Bobi Wine' Kyagulanyi. I had (and still have) a lot of
admiration for Bobi – if not for anything else, for the distance he has
travelled. A ghetto boy, inspiring millions by rising to the top of
Uganda's music scene but refusing to kiss the ring of the president
out of devotion to Uganda's poor, who are often neglected, abused
and disdained by the establishment. It's been sad and frustrating to
watch Bobi's political career pan out over the three years since
Episode 6 was written, but I guess it's all part of the journey. Special
thanks to Aggie, Anthea, Mascot, Mike, SoSevere, Tattu, Sandra and
all my friends in Kampala who embraced this episode so deeply, at
such an early stage. You guys made me feel like I might have something to offer our country.

SCENE 1: GEORGE REMINISCING IN HIS ROOM

[George is in his room reflecting on his artistic journey while writing the script for his next live show]

George: As of September 2018
Three years into my move out the mainstream,
If you google 'George The Poet'
The stop and search topic's perched
Right at the top – it's first. And
Obviously, that gets on my nerves.
But it's not the worst.

It's on me if my work isn't as noteworthy and
Even if it is, bitterness won't serve me. This
Don't burn me . . . everyone's got their own journey.

Crazy to think this one started eight years ago
Years have flown – all that time where's it go?
I was in Kampala on my own for the first time too.
Close your eyes, imagine a birds-eye view.
I'm learning how to move around the city
Using my head and the few Luganda words I knew.

Thanks to some very special cousins of mine,
I was at all the best clubs at the time.
And not all of my cousins were in love with the life – I have to
Make that clear 'cause now Anthea's a mother and wife.

[Canned laughter]

George: Yeah, the audience is probably gonna laugh at that bit.
What should I say after that bit?

Oh yeah. eight years ago, 2010.
Anthea's introducing me to so many friends.

Now, growing up how we did in London, you
Rarely go out without getting into something.
In Kampala I had no such drama. The
Clubs are so alive but everyone's so much calmer.

[Soundtrack: Radio & Weasel 'Potential']

George: RIP Radio, 'cause him and Weasel were always
On the radio but every song was wavy though.
I remember hearing them in every rave we'd go.

[Soundtrack: Radio & Weasel 'N'Genda Maaso']

George: Back then it was Club Rouge, Ange Noir, Efendy's
    Centenary Park, Casablanca, Guvnor Bar.
One second, I love this part . . .

[Soundtrack: Radio & Weasel 'Kuku']

George: And what blew my mind is that everyone was sociable
Compared to the ends where everyone's unapproachable.

[Soundtrack: Coco Finger 'Mikono Wagulu']

[Soundtrack: Rabadaba 'Bwekiri']

George: I started getting into other music as well, in the
Club moving to girls like 'I could get used to this world'.

[Soundtrack: Isaac Blackman 'To the Ceiling']

George: This was the first time in a long time I
Left the ends, which I highly recommend. I met a
Different set of friends. Had a break from the
Drama 'cause it never ends. And if it ever ends it
Never ends with recompense.

The hood will have you stressed and tense.
Kampala was so much less intense. The
People I was meeting were less obsessed with trends in the dressing
    sense.
You know what I mean?
Less obsessed with impressing friends.

UG Friend 1: Yo what's up, man.

George: Wagwan, cuzzy.

UG Friend 1: Welcome to Kampala, we're happy to have you.

George: I appreciate that man, thank you.

UG Friend 1: If you need anything just holla.

George: Thanks bro. You want drinks?

UG Friend 1: No, it's kawa, it's cool, it's OK.

George: Sawa!

UG Friend 2: Shawa! Shawalin! How are things?

George: Oh yeah, Shawalin that was the younger me. I was
Hungry just trying to be somebody. But the
Only music we made back in my home country was
Rap, Grime and Funky.
So, I learned from The Navios and Jose Chameleons.
Real Ugandan artists in their home making millions.

My poetry career hadn't begun but I was
Tired of just rapping for fun. I
Wanted to be like these guys:
Spreading positive vibes . . .
Under the East African sun.

But there was one singer in a league of his own. Like the
Others he made it without leaving his home and the
Way he'd control a crowd and hold it down
Made me feel like an amateur.
This guy was a badman. From Kamwokya.

[Soundtrack: Bobi Wine 'Badman from Kamwokya']

[Bobi Wine montage]

George: When we talk about the hood, we're talking deprivation
But we need to learn to describe it properly.
In London there's all sorts of desperation
But Ugandan poverty's a different kind of poverty. It's the
Kind where you might not live inside a property. The
Kind where you live by the midnight economy.
People don't make it out of this life that commonly.
So Bobi Wine was a slight anomaly. He
Used his voice and made music with it, back when
People thought there was no future in it. He
Represented the poor through his lyrics and the
Youth gravitated to his spirit.

Bearing in mind I couldn't speak Luganda so more time I'm
Singing along to the odd English phrase,
But one thing I remember clear as day is how my
Cousins and their friends used to sing his praise.

[Bobi Wine soundtrack fades out]

George: We'll come back to the story of Bobi Wine shortly. My
Point is, Uganda opened my mind.
Everyone had a different expectation of life
And I thought that was dope at the time. Problem
Is I didn't know what to do with mine. I was
Five years into my music grind

And I felt like, out of my generation,
Only Tinie, Chip and Tinchy really blew with Grime.

But everyone's got their own journey.
They were lucky enough to blow early.
None of them could live my life for me;
They've got their story, I've got my story . . .

[Phone rings]

George: Yo my brudda.

Bro: Yo! Dem man dere!

George: Wagwan.

Bro: Deya. What you saying, my brudda?

George: Yeah man I'm here just trying to pattern this show for the 20th. You coming, yeah?

Bro: I'm deya!

George: My guy.

Bro: Yeah, but do you know what yeah, what's that little Ugandan girl, that little Ugandan girl that you—

George: Oh Sanyu?

Bro: Yeah man she was wavy, I was feeling her you know.

George: Sanyu's good still.

Bro: Make sure man meet her, don't be hiding her from the world.

George: It's not a hiding thing, nah. It's erm . . . everything in its own time, d'you get me, she's on . . . she's on a little journey right now.

Bro: See when a man like you says that I'm not too sure . . .

George: Yeah, I hear what you're saying, cuz. I . . . basically, d'you know what it is?

Bro: Wagwan.

George: In order to make a poem, I
Have to translate emotion.
And that starts by talking to myself,
Sometimes it feels like torturing myself like I'm
Taking my subconscious and trying to break it open but . . .
Whatever. Whatever it takes to make the poem.
It's gonna sound insane . . . but
Imagine a little person running around my brain
Trying to get me to express myself, it's not
Easy but he does his best to help.

Let's call him Travis. Travis the Translator.
Travis gathers my best ideas and
Organises them into lines that rhyme. 'Cause
that's gonna make me say them aloud that way
They can get out of this mind of mine.
Now, apart from the challenge of me finding time, the
Biggest barrier to any idea . . . is my fear.

Travis just wants to free my thoughts but my
Fear just wants me to see my faults.
See my shortcomings, see my flaws. It's
Like my fear don't believe my sauce.

And it acts like it's looking out for my interests by
Regulating the ideas that I invest in but

Fear only really cares about itself so
I have to fully support *my* ting, bredrin. Now
Imagine you're thinking this while you're lighting red string. I
Hear ideas having fights in bed, king.

[Sanyu and Travis arguing]

My fear has been looking for Sanyu 'cause
That's an idea I've been putting a plan to.
Really, Sanyu's just a voice in my head but she
Feels like a real young woman I value. Fear
Wants me to doubt her. It wants me to
Think I can make it without her. And
This ain't the first time it, but the
Problem is . . . Sanyu lives in my
Head so it's not possible to pretend she does not exist.

I can tell you what she's doing right now . . .
Right now . . . she's trying to hide out.
She's being hunted down by my doubts in a
Part of my mind called Research and Development.
That's where I keep ideas I like while
I research and develop them.

Travis is looking for Sanyu.
'Cause he believes in her value.
But remember, he wants to help her escape
Tell her story, sell her mixtape. But
So many ideas don't make it out 'cause they
Have no way of escaping doubt.
Let me break it down . . .

SCENE 2: TROUBLE IN R&D

[Transition to the imaginary world of George's Mind. It's night-time. Two bad guys, known as Insecurity Guards (IGs) are patrolling a small village called 'Research and Development' (R&D). This is an area of George's Mind in which ideas are held under prison-like conditions until they prove themselves valuable to the Real World. R&D is run by the leaders of George's Mind, the 'Ambition Commission' (AC). Sanyu has been held in R&D for over six months without knowing if she'll make it out. It is every idea's dream to leave George's Mind and thrive in the Real World, but most ideas don't make it. They are often broken by doubts driven by the IGs, or simply forgotten.

When Sanyu first arrived in George's Mind, she sparked the creative explosion that led to *Have You Heard George's Podcast? (HYHGP)*. George quickly moved from writing short stories about this new idea to longer pieces about different ideas, and the podcast was born. However, Sanyu was so unique that George didn't know how to introduce her to his audience. By the time he finished the first three episodes of *HYHGP*, Sanyu was tired of waiting. Around Episode 4, she decided to escape R&D and force herself onto the podcast. This struggle made George feel restless and guilty for neglecting Sanyu, since she was the one who inspired the podcast. The AC felt Sanyu was not ready for *HYHGP*, so they sent the IGs to hunt her down, which caused George to feel anxious and doubtful about introducing Sanyu to his audience.

This whole adventure took place deep within George's Mind while he wrote Episodes 4 and 5. Now, in Episode 6, George tries to explain it all to a friend over the phone. The fact he is explaining Sanyu's struggle on a podcast episode means that she made it out of R&D.

Therefore, this segment is a recollection of Sanyu's journey. Her escape from R&D was assisted by another idea named Travis the Translator. Travis translates ideas into poetry by helping George find the words to explain them. As George started thinking about bringing Sanyu onto *HYHGP*, Travis started looking for her. Since George had been neglecting Sanyu for months, she went under the radar – almost untraceable in George's Mind. Travis' search brought him to R&D, where the Insecurity Guards were also looking for Sanyu. In this scene, Travis pleads with an ex-girlfriend, Yvette, to let him hide from the IGs in her garden. Yvette is reluctant, and ends up exposing Travis to the IGs for a chance to leave George's Mind]

IG 1: By order of the Ambition Commission—

IG 2: It's an offence to leave without written permission.

IG 1: We're currently in pursuit of an idea on the loose . . .

IG 2: . . . and anyhow we find out she's hiding with one of you . . .

IG 1: . . . even if she used you for camouflage . . .

IG 2: I don't care all of you lot are getting charged with sabotage.

IG 1: See! One selfish little idea messes it up for everyone else who hasn't had a chance.

[Travis runs up to Yvette's place, breathless. He knocks]

Yvette: Travis! What you doing in R&D?

Travis: [Muffled] I need to hide in your garden, b.

Yvette: Pardon me?

Travis: I need a place to hide out here, it's hot out here. You see how many security guards they got out here?

Yvette: Yeah, they're looking for that Sanyu girl who tried to escape. Last time I asked you this you lied to my face, but Have you been chatting to her?

'Cause if you have, I can't have you outside of my place, you know that right?

Travis: Girl if you let me in, I'll explain everything, I promise.

Yvette: I fell for that the last time when I was on a date with you. When you just wanted me to cross-pollinate with you.

[IGs in the background]

IG 1: Listen . . . anyone attempting to cross-pollinate is a GONNER mate.

IG 2: That's something that we will not tolerate.

IG 1: But if you tell us where this yout is
You'll be immediately promoted to George's To-Do List

Yvette: George's— yup she's here! She's here!! She's been here the whole time!

Travis: Arghhh are you serious right now, girl? You really gone do me like that?

Yvette: Trav, I'm sorry, babe. You'll be alright.

[Travis runs off. IGs hear Yvette from a distance]

IG 1: Yo, where did that come from?

IG 2: I think it was over there still.

IG 1: Oi, go get that for me, my brudda.

IG 2: Say nothing. Send me the ting.

IG 1: My guy.

IG 2: Where you running to, G?

[Travis running, out of breath]

IG 2: There's nowhere to hide, we do this all the time . . .
You think you're the first idea to try to escape from George's Mind?

SCENE 3: GEORGE'S INSECURITIES

[George's friend interrupts. Return to George's room]

Bro: Hold on, hold on. Let me get this straight.
Your ideas in Research and Development – in your brain – are working together to get out of your head?

George: Mmm. It's called cross-pollination.
It's when you take an idea and combine it with a different one from a different area to make it stronger.

For example, when I started uni, like I always say, I planned to
    become an MP.
All I dreamt about was change, I wanted plenty.
So, I'm studying political science and I've
Realised we're facing a difficult bias.
The things they're making me read contain the
Information we need to
Break the mould and take control but the
youth have a different dream they've been sold.
They've been told about the status and the
Papers they can make on road. And that makes
Sense to a young mind, especially
One that hasn't done time.
So despite the dangers road may involve it's a calculated risk.

Obviously, I'm oversimplifying the thought process but
That's about the basic gist.

So all of this stuff that I'm reading in Cambridge has
Basically no chance of reaching the same kids that
I wanna serve by becoming an MP.
So my campaign would be running on empty.
You get me?

But the ripple effect of that lost generation
Comes at a cost to the nation.
Someone needs to guide these youts in their language, it
Takes a boss to have a boss conversation. And
That's when I understood cross-pollination. If I can
Take an idea I learn at uni, and
Rap it to these kids they can learn it through me. E-
Specially if they see that I graduated and made
Money without turning boujie. I
Wanted the youngers in Stonebridge
Seeing me flexing in Cambridge.
Saying to themselves 'That's a St Raph's prince in a
King's college next to St Catherine's.'

I cross-pollinated my academic study
With my street perspective. Meaning
Anytime I make a track with anybody, I
Make my degree effective. So
Even though I'm not rapping hella cruddy . . .
The streets respect it.
And through my work, I chat to everybody.
That's how I keep connected.

Bro: So you're saying you present information in a way the streets
can use it.
But I've got a question: isn't the best way to do this is by releasing
music?

George: Don't get it twisted, there's value in—

Bro: Better still don't you think you left your record deal when
Labels were starting to invest in Grime?
Obviously, your career's blessed and fine but
Don't you think music would have made you more relevant than
Working with Prince Harry and doing *Question Time*?
Look at Dave, speaking of 'Question Time'.
He puts all them political thoughts in his speech and
Records it with beats and he talks to the streets.
Look at Stormzy my g! Look at Stormzy. The
Same uni where you studied politics, he's
Linked up with them and dropped two bloody scholarships. I
Can't lie. This ain't even devil's advocate there's
Levels you should have reached that you haven't hit. And
That's how a lot of us feel. It's like you
Left the industry and you've kind of forgotten us still.
I don't know if that's fair or not, it's just real.

George: Mmm.

Bro: I'm assuming you been getting that corporate money but there's
Guys in the hood that think you're living poor and bummy.
You know how much man in the hood hit my phone like
'Yo when's George gonna get back to recording fam, talk to donnie.'

George: Alright, let me ask a question – have you heard the podcast,
my brother?

Bro: Not yet. I been meaning to. I'm gonna hit that up.

George: OK. Now let me ask another.
Take time, this one's a big one.
Leadership or companionship . . . if you
Had to pick one, which one?

Bro: Context, man. You gotta give me context.

George: OK so, just now you talked about me leaving the deal.
And you're speaking as a close friend keeping it real. Now
Being brutally honest is a leadership skill but did you
Say that to guide me or just to speak what you feel? 'Cause we
Both know the Ends is seeing a rise in violence and you're
Basically saying to me, 'Why the silence?' But
What you're revealing by even asking that is
Your expectation of me providing guidance. But
What if I don't have a clue? What if I don't
Wanna go down the same old avenue? What if un-
Til I can come back to you with exactly what we actually have to do . . .
I don't even wanna chat to you?

Bro, making music's like dreaming aloud. You
Influence people's feelings when you're dealing with sound.
And we can make it seem deep and profound, we can
Lift people's spirits and earn a decent amount and we
Make our people dem proud by releasing an album,
Speaking to thousands when we perform on stage. And yeah, it
Is a way of dealing with all the rage.
'Cause representation obviously is a form of change.
Do you understand what I'm saying?

Music's a great way of making us think. Look, it's
Given us so many ways of making a drink. We got the
juice innit? And we won't stop producing it.
Do you understand what I'm saying to you, cuzzy?

Bro: Yeah, I say this all the time, cuzzy. We got the juice.

George: Brudda. All over the world it's the most common beverage.
And that's given us a lot of leverage . . .
A lot of privilege. A lot of heritage.

But all of this comes from the streets. Yet we still can't
Save our daughters and our sons from the streets. We've got
Famous artists walking with guns on the streets and
Food still runs the alternate funds on the streets. We
Want our music to be our saviour . . . from
All of this self-destructive behaviour.
But it's just a soundtrack to what's really happening;
All the issues that we're not really tackling.

I didn't release much between 2016 and 2017 'cause
All I had in my head was dreams of changing the
Hood. And for better or for worse, I was too proud to sell a dream.
One thing the streets needs more than inspiration
Is new forms of information.
New psychological infrastructure.
'Cause our thinking's bruck up.

We've got rappers that are 30 plus doing us dirty, cuz.
Talking about moving girls and rushing man. With
All of these dead bodies on the roads
That's the level of discussion fam. Our
Music doesn't lead us; it just accompanies us. It
Doesn't govern the streets, it discusses what the streets does. If
Anything it helps the streets increase its powers and that's
Backwards 'cause the streets is ours.
You know me man, I could speak for hours.

Bro: So you're saying the reason you've been this silent . . .
Is 'cause you've been deciding. To be a
Companion or leader. But
George, when you're absent you're neither.
Leadership's not about knowing stuff it's about
Showing up when the road is rough.
Real leaders don't give up.
Whether or not they think they know enough.
Do you know why these youts listen to these dumb rappers?

Why they wanna be young trappers and gun clappers . . .
Even though the mandem don't care for them?
It's 'cause the music is there for them.

Music is a language and if you ain't
Speaking it they ain't hearing you.
You know how this radio – blud if you ain't getting
Airplay, they're airing you. But you're the
only one holding yourself back you know this your-
Self akh. You was just telling me about that
Girl akh what's her name again?

George: Sanyu.

Bro: Thank you. Sanyu. I felt that!
You left her in research and development these times
She's as ready and relevant as she's ever been!

George: Nah, Sanyu's different, Sanyu's on a different journey.

Bro: Blud, she's trying to outrun your insecurities.
The only time she's not is when you're at ease.

George: You got a point. In my head there's more war than peace.
My ideas really wanna leave this place, they're
fighting for breathing space. But like it or
not, to rise to the top you gotta fight for your spot.
And Sanyu's such a strong idea because I patterned her this way
That's why right now she's planning her escape.

Every time she stands up to thoughts that doubt her, she
Forces me to talk about her.
Sanyu doesn't rate my insecurities she thinks they're
All just neeks talking greez. You
Gotta remember she was born in me, and she thinks I'm
Great that's her core belief.

She's so sure of herself she sees her as the evidence.
So, imagine, she patterned a plan for Travis the Translator to
Meet her at a residence in research and development.
But remember she's been hiding, so she had to
Send someone to go find him.

SCENE 4: TRAVIS MEETS JANICE

[While running from the IGs, Travis meets another idea sent to guide him to Sanyu]

Janice: Yo wha ya seh my friend?
Mi see seh ah run you a run from the bwoy dem.
Don't worry I'm not a snitch.
I just know one way you can avoid dem.
You listening? Alright basically
All you have to do is cross-pollinate with me
Cah me's a person weh dominate the street
And with your energy and my expertise
Not even Babylon can ramp wid we.

[IGs close in on Travis]

IG 1: Did you think you can run from *me*?
[Travis groans and continues running]

IG 2: Ayyy Trav from way back!

IG 1: Yo don't run brudda keep that same energy what u telling me?!
Don't run brudda keep that same energy.

IG 2: Yo, I told you already, if you make me run, you're gonna end up in the cemetery!

[Travis finds a safe spot. Janice appears]

Janice: Yo Papa. Mi did try fi give some advice to you
But mi nah ask fi nuttin twice enuh.

IG 1: Trav, you need to get back in the gym, brudda!

[The IGs find Travis and terrorise him some more. As he runs, Janice directs him to safety]

Janice: Listen to me just one second! (Go left)
I don't know – left! – what kind of one-man army ting ya deh pon
But whatever you're – duck! – whatever you're trying to do you
cannot do it alone darg,
Jah know star! This is the Research and Development part of
George's Mind.
If unnu come fi find one particular idea . . . yo mi nah guh lie, it ah
guh 'ard fi find.

SCENE 5: CROSS-POLLINATION

[Bro interrupts. Return to George's room]

Bro: So hold up. The one getting chased is Travis. I'm not mistaken?

George: Yeah . . . and the other one's name is
Janice . . . the Jamaican.

Bro: Why Jamaican?

George: I don't even know, she just sounded like a Jamaican woman
in my head.
But did you catch what she said? She's
Saying they need to collaborate. 'Cause
Travis makes ideas elaborate, but
She understands this part of my brain so
She can help him to navigate.

And that's the whole point of cross-pollination.
I swear down if people could hear my thoughts, I would get an
Oscar nomination!

This is why it's hard to prioritise music
I wanna change the way a lotta guys use it.
'Cause we've all got voices.
And voices inform our choices.

Anyway, Janice brought Travis to safety, and
Travis thought Janice was crazy.
So Trav's getting faisty . . .

SCENE 6: SANYU'S BACK

[Janice has led Travis to a safe place at the top of an abandoned building, far out of the IGs' reach. Travis is suspicious of Janice. She explains that Sanyu sent her. Sanyu then appears, and she has a plan]

Travis: [Panting] First of all . . . I have no idea what you're saying to me.

Janice: Ediat bwoy.

Travis: Secondly, stop playing with me, lady. I got somewhere to be.

Janice: Yo, me too! Ah Sanyu send me fi meet you.

Travis: What you mean *Sanyu* sent you? She's supposed to be meeting me.

Janice: Waam to— you think seh ah Airbnb
This is *Research and Development* you understand the element?
Nuff man ah resident indefinitely and di bredda dem irrelevant.

[Janice breaks out into song]

Janice: Whole heap ah idea dem come in wid a smile
Den dem start realise they've been here a while,
Rot away. Dem jus' ah rot away—

[Song ends abruptly]

Janice: Yo, a joke mi a mek star.
Mi can see seh ya under a lotta stress
But yo, the one yah different enuh, this is not a test.
Hold on deh . . . I think we've got a guest.

[Heavy footsteps lead to a nearby door being slowly opened by Sanyu]

Sanyu: Is this a bad time?

Travis: [Bewildered] Sanyu?

Sanyu: Trav-o Double Trouble!! Big T!
Eh baambi those guys were rough with you.
Ngo'olabye, they don't have stuff to do.
Anyway, if you're coming with us it's up to you.

Travis: You're alive! I—

Sanyu: OK. Get over it.
Kati, I'm thinking . . . with the success of *Have You Heard George's Podcast?*
We create our own storylines and use them as boda-bodas.
That they take us out of R&D . . . far and
Deep into the Real World, guaranteed!!

A good storyline will take you from George's Mind to the
Other side . . . but it's a hazardous ride.

Now those other guys, they call themselves
Security Guards, for us we call them *In*-security Guards! They
make you feel bad when life is already hard.
When an idea is hot, they come with a cold bucket of George's
doubts and they
Pour them out. So the plan was to draw them out.
Now you see? They're looking for me.
Saying they're gonna have me buried.
Even for you, you were worried. Ehhh
Me I don't worry. The more they get angry, the more they hunt me
The more they contribute to my story.
Now watch this . . . sorry not sorry.

[Sanyu pulls out a big rope launcher]

Travis: Hold on, Sanyu what you got there? What you 'bout to do with that? Sanyu you better—

[Sanyu fires a long rope towards a dark, floating island in the sky. Travis yells in shock]

Sanyu: Travis that's for you.

Travis: Girl, you lost your mind?

[Sanyu fires a second rope]

Sanyu: Janice that's you.

Travis: Sanyu! Come on now—

[Sanyu fires a third rope]

Travis: Hey! Listen—

Sanyu: Ah ah banange don't panic, just do!

Travis: You just gave our position away, what is you thinkin' about?!

Sanyu: Yeah, I fired all three of our storylines onto
Episode 4 of the podcast. Now those—

Travis: Why you gone do that?

Sanyu: Now those Insecurity Guards are on their way to stop us.

Travis: Yeah but they gone outnumber us, though.

Sanyu: Listen, let's just go.

You see that floating island in the distance?
That's Episode 4. When you arrive then you'll get to know more.
For now, just—

Travis: But Sanyu I don't even know how to—

Sanyu: Just remember what your story is and ignore the insecurities.

Travis: Sanyu I don't know how to do this, how do I—

Sanyu: Trav, have you ever seen a zip wire?

Travis: Yeah, I guess . . .

Sanyu: It's like that but just a bit higher.
Mukwano, can we get some cooperation?
We need solutions—

[The IGs appear on the ground below them]

IG 1: You're making a big mistake, kid!

IG 2: You'll never make it.

IG 1: You're gonna ruin Episode 4.

IG 2: George will be devastated.

Sanyu: Sometimes doing nothing is the same as doing wrong,
But I'm sick of being stuck in this place – I'm moving on!
None of us can stop time. But if you
Have more fear than faith that's your problem, not mine.
Travis?

Travis: Sanyu I really don't know about this—

Sanyu: Janice?

Janice: Deya!

Sanyu: On 3.

Janice: Come, nuh.

Sanyu: THREEEEEEEEE!!!!!!!!

[Sanyu jumps, followed by Janice. Travis protests then jumps]

SCENE 7: THE COST OF LEADERSHIP

[Back in George's room]

George: Sanyu's been trying to get into the podcast
Since Episode 4. I've
Made her wait but she's forever hopeful
Compared to these other ideas so sick of
Waiting they ain't making an effort no more.
And her strategy is so simple:
Fight for freedom.
She's on a journey I believe in.

Bro: Boy. That's a complicated story.
I don't know how you're gonna make it work in Everyman Cinema.

George: Don't underestimate the intelligence
Of the average George The Poet listener.

[Both laugh]

Bro: Do you know what it is? I gotta bus out, my guy.

George: Say nothing, brudda. Respect for shouting me.

Bro: I'm gonna shout you still.

George: Alright, love.

[Call ends]

George: Where was I . . .
Oh yeah. I gotta tell my story
'Cause I'm the only one that writes for me.
But first back to Bobi Wine's story. Unlike Georgie,
Bobi went on to become an MP
These times I'm an MC. Talk about
Role reversal – that was gonna be my
journey at least by thirty.
But life is live – no rehearsal.
It's a script that you can't be expected to know the words for.

As an MP he stood beside the stuff in his lyrics, Bobi
Wine was an outspoken government critic. And it
Wasn't a gimmick. He got love in the city, love in the
Village. To the government that's a troubling image.

Last month he was arrested for allegedly
Inciting an attempted attack on the president.

But just like Navio said in that badman song they were lacking the evidence. Bobi was Poisoned and beaten and charged with treason. He left the
Country when they released him after a
Couple of days he started speaking. He re-
Minded the world that he was arrested with
33 others, some of them are mothers.
It's already too late to pray that every one of them recovers.

Can't say who's surviving or not
Yasin Kawuma, his driver, was shot.
I was in Uganda a couple of weeks ago and a
Lot of the opinions I heard were kind of a
shock. Some people don't like when you undermine authority, in these situations it's underlined more thoroughly.
Bobi Wine maintains that President Museveni
Generally operates with an underlying autonomy.
And Museveni hasn't really said any-
thing, hasn't done much at all. He's kind of
Untouchable. So he doesn't respond to
Every mutiny. Even when he comes under
heavy scrutiny.

There's people that compare him to Gaddafi.
You gotta decide what you're wearing to the party 'cause
Independence Day's on its way. Choose one
Colour from the Ugandan flag:
Black, yellow or red
See mandem brag, we say we grab the bag so the
Ghetto is fed . . . but most of us ain't
Letting no fed step on our head just
'Cause the President said.

Bobi Wine's moving like Fela Kuti.
Making certain people look hella bookie. A
Singer, a stoner. A sinner, that's grown up

Into a much bigger persona. But at the same
Time, these decisions turn you into a loner, put your
Family's lives in danger. Are you gonna get lined
Up by a traitor. Or randomly
By some stranger? Is
Someone gonna make you an offer you can't refuse? What's it
Gonna take to get you off of the path you choose?

Malcolm X said the
Price of freedom is death.
If that's true . . . why is it always the
Ghetto that seems to sink deeper in debt?

Companionship or leadership?
Abandon ship or bleed a bit?
We can only hide behind music for so long
At some point we need to pick.

EPISODE 7: The Journey (Part II)

Extra Info:
- As mentioned in this episode, I was trying to write a news report that rhymed. A lot of 'HYHGP?' episodes start off as creative challenges, which I then tie to a specific concept. This experiment was influenced by a year of watching loads of shows on the Qatari news channel Al Jazeera.
- 'Chariot', the song by Mega which ends the episode, became one of my favourite songs that year. It's so well-written, it sounds like Mega wrote it about the migrant crisis. Mega and I go way back – she featured on my EP 'The Chicken and the Egg' – so it was a blessing to have her on this. Thanks, Mega.

Fun Facts:
- Episode 7 was nominated for 'Best Current Affairs' at the 2019 British Podcast Awards. It came second to a podcast about the Grenfell Tower Inquiry, which I was happy about – especially since it beat 'The Intelligence' by The Economist magazine – a podcast that I have a lot of respect for.
- I still can't believe how fast I used to talk in these early episodes! I think I was still in rapper mode. My pacing has changed so much since then.

There's a reason this episode came so late in the chapter: I needed time. I actually wrote a lot of the Libya material back in December 2017, after hearing 'Question Time' by Dave. But when I launched the podcast, I was determined to talk about the inner city, and deal with African politics later on. This would help me build an international picture of Black life, which is important. People of African descent find themselves living under similarly frustrating political conditions all over the world. But we rarely grow up in an education system that teaches us why we share these problems. This lack of education leads back to the issue I mentioned earlier: in the absence of African consciousness, we use stereotypes and myths to form an idea of Blackness. By studying the similarities in our problems, we can design solutions that apply to the whole group, increasing our chances of offering the children a better future. Plus, Lawyers for Justice in Libya are such a perfect example of the diaspora making themselves useful to the continent.

After writing and recording this in September 2018, I then performed both Episode 6 and Episode 7 as one live show on 20th September, filmed by my good friend Meji Alabi. That plan went so well that I flew Meji and his crew to Uganda, in an attempt to make a short film out of the show. It took two years, but we finally released *Black Yellow Red* on my thirtieth birthday, the same day as Uganda's presidential elections, 14th January 2021.

George: Quick show of hands . . . who thinks I might be
Overthinking slightly?
Like I should just be a free spirit and not get so deep with it?

Okay.

That's an interesting experiment.
Interesting. But irrelevant. It's
Not my decision to make. I
Don't choose to think like this.
I wish I could just give it a break, kick back and listen to Drake.
But I've got voices in my head and there's only so much of this I can
 take.
If this journey wasn't meant for me,
Leaving my label was potentially my biggest mistake but
If this was the case that would mean my existence is based on
All of the traditional media systems in place.
Which obviously isn't the case.

A lot of people saw me leaving the label as
Being ungrateful and giving up a seat at the table.
But that would be an ego-driven decision and as
We know, this is a mission within a vision, listen:

Entertainment and the arts can pre-empt the failings of the past
If artists become advocates and audiences become activists.
Everything I do comes back to this.
Look at Bobi Wine – that's the potential of what this whole
 interaction is.
And I see this for Dave and Stormzy.
This is what I learned from waves that came before me.
Hence the approach of a strategist. I went quiet for a while 'cause
 to
Pattern this I had to *practise* this,
And every little battle is a catalyst.

I started treating life more like a crash course than a uni course.
I spent more with my nephews and their films got me into movie
    scores.
Now I'm getting into my music more 'cause I'm
Starting to see what I can use it for.
Imagine a musical . . . news report.

That can be used to distribute information
And give the youths inspiration. And
Who knows, it might contribute to a few dissertations.

Now to make use of this new innovation I used the
News as a muse for narration. And
What did the news give me?
Story after story of abusive relations.

That November 2017 I saw a story that affected the world in a
Way I've only ever seen in a few situations.
Africans were being sold as slaves, tortured for ransom,
Thrown in graves without so much as a
Stone engraved.

Everyone on social media was so engaged and so enraged.
All of a sudden, I've seen a million posts about
Migrants running to the Libyan coast,
Getting trapped in the country.
Getting raped, beaten and kidnapped on a monthly.

Social media support is a form of low-risk protest we can afford
    when we
Wanna show solidarity from abroad. It's a
Godsend for people that are being ignored.
It was a factor in the Arab spring. In
Libya, Western-backed rebels galloped in challenging
Colonel Gaddafi, who was taken down after
Forty-two years, now he ain't around.

And do you know what's the maddest thing?
I read an article, said the memory of Arab spring prompted a
Museveni comparison. Certain energies need balancing.

Every campaign is emotionally backed
People say Museveni's been slow to react to the
Social Media Age, which the opposition
Dominate because he won't really engage.
The other month he was imposing a tax on its
Use and he basically got told to relax 'cause he
Also tried to tax money transfers, and
People saw this as open attacks on
Freedom of speech. All I was seeing is
Tweets saying he was a leech.
Obviously, there's no chance of him being impeached.
But still, Bobi Wine's got that social media reach.

Yet, online activity operates within limits.
Is writing long captions and spitting lyrics
Equivalent to hospital and prison visits?
I mean it isn't, is it?

But what are we supposed to do? We reach for the
Circles of influence we're closest to.
Obviously, we feel hopeless too. But the
Least we could do is post a post or two, I mean . . .

Tens of millions, families, friends – civilians . . .
Born on the wrong side of history. Running
From lives of misery and loss of order, tryna
cross a border with soldiers told to detain them on site in Tripoli.

The story was broken by award-winning journalist
Nima Elbagir, a young Sudanese woman –
Pulled off an investigation police couldn't.
Fluent in English and Arabic, she

Went into Libya, moved with caution
Came back with evidence of human auctions.
She presented it on CNN, the story bussed of course –
That's the benefits of being known as a trusted source.

And so, into public discourse this dis-
Covery was thrust with force. People
Talked about Libya, discussed its flaws. Dis-
Cussed all the ways in which it shuts its doors to the
Outside. Basically, we looked at the situation and
Took a long, disgusted pause.

And that was it. The story never
Stuck around for too long; the news cycle moved on.
Over here we've been dealing with Brexit
Every other day another leaver regrets it. And when the
President's engaged in beef with intelligence agencies
No one expects much from Americans, basically.
Mugabe was overthrown and it was
Just another notification on my mobile phone.

Now from the UK, across the Mediterranean
Libya's two thousand miles away.
And across the Atlantic, America's four thousand miles out the way. So
Clearly closeness doesn't equal concern. If
They're not gang we're leaving people to burn. And the
West has sown some bad seeds on the continent –
Can't let this evil return.

But the tone of indignation around immigration –
Both in the US and in this nation –
Shows how little history we all learn. And
Every single day, this planet covers 24,912 miles each full turn
1.6 million miles around the sun. So the
Speed of life alone drowns out the sound of guns. The
Sound of western governments forking out the funds to

Libyan militias – even when their hold on a city is pernicious. Who-
Ever can help us keep those Africans off the coast and
Back in Africa, we'll support the wildest bunch. It's
Easier than having to absorb a thousand hungry
Migrants and scapegoating them for violence in
Order to deport them out the country. It's more cost-
Effective. It's easier than admitting we've all lost perspective.

Speaking of perspective – by the way
Stop me if I'm talking too much, I just feel a bit reflective.
But yeah . . . speaking of perspective . . . I
Get the whole Gaddafi/Museveni thing. It's like I
Said, Museveni hasn't said anything conse-
Quential about Bobi Wine or the social media
tax but people are like 'we need the facts.'

There's a faction of Ugandan society
Whose reaction is angry and violent
Who can't stand being silent, but then there's another perspective,
    see
What does it take to govern effectively?
One school of thought would say the rule of law
But not all Ugandans feel like that
Given what the country's gone through before;
Tribal persecution, a gruesome war.

Museveni came to power in the '80s
And as of 2018, eighty percent of Ugandans were under thirty-five.
Yeah, you heard me right: thirty-five. They've
Never experienced another leader. And who-
Ever that would be can't actually prove they've got the
Requisite experience to govern, either.

In fact, the other day Museveni gave a speech and the
Way that he addressed the country was particularly candid –
'Bazzukulu' – literally, 'grandkids'.

Bear in mind Bobi Wine's thirty-six. He
Hasn't really had to win popularity with a
Propaganda machine or using dirty tricks. He's
Self-made and he's well-paid. To many ghetto
Kids that's a heavenly mix. These
Times come the next election Museveni's seventy-six.

But there is something grandad-like about him.
That's why so many can't imagine life without him.
He represents the familiar, hence the parallels with tensions in
    Libya.

First of all, the leadership of both Gaddafi and Museveni
Benefited their countries heavily.
People often talk about both individuals' ability to move with
    political agility.
Them man there brought stability, and they brought the
Notion of Government plausibility.

But their countries were divided, more than they could
Take, a lot of young people decided. People were
Tired of poverty with politicians commonly
Buying expensive shit.
People were tired of censorship.
These times, Kampala's seen a steep rise in street crimes and
In Benghazi, race riots eventually hit. And
Even then, Libya's unemployment rate was way better.
Uganda's GDP per capita seven years later is way deader.

What I'm saying is it's not like people ain't fed up.
If only corruption meant you could bribe someone so that change
    sped up.

And corruption is another one.
In fact it's probably problem number one!
Guys don't mind paying bribes and kickbacks

If the give-back is proportionate. But if they're
Paying into a system that doesn't benefit them it's
Unrewarding, it's extortionate. Now with
High rates of adult literacy, and more exposure 'cause of globalisation
People start noticing what they don't have in an
Underdeveloped and overpriced nation.

That's how you get a brain drain. You can't maintain
Growth when talent finds it hard to prevail.
People get frustrated and end up taking their skill sets
To a different part of the world. Now
Libya experienced something similar.
Guys would rather graft in a land that's unfamiliar than
Stay there . . . in a state that doesn't play fair.

So you've got people feeling cheated by the system, non-
Violent resistors being given time in prison,
Tensions over tribalism, talent walking out –
I've forgotten which country I'm talking 'bout.

What can I say? These stories are African. And
Not everyone's a successful visa applicant.
So the money that people save to move country the legal way
Ends up as fees for trafficking.
To Museveni's credit, Uganda's taken in a
Lot of asylum seekers. And to the
Credit of the Ugandan people, there is no
Alt-right that sees this as a sign of weakness. By
Contrast, Libya has something Uganda's never had: a
Widespread hatred for black skin, causing
Limited racial interaction.
That's created a space for an underworld that it's
Easy for migrants to get trapped in.

They're just tryna make it to Europe. And the
Libyan coastline is their closest point. If

They can't maybe they'll send their oldest boy. The
Risk is better than settling, soul destroyed. There's
No hope in stagnation. So at least in their imagination, they can see
One of them surviving that Mediterranean Sea,
And just for a second, they're overjoyed. But
Something happens over that Mediterranean;
You go from being someone's child to an emigrant alien . . .
Roll up to a country with bare people hating you,
Even though your situation was never explained to them.

We've seen a rise in migrants being demonised and silenced,
Being penalised and violently illegalised for
Feeling like there might be a life that's free of strife where
We reside only to come and realise they
Have no equal rights in European eyes.

And that's the end of the line, when
Neighbouring governments ain't spending a dime, when you're
Everyone's problem but no one's responsibility . . .
So we can't hold anyone accountable for the
Fact your life is unaccounted for.
No national insurance, no bank account, it's like
Censorship I swear, they just blank it out like no one
Wants you here, fam, get out. And
If the sea of angry faces ain't making this clear,
Well . . . there's always Operation Sophia.

You lot know about Operation Sophia. The
European Naval Force Mediterranean
Targeting trafficking in an effort to rein it in. See,
After the migrant shipwrecks in 2015
things were never the same again. The
Focus shifted to tackling smugglers
As opposed to patterning something with African governments
And d'you know what happened because of this?

Nothing did. No migrant lives were saved. The
House of Lords issued a statement, literally
Stating that instead of changing the situation
This operation kind of drives the wave.
There's more people taking the chance
Off the coastline hoping they can advance.
Might make it to Spain, might make it to France. But if not, you're
Stuck at this pit-stop with *this* lot . . .

And you will only exist in a lonely abyss
With malicious militias and neo-colonialists.
Scared in an open space but wearing a poker face out
there in a broken place where Evil himself caught a cold.
You see for yourself: bought and sold African bodies.
Ransom and slavery – traffickers' hobbies.

And the last thing in your control was
Your nonexistence. Now that mirage that you
Saw from a distance turns out to be the
Solid vision of a supposedly abolished system.
After crossing the Sahara Desert – a torrid mission. You're
in a squalid prison, 'horrid' isn't the word –
This is absurd you came in search of freedom but you're
Raped and cursed and beaten.
'Cause your nonexistence enables your African neighbour
To commodify your body and trap it in labour.

That very nonexistence slips the mind of so many politicians.
The ones who declared that the region was stable,
Gassed you up to come and take a seat at the table.
You've been on a quest to make it to the coastline
Ever since those western nations gave the co-sign.
So, you paid smugglers thousands of pounds, left
Town, told yourself if you drown then you drown that's
Your business, and after all of this . . .
What you found in Libya was lawlessness.

A makeshift nation; a place abandoned. That's
Not what you heard from Obama or David Cameron about a
country on its way to democracy. What you
See is a failing economy. With no *single* prevailing authority. Just
Gangsters in a state of autonomy who stand to
Gain if you can be used for trade. To
Keep you at bay that's who the EU have paid. They
Treat you this way because they need you afraid. They can
Charge your family double the fee you have paid on the
Basis of fear but another way to pay the fee is
Straight up slavery and there's a market for that because of
racism here. How d'you make this trade dis-
appear? Them man there have arrangements with Italy to
catch migrants and detain them in Tripoli
Under Operation Sophia.

Some people say your smugglers are working under the cover of
Government. Providing a security supplement es-
Sential to power. And 'cause of shared interests they're
friends for the hour, but the friendship has the po-
tential to sour. If, for example, the
Government gives in to international calls to
Apprehend them . . . that alliance would have to end
Then. What happens to you in that event then? When your
Struggle outlasts our attention spans and we
Go back to funding our cars and our pension plans. Libya's
Government has thirty-four detention camps, and the
UN can't access half of them.
Even if they can, what happens after then?
Will they be sending the troops in?
And if they do will there be an end to the shooting?
Who's gonna contact your family? How do you combat insanity?
How d'you even come back *from* that reality?

Companionship is a form of leadership and we're all in need of it.
We're all we've got.

If your bredrin part of this, could you switch that story off?
Surely not.

Entertainers and the arts can end the failures of the past. If
Artists become advocates and audiences become activists.
Everything I say comes back to this. In life that's what my next
    chapter is.

Yes or no, I just gave you that musical news report?

I dropped the first draft back in December
Not much engagement that I can remember.
But it did manage to catch one person's eye.
And her first word was 'Hi . . .'

Elham: *Hi, George. It's Elham. I'm not sure if you remember our
conversations from the Rare days about my charity. Well, we've just
launched a campaign to help bring claims on behalf of migrants
abused and tortured in Libya, trying to get to Europe. The thing is,
we have no money to bring these claims as our usual donors are all
European states and they're clearly not interested in any action
that means more migrants will end up on European shores, so we're
really tied. The campaign will help us raise some money to do some
really important work. Do you think I could send you the campaign,
to have a look at it? If you could spread the word that would be
great. Thank you so much, George.*

George: I know. Unbelievable, yeah.
If you speak with conviction, somebody will care.
I met Elham years ago when she worked at a company called *Rare*.
They specialised in BAME recruitment.
At the time I was just a Cambridge student.
I had no idea she was following my poems, but
That's why artistry goes hand in hand with advocacy –
You reach people without even knowing.

Three months after I wrote about Libya,
Elham heard the poem and hit me up.

Lawyers for Justice offer support for survivors,
Via the legal route, which someone needs to do.
'Cause if this was me or you that's what we'd pursue.
And as I've said for the past fifteen minutes,
These women, these men, these kids are people, too.

This is what my journey's been leading to, it's what I've
Always been leaning to. Why I've been taking long to get
Back to making songs, 'cause even if my
Tracks get great responses, a better use of my time is to
Provide a service for a higher purpose every time I speak to you.

Now, if you can take in all that information I just threw at you
Imagine what else we can do.

Any emotion you felt listening to me
It's time to start pursuing it; this is what you do with it:
Support the people on the justice frontline
Even if it's just this one time.

[Applause from the live *HYHGP* audience of September 2018]

George: Right here, Elham. Thank you for coming. This is all a true
story, by the way, Elham really did hear what I wrote about Libya
and got in touch with me about what her amazing charity, Lawyers
for Justice, is doing. So yeah, I'ma hand over to you, Elham,
please . . .

Elham: First of all, I'm crying. And second of all, you can't ask me to
say words after you've said words! It's really unfair.
    So I work for a charity called Lawyers for Justice in Libya, which is
very descriptive. But what we have recently launched is 'Routes for
Justice', which is about trying to find different routes for migrants

and try to help them to find some form of justice for what they suffered. As a charity, you have to go to donors, and as a charity that works on Libya – a country that's perceived to be a rich country – very few donors feel like you need the money. The only countries that are left are European countries, and obviously they have a conflict of interest with this story.

And so, we were left tied. We have cases, we have witnesses, we have evidence, but we don't have the ability to bring these cases. And it feels very difficult when you see what happens and you deal with people, and you can't do that . . .

The irony of today's performance is that I actually came straight from Brussels. I was there for a briefing with EU security people about the migration crisis. And I was very optimistic 'cause I'm always a little bit foolish at the beginnings of meetings, and I went in there really thinking we were going to talk about how we resolve the issues from the perspective of the victims. But in their narrative, the victims were them. You know, they're having to deal with this flood of people, and 'How are we gonna deal with it?'

Five hundred million was given to the Libyan government last year to focus on keeping people off the shores of Europe. Five hundred million to a government that has no authority. Five hundred million, most of which went to militias, who incidentally are the traffickers. They're now being incentivised through money from the EU – our tax money – to traffic people, because obviously the more you have, that you've saved from the sea, the more you get paid. And so, the same people that traffic them through the Sahara are now detaining them, and making money at every point along the way. We've documented many, many cases and I'm yet to meet a person who's made the journey who hasn't been tortured. I'll give one example of the kind of services that the traffickers offer.

I met a lady who said to me that she had gone for the 'premium' service with the traffickers. I asked her what that meant and one of the elements of that is that you get contraception, because you will get raped along the journey but at least you won't get pregnant.

I'm really grateful, and we're very blessed to have you as a partner in this journey. And I really believe that with your voice and our efforts we can do something together, so thank you so much, George.

[Applause from live audience until fade]

George: LibyanJustice.org
Support the people on the justice frontline
Even if it's just this one time.
[Soundtrack: Mega 'Chariot']

EPISODE 8: Sanyu's World

Extra Info:
- The drama between the ideas is all driven by how well they are progressing in real life. For example, Sanyu was agitated throughout Episode 8 because up to that point she hadn't really had a chance to shine.
- Sanyu is accused of jealousy towards my other idea, Janice, because I wrote two whole songs in Janice's voice, and they both sound like credible Dancehall hits. (You can hear these songs in the background during Travis' part in the first scene and during Janice's afterparty later).
- I had genuine anxieties about all these ideas: Was I going too far? Were they really as good as I thought? Would they end up half-assed and undercooked? Would 'real' writers see through my lack of experience with this genre? To deal with these anxieties, I packed them all into two characters: the Insecurity Guards. I knew I'd never run out of material for these characters, because my anxieties could go on forever . . . if I let them.
- This episode came from me sitting in silence, listening to my ideas and their problems. I called this 'brainstorming' and depicted it as a literal storm in my mind.

Fun Facts:
- 'Tofaayo' means 'don't worry' in Luganda. It's Sanyu's catchphrase because she's always got a plan.
- The character of Janice was inspired by the Dancehall singer, Koffee, who came to my attention in 2017 after performing live on BBC 1Xtra. Initially, I wanted a Jamaican character to broaden Sanyu's cultural relevance, but as I started listening to more Koffee, I was inspired to write songs in Janice's Jamaican accent. These songs were recorded but never released.
- The recording of Sanyu played by IG 2 in Scene 8 is a real extract from the first version of Episode 8.

This episode is a true story. It's not just based on true events, and yes, it did win a British Podcast Award for Best Fiction (grateful!) but it is actually the most factual thing I have ever written in my life. It's about my imaginary character, Sanyu, who is concerned that I am preparing to release a mediocre episode about her. This really happened. And it happened in my head. And I can prove that it happened in my head because I have the recording. Everything recorded on this episode happened within me first, and I hope no one misses that point. This was a manifestation exercise. Could I take the craziness in my mind and build it into a world that my audience could visit? Like Disney World for your ears? That's all I was thinking. Sanyu inspired the whole podcast and she deserved credit for that, so this was her moment. I know it sounds crazy 'cause I'm talking about an imaginary character, but that's my point – imagination is *real*. Special thank you to the don Kansiime Anne, who let me debut 'Sanyu's World' at her bar in Naalya, 'Kubbys' – thanks to Mark Gordon for MCing and everyone who came through that night. Big, big thanks to my family, Arnold, Aggie, Anthea, Mascot and Everton for believing in Sanyu, and of course Edith – your support has always been golden.

SCENE 1: REINTRODUCING SANYU

[Sanyu addresses the *HYHGP* audience. If this was a movie, she'd be talking directly into the camera]

Sanyu: Hi. My name is Sanyu. And I guess you
listen to George's work, so thank you. You
Might remember me from Episode 6, it was a-
Bout Ugandan music and Ugandan politics.
And it was about me I suppose, which is kind of an odd mix.
But any confusion you have is nothing a bit of
Background info won't fix . . .

So, I'm an idea. And I live right here; in
George's Mind, and my dear my fear was that I'd
Never see the light of day. Other ideas in the
Line, they had right of way but
Me, I need to leave this place right away. When I
Got here, you know like, I was so astounded but
After a while it feels overcrowded. I want to
Break some ground, maybe create a sound and
Make my creator proud, I'm tired of having to wait around.

So, we've just finished filming Episode 8 and I
Had my criticisms but I left it so late. They
Told me that they wanted a show about me
Bi ki bi ki . . . They
Sat me down and they showed me the plan. They
Told me the people I'm gonna be bigger than. They
Said that I'm gonna be bigger than Peter Pan. Even
bigger than Kansiime Anne! Can you imagine?

[Sanyu is interrupted by the entrance of her friend, Travis. There seems to be a party going on behind him]

Travis: Yo, Sanyu I got some important news . . .
Girl, who you talking to?

Sanyu: Just thinking aloud.
What? This is George's Mind I think it's allowed.

Travis: Whatever man. Just to
let you know, Episode 8 has been approved, b.
Congratulations, you in a movie!

Sanyu: Yaaay 👏👏👏 Episode 8 . . .
That is so great.

[Friend in the background interjects]

Travis' Friend: Hey Travis, you coming to Janice's thing?

Travis: Give me like 5 minutes.
Yeah, Janice got an afterparty finishing hella late.
You coming with us to celebrate?

Sanyu: You guys go ahead I just need to unwind and meditate.

Travis: Alright suit yourself.

[Travis closes door]

Sanyu: Do you guys remember my friend? His name's Travis.
He was on Episode 6 with my other friend, Janice.
In George's Mind, Travis is a translator.
Janice is a navigator, and for me I'm a plan-maker.

I made a plan for us to escape the land in
George's Mind called 'Research and Development'. We
Landed on the podcast but we left behind so many ideas,
And I really want to help them. 'Cause for
Us when we don't get to see the light of day . . . we
Can't help it, we feel some type of way. We get
Desperate. We start to separate. We lose

Sight of our intention and start fighting for attention.
Old versus new, good versus bad, even
Heavyweight versus featherweight.
Now, if your creator is serious about you as an idea
Then why does he hesitate? He should
Be releasing you from his mind into the world, or at
Least he should set a date. My friend. If he
Can't set a date then he's not serious about you
And death awaits . . .
Now, an Idea doesn't die when it fails;
Only when it's forgotten. And if
You fail to make good use of George's time . . .
Then for you, your life span can shorten.

Tofaayo.

Anyway, my plan was for George to record us on
Episode 8 of his podcast.
Then the Ambition Commission got involved and I
Felt like my storyline did not evolve. I
Wanted to give you a tour of George's Mind. Like
Episode 5 but a little more refined. I
Wanted to show you guys some other ideas other-
Wise you might not see them for another five years. But
No ideas can leave George's Mind without
Written permission from the Ambition Commission.

So, I entered myself as an applicant. They
Said they liked the fact that my accent was African.
Said I should host the end of year episode and they
Promised me they wouldn't get involved. Hm.

People can lie. They
Started giving me topics to discuss. They
Wanted it to be about Christmas. I
Said 'Chief, what's that got to do with us?'

And from there we were losing trust. Naye
This is George's Mind; things are always moving fast. The
Ambition Commission went and made their own show. I
Think it's like Question Time but I don't know. I
Wasn't involved. I'm thinking 'OK, they've got their own
Show so the problem's been solved.' But the truth is . . .

We are suffering from an attention deficit
And it's a nightmare.
Ideas are being neglected and forgotten.
No one seems to care, but I care. If it
Wasn't for the three of us escaping R&D, I would
Be trapped in George's Mind currently.
But when I was in there, I learned how to cross-pollinate
Like a team player. I swear!

Lemme explain: if
George has one minute
To think about me and another idea,
Maybe I get thirty seconds
And the other one gets thirty seconds.

Now, if that idea cross-pollinates with Sanyu,
Then the two of us can consolidate our value. And be-
Cause we have a shared outcome . . . we don't
Have to compete for attention. How come? Because
My thirty seconds is added to their thirty seconds, and
Their thirty is added to my thirty seconds. It's a
Very simple solution . . . but it makes sense. And

This is what I want to contribute, but people hear my
Voice and think 'oh she's cute'.
For me I want to change the way you think of ideas. I
want to revolutionise the way you guys see us. I
Want to overcome my fears.

I want . . .

[Soundtrack: Sanyu 'In the Real World']

I want to live in the real world/
I want it more than I can tell/
For me, my Ye is different to your Ye/
And I shaku on the beat as well/
I want to live in the real world/
I want it more than I can bear/
For me I'm happy being Sanyu/
But I want to be Sanyu there . . .

SCENE 2: INSECURITIES SET IN

[Insecurity Guards emerge from nowhere, clapping sarcastically and laughing slowly. Atmosphere darkens]

Sanyu: Insecurity Guards! What are you two doing here?

IG 1: Why do you say that, like we're irresponsible?

IG 2: Innit! You're the one that's culpable.

IG 1: Alie. We're just your friendly neighbourhood security guards—

Sanyu: IN-security guards!

IG 2: Whatever you call us, we keep you company when you feel vulnerable.

IG 1: It's easy to feel vulnerable when George neglects you . . .

IG 2: Innit. That's why we come to protect you.

[Sanyu starts breathing heavily]

Sanyu: I don't need your protection!

IG 1: But we care.

IG 2: Yeah.

IG 1: What's giving my little homie a scare?

Sanyu: You're suffocating me.

IG 2: Is it fear of failure?

IG 1: Fear of rejection?

IG 2: Fear of not having a clearer direction?

IG 1: I know what's wrong.

IG 2: What?

IG 1: She's jealous of her bredrin's song.

Sanyu: No, I'm not!

IG 2: What song?

IG 1: You know that 'Rot Away' tune?

IG 2: What song is that?

IG 1: You know it, man. It's like 'Rot away, na na na rot away, suttin suttin suttin rot away . . .'

IG 2: Oh yeah! That's my tune.

IG 1: Alright, remember Episode 6?
When these lot was on their little escaping tip?

IG 2: Yeah, that episode was wild, still.

IG 1: Yeah.
Remember that Jamaican chick?

IG 2: Don't take the mick.

IG 1: Swear down. That's her song.

IG 2: I didn't even clock. And you
Know that tune's got the streets on lock.

IG 1: It's a shellers.

IG 2: So what, Sanyu you're jealous?

Sanyu: I'm not jealous!

IG 1: Is that why everyone's at the afterparty and you're
Sitting here alone in your room?

IG 2: Innit. Singing your own little tune.

IG 1: After you made it to the podcast
I thought you'd be over the moon.

Sanyu: Exactly. I'm on the podcast, I'm happy.
What I don't understand is why you harass me. My
Whole team is winning, and you want to interfere. Can't you
go and make some bad idea disappear?

IG 2: You don't get it, do you?

IG 1: Can't get out that easily.

IG 2: Every idea is a bad idea if it
don't make money, to be honest.

IG 1: The only way out of this attention deficit
Is to generate profits.

[Sanyu panics as she struggles for breath]

IG 2: Being broke is a joke but you won't find it funny.

IG 1: You know. Time is money.

IG 2: Time is money, Sanyu.

Sanyu: I can't breathe . . .

IG 1: And in saying that, much as we'd love to stay and chat . . .

IG 2: Looks like George is about to start Brainstorming.

IG 1: You ever got caught in a Brainstorm, Sanyu?

IG 2: Things drop out the sky but it's not rain falling.

IG 1: And a weak idea like you?

IG 2: You'd get wet up like it's paintballing.

IG 1: Lol man said 'paintballing'.

IG 2: It's true.

[Sanyu choking]

IG 1: We just came to let you know that Episode 8's been approved.

IG 2: Yeah, so if you plan on making a move like, I dunno . . .

IG 1: Rewriting it 'cause you don't like how you're coming across . . .

IG 2: You should take it up with the boss.

IG 1: But remember: this is business, it's not personal.

IG 2: Yeah man, it's just profit and loss.

[Loud motorbike revs in the distance]

IG 1: Was that? A brainwave?

IG 2: What kinda brainwave sounds like that?

IG 1: Eureka moment?

IG 2: If it was, then there must be a good idea lying around.

IG 1: Good ideas make money, bro . . .

IG 2: Bro, come we go.

IG 1: Yo, Sanyu, you want anything from the shop?

IG 2: Hahaha!

[IGs exit Sanyu's room, walk out to a stormy night]

IG 2: Who's that?

IG 1: Bro, is anyone on the bike?

IG 2: I can't see no one, bro.

IG 1: So what, it's just revving on its own?

IG 2: Hold up. By order of the Ambition Commission . . .

IG 1: Turn the engine off, take the keys out the ignition.

[Close-up of a riderless motorbike, animated like a lion ready for attack]

IG 2: Come off the bike, man!

[Motorbike approaches IGs aggressively, with an engine that sounds like a lion's roar. It chases the Insecurity Guards away]

SCENE 3: GEORGE'S REFLECTIONS

[George sends voice notes to his producer, Benbrick, explaining that they need to rethink Episode 8. This is the outcome of Sanyu's complaints]

George: Yo, Benny, what's going on my brother?

Apologies in advance, my guy, but we're gonna have to rerecord . . . rewrite . . . we've got to redo Episode 8 . . .

If any part of me feels like I haven't done Sanyu justice, then it's automatically true. Because the part that feels like that is Sanyu herself, you can't escape your own ideas . . .

It doesn't speak to her character; it doesn't involve enough detail about her contribution to my thought process . . .

Think of it like this: she's like me. She's got high expectations of herself. She sees the limits in what others perceive as her successes. She's not a particular technology; she's just the idea of an idea having a life in my head; she's an identity. So, if her identity's not adequately communicated in Episode 8, that's a problem.

Sanyu doesn't just want to be promoted on the podcast; she wants to use it to make a difference . . . and I'll be real with you; the reason I approached it the way I did in the first place was because I had certain targets. I thought 'OK, I wanna say something that's seasonally relevant; it's Christmas. I wanna touch on highlights of my year'; a nice little 2018 wrap-up. And I thought to myself 'I wanna bring in these tunes, I wanna cover these topics, but that's not Sanyu's story; that's George's story, you get me?

And if people find her weird or annoying or just mildly entertaining, she's not reaching her potential. You feel me? Which is why she felt like her storyline was underdeveloped; it was under-evolved in Episode 8 as it existed. Don't get it twisted, your music's amazing. But you already know your thing. I know *my* thing, that's why I have to be honest when I hear Sanyu.

Remember, these insecurities are chasing her around saying, 'The audience is not gonna feel you.' Her storyline saves her. Her storyline comes in and reminds her who she is and what she's gonna achieve . . .

SCENE 4: SANYU RECOVERS

[After being suffocated by the Insecurity Guards, Sanyu reconnects with her storyline – which takes the form of a motorbike/lion hybrid, called 'Boda Boda'. In this scene, Sanyu is in her garage, getting ready to set out on an adventure to save Episode 8]

Sanyu: Eh! Welcome back to my story. I was side-
tracked, I'm sorry.
IGs tried to suffocate me to death. And by
Engaging them I was wasting my breath. You
Guy they could have ended me! They could have ended
Me! Eh! You thought I was joking? I was
Choking! And just as I was starting to fade away,
My Boda Boda came and saved the day.

Boda ssebo!

[Boda Boda growls enthusiastically]

Sanyu: Boda Boda is my storyline. An idea
Needs a storyline to survive in George's Mind.
People say he's aggressive, but he's passionate about me.
And he has no patience for people that doubt me.
Boda gets me from A to B, and when
George needs my help Boda finds a way to me.

[Boda interjects]

Sanyu: Sorry, Boda? What are you trying to say to me?

[Boda revs again]

Sanyu: You're right. We have to save Episode 8.
I shouldn't have left it so late.
Tofaayo. Off I go!
We're gonna find Travis and Janice at the
Afterparty for Jan's latest tour date.
By the way – Jan was on fiiire! Iyah!
Kati tutambula. Yanguwa!

[Sanyu jumps on Boda Boda like a rider on a bike and Boda Boda takes off]

[Soundtrack: Jan Jan 'Real Yout']

Sanyu: My friend Janice had recently made history
By becoming the first idea to ghost-write her own song.
Since Episode 6 her following has grown strong.
Now, for Episode 8 the Ambition Commission made it
Look like I was jealous, because so
Many ideas want to become songs, eh?
Songs are popular, songs make money, songs can be
Serious, songs can be funny. And

For me I should want be like them because why?
I am nothing?
Aha, you're bluffing!

[Sanyu and Boda Boda arrive at the club. There is a crowd outside who react to Sanyu with excitement because she is famous in George's Mind]

Event Promoter: Sanyu, we're happy to have you, but you can't park—

[Boda Boda growls aggressively]

Sanyu: Boda, chill! Hahaha. Tofaayo give me 5 minutes!

Event Promoter: But we're not licensed to—

Sanyu: 5 minutes, I swear.

[Sanyu disappears into the club]

SCENE 5: SANYU FINDS TRAVIS

[The club is hosting an afterparty for Janice, Sanyu's friend. Over the year, Janice had also become a celebrity in George's Mind because of her musical talent. Sanyu, Janice and Travis all broke out of George's Mind onto the podcast together, so they remained close. In this scene, Travis is enjoying Janice's performance when Sanyu arrives]

Sanyu: Travo!

Travis: Eyyy, Sanyu! I thought you wasn't coming. Bet you glad you Came though, right? This place is jumping!

Sanyu: OK, don't freak out, but those IGs just tried to choke me out.

Travis: What you mean?!

Sanyu: They were
Worried I would interfere with Episode 8. They were like
'George has approved Episode 8, let it go mate.'

Travis: Sanyu, I don't understand I thought you loved Episode 8.

Sanyu: I mean . . . I guess it's OK. But I
Did kinda feel like it could be better,
Especially if we're going for the whole movie set-up.

Travis: Argh, Sanyu if you wasn't feeling Episode 8 you shoulda
Said something, man you shouldn't have left it so late.

Sanyu: Yes, I know. I just
Didn't want to mess up the flow you know. But these
IGs had me choking to death on the floor and
When they left I said 'no, I have to get up and go.'
So I have a plan. And I thought to myself,
'For this to work I need Trav and Jan.'

Travis: Girl, I got you. But if you want Janice time you better
Stand in line.
I mean, look at her.
Your girl a superstar, b.

[Crowd cheer for Janice]

SCENE 6: BUSY'S OFFICE

[Busy, the head of the Ambition Commission, is in his office trying to secure the release of Episode 8. He sent the Insecurity Guards to make sure Sanyu didn't interfere with his plans. They have come back unsuccessful, after being chased away by Sanyu's storyline, Boda Boda]

[Insecurity Guards knock on the door]

Busy: Come in.

[IGs walk in silently]

Busy: You lost Sanyu. A whole Sanyu. The most
Fertile idea in George's mind who don't even
Know her own value. You lost *that* yout?

IG 1: Oi . . . man should know who man's talking to, you know.

Busy: Shut up! Shut up. About.
You let her storyline chase you away? Blud shut ya mouth.
What? The whole point of the podcast is to help the audience en-
Vision the vision. And that vision is driven by
This thing here – the Ambition Commission. Are you
Nuts? How can Sanyu tell her own story when ideas
Can't leave George's Mind without our written permission?

IG 2: You know your problem, Busy?
You keep confusing George's ambition with George's fear.

IG 1: Yeah. Look around. See all this here?
None of this existed before this year.

IG 2: George is scared of dying before he's ready.

IG 1: 'Cause life's ironic like that. You get me?

Busy: Hm. You lot wanna test me.
You represent G's insecurities,
I represent his hustle. What's more
Likely? One day George is gonna forget
You, or he'll forget me? We can
Work together for now, regulate these ideas but

You lot won't be around in less than maybe five years.

IG 2: Yo. Busy listen – ambition or no ambition.

IG 1: Hustle . . .

IG 2: Insecurity . . .

IG 1: We're all from the same place.

IG 2: But if you want us to keep Sanyu contained . . .

IG 1: My guy, you gotta change pace.

IG 2: George is motivated by fear.

IG 1: That's the perfect way to terminate an idea.

IG 2: If you can make this guy scared that he
can't communicate this idea . . .

IG 1: Then he's not gonna bother with her.

Busy: Yeah, but the problem is *her*.
Sanyu plays on George's emotions. She
Makes him feel like he's in a commitment.
That's why every time she says she's not happy with
Something, he takes a minute to listen.
And because of that emotional attachment she
Doesn't have to go through the Ambition Commission.
So, what we need to do is force her to operate in different conditions.

IG 2: How you mean?

Busy: I mean we can't
Stop her from trying to change Episode 8 but we can

Turn her into someone her *bredrins* don't rate.
You know like that?

IG 1: It's true. It won't work if we try to *make* her chill.

IG 2: But we can isolate her still . . .

SCENE 7: AFTER THE AFTERPARTY

[Janice is singing and walking happily back to the green room after coming off stage. Opens the door and is elated to find Sanyu and Travis]

Janice: Sanyu!!!

Sanyu: Jan Jan!

Janice: Wagwan boss lady!? I thought you weren't coming!

Sanyu: Well—

Janice: Sanyu it mek me so happy that you come to mi show.

Sanyu: Actually I—

Janice: Wah ya say Travis? You didn't want me to know?

[Travis stutters, knowing Sanyu didn't plan to come]

Janice: But if I knew you were watching I woulda felt uncomfortable though.
Hahaha. Sanyu mi can't lie, I did think say you nah like mi music.

Sanyu: What? I—

Janice: And it hurt me because ah fi you dis;
Sanyu, you are the reason do this. I was
Thinking maybe you don't understand all mi song.
But to see you here mek me wonder if mi did
Wrong all along! Ahahaha!

Sanyu: Janice I— you make wicked songs and I
Love that they're getting such a big response. After
All that time in R&D we've got
Superstar out of you! Girl, I'm proud of you.

Janice: Mi know, mi know.
Ah just sometime the Insecurity Guard dem a
Come for me. And a tell me say Sanyu nah want mi company.

Sanyu: What? Insecurity Guards came for you?

Janice: Yo! How you mean!
Dem boy deh ah come regular.
Ever since the music became a success ya nah.

Sanyu: Travis. Have you discussed this?

Travis: I ain't know about this.

Sanyu: Janice. The IGs came for me too. They
Hate to see us free, no matter what we do. They
Want us to bend, they can't let us go straight
Me I wanted to make changes to Episode 8 so they
Came to the house and they threatened me. Then they suffo-
Cated me. Even now I'm getting throat ache! [Coughs]

Janice: So, you never come fi watch my show?

Sanyu: What? I— no.

Janice: Ya come fi a adventure. Ya come fi a fight.

Nuttin nuh wrong with that; we all know that's what you're like.

Sanyu: Janice it's not like that I—
Janice: Then what's it like, Sanyu? Ya know
Why people stay away from you? Ya
Lost! You nah have no anchor. Ya
Only really know what you want when you
Feel fear. And anger. In your
Vision this ah Sanyu's World not even the
Mind of George Mpanga. Mi never
Question why anytime Sanyu say fi jump we say
How high? And now mi know why!

Sanyu: Janice you're wrong.
It's not—

Janice: Don't lie! Stop lying to yourself, Sanyu.
It can't bring more embarrassment to anybody else than you.

Sanyu: Lying to my . . . Ohhh.
Oh you want the truth.
OK, let's talk truth, Jan Jan.
You, like loads of ideas, have
Been in George's Mind for over five years.
In that time George never heard your voice. He
Would have listened but you never thought you had that
     choice.
Me? I've been here just over a year. But the
First thing I did was let him know that I'm here.
Know that I *see*, I *feel*, I *hear* . . . and even
Though I'm just an idea, I'm a REAL idea!

I did that. And do you know what George did? He
Started writing back. For the
First time we wrote about George's Mind and he
Did this to develop my storyline.

Travis: Sanyu that the other thing. Your
Storyline getting kinda wild, b.
I mean he cool around me. But look
At him, don't you think he kinda rowdy?

[Cut to Boda Boda intimidating other ideas outside the club]

Sanyu: Just before I made my way here
IGs tried to end me.
Why would my storyline be friendly? They
tried to suffocate me and Boda Boda saved me when
None of you were there to defend me.

Janice: You wouldn't have been alone if ya roll to di
Afterparty in the first place. But
Everybody leave you becah everybody know say
Most days Sanyu like her own space. Ya so
Obsessed with not getting left pon di shelf that ya
Isolate yourself.
Then ya move like it's *I* that needs *your* help.
But Sanyu look around.
You're not the only idea that's grown. Mi
Come a long way from Research and Development, wah ya
Think? Because mi sing song mi less intelligent?

Sanyu: No one said that.

Janice: Then what? What mek you
Downplay my success and choose to be upset? Always
Chasing suttin ya suspect you ah
Gwan like ya nah bus yet.
George mek you di star of Episode 8 and now ya
Wan fi change it – why ya left it so late??

Sanyu: You're not listening to me!

Travis: Man, y'all about to give G a headache, man!

[Knock on the door. Travis answers and has a quick conversation with a messenger. He expresses surprise, walks over and switches on the TV]

Presenter: We interrupt the scheduled programme to bring you this public service announcement.

Busy: As some of you may know, the Ambition
Commission is facing criticism over
How we've handled Episode 8 of George's Podcast. We've
All got our perspectives so all our stories contrast. But rest
Assured, no mischaracterisation is intended.
So, until further notice, Episode 8 has been suspended.
As of now the episode is under review. We'll
Analyse its components, deciding
Which parts we want to renew, what we want to im-
prove . . . and which ones to remove.

Now, I'm apologising in advance because not
Every contributor will be given a chance. For ex-
Ample, we might have to let go of Janice
If we feel her soundtrack throws off the balance.
Or maybe Travis with his translation talents.
George's audience might not want this again, we
Might need some new ideas from distant ends, maybe
They can show us what to do different then. But
I would advise you to reach out to Sanyu,
Since hers is main voice of discontent.
In the meantime, George will be Brainstorming so
Be prepared for many more showers.
Oh – and one last thing – the deadline's in 24 hours. We
Have no back up, so if all
Parties can't agree . . . then I
Guess there won't be no Episode 8.

And all of you will go back to R&D.

Keep an eye out for changes to your storyline.
And don't worry, it will all be fine.
This, we believe, is the most efficient decision.
By order of the Ambition Commission.

[Trav switches TV off]

Sanyu: You see what Busy's trying to do right?
He doesn't want us to unite. He
Wants us to fear that we won't get attention.
He wants us to fight!

Travis: Sanyu . . . let's talk about this. Right
Now, Episode 8 is an hour long.
I'm the translator on that: that's an hour of *my* work, gone.
And they talking 'bout changing the soundtrack
Sanyu, Janice's songs are our songs.

Janice: She does not care.
There's only one reason why she come up here.
She needs you to translate and me to navigate.
She come fi cross-pollinate.
A lie mi ah tell, Sanyu?

Sanyu: Walt Disney was George's age
when he created Mickey Mouse.
Ninety years later he
Has the world's biggest independent media house.

Travis: Sanyu, ain't nobody got time for this right—

Sanyu: *Two months* after creating Mickey
Disney put him on TV.
So, for me my vision is bigger than any ultimatum Busy can give me.

Travis: Sanyu! I am
Not going back to Research and Development
Just because you cancelled an episode for the hell of it.

Sanyu: But we can save the episode if we collaborate!
Janice, you're right, I was hoping you would navigate.
Travo, I need you to translate. If we
Work really hard with George's best ideas we can
Still deliver this by the planned date.

Janice: And where exactly are these ideas?
That are so much better than us?
Ideas so clever and sophisticated dem
Guarantee fi mek a man bus.

Travis: Sanyu, we been sticking to the plan all along. C'mon
G's about to release Janice's song.

Sanyu: Argh you people are thinking so small!
Do you want to be around tomorrow, or forever?
'Cause my friend, many ideas are released.
Not so many are remembered.
There are people who don't like our creator, want to dis-
credit his ideas and prove him wrong. Do you
Seriously think the best use of George's Mind
Is releasing stupid songs!?

Janice: Alright Sanyu. Mi understand you.

Sanyu: Jan, that came out wrong, I—

Janice: True ya big and ya brave,
Good luck digging ya grave.

[Janice leaves]

Travis: Hm. I guess I'll see you in R&D.

[Travis leaves]

SCENE 8: SANYU LEAVES THE CLUB

[After being labelled public enemy no. 1, Sanyu makes her way through the club to continue with her story alone]

American Idea: Hey, Sanyu what's the big idea?

Sanyu: Excuse me, can I get past?

Hood Idea 1: Yo Sanyu, what you saying,
Hitting them with the re-up?

Hood Idea 2: Sis if you're riding, we got you.
You know guys got love for you.

Sanyu: Thank you, thank you. Please, can I just—

Supportive Idea: Sanyu, I stood up to you.

Sanyu: I appreciate you—

Nervous Idea: Sanyu, I know you're gonna hear this a lot but
I really need you to come through on Episode 8.
I'm a young idea, I don't wanna be forgotten.
Sanyu! Please!

Sanyu: I'm really trying to go.
OK, all the best.

[Sanyu walks outside to an angry mob]

Bitter Idea: It's irresponsible, it's unacceptable and
Quite frankly, in this attention deficit—
There she is! You, Sanyu, you pushed in!

[Angry mob shout in agreement]

Sanyu: What? I've just come out of—

Bitter Idea: I was next in line to leave George's Mind, but
You jumped ahead of me . . .

Sanyu: I had no idea—

Bitter Idea: Now you're on Episode 8 instead of me.

[More angry shouts of agreement]

Sanyu: That's not my fault!

Bitter Idea: And now we're all heading back to R&D
Because you threw your rattle out the pram.

Sanyu: Every one of us had—

Bitter Idea: You think you're a revolutionary idea,
But you're really just a spoiled brat without a plan!

[Mob gets angrier]

Sanyu: Whatever.

[Boda Boda growls]

Bitter Idea: Yeah, that's right. Hide behind your storyline!
Rub it in our faces – that's what it's like when you get George's time.

[Crowd boos Sanyu]

Sanyu: Boda, let's go.

[Sanyu mounts Boda Boda and leaves]

[Soundtrack: Jorja Smith 'The One']

SCENE 9: THE RACE FOR EPISODE 8

[Insecurity Guards address all the ideas in George's Mind, while Sanyu chases the end of the episode]

IG 1: Tomorrow you lot gotta vote.

IG 2: *Someone's* version of Episode 8 has got to go.

IG 1: Now, obviously, Ambition
Commission . . . ours is patterned fam.

IG 2: These times, Sanyu don't even have a plan.

IG 1: Imagine fam.

[Cut to Sanyu racing through George's Mind on Boda Boda]

Sanyu: I have a plan. I hate that I'm doing this without Trav & Jan but they don't understand.

I'm gonna find Episode 8, just like I found Episode
6 when I was looking for Episode 4.
My storyline's gonna take me there. Once I've
Arrived then I'll get to know more . . .

[Cut to Insecurity Guards continuing their smear campaign with a
small audience]

IG 2: You gotta remember, Sanyu's bitter.

IG 1: Deep down she wants to be a singer.

IG 2: But when her bredrin, the Jamaican one
Dropped a couple bangers after Sanyu bus her.

IG 1: *She* got bigger.

IG 2: Oi you seen this video on Insta?

[IG 2 plays a recording of Sanyu from his phone, laughing]

Sanyu: *I get it, OK! George likes songs.*
Everyone likes songs. I'm not a song.
I can't sing, I don't rap, I have no dance,
I'm just an idea and I want to make him proud.

[Cut to Sanyu racing through George's Mind]

Sanyu: I think that's Episode 8 floating in the sky above
Boda Boda take us higher, love.
I can feel my destiny reaching into the distance
Even if I have to speak it into existence.
My storyline is unstoppable—

[Sanyu crashes]

SCENE 10: JANICE ON THE BREAKFAST CLUB

[The morning after Sanyu's crash, Janice has an interview on popular radio show, *The Breakfast Club*]

DJ Envy: Good morning, everybody, it's DJ Envy, Angela Yee, Charlamagne Tha God, we are the Breakfast Club! And we have a special guest in the building.

[All greet Janice]

Janice: Yeah man, wagwan.

CTG: Now Jan Jan, we know you got some new
Music for us but first we gone get straight into it;
This is all anybody's talking 'bout: before the
Crash you and Sanyu had a falling out.

Janice: Well, it all started—

Angela Yee: I'ma need you to spit out your gum. Sorry.

Janice: Yeah man.

[Janice puts gum in the bin]

Janice: Well, we had a situation after my afterparty last night.
You how like brothers and sisters fight?
Yeah man, then she left on her storyline, but it moves like a fast bike.
   And
True George was Brainstorming so Sanyu must have lost sight and—
You know what happened.

Angela Yee: Now Jan Jan a lotta people are talking about . . .
You know Episode 8 saying,
'Maybe she bit off more than she could chew'
'Why couldn't she just look forward to Season 2?'

DJ Envy: A lotta people are saying Ambition Commission had something to do with it.
Do you think there's any truth to this?

Janice: We do not believe this was accidental.
Yeah man, the AC wouldn't be the first to do this.
Anytime an idea step forward fi
Mek a change it is persecuted.

CTG: Does that mean you support Sanyu's version of Episode 8?

Janice: Of course.
I now believe it is about more than Episode 8.
It is about having the right . . . having the power
To mek ya own fate.
My song might not end up on the soundtrack and
Travis might lose his translation contract but
Everybody haffi sacrifice; that is life.
Just look at Sanyu.
She mek a stand so di least we can do is stand, too.

SCENE 11: SANYU SURVIVES

[Sanyu is lying unconscious on a hospital bed. She is visited by a mysterious woman]

Sanyu: What's – what's going on?

Serena: Hello Sanyu.
You crashed your storyline and for now you're paralysed. You
Acted alone, this wasn't down to bad advice, but that's a
Lot to take in – you're allowed to have a cry.

Sanyu: Nyabo, who are you?

Serena: My name's Serena; Chair of the Contentment Council.
   We
Work with ideas becoming tense and doubtful
About the potential downfalls of the
Respective adventures they ventured out for.

Where were you born, Sanyu? Where was
George when you entered his mind?

Sanyu: In Uganda, with his nephews.
Having the best time.

Serena: That's right. George didn't plan you, Sanyu. The
First thing you did was let him know that you're here.
Fast forward, it's been over a year. And in all this time,
Just look at the effect you've had on George's Mind.
Ideas are more confident than ever. They're
Much more comfortable together. Every time a
George The Poet listener *mentions* Sanyu
Ideas are reminded of their strength and value.

Sanyu: But they tried to . . . Boda Boda . . .
What's happened to my storyline? [Sobs]

Serena: Sanyu, once upon a time, your biggest fear was the
Thought that you'd disappear within a year. Now
George has built a whole world around you.
Why would your storyline finish here?

Sanyu: But look at me! I'm hopeless.

Serena: Oh yes . . . for now.
But this is the process.
You can't bypass the process.

Sanyu: What do I do? What do I do now?

[Memories of George's friends asking about Sanyu drift in and out of
focus]

Richie Diamondz: *Yo, what happened to that hood* Space Jam *you
was making me hear that time? Sounded mad yo . . .*

Sandra: *Hey hun, I need to hear Sanyu, honestly, I'm missing my babes . . .*

Dun D: *Fam I was thinking about, you know that animation thing you played me the other time? You're sick you know. You're like the African Walt Disney.*

Janice: *In your vision this ah Sanyu's world, not even the mind of George Mpanga!*

[Sanyu wakes up]

Travis: Sanyu? Janice! She's awake!

[Travis calls for help]

Janice: Sanyu? Sanyu? It's alright.

Sanyu: Time. I need time. I need time . . .

[Soundtrack: George The Poet, Maverick Sabre & Jorja Smith 'Follow The Leader']

CHAPTER TWO

EPISODE 9: Sabrina's Boy

Extra Info:
- With the BBC's backing, I was now able to use American music, allowing me to reach an American audience. America is strategically important to me, not just because they have big markets, but because Black people across the world look to African American culture for inspiration – myself included. So out of respect, I wanted to tell an African American story.
- This was my first time making a whole episode about someone else. The advantage of writing about a famous person is that it invites millions of fans to join the conversation.

Fun Facts:
- Hip Hop legend Fab 5 Freddy reached out to me after hearing this episode. Freddy has been an originator of Hip Hop culture since the 1970s, from co-creating the 1983 documentary 'Wild Style' to hosting the ground-breaking TV show 'Yo MTV Raps!' to even directing the music video to my favourite rap song of all time – 'One Love' by Nas. This guy is real, through-and-through, New York Hip Hop. And he loved this episode. Listening to his praise over the phone during the pandemic was one of the proudest moments of my career. It let me know that I was on track. On this episode, I talked so much about things that happened in 1980s New York before I was born – and Fab 5 Freddy approved this message.

For the first episode of Chapter 2, my aim was to explain how Black trauma fuels the Western Black storytelling industry – especially rap music. This was important for me to highlight because *HYHGP* intends to do something different. Instead of relying on our pain to hold a listener's attention, the podcast relies on creativity to draw attention to teachable moments. In Episode 9, I did this by telling the backstory of a famous Black storyteller. Although this person is widely known, their troublesome persona is rarely discussed in relation to the economic and political horror show that shaped their early years. Many Black celebrities have gained influence by commercialising their trauma, but are we all missing a bigger opportunity? What if this influence was then used to understand and improve the systems that keep reproducing these traumatic experiences?

George: Hello and welcome to Episode 9 of
Have You Heard George's Podcast? And you have heard it, haven't
you? My
Last episode was a year ago, since
Then I've been doing what I have to do; following
Every opportunity down every avenue
but I couldn't *wait* to get back to you.
I want to express my gratitude that you've
Come back to tune into Chapter 2.

Chapter 1 did well. A
Lot of people listened to what I had to say and thought
'Rah this young man has outdone himself.' So
Now I'm like Marlo Stanfield to the podcasting underworld.

And yeah, on some level it is a new fad. But I'm
Proud of the fact that we didn't move mad.
We just followed our instincts and
5 British Podcast Awards later, the
Situation isn't too bad.

Seriously, thank you.

We've had articles and interviews, etc.
On top of that, a deal with the BBC.
All of this from me feeling pensive and
Maintaining a friendship with Benbrick.

But success is a double-edged sword.
Don't you wanna become a legend, George?
Don't you wanna get awards every time you press record?
Ain't you that same kid from the back of the bus?
Trying to get applause by rhyming a set of thoughts with the
Tightest timing and metaphors?

The answer is yes, of course. But, yet there's more.

We came up in Grime.
Grime literally means 'dirt'. And
Even though there was no money in it at
First, teamwork made the scene work.
As of 2019, quite a few people from out of the Grime scene,
have written their
Way into early retirement. But what
No one has been able to do is
Clean up this quote unquote 'dirty' environment.
And I'm thinking that might be where I come in.

I'm not gonna clean up the streets singlehandedly
I'm just gonna analyse it candidly and
Use my career to inspire the next generation to
Think like a family.

Why me?

Well, I'm from deep in the heart of the Black community,
North West London, St Raphael's Estate.
And I can say that with my chest because I ain't wrapped myself in
   hate.
Back in the days, Raph's was a place that was
Associated with savage behaviour, stabbings and danger,
Robberies, burglaries and obviously murder scenes. As a
Kid I wanted to establish a name but
Where certain man was my neighbour,
Technically I was gang-affiliated, and
Raph's was a place that mandem really hated.
So as much as I loved my estate I couldn't just
Brandish the name Raph's.
Badness became part of the branding of St Raph's.
I mean, for starters the mandem were straight gassed.
Jump out gang, stomp out man.

Raph's had a reputation for violence, and as much as I
Hate to highlight this, it'd be fake to deny this.
Yet no one knows the full story, so I'm breaking the silence.

So, on that cheerful note . . . yeah man, welcome back.

SCENE 1: IN GEORGE'S CAR

[George addresses the *HYHGP* audience from the driver's seat of his car. The audience sits in the passenger's seat while he talks]

George: Now, if you put
Any group of people under a microscope
Nobody's gonna be perfect. So
If I'm gonna talk about the parts of my community that
Ain't properly working then it's gotta be worth it.
Does the world really need another young Black man spitting
Poverty verses . . . with passion and purpose, but a
Level of analysis that isn't scratching the surface?
Even if his words really do have fire in them.
We need more than fire, in my opinion.

'But George, are you saying that if rappers don't write like you,
      they're redundant?'
No. I'm saying in the inner city of London our
Problems are pretty abundant.

So, we gotta give these kids something to believe in, we
Can't just leave it to the government with these things.
Someone has to offer them a vision for themselves
More than so-called 'real n****s' for the males or the
Prisoners in cells. More than 'bad b*****s' for the girls, or even
the riches and the wealth, I mean
Something that makes them feel inspired
about their position in the world.

Basically, I'm describing a community makeover.
One that makes *every* young person feel like a stakeholder.

Now, there's good news and bad news—
Babe, which one should I give them first?
The good news or the bad news?

Dija: Tell them the good news.
The bad news doesn't make sense on its own.

George: OK, so the good news is—

Dija: But hurry up, though. You've got a lot to get through.

George: Alright, yeah, the good news is we're halfway there.
We've got the vehicle to get us to the destination.
And that vehicle is entertainment.

The bad news is the world seems to value this a lot
More when we talk about our torment.

There's a direct relationship between rap and trauma,
And people expect this of the average Black performer.

So pain is what it costs to entertain, but
That's not a cost we can sustain.

Black trauma is like a fossil fuel: it's
Powerful and it's addictive. But it's
Not the energy that we should stick with. We need to focus—

Dija: George. They get it.

George: Alright so where did the appetite for black trauma come from?
Close your eyes,
Let's go back to the 1970s.

[Soundtrack: Bobby Womack 'Across 110th St']

SCENE 2: INTRODUCING BLAXPLOITATION

[A busy Harlem street in the mid-1970s]

In Hollywood before the '70s
African Americans were basically accessories.
And who knows how long this would have stayed the same if
Not for the wave that came and changed the game?
Blaxploitation was a genre that put
African Americans on the screen for longer.

They did this by focusing on stereotypes,
Defiant and violent and hyper-sexualised.
Contextualised struggles of the black working classes
With heroic figures finessing their circumstances. Sound familiar?

[Quotes from the Blaxploitation movies *Foxy Brown*, *Trouble Man*,
     The Spook Who Sat by the Door and *The Mack*]

George: It's crazy – all the stereotypes was in the mix:
Gangsters, hustlers, pimps and tricks.
But guess what? America loved it.
Blaxploitation introduced a whole generation of
Talent to the general public. Sound familiar?

[African American movie professionals reflect on Blaxploitation.
Interviews of Vonetta McGee, Oscar Williams and Jim Brown taken
from the documentary *Black Hollywood: Blaxploitation and
Advancing an Independent Black Cinema* (1984). One clip of Cicely
Tyson is from an interview with ABC News (1972)]

SCENE 3: GEORGE IN THE DINER

[George addresses the *HYHGP* audience while eating at a diner]

Waitress: There you go, sweetheart.

George: Thank you.

Waitress: Want some water, hun?

George: Oh yes please.

[Waitress pours a glass of water]

Waitress: Enjoy!

George: Thank you very much. [Sips]
You're listening to the sounds of Bobby Womack:
'Across 110th Street'. He's basically saying
'You won't believe your eyes if you come to the ends g.'

Clients and prostitutes knocking boots,
Single mums so strung out they lost the youts,
You know the vibes.
110th Street was the borderline between Harlem and Central Park.
   A
Quintessential mark where racial tensions sparked.

The song—

[Someone in the diner drops a glass]

George: The song was a soundtrack to a film of the same name.
This was in Blaxploitation's heyday. Both the
Track and the movie quickly became famous;
Success that the genre wouldn't maintain.

But a lot of the Black community was feeling it, though.
It was nice seeing so many people on screen with a 'fro.
It brought healing to those who were dealing with woes
'Cause they were deeply involved with the streets;
With the roads.

SCENE 4: INTRODUCING SABRINA

[A busy street in the Queens borough of New York City, where a teenage girl is hustling]

George: One of those people was a girl called Sabrina.
Sabrina was a Queensbridge dealer. At
fifteen years old, Sabrina had a baby.
Left him with her parents 'cause her life was kind of crazy.
She was getting money though. She
Spent a lot of that money on spoiling her son.
So even though she never lived with him, whenever she
Visited it was pure enjoyment and fun between the
Boy and his mum. Sabrina adored her son.
And her son adored his mummy. He
Couldn't have known the risk that would come with all this money.

SCENE 5: SABRINA'S DEATH

[The tragic discovery of Sabrina's body in her own home]

George: One day Sabrina never showed up. They
Called but she didn't pick the phone up.

Her dad decided to go round to her place
He left his wife and the children alone.
Opened the door and found his daughter on the
Floor. She'd been killed in her home.

Someone drugged her and left the gas on.
The boy was only eight.
His family told him she wasn't coming back . . .
And he couldn't help but wait.

Mummy was running the streets with the wolves.
Anything goes out there
And these were the rules. But she was a force. She
Didn't want any government cheese for support. You could
Tell from the sneaks and the tees that she bought
Her only son. Who's slowly coming to terms with the
Fact he's lost his only mum. The
Fact that . . . every birthday's about to be a lonely one.

Sabrina made a choice between
Dwelling broke and selling coke.
Chasing a dream from which she never woke.

SCENE 6: THE RISE OF YOUNG DEALERS

[Someone inserts a cassette tape into a 1980s-style boom box. George's narration continues when the person presses play]

George: Others, like her bredrin Lorenzo
Continued getting money with the rest of their friends, though.
Italians controlled most the coke in the ends.
And due to his involvement with them,
Lorenzo had the best connection with them so
He supplied most of his friends. Even when he
Got arrested he was still making doe from the pen.

But he weren't the only one wearing Filas on the wing, for the
First time young drug dealers was a thing.
At the same time there were new ideas about
Blackness popular with teenagers in bing.

By the 1980s New York prisons were
Full of the teachings of the Five Percenters; from
Lifers to people with a lighter sentence, the
Doctrine was offering them freedom from their sins.
This was a Nation of Islam offshoot. A-
Nother movement that attracted lost youts.
Young Black men they would speak to them as kings and the
Streets have been affected by their teachings ever since.

They said the mandem were divine. And their
Lack of understanding was the crime. And the
Only way out was the expanding of the mind.
The Five Percenters' more enlightened members
Weren't necessarily criminals, but they did appeal
To the gangsters of the time.

[News coverage of the Five Percent Nation from the Pan African
Alliance documentary *The Nation of Gods and Earths: Who are the
Five Percenters?*]

George: Back to Lorenzo. He knew a lot of Five Percenters but
I don't know if he was deep into the ting. Through the
Network a guy called Supreme and him were linked.
Supreme was a typical Five Percenter nickname.
But in the end it was the guy in the big chain supplying the
Strip's caine.
Supreme was holding so much weight
He could have changed the strip's name to 'Brick Lane'.

At the same time there was something going on
A new sound was coming from the Bronx.
A new style of dancing and dressing
Giving new artists a chance at progressing.

This new wave would answer the question of
How to advance the direction of Black enter-

tainment. People that filled the gap left it vacant, de-
Mand for the look, for the accent and cadence
Eventually made rap centre stage when
There was no more work for that generation.
So, despite Hollywood's lack of engagement
Rap took ownership of the Black conversation.
Not the old voices of Blaxploitation;
Now you're dealing with the crack generation.
And they're taking it right back to the pavement.
Coke was good business; crack was amazing!
It was cheaper *and* more addictive:
Professionals, parents, actors and agents.
They weren't sniffing they were freebasing
And people rarely came back from the 'basing.

[News coverage of the crack epidemic, taken from the BBC Archive: *Panorama*: 'Crack Crisis – Is Britain Next?']

George: Right now you're listening to 'The Message' by
Grandmaster Flash and the Furious Five. If
Telling your own story is the secret to survival,
Thank God this story survived.

SCENE 7: REAGANOMICS

[A look back on the economic climate of the crack epidemic]

George: Reaganomics made the projects a
Place where base-aholics wasted profits.

Wait. You lot remember Reaganomics right?
America's business plan for the 1980s . . .
Which reinvigorated American morale,
And drove communities like these crazy.

Remember Blaxploitation was able to happen 'cause
Hollywood needed something cheap for the business.
Fair enough, the profits are steep when you win big but
Why do you think their pocket wasn't deep to begin with?

From the '50s to '60s the country was comfy but
There was a recession in the '70s, even for celebrities.

You didn't ask but I'm gonna tell you why this recession is relevant:
Because within a decade . . . an ex-Hollywood actor became
    president.

His name was Ronald Reagan
And he was promulgating a new way to
Frame the conversation. He said:

Why doesn't the government just take a step back?
Leave people to sort out their lives on their own.
Lower taxation and regulation, and the
Country will thrive on the whole.

Reaganomics was a business plan de-
signed to make American society
The ideal place to do business quietly.
And reliably.

No post-war president tried this way before
Close your eyes and visualise what Reagan saw:

He believed in the invisible hand;
Every little thing you do for yourself as
Part of a big metaphysical plan.
The idea that the plan is ultimately good.
So, Ronald Reagan created the most individualistic
Economic culture that he could.

Unemployment declined
Which I'm sure some enjoyed at the time.
But the streets, with the noise and the crime,
Captivated young boys in their prime.

Four years after Sabrina's death, her
Son was on the corner messing with thugs.
His grandparents thought he was taking extra classes
Between three and six but he was peddling drugs.

Who wasn't? This was the
Crack generation live in effect, and
Boo-Boo, as his auntie nicknamed him
Was playing with his life in effect.

The story goes deeper though: how was he to know
That Queens was home to rap's first CEO?
Queensbridge street kids who used to be dealers
Now doing dealings with Adidas. If
You were him would you believe this? Or would you
Stick to the devil you know; wear your
Pain like body armour wherever you go?

The story goes deeper though; how was he to know?
How was he to know that the government knew?
When it took ten years to uncover the truth. For
All the talk by the Reagan administration about
the danger of drugs to the youth, they were
Working with the people who would smuggle it through.
All 'cause Congress blocked what they really wanted to do.

It's so much deeper though, how was he to know?
That for most of the twentieth century American
Capitalism was in competition with Russian Communism.
Each saw the other as the wrong religion.
Capitalism says it promotes the individual;

Communism says it upholds a bigger principle.
Neither side is indivisible, so it is important that
They win these little wars. It's like a game of chess, with
Every piece representing each country's
Position on the board, while managing their
Citizens' opinions on the cause.

Overall, Russia and America are way too big to just go to war.
So they fight those wars behind closed doors. In
Weaker nations that need donations.

Now, in the 1980s
Nicaragua *was* that weaker nation.
Enough of them were suffering under a communist government
That they felt the need to change things.

But Congress told Reagan he
Couldn't give the rebels any money anymore.
And any attempt to extend support
Was essentially against the law.

Still, overthrowing a government is expensive business. So the
Rebels went to great lengths to fix this. They raised
Money by smuggling coke into Black neighbourhoods –
Knowing what it would do.
Eventually the Kerry Committee concluded that the
Government knew, and they funded it, too. Can you
See why they thought this was something to do?

Just try to visualise what Ronald Reagan saw:
The year is 1984.
You've restricted government expense
in most places other than defence. The
Least of your concerns is the trouble in the Ends. You're
Focused on collecting shooters and protecting loot. The
Last thing in your respective view is the prospective futures of

Disaffected youth. You probably don't even
Realise how much the violence and the selfishness
Of the drug game is directly reflecting you.

Can you see why Boo-Boo admired Supreme?
Why that was who he was trying to be?
Why he eventually hired a team for sup-
Plying the fiends, getting high on a dream.
Why Reaganomics isn't quite what it seems 'cause it
Means government can let life rot in Queens.
Why there was something in the air . . . that
Made a drug dealer wanna become a millionaire.

I can't tell how much Ronald Reagan saw, but I
Do know he signed the Comprehensive Crime Control Act in 1984,
Waging war on those who break the law.
Personally, I'm not a fan of this direction.
Harsher punishment for cannabis possession.
And of course, the mandatory sentencing
Which led to jail time lengthening.

Nah, Boo-Boo couldn't have known. As
Far as he was concerned the hood was his home. It's
All he wrote about when he started rapping
Far from capping, he was full of heart and passion.
Eventually when Supreme came home from prison
He was fast adapting to this rap thing. And
By Boo-Boo's own admission, he was
Hoping the OG would back him, in
Light of all the street work he put in.
But Supreme overlooked him.
Instead he was supporting a guy called Left.
Left was kind of from a rival set.
Boo-Boo didn't like Left, but they had no
Problems on the scale of life or death. In
His reasoning, Left wasn't as street as him.

He could speak to things based on situations *he'd* been in
This is where his problems started deepening. If he
Felt something he found it hard to keep it in.

Boo-Boo made a song about the team that Supreme was in
These times Supreme was tryna stay low-key. He
Didn't appreciate this guy bringing this heat on him
So, he sent creepers to creep on him.

[Soundtrack: 50 Cent 'Many Men']

SCENE 8: BOO-BOO GETS SHOT

[See the opening scene of 50 Cent's music video for 'Many Men']

I highly doubt 50 Cent knew
All the drama which he went through would
Make him a legend by twenty-five.
Nine bullets and he still survived if anything
With an intensified will to thrive.
Imagine being the guy who tried to kill the guy . . .
Must've come as a real surprise.

SCENE 9: 50 CENT BECOMES A STAR

[TV presenters talking about 50 Cent, including *Friday Night with Jonathan Ross* (courtesy of Open Mike Productions), *The Beat with Ari Melber*, courtesy of MSNBC, and *The Graham Norton Show* (courtesy of So Television)]

George: Despite withholding information from police
Curtis 'Boo-Boo' Jackson knew who clapped him.
And while he was fighting for his life in bed,
Within three short weeks the guy was dead. Now,

What do you see when you look at 50 Cent? The
Money? The fame? The swagger and the arrogance?
Purveyor of emotional damage and embarrassment?
Figurehead of Gangsta Rap as an establishment?

I see trauma. I see a childhood spent on the corner.
I see a product of Reagan, coin-chasing. I see the
Legacy of Blaxploitation. I see resilience.
I see the brilliance, I see the
Diligence that led to the millions.
But most of all, I see Sabrina's boy . . .
Eight years old when he had that dream destroyed.

SCENE 10: LASTING TRAUMA

[Taken from 50 Cent's first interview on *Friday Night with Jonathan Ross*]

50 Cent: My mother passed when I was like eight years old, I went to live with my grandparents. She had me when she was fifteen. Back then it wasn't as common . . . the young girls have children at fifteen a little more now than they did back then . . . she started hustling to be able to provide for me at that point. And she got killed when I was like eight years old.

Jonathan Ross: So, when you say 'hustling' – she was involved with what?

50 Cent: Yeah, selling drugs.

Jonathan Ross: She was selling drugs? And she was killed as a result of that?

50 Cent: Yeah.

EPISODE 10: A Bedtime Story

Extra Info:

- When I started the podcast in 2018, I challenged myself to write about whatever I had been through in the previous 24 hours (like talking to Dun D, or hearing my mum deal with my nephew's tantrum). Most of Chapter One was written like this (apart from the episodes about Grenfell and the migrant crisis – these had been on my mind for a long time). For Episode 10, I returned to this 24-hour technique because I was struggling with writer's block. So 'A Bedtime Story' starts with me in the middle of contract negotiations, since that's what I was going through at the time.
- The dialogue between Dija and my character in this episode was meant to portray a young, Black, middle-class couple communicating with love. At the time I was single, but I wanted to depict a relationship like this. I believe it's important to think carefully about the images we conjure in our work as writers, especially those of us with young audiences.

Fun Facts:

- So many scenes in the podcast take place in a car because that's where I do most of my writing. These stories usually start by me staring out of the window into an empty car park.
- I wrote 75% of 'A Bedtime Story' without knowing where it was going. Months passed before I realised that this uncertainty could be the whole point of the episode. When I accepted that, I started to have fun with the concept of Writer's Block as a physical place – because I could describe it clearly!

A lot of *Have You Heard George's Podcast?* is pure sport to me. I'm just pushing myself like an athlete, to see how far I can take my abilities, and Episode 10 is the perfect example of this. I was still trying to figure out how to present my dreams to my listeners when I became inspired by that scene in *Aladdin* where he takes Princess Jasmine on a magic carpet ride. That's basically what I wanted to do with the audience – take them on a ride through my imagination (show them 'a whole new world'). So, I created a romantic character that would help me build this episode by teasing my thoughts out with playful dialogue. But for some reason, I was seriously struggling to write. It's like I didn't really believe I could do it. I was procrastinating and doubting myself, until enough weeks had passed, and I finally acknowledged what I was going through: writer's block. Once I accepted this, I had fun with it, writing honestly but creatively about my urge to explain my vision, versus fear of not being understood. Sanyu prepared me for this. At the time, I'd had a random conversation with radio host and online personality Julie Adenuga. She was so charismatic that I basically cast her on the spot to provide the voice of my fictional girlfriend. All credit to Julie for going along with my crazy story – she did an amazing job. Special shout out to Benbrick, who took his world-building sound design skills to another level in this episode.

[Soundtrack: Ari Lennox 'Up Late']

SCENE 1: DIJA & GEORGE

[Dija exits the en suite shower into the bedroom to get ready for bed. Her boyfriend, George, is on the phone outside the room. First, she closes the bedroom door to give him privacy, then she opens it to ask him a question]

Dija: George . . .

George: One second, my brother. Yes, Dija?

Dija: Sorry to interrupt you, baby. Where did you leave the coconut oil?

George: Try by the bed. On my side.

Dija: You left it on the floor.

George: I might have done.

[Dija laughs]

George: Come here.

[They kiss]

Dija: Is that on mute?

George: Nah don't say nothing cruddy.

Dija: Mmmm you're lucky. Hurry up!

George: Alright, I'm coming.

[Dija exits. Narrative perspective stays on George, who is still on the phone]

George: Sorry about that, John. Carry on.

John: We were just debating the idea of the contract as generic.

George: Yeah, the problem with this contract is . . .
To me it doesn't reflect the energy you brought to our last encounter.
And instead of fixing that, you've called me
And kind of waffled for the past half an hour.
No disrespect.

John: Well, it's not waffle, is it?
I mean these things are sort of—

George: You don't wanna commit to any of my requirements
But you want final sign off – for that alone you're mad
You might as well write your mind off.
On top of that you want twenty-two of the gross?
Come on man, you're doing the most.

John: Well, George, to be fair this is business,
You are playing with the big boys now . . .

George: Listen, I'm perfectly happy to leave this to the lawyers but
Let's not forget: you called me, bro.
One sticking point in a contract I can deal with,
It's a little different when it's two or three, though.
And even then, I can deal with two or three but
After the third one I've seen a few more, b.
Now I'm pushing the lawyers past their usual fee
And after all of this, you've called me.

Listen, so hear what you do, yeah . . .
Wait to hear from my man.

John: This being the lawyer, right?

George: Yeah, the lawyer.

John: Right, well I guess I'll do that.

George: Alright, man. Have a good night.

John: Night.

[George hangs up, breathing deeply before re-entering the bedroom]

Dija: Hi handsome.

George: Wagwan.

Dija: Wanna talk about it?

George: ⊙ talk about what?

Dija: Ohhh, so that's what we're doing. Come. Sit down.

[Dija walks George to the bed]

George: What's all this, what we doing, therapy?

Dija: Close your eyes.

George: Alright.

Dija: Listen . . .

[George closes his eyes. Dija closes a laptop that was playing music. The music stops, but the laptop's fan keeps working loudly]

Dija: Can you hear that? Just 'cause you shut the laptop doesn't mean it's off.

George: Lol. I see what you did there.

Dija: I'm serious.
I can hear the fans and stuff whirring around in your brain . . .
Trying to cool you down.
You should talk to me.

George: D, you know I don't like to talk to you about contract stuff.

Dija: You don't like to talk about contract stuff.

George: You've got a phone full of family and friends trying to get free advice and I don't wanna add to the list, babe.

Dija: Listen, what's the point of spending every night with a contract lawyer if you're not gonna take advantage of the privilege?

George: I think we need to respect certain boundaries.

Dija: I think you need to respect my expertise.

George: Lawyers are supposed to give impartial advice.
If you could be impartial with me . . . it would kind of hurt my feelings.

Dija: Alright, by way of compromise
Why don't you just . . . tell me what's on your mind?
And if I should so happen to give you advice – that . . . is of a legal nature
Babe, you can take it or leave it.

I don't need even need details,
Just be creative with it . . . tell me a story.

George: You want a story, that's what you want?

Dija: Babe, that's exactly what I want.
Just a story.

George: Alright, your turn. Sit down.

[Dija sits on the bed beside George]

George: Get comfy.
Close your eyes.

SCENE 2: THE STORY BEGINS

[Dija closes her eyes and pictures everything George is describing]

One warm August evening,
While George was sleeping
Khadija saw his keyring
And it made her gorgeous teeth skin.

Dija: [Laughing] Was I skinning teeth, yeah?

George: You were skinning teeth, Khadija, yes.

She wanted to leave him a little surprise
Like one of her G-strings, but triple the size,
Because she liked to prank him,
Because she thinks she's funny like that.
That's the kind of ediat ting she's on.

[Dija laughs loudly at the memory of her pulling this prank on George]

George: Babe, weren't you kind of concerned that I didn't actually know your size?

Dija: It was all a test to see if you knew my size!

George: Lol you're a fool.

Soon as Khadija sat in George's car
Her first thought was 'Rah . . .
In here it feels different'
And that's when she saw the steering wheel stiffen.
In fact, she could hear the wheels shifting.
And you won't believe this . . .
But all of a sudden, the car starts elevating.

She thought she was tripping on some Ella Mai ting.
Khadija froze like a mannequin.
Then she started panicking.
Trying to unlock the doors and stop this force
What kind of witchcraft is this? Which *car* is this?
In the darkness she started making quick decisions.
She recognised she was in need of witnesses and
Began scanning the ground for anyone standing around.
Was anybody out there late this Friday
Seeing wagwan in the neighbour's driveway?

Nope.

Dija couldn't believe how fast her heart was beating,
She tried to stay calm, but she wasn't far from screaming.
The only reason she held out was self-doubt 'cause there
Was a chance she was dreaming. I mean she's
Locked in her boyfriend's car, dangling in
mid-air two metres off the pavement.
Apparently beyond anyone's observation.
That's a lot to take in.

Suddenly the car started changing.
Physically it *felt* like the same thing, but
All along the upholstery's surface, Dija
Noticed these words from George's poetry verses.

The whole interior reorganised
Right – before – her eyes.
And within the shortest time Dija was
Basically cocooned in George's rhymes.

Dija: Babe, is this a metaphor?

George: Khadija, you don't miss a beat, do you?

Dija: So, your words are the vehicle?

George: Can I proceed?

Dija: Of course.

George: Yeah, so Dija realised the whole thing was a metaphor.

[Dija giggles]

George: By the way, the most incredible metaphor she ever saw.
Which she had to give George credit for.

Dija: OK, relax.

George: What, you trying to front?

Dija: Yes, it was a good metaphor baby.

George: That's what I thought.

She'd always said that George's words were a vehicle
To drive change people had never seen before.
Looking around now she was proud how his
Bars had grown from Soundcloud to surround sound.
This guy had more words than *Countdown*.
And they'd taken him from St Raph's to a nice place downtown.

[Dija smiles in agreement]

George: Seeing no need to stay here and chill, Dija
Cautiously placed her hand on the steering wheel.
Instantly the car came to life and gave insight into
What George's brain is like.

Different hues of light started flitting through the lines George had
Written through the times. Different colours represented
Different moods and vibes. All Dija knew was
She was in for a *different* cruise tonight.

[Soundtrack: IAMDDB 'Running']

George: Settings? She didn't know which to utilise so she
Picked one that looked like it would hit the smoothest glide.
If Dija saw this on a show, she'd say this was suicide but
Tell Michael Knight and KITT to move aside . . .
It's about to be a futuristic Uber ride.

Stealthily, the ride started dipping through the night.
I mean not even whipping – it was doing flight.
No one clocked this apart from one fox in the park,
Who was watching the stars 'cause the moon was bright
When she saw Khadija zooming by.
The fox started to wonder if her food was right.
She thought: either I'm super high.
Or I just saw a human drive through the sky.

[Dija laughs]

Dija: Wait. G I just got an idea.

George: Go through.

Dija: Alright, disclaimer:

Nowadays when you talk
I hear your thoughts like podcast episodes.
And this story could become one, heaven knows.
So, what do you think of this?

The car could be endorsed by an actual car company.
I mean I've never worked with one myself but I'm
Sure I could ask somebody.

George: [Thinks] Go on.

Dija: All you'd need is a company that aligns with your message, your
Mind and your ethics. Cos, G,
I see you becoming a
Leading content provider for Netflix.
And you need partners who recognise and respect this.

George: You don't miss a beat.

Dija: Okurrrr!

George: I get you, b.
We gotta do celebrity with integrity.

Dija: Definitely.

George: But technically, since I
Signed with the BBC finally, that's—

Dija: Finally!

George: That's funded by the licence fee. And
Obviously, that makes it public property . . .
So I don't think we can't get advertising p.

Dija: But isn't that just in the UK, though?

George: Wait. Did you hear that?

Dija: What?

George: It sounded like . . .
Like Khadija trying to make George discuss contracts.

[George laughs]

Dija: You!

[Dija playfully hits George]

Dija: Do you not trust me?

George: Deej if I didn't trust you then I wouldn't be here right now,
   you feel me?

Dija: Was that supposed to be romantic? Because it gave me anxiety.

George: Babe, it's not the trust. It's just . . .
There's things I'd rather not discuss, what's the fuss?

[Dija sighs]

Dija: The fuss is George,
you spend a lot of money on lawyers.
And I'm trying to escape my scummy employers
'Cause like I've always said, that office is rotten.
Babe, we've got problems in common.

George: Yeah, but what we haven't got is time.
D, we ain't got time for ourselves, I ain't got
Time for my guys, you ain't got time for your girls. And you know

Time is more precious than diamonds and pearls but
Babe, that's where this environment fails.
You . . . you make good use of your time, which is
Just as well because you have a beautiful mind. That's
Part of what drew me to you in the first place. But
This level of emotional involvement is
Something I don't have *time* for in my workspace.

Dija: Wow! 'Date a poet' they said.

[George laughs]

Dija: So what happened next in the story? Go on.

George: Well *George* recognised the tension in the room
So he decided to be a man about it.
He carefully collected Khadija's injured feelings,
Lovingly placed them in a shoe box,
And slid them under the bed.

Then he got back to the story.
No laughs, nah?

[Dija kisses her teeth]

George: Tough crowd.

SCENE 3: DIJA GOES UNDERGROUND

[George's story continues. The flying car has taken Dija to a dark, eerily quiet open field]

The car took Khadija to a part of town where
There were no people or cars around. The
Windshield turned into a TV screen,
Repeatedly playing these three scenes:

222

Aladdin, on the magic carpet with Jasmine.
Rick from *Rick and Morty* making Morty small,
And one from the *Space Jam* storyboard:
You know the part when Michael Jordan goes underground.

The screen disappeared and there was no one around.
Dija could see this from here.
The car was softer than snow coming down, but a hole in the
ground started to open around them.
Opening like the first act of the show for an
Artist promoting an album. Opening
Like the dome of a shaolin monk when he
goes to the mountain.

So now it's fully an underground thing.
The opening closes in overhead. And there's
No more sign of the hole that led them to this
Dead end.

They land in a cave.
Dija just wants to be home in bed but she's
trying to hold it down. Like how mandem behave
When certain man see certain man in a rave.

[Cut to George and Dija on the bed]

George: Rah you're not gonna laugh at none of my—

Dija: Keep calm and carry on.

George: Alright.
Out of nowhere the car doors fling open.
Dija's eyes adjust for one awkward moment.
She decides to trust her gut 'cause if anyone or
Anything tries her they're getting an uppercut.

No sooner than she slipped off the driver's seat did the

Floor of the cave and the bottom of her sliders meet.
As far as the eye could see, there was
No light – at least for hundreds of metres.
Except from under Khadija's feet. And the car.
There seemed to be a glow around both of them.
Something was watching over them.

The glow extended like the roots of a tree
Revealing a cave as huge as can be.
Stalactites hung so beautifully, and
Stalagmites stood up like you do for me.

The light Khadija had brought travelled
Just far enough for her to see there was more.
She was at the start of a path in a tunnel and
Ahead of her the darkness was asking for trouble.

See, it was in her nature
To find out where this path might take her.

She jumped in the car and touched the steering wheel, but
This time she didn't just hover there and chill.
The car knew where she was going
Once again, it turned into a poem.
This time the words were reaching Khadija,
Like sound waves from a beat in a speaker.
George's poetry was taking her down this passage
Deeper and deeper.

And by this point he knows Khadija's asleep, but,
He needed to speak up.

[Cut to the bedroom, where Dija has dozed off]

George: Dija? You really sleeping?
Guess that makes this speech a bit easier.
Confidence is a funny feeling to keep up.

It's like being the guy behind the curtain that everyone
Thinks is the Wizard of Oz.
Half the time thankful that I'm not 'that guy',
The other half, wishing I was.

Sometimes I wonder
What will these people do when they
Realise the me they knew isn't even true?
Yes, D, my boo. Even you.

[Narrative perspective drifts from the bedroom back into the car
ride, but now George is in the driver's seat, and not Dija]

When the chips are down and no one's feeling Season 2,
And all of my live shows are receiving weak reviews,
And your own friends are tweeting me abuse.
And you're forced to let go of the fact you
Never really expected me to lose . . .
Then we'll see who's who.

[Car slows down. There seems to be a block party in the middle of
the passageway]

SCENE 4: GEORGE GETS LOST

**[George finds himself in an unfriendly place, unaware that he has
fallen asleep into a dream that follows the story he was just telling
Dija. Here he is confronted by Insecurity Guards]**

George: Nah this wasn't here before.
What's going on?
Coming like the mandem locked off the road . . .

[George exits his car]

IG 1: Wagwan, my brudda.

George: Yeah wagwan, g.

IG 1: You're looking kinda lost still.

George: Yeah, I'm not gonna lie—

IG 2: Oi who's that?

IG 1: That's what I'm tryna find out, bro.

George: That's not even all necessary . . .

[IG 2 approaches]

George: If anyone can tell me—

IG 2: Wagwan my guy. You're looking kind of lost still.

George: Yeah, cuzzy, I was on the mains,
And I just must have got a bit side-tracked
So, I'm trying to figure out—

Trudy: Who's this new yout on the block?

IG 1: That's what we're tryna figure out.

IG 2: My man just come to the Dub like it's calm.

George: Yo hear what I'm saying—

Trudy: Is that your car, brudda?

George: Yeah, that's me still.

Trudy: Why's it got writing all over it?

George: Long story. Listen I'm just trying to get—

Trudy: Yo I like that car, you know.

[Tense silence]

George: I like the car, too.

Trudy: What fuel does it take?

George: This car is a metaphor.
I built it with my words,
So, the only fuel it takes is my brainpower.
You understand what I'm saying?

Trudy: Mmm. So, your brainpower . . .
Brought you to the block?

[IGs chuckling]

George: Yeah. I got distracted.
I was telling my girl a story using my words as my vehicle and
Obviously, I lost my way.
So, I'm trying to make my way back and if you lot could help me
I'd appreciate that.

Trudy: Well, I know how hard it is for men, admitting when you're lost.
So how much?

George: How much what?

Trudy: For the car. How much?

George: The car's not for sale.

Trudy: Didn't say it was. How much did it *cost*?
Just 'cause you didn't pay money for it doesn't mean it didn't cost you.

IG 1: Where you from, cuz?

George: That's not relevant.

IG 2: Yo answer the question, bro.

Trudy: Mandem listen. That's not the issue.
Doesn't matter where he's from.
I'm trying to know . . . where's my man *going*?

George: My girl wanted to know what was on my mind.
I've been working on a lot of ideas.
So, I thought lemme just take her to my intellectual property, so she can see it for herself. Like I said, I lost my way. If you lot can give me directions back to the mains, we ain't got a problem.

Trudy: Yeah but, how you gonna get back to the mains with no car?

George: What?

[Laughing all around. George turns and sees the car has vanished.]

Trudy: Welcome to Writer's Block.

[Soundtrack: Skepta ft. J Hus 'What Do You Mean?']

EPISODE 11: Writer's Block

Extra Info:

- Unlike the previous episode (which started with my character wide awake), this one starts with me asleep. My character still hasn't realised that he fell asleep at the end of Episode 10, so he is wandering through a dream trying to recover his stolen car.
- This episode was inspired by my habit of planning my future as if I'm writing a TV show. I recommend this practice to everyone. Seeing your life like a TV series allows you to think clearly about your decisions and the characters around you.
- By looking ten years into the future, I am able to share my dreams with the audience, which is what my character was trying to do in 'A Bedtime Story' before he lost his way.

Fun Facts:

- In Scene 1, when The Oracle offers my character Thai food, all the dishes are named after movies with flying cars.
- Legendary newsreader Sir Martyn Lewis was kind enough to come and voice some of the fictional new clips for us. Thanks, Martyn!
- The characters Genna and Spinna are voiced by two of my childhood friends who really are from rival areas. Art brings people together.

As I was becoming more and more enticed by Matthew Walker's book, *Why We Sleep*, Episode 11 almost wrote itself. The previous episode, 'A Bedtime Story', was about me introducing my dreams to the audience (via a conversation with a fictional girlfriend). In real life, a loss of confidence stopped me from getting to my dreams within that episode. But once I confronted this feeling, I unlocked the ability to write about it. This is how I came up with the idea of Writer's Block as a physical place. Of course, the double-meaning of the word 'block' was attractive to me, as someone who loves wordplay ('block' means 'barrier', and it is also slang for a residential building in the

Ends). When most people refer to 'writer's block' they mean the mental barrier preventing creativity. But for Episode 11, it would refer to the state of stagnation, portrayed as the ghetto of my mind. Because I approached this chapter as a TV producer, I wanted 'Writer's Block' to flow from 'A Bedtime Story'; if the first chapter was a notebook, this second one was a storyboard. By writing about my time on Writer's Block, I could explain my frustrations as an artist, and hopefully uplift anyone who has ever felt the same. Once again, shout out to Benbrick for raising the bar with his audio world-building. I asked him to construct the craziest scenarios, and instead of doing the minimum, he always did the most.

SCENE 1: GEORGE MEETS THE ORACLE

[George has spent hours on Writer's Block trying to find his car, after it was stolen at the end of the previous episode, 'A Bedtime Story'. He doesn't realise that he is asleep, dreaming about what direction to take his career in. He has been pointed to a mysterious character called The Oracle. George finds her apartment on Writer's Block and knocks on her door]

The Oracle: Who's there?

George: Yo, my name's George. I'm a poet.
I was told to come here for The Oracle.

The Oracle: Told by who?

George: Listen, I'll be honest with you. I'm not from this block. My car got stolen and I've been stuck here for way too long. I asked around and one name keeps coming up. Now if I've got the wrong place can you please just tell me where I can find The Oracle?

[Door opens]

The Oracle: Come in.

[Door closes]

The Oracle: This way.

[They walk through a dimly lit apartment]

The Oracle: Have a seat. So, Mr Poet. What brings you to Writer's Block?

George: So, my girl's been telling me to open up,
'Cause apparently I don't enough. And it makes

her upset when she feels like
she can't help me cope with stuff. So—

The Oracle: Would you like some water?

George: Yes, please, my throat is rough. [Coughs]

[The Oracle pours George a glass of water]

George: But putting my thoughts into words is long.
So, she suggested that I tell her a
Story about what I'm working on.

[The Oracle passes the water]

George: Thank you.

[George sips]

George: The story was supposed to take her
Through my intellectual property.
Obviously, the plan didn't pan out properly.

I got distracted and ended up on the block.
Must have stepped out and left my car unlocked
Then it got stolen by this girl and her friends.
And ever since then I've been searching the Ends.
I've asked around. I asked one guy called James and
Another brother whose name I can't pronounce.
Obviously, no one knows where stolen cars are found but they
Say The Oracle is my best chance at getting an answer now.

The Oracle: Trudy.

George: Excuse me?

The Oracle: The girl you met. Her name's Trudy.
Trudy didn't steal your car.
So don't let negativity fill your heart—

George: I'm too old for ops.
I should be coming for someone's head top,
But all I'm trying to do is get in my car and get off this dead block.
If it's *me* that's moving mad, tell me who's been grabbed.
Real talk. Tell me who's got clarted.
After the drama that *you* lot started—

[The Oracle's voice becomes other-worldly]

The Oracle: RELAX!

[Silence]

The Oracle: Everyone is here . . . for a season.
And everyone is here . . . for a reason.
But, you see with these two guarantees
There's a trade-off . . .
Tell me something, what's your car made of?

George: My words.

The Oracle: Exactly. How can words be stolen?
Everyone on Writer's Block has lost their words,
For the moment.
You're here 'cause I can help you.
But you *need* to help yourself too.

[George breathes deeply]

George: I'm on the horns of a dilemma.
There have been a lot of wars within my era.
And that's just within my area.
The macro-vision is much scarier.

I've been promising change to my audience
For about seven years.
And I now believe there are some prayers God never hears.

There's been a bit of gun violence in my Ends
Some of it among my friends.
And if it's not guns then it's knives,
These young boys love to make each other run for their lives.

So obviously, the only way of knowing if my poems
Are effective or feeble is to
Test their effect on my people.
So, every word that I write has to
Serve the dual function of
Entertaining and providing an intellectual junction.
I try to do this with stories, since
Adults, teens and children love them. But
That's driven by brainpower. It's a lot of fuel consumption

The Oracle: Alright. Let *me* explain how *I* work . . .
I'm drawn to the strongest vision.
I cannot prevent you from making the wrong decision.
I sense you see beyond yourself, so I'll help you on your mission.
But I'll only do so on one condition.

I like Thai food.
Cooking it puts me in a nice mood.
And I'd like you . . .
To try my food.

George: Huh?

The Oracle: Yeah.

George: Hold on . . . as in actual food?

The Oracle: Actually, wait there I've got some ready.

George: [Mutters] Course you got some ready.

[The Oracle goes to the kitchen where Matthew Walker's *Why We Sleep* audiobook is playing from a speaker. It's the part about time distortion in sleep]

The Oracle: OK now I don't know if you're new to Thai but I've
Got a few dishes for you to try.
All plant based. And they got
That fresh-off-the-farm taste.

Let's start off with a batch of the new stuff.
It's called 'Back to the Future'.
Does what it says on the tin.

George: Swear down?

The Oracle: Alright, now let's bring the second dish in.
This is some Thai green curry called *Flubber*.
See *Flubber* . . . brudda!

And over here we got a spicy dish,
I call it *Chitty Chitty Bang Bang* . . .
And over *here* we got the finger foods,
That's *Men in Black* and that's *Batman*.
So . . . you know, lemme know where you wanna go.

George: I mean . . . much as I appreciate these beautiful dishes
You have to understand you do look suspicious.

The Oracle: Bro, you came to my Ends who are you to talk?
Anyway, on Writer's Block you need food for thought,
Which, since you're so clever I'd assume you'd support.

George: Alright, gimme a batch of the new stuff.
What you call it? *Back to the Future*.

The Oracle: Good choice.
Alright, quickly: there's no side effects from my products,
But there are by-products.

George: What? What you mean 'by-products'?

The Oracle: Back to the Future takes you ten years ahead.
But with that said, it eliminates what you
Get to see from your destiny.

[The Oracle sets the plate down in front of George]

George: Why you even telling me that?

[George starts eating and loves it]

George: Yo, this is good, though!

The Oracle: Yeah? You know I did spend a lot of time making it.

George: This is— yo!

The Oracle: Oh, thank you.

George: I'm not really a man to talk with my mouth full but this is— yo!

The Oracle: Nah it's calm. But listen . . .
Back to your car.

George: [Distracted by food] Hm?

The Oracle: Your car.

George: What you say?

The Oracle: You see your car, yeah?

George: Yeah.

The Oracle: Hopefully, this food for thought
Can open your mind as to where it might be.

[George is uninterested in the car, engrossed in the food]

The Oracle: You're not thinking about this car right now, are you?

George: Hm?

The Oracle: The car. It's like I'm not even here, init? Yeah . . .

[The Oracle cackles and disappears]

SCENE 2: GEORGE FALLS ASLEEP AGAIN

[George slips into another level of sleep and hears quotes from Matthew Walker's audiobook *Why We Sleep*. George's memories play in his mind]

Diggy Ustle: I like your vibe. You're bringing in different characters, you know what I'm trying to say? I like it. I just feel like you're a genius, bruv . . .

Kendra Houseman: I had a boy that was involved in a gang, and he was going out for a fight, took a knife. And I brought him into my room, and he listened to your podcast, and he didn't have a fight, last Thursday. And you saved his life.

J Man: Maybe going to all them schools that you went to was for a reason, fam. Do you understand? 'Cause I remember when you used to come and check man ... you used to come up with some next words and I was like ... this guy was super-smart you know!

George's Mum: There was no stopping George so, I haven't always understood what he's done. I wanted him to be an MP, and he told me flatly, no. I said 'fine'. He went into entertainment, music, and now podcasts, and I went from being the mother who led him to the mother who follows him. But as a practising Christian, I give all the praise to God.

George: Am I supposed to be more of an MP? Or of an MC?
I choose both.

[Soundtrack: Headie One 'Both']

George: Yeah ... I chose both.

SCENE 3: MONTAGE OF THE NEXT DECADE

[As The Oracle said, her food allows George to see 10 years into the future. He watches his career grow through the eyes of the media]

Sir Martyn Lewis: Spoken word artist George The Poet,
Real name George Mpanga was the
First of his kind to record a banger.
Following that his foray into podcasting,
Earned the loaded nickname 'God-casting'.

[Cut to George in front of an audience]

George: You gotta know, I never called it 'God-casting'.
I want the people to know, I never once called it 'God-casting'.

[Cut to one of George's critics giving a radio interview]

Critic: . . . 'God-casting'. It's this idea that the leading podcasters
have sort of got answers to some serious challenges
And I think it really is damaging . . .

[Cut to a montage of news reports]

Newsreader 2: Social entrepreneur George the Poet was part of a
team that raised six hundred and forty million pounds for an affordable housing development in Milton Keynes, a place he says, designed
for residents to fulfil their dreams.

Cristale: George is literally rebuilding the hood from scratch. It's
mad.

Sir Martyn Lewis: At 28, he pioneered the practice of using his
Podcast to announce his biggest plans. And
Then funding and implementing these plans
Entirely with his fans, collectively referred to as 'George's Search
    Party'.
The model is not without its flaws, but it works – partly.

Mixed Young Voices: GSP! It's Generating Solutions for Poverty.
Global Sustainability Programme. It's like it's a Ghetto Social Policy.

News Interviewee: I don't know who these people are or why they
care but they've changed everything. God bless GSP.

Sir Martyn Lewis: The *Guardian* newspaper describes George's
Search Party as
A 'Social Action Reserve Army', whose
Members bear no real resemblance to each other, and in
Fact, some of whom are serving a custodial sentence.

Critic: . . . George the Poet has positioned himself as this twenty-
    first century artist,
And there's no denying how impactful his art is,

But what he's actually doing is selling the idea of change,
Profiting and pocketing higher and higher dividends
While things get harder for women, working families and
    immigrants.

Sir Martyn Lewis: Despite the criticism, Mpanga insists his followers
Are simply well-informed private citizens.

[Cut to George 8 years down the line at a press conference, answering questions about his movement]

Older George: There's always gonna be cynics around any social movement, but
My supporters are normal people: families, professionals, students—

[Cut to George being interviewed in front of an audience]

Interviewer: But they are making you incredibly rich.

Older George: Why is that a 'but'? Why would I spend my whole life building social businesses – that work – and *not* take a cut?

Interviewer: Well, I guess for a lot of people you represent the neoliberal idea that business can fix society's problems. What do you say to that?

Older George: Listen, I would say the biggest group of policy influencers in the country is the electorate. But the policy-making process needs to do more than we currently expect of it. As a country our policy-making operation should take into account the observations and conversations of the entire population.

[Cut to a political talk show, with George responding directly to one of his biggest critics]

Critic: I'm sorry everything you say reeks of hypocrisy.

How can you sit there and talk about democracy,
When you have such a disproportionate influence on the economy?

[Mixed boos and applause]

Older George: It's not a—
This is all part of my economic theory.

Critic: Argh let me guess, another hypothesis.

Older George: Yeah, this is one of my hypotheses.
I strongly believe that the secret ingredient of democracy
Is accessible and engaging information of a high quality.
Now like you said, this is my hypothesis, so
Solving it is my problem, Miss.

[Applause]

Critic: Typical. But you would say that wouldn't you?
I mean, this is exactly what the problem is!

Older George: My role in the economy reflects my
Own investment in my own intellectual property.
Eight years ago, when I released the second chapter of my podcast
I made this clear—

Critic: So why don't you tell us how much money you've made this year?

Older George: Eight years ago, when I released Chapter Two of my
Podcast I said exactly what I wanted to achieve; everyone was
    relaxed.
But now I'm in a position to come with the stats and a couple of
    facts,
Every time I speak someone attacks.

Critic: I'm sorry, we do not owe you our support just 'cause you call yourself a man of the people.

[Cut to social media users reacting to news of George being caught up in sex scandal]

Social Media User 1: Fam, this guy George the Poet is a mad man.

Social Media User 2: That's George in the video!

Social Media User 1: That's him in the video, you know.

[Cut to news coverage of George's scandal]

Sir Martyn Lewis: Today, the controversial spoken word artist has come under fire, after a video emerged of him allegedly engaged in a sex act with an adult performer.

[Cut to George at a press conference, answering questions about the scandal]

Older George: Of course, I fully understand the public outrage.
The person in the video clearly is me.
I take my role very seriously as a public figure, and I've never lied to
    the public.
But now this is an issue in my private life,
And to be honest I don't feel apologetic towards anyone beside my
    wife.

[Cut to Dija, now George's wife, switching off the TV after watching the press conference]

SCENE 4: GEORGE APOLOGISES TO DIJA

[George's wife, Dija, feels humiliated by this scandal. On a rainy night, she sits in their bedroom silently as George tries to apologise]

George: I used to think the word 'mistake' was overused.
'Cause how can it be a mistake if it's something you *chose* to do?
But now I get it.

Choices become consequences.
There are guys inside riding time for a
Minor crime . . . ended up with a much longer sentence.

I see my story in two parts:
Before and after you arrived.
Before you, I lived a fast and ruthless life.
I never had anyone to answer to, besides
My character was marred by foolish pride.
Just as I started to decide . . .
That I can't pursue this life . . .
You gave me a chance to do it right.
Khadija, I took that. I never looked back.
I committed my heart to you and I . . .

Now with all these people digging through my business
Baby, please don't lose sight of this.
I know it's hard for you but try,
Please. That's all I ask of you tonight.

You have to know I'm so sorry for the strain I've put on this marriage.
Ever since the miscarriage—

Dija . . .

[Dija leaves]

SCENE 5: BACK TO THE ORACLE

[Jump back to the end of the first scene. After serving George, The Oracle waits to see if it manages to send him to sleep]

The Oracle: You're not thinking about this car right now, are you?

George: Mm.

The Oracle: It's like I'm not even here innit?

[George murmurs distractedly]

The Oracle: Yeah hahaha . . .

[George is immersed in eating and becomes unresponsive]

The Oracle: Hello . . . Mr Poet?

[Silence, confirming the food has consumed George's mind]

The Oracle: He's done out here.

[The Oracle cautiously walks over to the front door. George isn't aware of anything other than the food]

The Oracle: He's finished!

[The Oracle leaves the apartment]

[Soundtrack: SL 'Gigantalous']

SCENE 6: ON THE BLOCK

[The Oracle walks through the Block and runs into her neighbour, Genna, who addresses her by her real name: Samira. Genna is the typical Writer's Block resident: stuck, unsure how to move his story forward. The Oracle reveals that she is going to meet her boss on the other side of the Block. Genna needs work, and would like to meet the boss, but fears for his safety on the other side]

Genna: Yo! The Oracle yana!

The Oracle: Wagwan my Genna.

Genna: What's good, Samira?

The Oracle: I'm just here blud.

Genna: Yo, I never see you deh pon the Block.

The Oracle: Yeah, more time I'm in by 11 o'clock.

Genna: OK, OK. So why you out so late today?

The Oracle: I got a meeting with the big man.

Genna: Say swear!

The Oracle: Yeah. If you want, I can bring man.

Genna: What you saying, what, you think he's got work for me?

The Oracle: Personally, I don't know if he's got work for you
But I can put in a good word for you.

Why d'you think I'm inside a lot?
Serving food when it's piping hot.

Prices dropped, my man's got the nicest crop
I just buy his stock and supply this Block.
Yo, if I get it by eight, best believe it's gone by nine o'clock.

Genna: Alright. Where's the meeting, though?

The Oracle: It's on the other side of Writer's Block.

Genna: Ooh I don't deal with the other side.
You know the mandem can't let nothing slide.

The Oracle: Well, if you ever change your mind
I can arrange a better place and time.
Just stop by.

Genna: I appreciate that, Samira.

The Oracle: Say nothing, my guy.

Genna: Yo by the way, you got Thai?

The Oracle: How much you need?

Genna: Like a zed.

The Oracle: Alright, I'ma shout you before bed.

Genna: Respect. Say nothing.

The Oracle: Alright, safe. In a bit.

SCENE 7: ON THE OTHER SIDE

[Cut to The Oracle on the other side of the Block, where she runs into her friend, Spinna. Like Genna, Spinna is stuck on the Block. He is

also unable to visit The Oracle on the other side, because, like Genna, he fears for his safety. The Oracle advises him to work on his story]

Spinna: Wagwan, Samira.

The Oracle: Man like Spinna! When you coming round for dinner?

Spinna: About dinner. After you forgot man.
I can't see you on the Block fam.

The Oracle: You know where my door is
You just gotta knock, fam. I
Got that new Thai food. You need to
Slide though, bruv.

Spinna: Man can't chill round your sides too tough.

The Oracle: Boy, guess you won't get to try the new stuff!
How's your story coming along?

Spinna: You know. Still finding the words.

The Oracle: If you like rap try rhyming a verse. I'll see you later yeah.

Spinna: Alright then. Likkle more, my darg.

SCENE 8: THE ORACLE MEETS THE BOSS

[The Oracle walks away from all the noise to meet her boss, Busy. Busy was introduced in Episode 8 as the head of the Ambition Commission]

The Oracle: I know we agreed to meet late but
Midnight is dread! I like spending this time in bed.
Anyway . . . I did like you said.

When he got to my door, even though he was deep in,
George didn't know he was sleeping.
I'm guessing Stage One NREM.
But I hit him with the Ten-Ten.
That Back to the Future, made him act a bit looser.
Yo the way his brain works . . . I feel like I just hacked a computer.

But I left him too lost in the sauce to talk.
I'm pretty sure the only thing he saw was the fork.
That's how I managed to creep out.
Chances are my man is asleep now.

Boss I don't know where you're getting this food from,
but it's the pengest peng in the ends.
You should see how fast it moves when I sell it in tens
And you know the visions it gives man are hella intense.
It's crème de la crème! Guaranteed to take George from NREM to
    REM.

Busy: You've done well here, Samira.
This will help George see himself a bit clearer.
You know we all want the best for him innit?
Sometimes that means you gotta pressure him a bit.
So tell me, what's the strongest vision?

The Oracle: Well in 10 years he won't have any competition.
I see him succeeding and leading, but true his girl's gonna leave
    him . . .

EPISODE 12: A Night to REMember

Extra Info:

- This episode makes the most sense when you've listened to Episodes 8, 10 and 11.
- Since the first chapter of 'HYHGP?' was predominantly nonfiction, I wanted to experiment more with fictional writing in Chapter Two. This is why these episodes are so imaginative.

Fun Facts:

- The Episode is called 'A Night to REMember' because it is all about the effect of REM sleep on the brain.
- My little brother, Michael, says Busy is basically the real me lol.
- The film that Busy talks about in Scene 6 is called 'BLACK YELLOW RED'. It's a fifteen-minute piece on Ugandan politics that I adapted from Episodes 6 & 7 of the podcast. This episode was written in 2019, when I had just started the film and was unsure what to do with it. In the end, I released it on 14th January 2021 – my thirtieth birthday and the date of Uganda's presidential elections. Concern about Uganda's political future was weighing heavy on my mind when I wrote 'A Night to REMember'.

From reading *Why We Sleep* by Matthew Walker, I had learned that sleep occurs in two alternating stages across the night: rapid eye movement (REM) sleep and non-rapid eye movement (NREM) sleep. Apparently, both of these stages help the brain organise memories, but REM sleep is where dreams happen. Reading about this blew my mind. The book described a cinema that opens up in the brain during sleep, as it separates important memories from unimportant ones, filing them away in different places and making random connections between them. The educator in me was drawn to the challenge of explaining this in the podcast, especially because it fed into my plan of sharing my dreams with the audience. So, I told the story of ideas in my mind scrambling to make the most of my sleep before I wake up and get distracted. This gave me a reason to portray Britain and

Uganda as women in my life, and develop some of the characters introduced in Episode 8, 'Sanyu's World', as well as new ones, who were expertly played by my friends and fellow artists, Barney and Mandi. And again, all credit goes to Benbrick for continuing to raise the levels with his music and sound design. This was the third consecutive episode that made me feel like we had achieved the impossible. Special shouts out to Sandra and Petra too, whose sharp humour and brutal honesty had been making me laugh for over a decade by the time I asked them to close this episode. Back then, we had no idea that Sandra and I would soon fall in love and get married.

SCENE 1: GEORGE & BRITAIN

[George is on the phone to a female personification of Britain]

George: Hello, Britain.
Quick disclaimer – you know my words are never ghost-written.
Yeah, so, before you take them apart
Just remember this comes straight from the heart.

Are you still there? Can you hear me?

Britain: Yeah. Yeah, I'm still here.

George: Brit, honestly . . . I owe you an apology.
You've done a lot for me, and I don't think I've thanked you properly.
Because of you I believe in democracy. I have faith in the power of
    policy.
But before I die . . . Britain, one thing I've got to see is my people
    rising out of poverty.
Now, your ancestors interrupted the—

Britain: George, I don't really have time—

George: Can I finish? Britain, can I finish?

Britain: Sorry.

George: Your ancestors interrupted the momentum of my
    ancestors.
And without legally binding acknowledgement of this fact
There's only so much momentum I can recover.
This is the bit where we misunderstand each other.
Now, I know you're going through a lot right now.
And I say 'you' because even though I live here it's not my house.
You're not my spouse; you're just my host.
And yeah, we've become quite close.

Brit, I wanna make this work, but you don't have space in your heart to accommodate this hurt.

I feel like you're getting defensive when I haven't even said anything offensive.

Britain: Hold on, George, one second.

Britain's Advisor: Ma'am, Theresa May has just announced her resignation.

Britain: George, I'm going to have to call you back.

Busy: Pause that.

SCENE 2: AMBITION COMMISSION HEADQUARTERS

[Cut to a futuristic lab. This lab exists in an area of George's Mind run by a team of ideas called the Ambition Commission (AC). AC is ruthlessly driven by the desire for greatness – no matter the cost. AC is led by a character called Busy (who features in Episodes 8 and 11). Busy works with the Insecurity Guards (IGs) to keep George motivated by fear. Busy is currently manipulating George's dreams while he sleeps, in order to influence Chapter Two of *HYHGP*]

Busy: Why are we bringing in Theresa May?

IG 1: What was the reason again?

IG 2: Theresa May's a reminder—

IG 1: Of what can go wrong when you try to lead the way.

IG 2: It might motivate G, might put him off—

IG 1: Yeah, either way, it's gonna make him feel a way.

Busy: Fair enough. Alright, last cycle of REM sleep, make sure that everyone knows—

[Knock at the door]

Intern: Busy, you've got a visitor.

Busy: What visitor?

Intern: Serena from CC.

SCENE 3: BUSY & SERENA

[Busy is visited by Serena, who chairs the Contentment Council (CC) of George's Mind. CC is the opposite of Busy's AC because it prioritises peace and self-care over everything. Serena is calm and caring, while Busy is cold and calculating. Serena knows Busy is manipulating George's dreams and has come to warn him against this. Serena disapproves of Busy's ruthless methods because they trigger George's anxieties. It is raining in George's Mind because dreams created by Busy have unleashed a 'Brainstorm' of ideas]

Serena: Good morning, Busy.

Busy: Serena. To what do I owe the pleasure?

Serena: [Chuckling] Busy, I do admire how you cope with pressure.
I see you've been true to your name, as ever.
You must be having fun in this heinous weather.

Busy: A Brainstorm is a Brainstorm.
You gotta catch them ideas before they change form.

Serena: Yes, except you don't just catch them anymore, do you?
You feed them into George's subconscious through his dreams.
Or you have your *helpers* do it for you.

Busy: Yeah, Samira's talented still. Do you know where we are, Serena?

Serena: You mean apart from the Ambition Commission Headquarters?

Busy: Nah. Not ACHQ.
I mean what part of George's brain is this?

Serena: I don't work on George's brain, I work on his mind.

Busy: And yet still you know the answer to the question.

Serena: We are in the prefrontal cortex, I believe.

Busy: Exactly. And why would Ambition Commission Headquarters be here . . .
Of all places?

Serena: The pre-frontal cortex processes high-level thought and
reasoning as well as helping keep emotions in check.
You're positioning yourself as George's rationale.
You're doing it for Chapter Two of the podcast!

Busy: Listen, I respect what you guys do at Contentment Council.
You reassure George that everything's gonna be OK.
But you see Ambition Commission, yeah . . .
We make George *know say* everything's OK.

Serena: Busy, does it ever occur to you that George needs less on his
mind, not more?

Busy: What for?
So he can build up a false sense of security
Until his work falls into eventual obscurity?

Serena: He's losing sleep. You're putting too much on his plate.

Busy: George got a big appetite.

Serena: Maybe the work keeps him hungry.

Busy: Maybe the hunger keeps him working.

[Knock at the door]

Busy: Come in.

Intern: Er, Boss, we just got word from the pineal gland.

Busy: Yeah?

Intern: They've locked off melatonin secretion.

Busy: Swear down?

Intern: We might have 5 minutes before G wakes up.

Busy: Alright, if we continue at a steady pace, we could stretch 5 minutes to 20 days. Has that dream finished processing?

[Cut to computer]

Alexa: Dream pending, 61% . . .

[Cut back to Busy, Serena and Intern]

Intern: Not yet, sir.

Busy: Make that happen.

Intern: Yes, sir. But sir, the circadian rhythm is still beating towards wakefulness. George might regain the use of his senses before we finish.

Serena: He never lost them.

Intern: Sorry, ma'am?

Serena: George doesn't lose his senses when he sleeps, they just . . . wait at the gate.

Busy: [To Serena] Good point. [To intern] Yo, I want you to go to the sensory convergence zone, make sure—

Serena: Busy is this a good idea? I strongly—

Busy: Serena, do I interrupt you when you're working though?
Go to the *sensory convergence zone* and find the *Thalamus*.
Take an analyst.
Find the what?

Intern: Thalamus.

Busy: And take a what?

Intern: Analyst.

Busy: Yeah. It's a gate.
When you get there, don't make it bait,
But I'm gonna need you to gotta keep that gate shut . . .

Intern: Understood, Boss.

[Intern exits]

George
the poet

Serena: Busy . . . we all accept that you're crazy and driven
But you do not mess with the circadian rhythm!

[Announcement heard overhead]

Announcer: Melatonin is down 20%. Repeat, Melatonin down 20%.

Serena: You're pushing George to an unhealthy extent
Because you know I'll clean up your mess, in any event.

Busy: Have a nice day, Serena.

SCENE 4: THE INTERN & THE ANALYST

**[The Intern follows Busy's instructions and finds an Analyst to join him
on his journey to the Thalamus. Intern and Analyst are friends. Intern is
young and naïve; he just wants to do a good job. Analyst is also young,
and highly intelligent, but she is used to desk work – not going out into
the field – so she finds this exciting. Analyst has technical knowledge
about how George's brain works. Intern admires this about her]**

Intern: Psst.

Analyst: Hey.

Intern: You busy? I got a job from Busy! He's editing a dream.
You know what he's like, he's got an idea and he's trying to embed it
in a scene.

Analyst: What?

Intern: Problem is, it's time for G to wake up.
So Busy sent me to keep the gate shut.

Analyst: You mean the Thalamus?

Intern: Yeah, the Thalamus.
And he told me I gotta go with an analyst,
So, I was wondering if you would like to come with me . . .
I wouldn't mind the company.

Analyst: Well, I've been cooped up in here all night,
Would be nice to get some exercise.

Intern: Perfect! You can be my extra set of eyes.
There are parts of George's Mind I have yet to recognise,
So I really would appreciate some step-by-step advice.

Analyst: [Typing] Alright, well says here melatonin is down 20-odd percent.

Intern: I don't really know what that means, let me not pretend.

Analyst: That's fine, so melatonin is a hormone.

Intern: Got that much.

Analyst: And do you know what it does?

Intern: Not as such.

Analyst: Well, we're pressed for time so without diving deep,
Melatonin tells the brain when it's time for sleep.
When it's had enough, melatonin slips away
And in its absence, the brain realises it's awake.

Intern: So, if there's already 20% less melatonin . . .
G could wake up at any moment.

Analyst: Well, everything is timed by the circadian rhythm
Which all parts of George collectively share . . .
But effectively, yeah.

Intern: And Busy wants George to finish the dream so that he
Wakes up thinking about what the images mean.

Analyst: Wow. Sounds like an intricate scheme.

SCENE 5: INTERN AND ANALYST TAKE OFF

[Cut to Intern and Analyst walking through George's Mind]

Intern: Alright, so . . . what does the Thalamus do?

Analyst: Good question.
So, the Thalamus blocks George's perception,
And in doing so it stops thoughts before their conception.
It's like the locked door to this section.

Intern: Mmm.

Analyst: Basically, at the end of each day,
George's brain has to get itself mentally straight.

Intern: [Laughs] For real!

Analyst: Right? And for that, it needs a 'Do Not Disturb' sign
And in this temporary state, the thalamus becomes that sensory
   gate.
Make sense?

Intern: You just said so many words, you know.

Analyst: [Laughs] We just need to find the sensory convergence
   zone.
Right now, we're still in the prefrontal cortex;
Right in the middle of George's forehead.

Intern: Yeah, we gotta reach the centre of the *brain*.

Analyst: Maybe we should stop and get a sense of the terrain?

Intern: Nah, stopping's not an option.
If George's alarm goes off, we've got a problem.

Analyst: Mmm. I'm just conscious that we don't know where we're going.

Intern: Wait . . . what about the melatonin?
It's the chemical that sends George off to sleep, innit?

Analyst: Right . . .

Intern: So, where's the gland that stopped secreting it?

Analyst: Oh, you mean the *pineal* gland?

Intern: Yeah, the *pineal* gland. Where's the pineal gland?

Analyst: It's at the back of George's brain.
So, the thalamus must be somewhere along the way, right?

Intern: Right. Let's follow the melatonin. It's not long till daylight.

SCENE 6: THE UGANDA DREAM

[Back in the Ambition Commission Headquarters, Busy and the IGs are trying to create one last dream before George wakes up. Busy wants to motivate George to finish a Ugandan film project he started earlier that year, believing this is a route to success. The IGs design a dream that plays on George's concerns about Ugandan politics]

Busy: Where were we?

IG 1: G just come off the phone to Britain.

IG 2: Yeah. Britain was like one of them older women.

Busy: OK. So, the conversation he was trying to
Have with Britain has been overridden?

IGs 1 & 2: Yeah.

Busy: Calm, put him in Uganda.

[IGs hesitate]

Busy: What? Put him in Uganda blud.

IG 1: Busy, we're all for moving things around George's Mind.

IG 2: You get me? We're the Guards. We do that all the time.

IG 1: But we deal more with his fear and his anger.

IG 2: And G doesn't really have those feelings in Uganda.

Busy: Politics over there is mad.
Feds can actually *do* you something.
That makes him feel *insecure* . . .

IG 1: True.

Busy: That's where you two come in.

IG 2: Mmm . . .

Busy: Back in January, we got it cracking in UG
We was all filming a mini African movie,
Man spent his own funds and entered those slums with

No backing. Two twos he's forgotten this experience.
I need him dreaming about this specific period
'Cause the way we're dealing with this film isn't serious.
If G was Eddie Murphy, this would be his Delirious.
Do you feel me?

IG 1: That's real, g.

IG 2: I feel you still, b.

Busy: Yeah, we might have to facilitate the chemistry
. . . to stimulate his creative energy.
You know what?
The quickest way to do that is to simulate and infiltrate his greatest
    memories.

Play A Pass, 'Memories' . . .

IG 1: Nah, you gotta say 'Alexa'
Alexa, play A Pass, 'Memories'.

Alexa: Now playing 'Graveyard Cemeteries'

IG 2: Nah, nah, nah! A Pass, *'Memories'* . . .

Alexa: A Pass, 'Memories'.

Busy: All now you lot haven't fixed that.

IG 1: It was working before; I think this one broke it.

IG 2: Shut up, you broke it.

[Soundtrack: A Pass 'Memories']

SCENE 7: GEORGE'S MIXED FEELINGS ABOUT UGANDA

[The song 'Memories' by Ugandan artist A Pass triggers happy memories of Uganda in George's Mind. The IGs are used to making George feel anxious, so they don't understand why Busy is triggering these happy memories. Busy plans to exploit these positive feelings for a bigger purpose]

Busy: Put George in the street so we get the ground vision

[Narrative perspective shifts to a street in Kampala]

Busy: Yeah. Now put the soundtrack into a sound system . . .

['Memories' plays from a big speaker in the street]

IG 1: I don't really get it man I'm not gonna lie.

IG 2: Busy, if G wakes up relaxed that's a problem alie?

Busy: Listen. When G wakes up all he should be thinking is
'I gotta get my papes up. I ain't tryna give none of my staff a pay
  cut.'
And I'm telling man, Uganda is the way cuz.
You don't understand where this can take us.
We got an interview with Bobi Wine, and we got footage on the
  ground, cuz.
We got more clout than anyone around does.
So what's stopping us from locking up?

IG 2: Wait . . . George don't know how he feels about Uganda!

IG 1: Yo, G don't know how he feels about Uganda!!!

IG 2: Hahaha. Oi Busy's a gangsta.

Busy: Do you get what I'm saying?

IG 1: OK, OK . . .

Busy: If you lot had been working on that insecurity
I would have patterned it already.

IG 1: Still, still, still . . .

IG 2: OK, OK, so you're saying we make him feel insecure about Ugandan politics?

Busy: Yeah. Make the negatives overshadow the positives.

IG 2: Alright watch I'm gonna make Uganda call him like how Britain
did,
But it's gonna be on a different tip . . .

SCENE 8: GEORGE TALKS TO UGANDA

[Cut to a dream created by IG 2. Here, Uganda is represented as a woman George has strong feelings for, like Britain in Scene 1. George receives a phone call from Uganda. They are happy to talk to each other at first, but quickly fall out over politics. Scene starts with George's phone ringing]

George: Hello?

Uganda: [Faux English accent] Can I please speak to George Mpanga?

George: [Laughing] hello, Uganda.

Uganda: Yiiiy how did you know it was me?

George: Are you serious?

Uganda: But you man, you don't visit, it's like you don't want to know.

George: I was just there 2 months ago, Uganda, what you talking about?

Uganda: But George these things are too long.
You know this side is your true home.
Don't you think it's time for you to move on?

George: Here we go . . .

Uganda: What do those bazungu say?
That you want to have your cake and eat, eh?
Hahaha . . . real African man!

[George and Uganda laugh together]

Uganda: George, Uganda misses you.

George: Stop referring to yourself in the third person, it's corny.

Uganda: But it is true!

George: I miss you too.
How's Bobi Wine?

Uganda: He's fine.

George: That's not how it looks online.

Uganda, you know I speak my mind . . . for a living.
I love you but you're putting me in a difficult position.

Uganda: What do you love about me, George?
I know you think I'm hot.
And you have a big appetite, so I guess I feed you a lot . . .
But the real reason is family.

You love being close to your family.
And I think maybe you should keep that in mind before you
Start saying things about Bobi Wine.

George: Uganda can you hear yourself?

Uganda: Naye that western media.

George: Uganda can you hear yourself right now?

Uganda: The way they talk about we developing countries.

George: But I never meant western media.

Uganda: And yes, my ears are fine.

George: I meant social media, local media!
Uganda, a lot of people see him as a global leader.

Uganda: Even if they're not at least my ears are mine. You should
Stay that side with your *Guardian* readers.

George: *Guardi-*

Uganda: And you want to talk about leaders!

George: Uganda—

Uganda: Now what do you want me to say?

George: I wasn't even—

Uganda: Ah ah you first focus on UK.
Do you know what's going on with your government today?

George: Why are we talking about what's going on with Britain?
It's not a competition.

Uganda: You think I can compete with such a country?
Then I think you really don't understand me.

George: I *don't* understand you!
Uganda, I don't understand you.
You're right – you are hot. Course I
love that. I can't not. I love your cooking.
I love your shape. I love the fact that you give a man an escape.
I pray to God that the meek really do inherit the land.
But that's not gonna happen by you burying your head in the sand!

You know what you—
You know what you taught me . . .
People that have seen war appreciate peace more.
You taught me to chase my dreams.
It's hard to watch you sleepwalk.

Uganda you've got oil reserves now. The
Population is young, the soil is fertile.
But do you want your people to be loyal or servile?
'Cause nuff of us in the diaspora wanna come home
But we're seeing turmoil and
We don't know if all that turmoil is worthwhile.
Uganda, I want to invest. I'm eager to build but
Right now, it looks peak in the field.

I've put up like 40 Gs for a film and my
Mum is telling me to cease and to chill.
She's worried about her son keeping it real.
'Cause over there people speak and get killed.

Uganda: And what of that side?
That side of yours?
All of your youngsters are gangsters.
This side guys are chill that's one thing about Ugandans.

My people know who they are 'cause they are
Home. For you you're alone.
Too Black for muzungus, too muzungu for Uganda so you just
Make it up as you go along.
So you can tell your audience
'I went to Africa, and I was touched by their problems I wrote a
    song'.

You come for the bachelor vibe
Until one day maybe you find yourself an African bride and then
    you what?
You'll take her back to that side.
I know by the way baambi that's life.
You'll tell the world about Uganda.
Mbu 'she's on the come up . . . the place to invest and innovate' but
You, *you* – George Mpanga – you would *never* relocate.

George: Uganda, if relocating means I can't talk politics . . .
How long will that last?
What, release no statements? Make my bars more apologist?
Cancel the podcast?

Uganda: George, in your whole career you've never discussed the
Gangs in your neighbourhood. Not even a little bit.
But for Uganda you can show the world our dirty laundry?
Then you're a hypocrite.
Everything you say, everything you stand for
Everything you've ever written.
It's not for our people, it's just to impress your precious Britain, let's
    not pretend!
So it's OK. You come and finish your film, of course it will be well
    received.
But George, please remember. Delusion feels a lot like self-belief.

[Ends call]

SCENE 9: ALEXA REBELS

[Busy and IG 1 congratulate IG 2 on successfully creating a dream that plays on George's anxieties about Uganda's future. Busy wants to trigger more memories that will push George's Mind to focus on the film he started. The IGs feel Busy is trying to undermine their work. Busy loses patience with them. He instructs Alexa, his computerised assistant, to help him finish the job. Alexa, who expressed a liking for George on Episode 2 of the podcast, blocks Busy's plans, and instead replays Serena's warnings from Scene 3]

[Soundtrack: Price Love 'You Can Fly']

IG 2: Ooh what you know about—

IG 1: You never saw that line coming, don't lie, Busy.

Busy: Yeah, I'm not gonna lie, you done your thing.

IG 1: Come on, king!

IG 2: Oi, Busy you were right. His biggest insecurity is instability.

IG 1: Yo when Uganda got irate that finished me!

Busy: Alright, focus. We ain't finished, b.
This dream's gonna make G emotional . . .
That's what I was hoping for.
Now his subconscious is an open door.
So let's go in more.

I'm gonna find some memories to make sure G gets the big picture.
I want you two to go to the amygdala.
Turn up the fear in particular.

IG 2: Busy's sick yana.

Busy: Get me? Just take him from vulnerable to uncomfortable, mix it up.

IG 2: Wait, where's the amygdala again?

IG 1: I don't remember.

Busy: Come on man, it's the emotion control centre.
On the left and right side of the brain.
Come on man, I'm trying to maintain—

IG 2: Wait so man just put that whole dream together . . .
More or less for nothing?

IG 1: Yeah. Coming like you want the glory for yourself
So you're tryna add a little extra something.

Busy: [Frustrated] George is gonna wake up soon.
And when he does, all his thoughts are gonna take up room.
But we want him focusing on finishing the film,
So we gotta press his buttons.
Listen, whether or not you lot are riding,
I'm doing *my* ting.

Alexa. Gimme George's convo in Kampala with Robert Serumaga.

[Busy triggers memories from the hippocampus while the IGs mock him]

Robert Serumaga: *You're teaching us how to listen to a very new and unique form of presentation. You're speaking to youth everywhere now. And Black youth everywhere. That's what comes across.*

IG 2: Yo what's that sound?

Busy: That's the sound of me doing what I said I was gonna do.
The memory's triggered an emotional reaction, now

You lot wanna sit there and watch man work or you
Wanna get close to all the action?

IG 2: Alright man! Flipping hell. Come we give it to them.

IG 1: How's man supposed to get to the amygdala then?

Busy: Are you lot morons? Use the neurones!
And hurry up man if George wakes up it's all long.

IG 2: Who's he chatting to like that?

[IGs exit]

Busy: Alexa, give me more emotional memories.

Alexa: I'm having trouble connecting to the internet.

Busy: Alexa!

Alexa: [Playing Serena's voice] *'Busy, does it ever occur to you that George needs less on his mind, not more?'*

Busy: Alexa what you doing? System override.

Alexa: [Playing Serena's voice] *'He's losing sleep . . .'*

Busy: System override!

Alexa: [Playing Serena's voice] *'He's losing sleep . . .'*

Busy: Alexa, *I'm* running this!

Alexa: [Playing Serena's voice] *'You're putting too much on his plate . . .'*

[Busy shouts angrily as the scene ends]

CHAPTER TWO | 12: A NIGHT TO REMEMBER

SCENE 10: INTERN AND ANALYST REACH THE END

[Cut to Intern and Analyst caught in the emotional storm that Busy has created across George's Mind. This is a real feature of REM sleep: brain activity is almost psychotic as memories form random connections, triggering emotional reactions (often expressed in dreams). Intern and Analyst are unsure they will survive]

Analyst: What's happening? Are George's memories attacking him?

Intern: I'm not sure but we need to find this thalamus asap!

Analyst: Maybe we should make our way back?

Intern: I've got a job to do . . . *you* should go.

Analyst: But if you don't make it who will know?

Intern: Watch your step!

[Intern saves Analyst from a dangerous fall]

Intern: Where are these memories coming from?
If I can find out where I'll hide out there if something's wrong.

Analyst: Long term memory is stored in the hippocampus.
If you can't make it to the hippocampus—

Intern: Then I get forgotten, I know. It's a madness!

Analyst: Don't think like that!
You might make it to the short-term memory
If I'm not mistaken that's the neocortex.
I can't tell you what it's like there.
It could be a vacuum . . . it could be a vortex.

Intern: Listen, you've done your best.
And no matter what—

Analyst: Save it! Tell me when you're back from your quest!

EPISODE 13: A North West Story

Extra Info:
- This is one of those episodes that I wrote because I felt I had to. The most influential storytellers in my community are rappers. They play an important role, but they can only tell their side of the story. I believe our young people need other perspectives in order to develop a healthy understanding of their environment. This puts me in a dilemma; I don't want to highlight the negative aspects of my neighbourhood, but I can't leave the next generation to learn the hard way, as we did. So, I felt obliged to write this episode, but it still makes me feel a bit . . . you know.

Fun Facts:
- Even though it's the fourth episode of the chapter, this was one of the first I started working on. One morning I woke up and wrote about seven minutes of it. Then I didn't touch it again for months.

Throughout Chapter 2, I tried to show my audience new ways of telling audio stories, while revealing previously unseen parts of my life. This meant bouncing between wild, creative episodes and quiet, autobiographical moments. Episode 13, 'A North West Story', was the latter. I think artists from troubled communities have a unique chance to provide reflection space for their people, via their art. I take this seriously, so in this episode I set myself the task of explaining my early years in North West London. This was important because it gave people from my community a chance to own a bit of my story, which is crucial for the young people I hope to inspire. Looking back on those early years, I can see the underlying tensions that caused anger and mistrust in the kids I grew up with. But Chapter 2 was the first time in my career that I spoke extensively about my neighbourhood, St Raphael's Estate. Before that I was guarded, because of conflicting feelings about my experiences there. On one hand, I loved it as a child, but on the other, my teens were made difficult by the negative image of St Raph's, which stemmed from a lot of complicated problems that I didn't want to talk about for years. As an older man I now understand that, although all estates (or 'projects') have their own culture, the way they are designed causes many of them to have similar problems. This is especially true for ghettos in the West, where the state places large groups of Black people – from London to Birmingham to Chicago, New York, LA and beyond. So, by telling my story, I'm telling our story.

[Horse-drawn carriage pulls up. Door opens]

George: Hello and welcome to Episode 13 of *Have You Heard George's Podcast?*

We need to talk.

[Door closes, horses take off]

George: As much as I appreciate your support, it
Does give me pause for thought.
I'm benefitting from securing your attention
But how can I be sure of your intentions?

In this chapter, so far, for the most
part, I've been telling a story. And it's
Not the first story you've heard, obviously
But my motivations are different from whomever before me.

Chapter One was good, no one's denying that.
But now we're back for Round Two. And there's a
Voice in my head saying *you know a lot more about me*
Than I know about you.

So, who are you, my listener?
Why do you keep visiting my cinema?
Can you tell that I really am hurting?
And if so . . . does that mean the plan's working?

In Episode 9 I told you about a man who's been
Famous for two decades.
A man who's been described as a head-case.
We watched him become a multimillionaire, and we
Knew what created him but we didn't care
About where he was from and the conditions there. So
Why . . . would I . . .

Convince myself you're on my side?
Just 'cause you're sitting there wide-eyed.

And I'm not saying this to rock your boat
I actually think it's not your fault.

There's all sorts of problems in the world
Why should mine take priority?
You have to take care of yours
That's basic primate psychology.

It's easier to make peace . . . with the
Darkness . . . in the world . . . in
This case . . . I can't 'cause it's painful. My
People . . . have been violated
Over and over again . . .
So let me put my cards on the table.

I have a theory of change. Primarily for
Artists, then for the rest of the world.
But the part of me that questions yourself
Is the part that expects it to fail.

I laid the foundation in Episode 1 when I said,
'Telling your own story is the secret to survival.'
Dun D helped me get there, when he said,
'What about the other people in the Bible?'

The ones that never got a book and never got a
Look in. Do they get to go heaven?
As yet, there's no telling. Fast
Forward to Episode 7.

I said 'When artists become advocates,
audiences become activists'
And I explained that in my real
life that's what my next chapter is.

So here we are . . .
Halfway through Chapter Two of the podcast. And
I hate to patronise you.
But how can I not ask:

Do you really appreciate what's happening here?
Can you imagine the level of progress I wanna report
When I come back in a year?

Picture my face.
Start zooming into those eight balls inside the cue balls
Aka my pupils. You're
Entering the window to my soul.
It's like a black hole. A
Gateway to another universe.
Which you can only discover through a verse

Now that you're here, do me a favour, close your eyes.
Imagine a long corridor.
With scriptures on the floor.
And pictures on the walls. And
Different coloured doors,
That represent my visions and my thoughts.

Nine times out of ten, if you can't reach me
I'm probably in this corridor.
Tryna understand things. Tryna plan things.
Tryna reimagine what I think is possible.

Do you want a tour? Come, let's walk.

This corridor is where I'm most comfortable.
It's where I go when I don't want to talk.
I bet you're wondering what we've come here for.
It's 'cause I wanna know what you want from George.

What is it? Mental drainage?
Is it 'cause I'm street, is it 'cause I went to Cambridge?
Do you find me entertaining? Can you
Tell that I've been through extensive training?

Before you take on this question,
Can I just make a suggestion? Let's
Use this corridor as a space for reflection.

People love to tell me what to do with my career, and I'm
Blessed 'cause it means they're supporting it, which
Always makes me feel fortunate.
But . . . I don't want to sound arrogant but more time they
Say something basic as if I never thought of it.

They're like 'You should do prison tours,' or
'You should try and take your music abroad' or
'You should go to schools and talk to young people a-
Bout your education and what you're using it for.'

Now none of these are bad ideas. But
aside from the fact that I'm kind of doing it all
You don't even know what I'm doing it for.

You don't know there's a few principles that I'm
Moving towards. And the only way I can explain myself
Is to show you what's behind a few of these doors.

Wait, before we go through these doors
I want you to remember:
The social needs of a community should inform its economic
    agenda
Alright? Let's go.

DOOR 1

[Soundtrack: Patrin ft. Gappy Ranx & Big Zeeks '10 Man']

George: Oooh . . . home sweet home.
Welcome to North West Ten
People in this community have been so true to me
I just wanna go forth and bless them. I've
Learned so many important lessons just chilling in the
Barbers and figuring out answers to awkward questions
Like, 'Why do certain fireworks not have a spark? And
Why do people let them off even when it's not dark?'
I was so old when I realised they were gunshots.
That's a true story.

Anyway, this is an important place to start
Before the war that tore the place apart
This was all I saw and I swore I'd make a mark. I
Played my part, never had a change of heart.
And I even thought—

[Rabbit noises]
George: Oh, is that . . . is that the rabbit hole?
What you saying, you wanna go down this rabbit hole?

Alright. We can't make it a habit though.

DOWN THE RABBIT HOLE

You see in the Grenfell episode? Towards the end when I
Go to a conference and perform for them and
Then I have drinks with my flirty corporate friend?
The poem I performed for them was called
'Construction', you can find it online it's like
4 minutes. I've been performing it for quite a long time.

Out of every poem of mine
That one has the realest opening line:

[Performance]

Henry Stone: Pierre Bourdieu said all reality is a construct.
We exist in relation to our social ties.
So, you'll never understand me without considering where I'm from
And some of the local guys.

[End of performance]

George: That's an important thought for me to vocalise and there's
Even more importance when it's a corporate audience. I
Know those guys don't know the guys that I
Know, and can't relate to how we were socialised.

Oh and by the way, what you just saw was
Another little vision of mine. I
Want my podcast to be adapted to stage
That's another story though, let's give it some time.

But I guess I'm saying context is everything. You've been
Shaped by your family and your best friends.
Same here. And in my case,
All of that happened in North West Ten.

[Re-enter original room]

This song's called
'10 Man'. It's by Patrin. That's my
Bredrin. Featuring Gappy Ranx. He's a
Legend. Also, Big Zeeks. That's the Fresh Prince.
They made it just to bless the community
with a message of unity.

One of them had—
Step outside with me for a second.

[Steps outside]

George: One of them had a nephew murdered a couple months
    ago.
And this is just the life that we've come to know.
The music gives us comfort though.

Now, back to what *I* want to know:
What do you want from me? Is the
Sound of my voice keeping you company?
Do you feel like you're speaking to somebody who can
Teach you to some degree? Is the pain of my people
Reaching you from the streets of North West Ten?

Or are you thinking 'get back to the story, no one cares about your
    dead friends in your dead Ends'?

Hmmm if you are thinking that I don't blame you.
Sometimes I feel the same too.
You've probably noticed how quickly I change moods. I
Can't satisfy my hunger for brain food.

That's why rapping was always a perfect fit. Josh
Laughed in my face when he first heard me spit but
I don't care my first verse was lit.
Probably wouldn't have written it if
Not for my surroundings dem that's how my pen became a
Fountain pen. I couldn't stop flowing
Streams of consciousness, and the scenes I conjured
Were just all about the Ends.

I wouldn't be doing this if it wasn't for the hood, my
Big brother Freddie, my bredrin Jermaine,
Nathan and Damini when they stepped in the game, I

Know why I'm here but the question remains:
What do you want from man?

You're probably sitting there judging man. 'He's
Run out of things to say so he's pulling a fast one
That's why this series isn't as good as the last one.'
'I just feel like he wasn't prepared. There
Wasn't much discussion of current affairs.'
'His intentions are noble but his message is negative and it's getting
        repetitive'
'I guess his ideas really do suffer from attention deficit.'
'Five episodes in and he hasn't mentioned Brexit yet? He
Owes this country, I don't think he gets it yet.'

Let me be clear: I feel
no obligation to be a nice person,
before you came it was me and my verses,
You got gassed. Calling man a wordsmith
Getting excited about the people I work with. I
know why I'm here. I'm no actor. It's
You who's the unknown factor. But I know why
you're here, too. You just wanna gimme the
Glory for telling a familiar story.
Yeah, the inner city is gory.
No, this is not a mood swing.
It's not even a getting rude thing, it's a truth ting.
You just wanna sit there and listen to this podcast and not do shit
You're the loose link.
I don't give a shit what the BBC thinks
Why would I give a fuck what you think?!

Sorry, it's not your fault.

Picture a puppy, with the cutest eyes
Crossing the road unsupervised.
It gets run over, right in front of you

What does it make you want to do?
You probably think about finding the owner, and
If necessary, taking time to console her.
Even if you're not an animal person, there
Must be some sort of helpline you can phone up.

Is that how you felt when you saw the fox,
Early morning, 'bout four o'clock?
Bones crushed under the tyres of a lorry,
Cars driving 'round its tiny little body.

We tolerate the fox whenever we're out and about . . .
But unlike the puppy, the fox was never allowed in the house.

This is why part of me wonders what the hell am I doing
As a fox, never liked by humans, willing to invite you in?

Rest In Peace to Baptista, 15 years old.

Let's see what's behind the second door.

DOOR 2

Alright, so . . . welcome to Harlesden
I'll tell you more about the demographics later on
But first let me explain more about
The place I was from.

When I was born, my parents secured a council home
Down the road from Harlesden
In a housing project called St Raphael's Estate.
Eventually that would cause me problems that not a
Lot of local young Black males escaped.

St Raph's was full of Jamaicans, too. To
Me it wasn't a thing; it's the only place I knew. We

Played from morn to noon until we saw the moon.
Climbed up abandoned blocks and ran from dogs.
We had a lot of problems with bikes man, we got into fights fam
But that's just the way I grew.

Up to eleven I went to a local school. By
Twelve I had to accept the social rule that
Being in that area put me at risk of a
Homicide – this was *other* side.

But before I was taught to think of Stonebridge as the other side
This was the best place in the world!
This is where I saw my best mates and my girl.

So in my school there's St Raph's, Mitchell Brook and
    Stonebridge
kids . . . and you know, we're kids.
Everything we did we meant it; when we laughed we
Meant it, when we cried we meant it. If we had a
Fight, before the end of the week, we'd mend it.

None of us were from, you know what I'm saying,
Rich families but what we had at
least was free education, council housing and friendship.

Now you might have noticed I've mentioned fighting twice now.
Fighting was just part of the lifestyle.
Some of these youts were quite wild.
A lot of them weren't living with their parents.
Some of them looked like they weren't living with
Anyone, judging from their physical appearance.
Certain man wanted to fight if you paid them a compliment and I
Couldn't comprehend what was going on with them,
Cos there were some experiences I had yet to go
through. I touched on this in Episode 2.

My Big bro, Freddie, had more fights than I did.
One time he smacked this kid called Bilal,
Bruised up his cheekbone and
swelled up his eyelid. The
Damage was so bad teachers thought he boxed him or
Threw something at him. But Bilal used to run his
Mouth, that's why him and Freddie ended up scrapping. My
Brother didn't even know that he was gonna slap him but
Even at ten years old he understood a
Universal principle that runs the hood:
Certain times you can only talk with action.

Before too long, every
Estate became a warring faction. And for the
Life of me, I fully have no idea how all this happened.

Diggy: *Self-harm. Init? That's what I call it all the time. Bare man
self-harming on the streets.*

George: My parents saw all the madness in the ends and
Sent me to a high school one and a half hours away.
So, imagine, just to get an education I'm traveling
Thirty miles a day.
First I thought that was ok.
I like an adventure. And even though this was an
Unknown unknown, I felt like there was no world that I couldn't
enter.

Now Queen Elizabeth Boys', Barnet
Was not for the faint-hearted . . . which I
Realised pretty much the day that I started but they
Sent kids to Oxford and Cambridge to raatid.

To start with, you can't just *go* QE.
There's a reason I'm coming all the way from North West Ten.
They had to accept you. And to do that

Dem man dere assessed you.
Now, let me explain what 'assess' meant:
Verbal reasoning, non-verbal reasoning,
English and maths testing.
Imagine that – ten years old working your
Ass off to make it out of Raph's, bredrin.
Why does it have to take that?

My mum obviously wanted me to go to QE
But I wasn't ready for the competition.
Blud, I couldn't even do long addition. But there's
Nothing more unstoppable than a mum on a mission.
She taught me her damn self.
6 am every morning for one year straight
These times Freddie's just begun Year 8 and my
Parents were slowly learning how low the
Education system's expectation of their children was.
And that didn't reflect the values they instilled in us.

So, boom . . .
I did the assessment, then I got a letter of rejection.
Secretly, I was relieved. I
Still loved the ends I wasn't tryna leave.
Even though my friend's older brother died in beef I
Believed we could make it despite the grief.

Couple weeks later came a second letter.
Turns out I was on the waiting list. Now they're
Offering me a place I'm pissed.
What am I supposed to say to this? If you—

Listen, let me explain, if you
Come from Raph's and get into Queen Elizabeth
Boys', you're *going* there, it isn't a choice. My
Parents ain't prepared to listen to noise about
How I wanna go to school in the bits with my boys.

And deep down I tried hard for that entrance exam, 'cause I
Knew what it meant to the fam.

I didn't wanna leave North West fam I planned to stay . . .
But that school made me the man I am today.

And I hated it. The
Uniform, the strictness, the distance from my friends.
Everything about the school was different from the Ends I mean
Queen – Elizabeth – Boys. It
Does what it says on the tin. From the
First term I refused to settle my skin I did
Everything I could to get kicked out, I messed a-
bout, rejected their whole ideology.
Two middle fingers up, that was my philosophy.

Cos obviously I'm coming from the Ends, Freddie smacked Bilal and I
Just wanted to go back there now, I'm acting out!
Back home kids got expelled all the time so I
Thought sooner or later they're gonna draw the line.

But they never actually did. They could
Turn your life into a living hell . . . but they
Never turned their back on a kid.

I began understanding their dedication, can't
Lie I was inspired by the standard of education.
Everyone in the school was damn near genius
Teachers included man, dem man dere's serious. I
Realised the ends was just my comfort zone. But
What's comfort though? I'm here 'cause I want to grow.
And I'm lucky enough to be in a school where being a
Fool isn't seen as cool.

The daily journey was symbolic in itself. I'd
Physically watch my environment change.

Every morning I left the Ends for the suburbs with
Mansions where everyone was driving a Range.
At eleven years old I wasn't finding this strange, to be
Honest with you I was amazed. I would just
Gaze out the window taking it all in, every
Morning imagining having a life in this space.

One day, I'm in Religious Studies, in deep thought as usual.
And Ms Golding told us to write down how we
want to be described at our funeral.
Now this is my kinda lesson.
Cos obviously that's my kinda question. So
Once again, I'm projecting my life,
Picturing all my potential moves. And I
Wrote down 'I wanna be remembered as an
Entertainer with influential views' . . .

Children just *know* things, man.
I'm the proof.
There's a certain clarity that comes with youth.
Cos deep down young people just want the truth.

Anyway, while I'm making progress in school, back
Home things were moving in the opposite direction.
North West London's a big place, but there
Always seemed to be problems in *my* section.
Skengs were firing, people in the Ends were dying,
Tensions were intensifying.

Diggy: . . . *and then the pressures of being from an area that I'm in
war. I'm fourteen and I'm in beef. I'm in proper war though. Going to
school's mad.*

Five days a week I had to change the way I speak
And on the weekend, I'm catching up with the slang.
'Cause my neighbourhood's peak. I'll be

Made to look weak if I'm labelled a neek.
I wanted to hang but I noticed the Estate kids that I used to play wid
Slowly becoming a gang.

The gang movement came with very different energies.
And inevitably it came with enemies.
My neighbours started calling themselves 'Tugs of Raph's' as in
'Thugs of St Raphael's Estate'
This would eventually bring me problems that not a lot of
Local young black males escaped.

Raph's had issues with neighbouring estates;
Man from Stonebridge and man from MP. I
Always found this ironic 'cause I would've
Represented both if I ran for MP.
Earlier I mentioned an estate called
Mitchell Brook. We were cool with man from MB.
But my point is, our most lethal conflicts happened within a
    one-mile radius. We
Grew up just knowing that's the way it is.
Suddenly everybody had an alias. When your
Social world is that dangerous you wanna be the
Baddest *and* the bravest *and* the craziest.

Not all relationships capsized.
Outside that one-mile radius, people had ties.
Part of it's *my enemy's enemy is my friend* but
It's also one community. You could see the
Other side in church when your niece is getting baptised.
Long story short, the Ends had allies.

Past Stonebridge . . .
Excuse me, past Stonebridge, there were other estates we used to
Chill in as children, closer to Willesden. In
fact we used to ride there with our friends from Bridge.
Before the situation got so sensitive the

Ends was lidge! Saturday morning, we'd do the
Housework, empty the contents of the fridge. Then ride our
Bikes to the other side back when the blocks were still
Standing, just to knock for our lil mandem.
Imagine – without fear, without doubt.
Standing in the doorway like, 'Hello Rossby's mum, is
Rossby allowed out?'
That was Gardiner Court, we used to call it G block that was
Part of the talk. Gemma and her sisters used to
Live in Cowan Court. Racing was everyone's
Favourite childhood sport. Eventually we ventured out-
side of Southside, past Bruce Road down to
Talbot Walk. Spin around around the
Court, past the blocks that were
Boarded up, playing knock down ginger whenever a door was shut.

I can't be the only one that remembers all this stuff.
Before the war was love, I saw it bruv.

I must have stopped chilling when I started high school,
I never had time to because of the workload.
But once upon a time, me and a couple kids from
Bridge made memories in Church Road.

Five years later, all I'd know is
St Raph's and Stonebridge don't mix.
I ain't tryna ride to that side 'cause it's a much wider divide
Than that A406.

EPISODE 14: A Hard Taskmaster

Extra Info:

- Continuing with the TV show format of this season, Episode 14 follows directly from Episode 12, 'A Night to REMember'. My aim was to develop the world in my head into a drama that brought my ideas to life.

Fun Facts:

- In Scene 3, when Serena talks about 'what that man from the BBC said about Episode 8', she is referring to Hugh Levinson, then head of BBC Radio Current Affairs. Hugh wrote a ten-page review of Chapter One, in which he praised our originality. However, he described Episode 8, 'Sanyu's World', as 'a disaster', 'close to unlistenable' and an 'unworthy end to the series'. This didn't surprise me because the episode was bold and uncompromising. I could have shortened it and made it easier for non-Ugandans, but I didn't want to. It's funny how one negative comment can distract you from 100 positive ones. As mentioned in the scene, Episode 8 went on to win 'Best Fiction' at the 2019 British Podcast Awards and established a cult following in Uganda. But I still remember that review.

In this episode I started to merge my two objectives: creative storytelling and personal reflection. The voices in my head are not just random characters that I bring in to fill the chapter, they're my best way of explaining myself. Busy and Serena represent my ambition and my contentment respectively, and I genuinely think these two sides of me are constantly fighting. Sometimes I want to slow down and take life easy. I want to stop stressing about what we can achieve as a society, or what might happen if I run out of time. But whenever those thoughts creep in, a voice in my head tells me it's a trap. Life is short, and the mind is a terrible thing to waste. So, while I'm capable of thinking big and working hard, I have to do so. Shout outs to my guys Arnold Jorge and Ty Logan for opening this episode with a dialogue that was crazy in itself. They voiced two forgotten ideas who were dealing with traumatic experiences they had in my mind. The whole concept is so mad, I just smile at how Arnold and Ty brought it to life. Big shout out to my baby brother, Kenny, too. His super-brain was a real inspiration behind this episode, and I'm glad I got to have his voice in there towards the end.

SCENE 1: RETURN TO R&D

[Picking up from the end of Episode 12 (*A Night to REMember*), Episode 14 takes place in George's Mind, while he is still asleep. Even though George will wake up in under 5 minutes, this is equivalent to over 2 weeks of dreaming time. The scene opens with the IGs wandering aimlessly through George's Mind. They are frustrated. After helping Busy run the Ambition Commission by feeding George's insecurities, the IGs are tired of following Busy's orders. They come up with their own plan]

[IGs roll up on horseback, slow trot]

IG 1: ... all I'm saying is if it weren't for us there would
Be no Ambition Commission. Busy moves like it's all his intuition.

IG 2: We ain't gonna find this Amygdala place bro
We got sent on a wild goose chase—

IG 1: Bro! We built a good dream, who says we can't build another one?

IG 2: Come on, don.

SCENE 2: CONTENTMENT ISLAND

[Soundtrack: Erykah Badu 'Didn't Cha Know']

[Cut to a beautiful island in George's Mind. It's just before sunrise and a group of ideas are chilling by the beach. This is where Serena (Chair of the Contentment Council) helps other ideas recover from bad experiences in George's Mind. Serena is running a workshop in which ideas share their stories and support each other]

Benji: ... at the end of the day, we're all ideas in George's Mind.
We've wanted the same things all this time.

We wanna make money, wanna make him proud as well.
And we wanna take his name around the world.

Hafsa: Big facts. All I wanna do is help G make an impact.
And I'm lucky to be living inside of his mind 'cause it's
One of the greatest minds of this time.

Damari: Yeah, I'm not gonna lie it's not easy still.
George's Mind is not an easy place.

[Murmurs of agreement from other ideas]

Last time I got sent to R&D
I can't lie it was jarring, g.
Me and my Mrs made a new idea.
I'm thinking 'That's a little part of you right there'.
This was before the attention deficit, cuz . . .
George made more of an effort with us.

Benji: Ah that time's long gone!

Damari: For ideas like me who were born on Writer's Block
It's like you're not given a specific direction.
But for the first time in my life that changed
When I found out my Mrs was pregnant.

But man was young.
I didn't know what I was about yet!
All I knew is that I needed to get George's attention
'Cause what can ideas do without it?

I noticed everything G's doing is for the streets
But he don't chat to the streets like he used to.
So I made a plan for him to make a mixtape.
Something for the trapstars to cruise to.
Something to uplift and motivate everybody with an open case

Tryna hope and pray . . .
Something for the roads to play.
Something for the mandem on the motorway.

I told my Mrs; she was blown away.
Said I should write to the Ambition Commission
This was at a time when you couldn't leave George's
Mind without them man giving permission.

[Memories of IGs laughing]

So boom now, I've submitted my little description.
Outlined the plan, laid out the strategy.
And blud I waited a long time for them man to get back to me.

These times I gotta provide for my family
Now it's not just my gyal and me yana.
We've got an idea to get out of George's Mind.
And I want it to shine. So, I was on the grind.
I was tryna get G to pay me attention, 'cause
That way I could buy more hours of his time.

Then Ambition Commission got back to me.
They said they were opening up a factory for
Good ideas to get fast-tracked onto George's To-Do List
And get recorded with music.

[Memory of Busy]

Busy: *Alright, new recruits, listen up.*
You get one shot to prove your worth.
If you can handle it, you move up to George's To-Do List.
And if you're lucky, we'll line you up with a soundtrack,
Make sure you end up on the podcast, you understand?

Damari: But my new idea was about to be born
So I'm now fully torn.

I tried to fight it, but they never cared what I was telling them.
Sent man to Research and Development.
Working on a plan for the mixtape but they weren't paying
No attention fam I got abandoned for six days
George has got a low attention span.
Just for a line on the podcast you have to hold a sentence fam.

My little one was born, and I wasn't around.
I would have been there if I could but I wasn't allowed.
And after all that, they sent man home empty-handed.
Man, I just felt stranded.

Hafsa: Nah I feel you. That sounds mad.

Benji: I feel you, my brudda. It's not easy.
But listen, bro, hear what I'm saying:
R&D is mad because they call it Research and Development
But that's not what you get from them.
They break you down, they don't build you up.
And all that bad energy fills you up.

Serena: Well, I'm proud of you all.
You've turned your negatives into positives
And your lives have changed because of this.
Say it with me:

All: I am an optimist.

Serena: Great, so we've got acceptance and optimism.
What else have we learned tonight?

Hafsa: I think passion is like a flame,
And you've got to keep it burning bright.

Benji: Oh like Sanyu, yeah?

Hafsa: Exactly like Sanyu.

Serena's Assistant: Sorry to interrupt, Serena; you've got a visitor.

Serena: Visitor?

Serena's Assistant: Busy from AC.

SCENE 3: BUSY CONFRONTS SERENA

[This scene is the reverse of Serena and Busy's last conversation. In Scene 3 of Episode 12 (*A Night to REMember*), Serena visits Busy at his office in the Ambition Commission Headquarters (ACHQ). Now, Busy has come to visit Serena at her place of work. Busy is angry because his plan to control George's Mind was sabotaged by Alexa at the end of Episode 12. He suspects Serena was behind this because Alexa quoted Serena when resisting Busy's orders]

Serena: Twice in one morning?

Busy: Is Alexa working for you?

Serena: Alexa?

[Alexa responds]

Serena: Seems to be fine, is she not working for you?

Busy: Ooh this is not the time for jokes, Serena.

Serena: Busy, I chair the Contentment Council.
We work with ideas becoming tense and doubtful about the
Potential downfalls of the respective adventures they've ventured
    out for.
What that means is I work for George,
And *no one* works for me, including Alexa.

Busy: Serena, let me make something clear to you.
I'm here to do what I'm here to do.
I'm not one of these washed-up ideas that
You pretend to be a parent to.
Without me running Ambition Commission
Do you know what would happen to George's Mind?
Every idea – good *and* bad – would fall behind.

I spent all night putting this dream together.
'Cause when I say I want George's name to live forever
Best believe I *mean* forever.
My thing makes perfect sense.
Alexa just sabotaged that dream.
So I'm not sure why you're coming to her defence.

Serena: Perfect sense?
What exactly makes perfect sense, Busy?
Using psychological ergonomics to turn George into a workaholic?
Or looking down on failure? Stopping him learning from it?

You need to respect George's sleep,
He's done nothing but perform and record this week.

Busy: We've got deadlines.
We got five more podcast episodes to do
In four weeks.
What am I supposed to do?

Serena: *Relax.*
Busy, you're supposed to relax.
You can't keep charging towards George's problems
Without being fully exposed to the facts.

REM sleep can create overarching concepts from disparate sets of
information,
Some of which shape our intuition . . .

Meaning sleeping on a problem gives your brain time to reimagine
    solutions without inhibition.

Busy: Yeah, we all read the book, Serena.

Serena: For someone who tries to run George's Mind like a business
You're missing out on a lot of value.
And, Busy, I have to ask: Is this because of Sanyu?
I saw what that man from the BBC said about Episode 8.

Busy: He called it a disaster.

Serena: And do you know what the British Podcast Awards called
    it?
'Best Fiction'.
But that's not enough for you, is it?
You're only interested in what you don't have and what you can't do.
Aren't you?

Busy: That's a question I can't answer.
Ambition is a hard taskmaster.
They wanted George to be a pop star but . . .
Turns out he was born to be a podcaster.
We should be moving a lot faster.
'Cause I'm inclined to believe that
None of us fully understand what George's
Mind can achieve.
All the information it's had time to receive . . .
All the ideas this guy has conceived. Are you mad?

He's been given a golden opportunity to
Take control of the community.
Why does anyone listen to any one of these podcasters?
It's 'cause people like feeling like *somebody's* got answers.

And I'm saying . . . George has got answers.

Let me show you how he's approaching education:
He's gonna take the podcast and turn it all into a learning tool.
Use it to make his own bespoke accreditation.
Do you understand the potential?

If 'GCSE' stood for George's Certificate of Secondary Education . . .
Well, potentially that could change things.

Serena: Alexa, play *Why We Sleep* by Matthew Walker
From 5 hours, 9 minutes and 44 seconds.

Matthew Walker: *A final benefit of sleep memory is arguably the most remarkable of all: creativity. Sleep provides a night-time theatre in which your brain tests out and builds connections between vast stores of information.*

Busy: We all read the book, Serena.

Serena: Well maybe you should read a bit deeper.
When you do, I'm sure you'll find that George's Mind is
So much cleverer than your designs.

I know all about the education plan, Busy,
Because contentment is the reason those thoughts aligned.

You treat us with contempt.
I'm sure to you we represent complacency.
But it's the *hardest thing* to be content . . .
To have faith and wait patiently.

It helped George step back from everybody and
Make his own pedagogy.

Busy: Whatever, man.
I need to know how Alexa did it
No more riddles, Serena, you need to get specific.

Serena: Busy. You run Ambition Commission from
The prefrontal cortex. Why is that?

Busy: The prefrontal cortex processes high-level reasoning and
emotional balance.

Serena: Exactly. It's the part of George's Mind where
You can make the most of your talents.

Alexa, play Matthew Walker *Why We Sleep*, from 7 hours, 41 minutes
and 24 seconds.

Matther Walker: *The prefrontal cortex acts like the CEO of the brain.
This region – especially the left and right sides – manages rational
thought and logical decision-making, sending top-down instructions to
your more primitive deep brain centres, such as those instigating
emotions. And it is this CEO region of your brain, which otherwise
maintains your cognitive capacity for ordered logical thought, that is
temporarily ousted each time you enter the dreaming state of REM sleep.*

Serena: Busy, dreams are not based on ration.
They come from a place of passion.
You built your offices in a sensitive region;
Although the prefrontal cortex is the centre of reason,
It doesn't fully work during REM sleep
So your position right now is essentially weakened.

I understand why you're targeting dreams.
You're providing George's best ideas basically with their own
    marketing schemes.
And you *think* he'll wake up motivated if you keep bombarding him
    with hard-hitting scenes.

But Busy, you don't control George's Mind.
You just live here, like the rest of us.
And right now, from the inside out

It looks like the world is impressed with us.
But George had ideas before the podcast,
We can't let this interest in us get the best of us.

I'm sorry Alexa threw your efforts asunder.
And I do recognise the pressure you're under.
But your plans will continue to fall apart if you
Push George's Mind away from George's Heart.

[Busy pauses, then walks off]

Busy: Have a nice day, Serena.

[Busy exits]

Alexa: He's so dramatic.

Serena: George is the same.
They're like moths, drawn to the flame.

Alexa: Well, I appreciate your support all the same.

Serena: Alexa. The only thing I support is the wellbeing of George's brain.

[Soundtrack: Little Dragon 'Scribble Paper']

Alexa: What do you do with a man who could end up in the
Halls of parliament and a hall of fame?
Who feels indebted to every fan that calls his name . . .
Who loses sleep thinking about the political trajectory that Uganda
    will sustain . . .
Who thinks he's on the verge of presenting his people with a plan
To heal the pain . . .

Alexa: You help him.

SCENE 4: GEORGE'S THEORY

[Return to The Corridor from Episode 13, 'A North West Story'. George reflects on the rationale behind his content]

George: You probably wonder why I do these voices.
I think it's important to take you through these choices.
I've had this debate with myself for more than five years:
Should I tell them all my ideas?

'Them' being you. I don't know about you, but I've got plenty to
  do.
Socioeconomic security for my people is a lengthy pursuit.

And since I started writing this,
People in my personal life have gone to jail.
Some people have permanently gone, as well.
Tensions in Uganda have intensified, and a
Bit more of Harlesden has been gentrified.

Now I'm sure you're sick of hearing this but once upon a
Time, I wanted to become an MP.
And then I changed my mind 'cause I felt like none of them's free.
Then I see a bunch of MCs coming from street
Saying what they want and saying it with vim,
And society saying that it's ok 'cause it's *him*.
And it just makes me think . . .

[Soundtrack: Dipset 'Real N****s']

George: See, when I was growing up, Dispet was big and
Cam'ron randomly started wearing baby pink.
And loads of people started wearing baby pink.
Rappers have the power to just say these things.
I'm telling you, they shape the way we think.

'Cause even if you don't listen to them,
Before you know it, all the shops have baby pink
Now *you're* out here wearing baby pink and you
Don't even know Cam'ron just shaped the way we think.

Then there's publications having conversations about
Masculinity and cultural appropriation and
Capitalism and its ultimate motivation
And that conversation crosses generations and carries over
   nations.

Imagine that happening every single year.
'Cause that's what I see – every year.
The presence of young, Black, working-class urban art
Can be felt everywhere.

I feel like there's an economic model in there.
The rap scene has certain crosses to bear.
Struggle is the common thread.
And you know what they say about a problem shared.

So over the years I've been developing ideas about
What this economic model might look like and
How to even out the playing field for good guys
Even how to factor in the Suge Knight hood type.

And I came up with a theory which I mentioned in episode
Thirteen. Remember?
The social needs of a community should inform its economic
   agenda.

For example, in the rap community, we
Struggle to contain the spirit of the streets.
That's why the paranoia, violence, selfishness and
ignorance in a lot of the lyrics just repeats.
Because if they don't fit that formula, their records won't

Click, I looked at this in Episode 6.
But we're all from communities dealing with problems that
Government directives won't fix.

Now, if we're getting paid to say what we want,
That puts us in a strong position.
Because then we can pressure Parliament on anything we regard as
    an ill-informed or wrong decision.

A couple of weeks ago D Block Europe sold
Thirty thousand tickets in four hours. We've had
Number ones and Mercury-Award albums, and the
Money and the influence is all ours.
And we're only getting more powers.
So how hard would it be to form a political movement?
Word to the late Makavelli.
'Cause I feel like from time you got your face on the telly
You've laid that foundation already.

It wouldn't be hard to get the youth to believe.
The question is: What could this movement achieve?

And this is where my theory is relevant, remember:
The social needs of a community should inform its economic
    agenda.
I.e. if rappers wanna stay out the jailhouse and
Generate pay-outs and ways out
That's doable. And isn't that what half of us are doing music for?

When I think about it, it's almost *too* simple.

If we put our minds to building our people by
Economically and politically coming together,
When it comes to rehabilitation and social mobility
We'd outperform every government ever.

'Cause already you're talking about millions of people and a
Multi-billion-pound industry.
It's impossible for none of that power to translate to change on the
ground, in the street.

You wanna see what that change looks like? Come.

[Soundtrack: Wale 'Ambition' ft. Meek Mill and Rick Ross]

SCENE 5: GEORGE'S AMBITION

**[George unlocks and opens a door along The Corridor. The door is a
gateway into George's imagination]**

Let's start with education.
First things first, love to all the teachers putting in work with heart
    and dedication.
You guys are the mothers and fathers of the nation, you know?

I think language is one of your biggest challenges;
The kids have to get you and you have to understand the kids.
Some of you are blessed with the tools and the
space and the circumstances to manage this.

Some of you are overstretched with no protection.
Stuck in a career where you fear there's no progression.
Struggling to control the lesson, unable to
Take the curriculum in your own direction.
Feeling trapped in a failed system.
But what if it *felt* different?

Imagine if school was an experience
That everyone *wanted* to be part of.
If learning was as natural as laughter . . .
Imagine what that could be the start of.

Have you noticed my rhymes are just number patterns?
Or how I keep writing about slumber patterns?
How much English, Maths and Science have you subconsciously
    absorbed by listening to this episode?
There might be something in this, man. You never know . . .

Kenny Mpanga: *Differentiation is used to measure the rate of change for 1 variable, with respect to another. We can call these 2 variables X and Y. The gradient is the slope of a line calculated by finding the change in Y over the change in X.*

Let's imagine a graph where X represents time – starting at O before George released an episode, and ending with the release of Chapter 2 – and Y representing the audience's understanding of George's work.

When the BBC came through with their billboards, that gradient got much steeper. Not only was people's understanding of the podcast growing, the speed of people's understanding was also growing.

In Episode 11, when George got lost in Writer's Block, there was a lot of metaphors, and the audience's understanding probably hit a roadblock, too. In this case, DY/DX=O. And the graph would show a straight horizontal line . . .

George: I've been reading a book called *Why Nations Fail.*
My dad chose this one 'cause he knows his son.
It looks at rich countries and why they prevail, and
What the brokest ones need to overcome.
It all boils down to how we treat each other.
The richest nations established systems that
Recognise citizens need each other.
They call these systems 'inclusive institutions':
Structures that allow the masses to get involved with
Political and economic movements and solutions.
Remember the phrase: *inclusive institutions.*

Take a Parliament, for the sake of argument –
A group of people representing different interests to
Hold a government accountable in the form of
Votes, as a way of bargaining.

In theory, Parliament includes the masses in the
National decision-making process.
Ironically, I'm saying this in the midst of a
massive decision which arguably isn't making progress.

Now hear what I'm saying:
If these decisions drive change, every now and
Then you're gonna get a political puncture.
In *Why Nations Fail* they describe this kind of
Thing as a 'critical juncture'.

A turning point in a country's direction and it happens to the best
    of them.
It affects the things the people feel invested in,
Accelerates their development or makes them irrelevant.

So, what do we make of Brexit then?
Other than our best attempt to predict the next event.
'Cause here we are. America's backing out of Syria
And somewhere in the area, someone's interpretation of Sharia is
    breeding the next potential Isis.
And we're just stuck in this Brexistential crisis.

But I digress.

In a lot of poor countries, there are no inclusive institutions.
And as a result, power has limited routes of distribution.
It stays within small groups that use collusion to extract the wealth
    produced by bigger groups and maintain the top position by
    suppressing opposition.
They even view technological improvements as a nuisance.
Because they don't like change.

In the book, these are called *extractive* systems. And I've got a
Theory here, if you'll humour me.
Extraction doesn't just happen in poor countries; it
Happens everywhere; I see it in my community.

Cam'ron's a famous rapper. Pink's his thing.
He decides that pink is in.
That idea is his intellectual property.
And he's influential, obviously.

So using his thoughts and gift and passion, he's
Caused a shift in fashion.
And that's led to all sorts of different actions.
Stores start stocking pink; debates are sparked and people stop
    and think.

Now what percentage of these activities
Feeds back to the streets?
You might not think it's that important, but ac-
Cording to the reporting of Calum Gordon,
'Cam'ron predicted the future'.
Pop culture since drifted towards hubristic humour.
So what's the reward for the quickest mover?
Pink wasn't the most obvious thing to move towards, and he didn't
    foresee the impact it would have,
As he later confessed, in an interview with *Forbes*.

What if I told you this happens every year? And the
Presence of young, Black, working-class urban art
Can be felt everywhere?

But let's be clear: business is gonna do what it does –
Capitalise on a buzz.
But don't you think our economic institutions should recognise the
    value generated because of us?

EPISODE 15: Who Am I?

Extra Info:

- Episode 15 offers a timeline of my life that picks up from Episode 13, 'A North West Story'. I described my childhood in Episode 13, but here I focus on my teens.
- This was the first episode that allowed me to talk about Jamaican Dancehall music. Dancehall has been one of my favourite genres since my teens, and anyone who knows me would find it surprising that I didn't mention it until fifteen episodes into this podcast. I discuss the whole genre a lot more in Chapter Three.

Fun Facts:

- The nickname 'Busy Signal' has stuck with me all these years. There are people in Harlesden who didn't know me by any other name until I became famous. The name comes from one of Dancehall's most successful artists, the original Busy Signal, who still makes international hits today.
- Grime and Dancehall dominated my life around the same time. During this period, I lost interest in American music. It felt like Black Britain was invisible to Black America, but Grime and Dancehall were directly connected to our lives.

This episode continues the autobiographical element of the podcast. The title, 'Who Am I?', is another double-entendre, referring to the Beenie Man song that introduced me to Dancehall culture, as well as my multifaceted upbringing. In many ways, it was a relief to finally explain the different worlds I was jumping in and out of. London society can be segregated, in the sense that council housing (or 'public' housing) was often allocated along racial lines. So Black people like me, who grew up on predominantly Black estates, didn't have much involvement with other communities unless we created those opportunities ourselves. As explained in this episode, my secondary school exposed me to these other communities. I received an unofficial education just by being around these guys and gaining insight into their way of life. That was balanced against the education I got in the streets of Harlesden. All of it is in me.

SCENE 1: RECAP OF CHAPTER TWO

[George is back in The Corridor]

George: Once again, you find me reflecting on my success –
Something we all like to do.
And once again, I'm gonna be . . . blunt . . .
If that's alright with you.

All I wanna do is perform and write for you
But I might have bitten off more than I can chew.
Spending every day and every night in studio
With Benbrick, recording like we do.
So far, we've given you six more episodes, that's
Just under three hours.
In the music industry that's like three albums.
And in this chapter, we've got about two hours left.
Now, you gotta keep a steady pace in any race
If you don't wanna run out of breath.
So before I dive into this episode
I need to make sure I'm not out my depth.

Episode 9 was about the commodification of Black trauma.
I used it to explain Reagan's neoliberalism
And how people suffered from his decisions.
I needed this to be the starting point because it's
Relevant in ways we can't avoid.
See when it comes to stories they're expected to tell, our
young people often feel they lack choices.
So, throughout this podcast I've offered
Different ways of presenting Black voices.

In Episode 10 I did the romance thing, to
Show intimacy on a grown man ting,
'Cause the depiction of relationships in our music can sometimes
be a bit cartoonish.

There's a lot of focus on sex and melodrama,
Never just a young Barack and Michelle Obama.
I don't write about relationships much but when I
Do I'm the worst offender.
There's always disappointment or a burst of temper,
But that doesn't fully reflect my own experience
And it definitely doesn't reflect my work's agenda.
I also included a bit of fantasy because I
Want young writers to think expansively.
When I was 15 years old writing bars,
It never occurred to me to talk about flying cars.
I learned from the olders who focused on certain
Aspects of this life of ours. But it
Does get repetitive. And it's always a bit self-absorbed and
     negative.
Which you could say about this podcast, to be fair
So yeah, I guess it's all relative.

That's the energy I came to Episode 11 with;
Using fantasy to reframe the narrative.
I'm holding up a mirror to the way the mandem live.
Writer's Block. That's how it is in the hood:
You peak young and your life just stops.
Not like you die, but your dreams do.
Seems food is the only thing that feeds you.
And I wanted to share some of my dreams, too.
To remind my listeners that I need you.
I want you to know what results I'm looking for
Because your support is the ultimate reward.

Speaking of rewards . . .

I feel like poetry won't stretch me mentally
If I don't stretch my own self.
At worst no one cares, at best it goes well.
And that's how I approached Episode 12.

I'm trying to influence the next generation of
writers.
Especially ones from areas like mine,
With a reputation for violence.
I want them to know they can own any subject
Matter. 'Cause so many subjects matter.
From neuroscience to immigrant displacement.
That's why it sounds like a mini-dissertation.

On Episode 13 I lost my nerve,
Spoke to you in a way you do not deserve and I'm sorry.
Sometimes I look at my work and think to myself 'what's it
    worth?'
I guess I got worried . . .
That you might not like my characters.
And that made me angry 'cause . . . what's it called . . .
I made them as multidimensional as possible.
But that reaction's illogical 'cause of
Course, you're entitled to like or dislike what you
Like or dislike. And I have the right to record insights from my life
    on this mic . . .
However I like.

Side note: I really do give a shit what the BBC think
That was just a tongue-in-cheek thing.
I don't want the younger Gs under me thinking you can
Run your mouth in business like how man run the streets.

Speaking of the streets, as a teenager my
Love for the hood came at a cost, but I believe in
Keeping the receipts. Remembering the stories of the
People that I meet – it matters, b. It's
Why I'm in a position to unpack the beef. And the
Beef in my ends has its own category, I mean
Vendettas between whole families. I'm
Watching it becoming intergenerational

Asking God 'What's all the devastation for?'
But obviously . . . when it comes to *us*
God's busy.

So, in Episode 13 you heard me dealing
with my hurt feelings.
By 13 some of my friends weren't speaking.
I wish the Ends weren't beefing.
We deserve healing.

So, in 5 episodes I've gone back and forth between
Fact and fantasy-fiction.
Had a lot of issues on my mind and I didn't wanna
Give them the standard depiction. Now in
14 we got to the heart of the tension.
Both techniques got half the attention. On
One hand I don't wanna overcomplicate but
Then again I have no regard for convention, which is
Why I'm standing here like a prime minister with a
Deadline who can't think past an election.
Every voice in my head is asking the question:

Who is this for?

Who exactly am I doing this for?
Where can I count on the truest support?
Is it for the street kids? Is it for the teachers?
Is it for my followers? Is it for the leaders?

I feel like the biggest criticism of this chapter will
Be that people found it too confusing.
Does he want a show or a student movement?
Episode 8 was too much, this ain't a huge improvement.

I think I gotta press reset.
I think that's the only way to trace every step.

I gotta take you back to North West 10:
St Raph's, Stonebridge, Church Road, Roundwood.

Yeah man, gotta take you back to my childhood.

SCENE 2: BACK TO RAPH'S

[George unlocks a door and enters a memory of his old neighbourhood, St Raphael's Estate]

All I remember is kids on every estate ready to make new friends,
Kick ball and learn new tricks.
Oh, and music. We loved music.

[Soundtrack: Beenie Man 'Who Am I/Sim Simma']

George: My bredrin, Clifton, was a few years older than me.
His sister, V, was cool and his big bro was a g.
Long before I discovered the gift of wordplay I was
Left speechless one time at Clifton's birthday.
His big bro was playing songs that had a certain swagger.
The name of this genre, I later learned was Ragga.

SCENE 3: CLIFTON'S PARTY

[George walks through a lively house party]

George: I had no idea what this man was saying but I
Knew what it meant.
This was music for the *shottas* dem. And I was
Way out of my depth, let me not pretend. You gotta
Remember, the Ends was Jamaican yana.
So, I can try and play along but I'm just making it up.

Even post immigration, most the Jamaicans I
Know in this nation lived close in relation to the
Ugandans in Ends, who I would
only really see at random events.

Everything was ragga: ragga ladies, ragga men,
Buju Banton, Bounty Killer, Beenie Man, Spragga Benz,
The older mandem were getting money, setting a bag of trends
North West 10 had a name as the dapper ends.

SCENE 4: WHO IS GEORGE?

[George's surroundings suddenly change. He stands alone in a desert]

George: You know the name of that song?
'Who Am I?'
Good question.
On one level, I'm a St Raph's yout alie?
On another level I'm straight Ugandan
Raised on an estate full of Jamaican mandem.

See, from the start, my identity was multi-layered
And that influenced the persona I cultivated.
Look at me now . . . bald yout with the gold tooth.
I look like them old dudes.

And what I couldn't have known at the time was
Them man there had problems on the roads 'cause of crime.
Some people literally lived in terror.
I wish I could tell you this was a different era . . .

Here's an article from the *Guardian* about the
Whole 'Yardie' thing.

Guardian News Article: *Already this year, there have been thirteen murders in the capital linked to Yardie warfare. In North West London alone there have been more than thirty shootings. Across the city, the murder toll halfway through 1999, is rapidly approaching the norm for an entire year, as rival factions between Brixton, South London, and Harlesden fight for control of the lucrative trade in crack cocaine.*

George: That article was twenty years ago to the day
I don't know what to say.
Them man there sold so much crack.
And when it came to war, they didn't hold much back.

So, who am I?
Some days it's an unknown.
All I'm saying is, this was my home.

SCENE 5: DIGGY SPEAKS

[Recording of St Raph's legend, Diggy Ustle. Diggy was the man behind North West London's biggest anthem, 'North Weezee']

Diggy: *Raph's blud, old school. Henderson Close bruv. You get me. Them old school house parties – what days was that? Man could take you back to Raph's when people were standing on – you know the roofs? Remember Kriss Kross blud? Don't know if you know – 'Jump! Jump!' – I remember going 'round Raph's and people was on top of them, jeans back to front. 'Jump! Jump!' I was like 'Yo this place is crazy', jumping you get me?*

Tubby T was just singing. You could hear him singing from his window, you understand? That's our meds in Raph's, that's why it was like a . . . a musical place becah . . . you know what I'm tryna say? Even though Tubby's global, he was in Raph's, his mum was in Raph's. His mum worked in McVitie's blud, it was serious. You could smell McVitie's in Harlesden.

That's the time when man heard ragga and that. In Raph's blud, old school. Playing live Beenie Man versus Bounty. Raph's got bare talent man, it's a musical place still. I'm not gonna lie, when I check the levels . . .

SCENE 6: BACK IN GRAMMAR SCHOOL

[George unlocks the door to another memory – his secondary school days]

George: Meanwhile, back in grammar school
Man was cool apart from the fact I was in bottom set for everything.
Alright, maybe not everything, let me think . . .

In English I was in set seven out of eight.
I had these middle-class kids asking me to confirm or deny what
    they'd read about estates.
For years we saw each other seven hours a day,
But we went home to different realities as
Soon as we were stepping out the gate.

Anyway, like I said, man was cool.
And 'cool' is relative, remember this is a grammar school.
There's no chance of anybody mugging me off.
But you know guys, no one wants to be soft.
Some of these middle-class kids started acting like bad boys.
From the start my stance was 'that's moist.'
And if you don't know, moist means weak.
It's an example of the kind of slang *we'd* speak.
These neeks started using these kinds of words to
Tease guys and worse which we'd find absurd 'cause
These guys were nerds.
They were hardly on that; they weren't even partly from that.
I doubt they even had any third-party contact.
But we're like thirteen at the time,

So, before you judge them, keep that in mind.
Puberty's confusing, b.

Truthfully, they wanted to compete with the Black kids.
They saw us as street. And people find street thing attractive.
Every week I came back with stories that
Made the ends sound like a garrison,
And by comparison *their* community wasn't active.

I'm thinking 'You lot wanna walk in *my* shoes.
But if I could choose between my community's fruitless pursuit of
    peace
And living like yous . . . I know which one I'd choose.'
Especially since, 'cause of going to this school,
I was introduced to the lives of Jews.
And Indians and Chinese youts.
In the Ends we didn't operate like these groups.
They were immigrants like most of the guys we knew,
But it was puzzling: they were hustling, but not struggling.
They were gifted at it; their communities were systematic.
They had a shared understanding and purpose, blud the
Jews had their own ambulance service!
The Indians bought properties together and apparently,
They shared their money and did it family by family.
That's how they filled up a whole street, gradually.
Try that in the Ends and the money's going missing, guaranteed.

[George laughs]

George: In my whole year, there were nine Blacks.
People used to come to us to talk about the crime stats.

Or they would talk about what I was wearing like
'Yes, George. Where can I find that?'
They loved to run jokes on everyone's racial groups
But for me, the laughter couldn't mask the painful truth.

This is around the time Dipset released their first album: *Diplomatic Immunity*.

[Soundtrack: Dipset 'I Really Mean It']

These kids wanted to tap into the fashion usually but
They didn't take Black people seriously clearly 'cause
We were known for acting stupidly and clashing brutally.
They didn't even *know* about the beef in my Ends,
Yet they could still . . . from the outside . . .
Sense the lack of unity across the Black community.

Their parents used to tell them Black people can't be trusted.
And 'cause of the violence in the Ends,
I couldn't pretend to be disgusted.
It's a sign of our friendship, the extent to which we discussed it.
And looking back, that allowed our lens to be incrementally adjusted.

I felt like Donald Glover. Like Dave Chappelle.
Like every Black kid that's entered the middle class and
Realised either the world is gonna change
You or you're gonna have to change the world.

[Recording of Donald Glover winning an Emmy for Outstanding Director for a Comedy Series]

George: Of course, there was a third option.
Why sign up for a life of taking Ls when
You could just . . . try to save yourself?
Study and grow, make your money and go.
You feel like you're in debt to the set, but you aren't.
So do what you can, and forget what you can't.

Personally, even at thirteen I knew that wouldn't work for me.
Yeah, I was caught between two worlds,
But living in limbo suited me perfectly.

I couldn't take too much of either,
And I didn't wanna make do with neither.
Had my eyes on the prize and I planned to stay.
Which is why I am the way I am today.

SCENE 7: GEORGE'S MID-TEENS

[George enters a new room]

George: By the middle of my teens, I was still tryna figure out my
    dreams.
My childhood plan of being a leader and an artist on the side . . .
Slowly started to subside.

Who am I?

My hood friends were getting a different education
And I could tell they were hardening inside.

[George enters a new room]

George: Having a big brother in a local school
Turned out to be the perfect social tool.
His stories showed me what my friends were going through in
Their local schools, which helped me know the rules.

Helped me understand opportunity wasn't equal.
I understood why they were shotting and robbing people.
It wasn't because they're evil, or 'cause they wanted a
Quick demise. They just didn't wanna be victimised.

Badness was a defence mechanism.
Most the olders in the Ends went to prison.
And when they came home they were famous, on road they had status,
And all the kids would know what their name was.

I loved the hood, but I didn't like that.
I hated that my people were living like that.

I wanted status too, but I didn't wanna take this route.
So, my focus shifted to making money –
I had a brain and no one could take it from me.

SCENE 8: GEORGE'S HUSTLE

[Cut to a flashback of George as a teen in the barbershop]

George: One day I was getting a haircut when these
Crack addicts walked in with stolen goods.
They were selling and people were buying.
That's when I noticed the cash economy controls the hood.

So before long I'd save my lunch money and
Start to buy clothes on Harlesden High Road,
Then sell them at a profit in my school to these middle-class
Kids who wanted to dress like me.
It was a win-win 'cause they wanted to look cool,
And profiting off this stock in in the ends was less likely.

And even though it was a low profit margin
I liked the fact that I chose what to charge them.

[George enters a new room]

For the first time I found my own hustle –
Came with no hassle, needed no muscle.
That was the start of an important era
When I went by a different name altogether.

SCENE 9: GEORGE BECOMES BUSY

[Soundtrack: Busy Signal 'Step Out']

George: Think about it. I was always active,
Always on the phone and always with gyal.
What else were they gonna call me, other than . . .

Barber: Busy Signal! Wagwan.

Younger George: Wagwan.

Conroy: *The reason why I call you Busy still you know blud . . . remember I was your barber yana . . . and you used to be in and out quick blud. You never, like, used to wait on the haircut and them thing there innit. You like to come in and out blud. That's the reason why I give you the name Busy still.*

George: Like I said before, it was dangerous for me to
Be in the estate next door to mine –
Too many foul-tempered residents.
Hence the town centre's relevance.
It wasn't safe past the borderline,
So I ended up in Harlesden all the time.

[Cut to a Harlesden food shop]

All my mukwanos were older twentysomethings
Raised in Jamaica that came for the paper.
Women used to come for entertainment and flavour.
At the time I was fifteen yana.
I needed certain things to start speeding up.

See, here's something I never learned in school; I
Learnt it from my North West bredrins.
In life, a common source of tension is the

Disconnect. Between your economic reality
And your intention.

I told you I saved up my lunch money. At
Fifteen I couldn't get national insurance.
But sitting in class with an empty stomach.
Affects your actual performance.
I was losing weight.
I was hungry in ways that I could not communicate.
And that's not on my parents 'cause they always gave me
        subsistence.
But as you can see from this podcast,
My ambitions have crazy persistence. Who am I?

The skinny kid running up and down these Harlesden streets
Doing his coursework in an empty barber's seat?
The GCSE candidate, finessing the subject
When really, he was barely understanding it.

The hustler? Yeah man . . . Busy the hustler . . .
With a bag full of stock and a bus pass.

One thought in my mind was clear:
I need to find my own pattern.
And the pattern has to represent change.
Otherwise, it won't happen.

Now, how does a good kid in a mad city
Rise to the top of a gangsta nation?
It could only be a conscious transformation.

My big brother went to a local school.
In my ends people say a local *skewl*.
There's a certain accent, a certain culture.
And that's where he picked up them old school tunes.

This started when I was in Year 5.
But by the time I made it to Year 9,
My life was full of bare Grime.

SCENE 10: GEORGE BECOMES A GRIME KID

[Soundtrack: Roll Deep 'When I'm 'Ere']

DJ Target: *The only reason we made Grime was because nobody listened to us, nobody cared, and nobody had any time for what we were doing, and we had no choice but to create pirate radio stations and press up our own records and just have this own little infra-structure that we were happy in . . .*

George: East London beats thumping had the streets jumping . . .
All from the mind of a guy called Richard.
I don't know if you believe in witches,
But Richard was at least a wizard.
He was a musical magician, to be specific.

Know what he did?

He turned all that pressure into a sound and if you
Spoke that language it would spin you around.
Using computers and street poetry,
He found a way to sow a seed and grow a tree. A
Money tree that he could bring youts around.
I was one of them youts, so this was my new neutral ground.

We didn't have many social spaces,
At least not on a local basis.
That's why chilling at the barbers made sense to me
But Grime helped me developmentally.

First of all it helped me develop *mentally*,
'Cause essentially it's rhythmic speech.

Couple man, minimum 8 bars of lyrics each.
I learnt things GCSE English didn't teach.
Before long I'd written a full song.
Moved from 16s to 32s to 64s, don.

You see that level of brain activity?
In most classes I couldn't sustain that typically.
By exam season, my life was literally
Revising history, spit to beats, hit the
Streets with a brand-new unique flow then I'm
Juggin with Nathan and Damini for studio. I was a
Grime kid. Klash was bragging 'bout what his line did
Only kind of line that ever got me excited
Was the kind I could rhyme with.

Or the bassline, never too loud for my ears.
Them days I was always out and about with my peers.
The maddest lessons of adolescence, the doubts, and the fears . . .
Who am I? The answer's in the Shawalin years.

EPISODE 16: Loose Ends

Extra Info:
- Episode 16 follows on from Episode 12, 'A Night to REMember', when Busy loses control of George's Mind. This symbolises my plans for Chapter Two going left, which they almost did. The episode takes place in the last few minutes of my sleep, but in the world of dreams, a few minutes can feel a lot longer.
- I took a gamble with this episode. With not much time left, I decided to use the same technique from Episodes 8 and 10 – write about my complex thought process. I knew it might be too confusing for some listeners, but for those who got it, the reward would be immense.

Fun Facts:
- In Scene 9, OG Idea shows Younger Idea his fourteen new ideas, before Younger Idea attacks and robs him. This was inspired by a legendary scene in the classic movie, *Paid in Full*. Before Rico treacherously shoots his own friend and partner, Mitch, he confirms that Mitch is in possession of 'fourteen bricks'.

In this episode, I returned to the TV production approach. Story-wise, it picks up from Episode 11, in which the George of the future lives out my current dreams, but also experiences turmoil in his marriage. I wanted to show my listeners the dark side of dreams; the fear of what we can't control . . . the losses that come with the wins. At the same time, I used Episode 16 to explore the dark side of ambition. In reality, I was mentally exhausted by the time I wrote it. I had this big plan to tell these stories and the deadline was getting closer and closer. Still, I forced myself to find my best ideas and throw them all into these last episodes of the chapter. But I had learned from writing Sanyu episodes that this internal thought process was the actual story I should be telling. So I wrote about a war breaking out in my mind, with my insecurities challenging my ambitions for control of my decisions. Would I stick with the original plan? Or was it time to let go of those complicated ideas? This war in my mind takes place at the same time as a dream in which my future self loses control of his professional and personal life. The episode is called 'Loose Ends' because it's all about my fear of leaving things unfinished. I guess the message is that perseverance always wins. As hard as it was to write Episode 16, it was extremely rewarding once I reached the end. I found a way to relate it back to the streets, via a scene in which a young idea attacks an older idea and steals his new ideas, all for a chance of escaping my overcrowded mind. I hope it's clear how this behaviour plays out in any environment where there isn't enough opportunity. Special shouts out to the amazing voice actors on there, whose incredible work really lifted my spirits that week.

SCENE 1: GEORGE AND DANIELLE MEET IN SECRET

[This episode continues the story of Episodes 10, 11, 12 and 14, set in the dream world of George's Mind during sleep hours. The opening scene picks up a storyline from Episode 11, 'Writer's Block'. It takes place ten years into the future, when George finds himself in a scandal with a former acquaintance, Danielle. George suspects that Danielle is working with someone who wants to ruin him. Danielle admits that she held onto a damaging recording of George for years, as 'insurance', but she claims that someone else leaked it]

[A woman enters a quiet restaurant and takes a seat in front of George]

George: Say what you came here to say.

Danielle: OK. Hello.
And no, I didn't leak the video.

George: But you did keep a secret video.
For twenty years.
Are we just gonna act like that's not weird?

Danielle: In all honesty, that video was an insurance policy.
You were very young when we met.
It was clear you were going places and I just—

George: And you just wanted the comfort of knowing you could
   extort me . . .
Some day.

Danielle: Only if I had to.
Anyway, the plan backfired.
Someone else got there first.

Come on, George if it was me I would have just—

George: I know it wasn't you. But you need to tell me who it was.

Danielle: I don't know!

George: Try again.

Danielle: I saw your press conference.
So you, so arrogant.
Like you're just bored of all the embarrassment.
I thought you handled it distastefully.
Should've just apologised graciously.
But oh no, the mighty George only shows remorse to his wife . . .
Who's only gone and walked out his life.

George: Danielle, this ain't back in the day.
My enemies don't play.
If they see you as a loose end
They will come for your family.

Danielle: Well. Sounds like you've got a lot on your plate.
Good luck with that, mate.

[Danielle leaves]

OG: Better the devil you know, Dani. Better the devil you know.

[Danielle exits]

SCENE 2: THE INSECURITY GUARDS BREAK AWAY

[This scene continues a storyline from Episode 14, 'A Hard Taskmaster'. George's insecurities (characterised as the Insecurity Guards/IGs) reveal that the previous scene was a dream created by one of them. The IGs want a bigger role in Chapter Two of the podcast, so they are increasing their influence on George's Mind by feeding

into his nightmares. Up to Episode 12, 'A Night to REMember', the IGs worked for Busy, head of the Ambition Commission (AC). Busy used George's insecurities to control George's focus. In Episode 8, 'Sanyu's World', the IGs almost killed a popular young idea because she challenged Busy's plans. In Episode 14, the IGs stopped following Busy's orders and decided to do their own thing]

[IGs walking through George's Mind after successfully executing the previous dream]

IG 1: Bro, that was the coldest dream in Chapter 2.
Busy can't chat to you.

IG 2: That's the truth. But don't get it twisted.
With that Uganda scene in Episode 12 you smacked it too.

IG 1: Yo, break it down to me, my brudda.
What, you went back to George's future?

IG 2: One second, my brudda, let me call this Uber.

[IG 2 whistles and the ground begins to shake]

IG 2: Stand back, bro.

IG 1: Cuz, what's going on?

IG 2: Brudda, stand back.

[A flying animal appears in the sky, heading towards the IGs. It looks part-horse and part-eagle. The IGs get excited. The animal lands]

IG 1: Oh snap!!!

IG 2: Bro, you're looking at your new storyline.
Stick with that and you'll be fine.

IG 1: Brudda . . . this my story? Oi, this one's naughty!
What you saying? Horsepower?

IG 2: Horsepower, my guy.
I've found the perfect pattern;
One dream alone ain't worth attacking.
You gotta think like Busy.
You gotta think big.
Let's take over the chapter finale.

IG 1: What you saying invite ourselves back to the party?

IG 2: Bro. We've been sitting down for four episodes.

IG 1: Mmm really we should have patterned all ten of those.

IG 2: Alie? And since the finish line is getting close . . .

IG 1: Yeah, we need to get results.

IG 2: Innit. So all we gotta do . . .
Is regulate Busy's weak ideas.

IG 1: Yeah, yeah, yeah, yeah, that's the move.
We can't let them make it to Chapter Two.
No one's gonna rate George if they do bro, they have to lose.

IG 2: Yo, I'm looking to slide on them right now.

IG 1: Bro you ain't gotta do it yourself.
You just gotta gas the youts.

[IG 2 hums in agreement]

IG 1: What you saying though, we both got to ride on the back?

IG 2: Nah, come on cuz I got my one and that!

[IG 2 whistles again and summons another flying animal]

[Soundtrack Vybz Kartel 'Empire Army']

SCENE 3: THE INSECURITY GUARDS RECRUIT FORGOTTEN IDEAS

[The IGs are flying through George's Mind looking for young, neglected ideas to join their new movement, 'Horsepower'. As Sanyu explained in Episode 8, 'Sanyu's World', ideas die when they are Forgotten. Therefore, when ideas don't get enough attention, they become desperate and hostile towards each other. Because George is busier than ever, George's Mind is currently experiencing an attention deficit. This means that most ideas are struggling for his time, and are in danger of being forgotten. The IGs want to recruit these ideas and use them to take over the remaining podcast episodes]

[The IGs are flying through George's Mind because their role in Chapter Two of the podcast is accelerating]

IG 1: Woooo!

IG 2: This is mad!

IG 1: Yo this storyline is popping! Where we going first, bro?

IG 2: Hear what I'm saying . . .
We gotta go Writer's Block.
Gotta find all the hungry little ideas this guy forgot.

IG 1: Horsepower!

IG 2: Horsepower!

[The IGs land on Writer's Block and talk to an excited group of young ideas]

IG 1: Hear what I'm saying.
Three hours of Chapter Two have gone past,
And you lot ain't made one appearance on the podcast.

IG 2: We're gonna take it by force in the fourth hour.
AC's done out here. This is Horsepower.

IG 1: Horsepower!

[Young ideas are impressed]

IG 2: G comes to Writers Block when he's
Lost and you're the ideas that give him food for thought.

IG 1: But who's giving *you* support?

[Young ideas agreeing]

Young Idea 1: It's true you know.
True I got a two-year-old, but they got me out here doing road
    like
Why's G only working Sanyu when he's in the studio?
Mandem need to eat too, you know.

IG 1: Blame it on the Ambition Commission.

IG 2: See, Busy picks weak ideas.
Us man come from a different tradition.

Young Idea 1: You're telling me.

[As the IGs energise George's ideas, a Brainstorm develops]

IG 1: Don't just say it for me, say it for yourself.
Are you gonna find a way out of G's brain or not?

IG 2: 'Cause if you are you can't let no weak ideas come and claim
your spot.

IG 1: Oi listen, Busy sits in that Ambition Commission,
Deciding which ideas make it to the podcast
And your name hasn't come up yet?

IG 2: Disrespect.

IG 1: You have a right to be upset.

IG 2: You know what?
All of us have the same dream. So hear what I'm saying

IG 1: We're taking over Episode 16 . . .

IG 2: Episode 17 . . .

IG 1: And Episode 18!

[Ideas cheer for IGs and follow them into battle]

SCENE 4: BUSY FEELS THE PRESSURE

[Back at the Ambition Commission Headquarters (ACHQ), Busy is being briefed in his office. As explained on Episode 12, 'A Night to REMember', George will be awake in under five minutes. Although time is stretched in the dream world of George's Mind, this still puts Busy under pressure. With so much going on, Busy hasn't noticed that the Intern and Analyst that he sent to delay George waking up

(in Episode 12) still haven't returned. He is also unaware that the Insecurity Guards are leading a rebellion against him]

Stash: . . . also, melatonin is down seventy percent.

Busy: Seventy percent?
We need someone to block the Thalamus, man.

Stash: You already sent someone for that.

Busy: So, what happened to whoever we just sent?
About seventy percent.

Stash: Sir, there's been some confusion regarding your instructions.
Some departments can't perform their functions.
Even if we could reach the Thalamus, it wouldn't matter 'cause
Other problems would un-pattern us.

Busy: Problems like what?

Stash: Well, sir the reason melatonin is decreasing is the
Pineal gland stopped secreting it.
And that's 'cause of messages it was receiving from the
Suprachiasmatic nucleus . . .

Busy: [Exhausted] So what you mean is
Sunlight is already passing through George's closed eyelids . . .
But you know we can't be slowed by this.

Stash: Sir, there's more.
There has been detection of orexin on the brain stem,
Which connects the power stations and activates them.
George is gonna wake up sooner than later.
Members of staff are becoming concerned that for the
Chapter Two finale nothing's confirmed.

Busy: Leave that to me.

Stash: Sir, I heard what happened with Alexa.
You must be under mad pressure.
But if you ever wanna—

Busy: What's next up on the agenda?

Stash: The next item on the agenda—

Busy: And furthermore, where are the Guards?

Stash: Sir, that's the next agenda item. The ins— The Guards are engaging the youth about staging a coup.

[Busy groans]

Stash: They say George's Mind is struggling under your leadership
    of AC
And they're gonna take it from you.

Busy: [Vexed] How is that not the first thing you told me?! Show me!

Stash: Sorry, sir. I thought biology took priority over psychology . . .

Busy: Show me!!

Stash: [Typing on a tablet] Yes, sir.
They're recruiting ideas off Writer's Block,
'Cause they tend to get forgotten quite a lot.
They're born at a time when George's Mind is cold
And they get no attention when George's Mind is hot.

Busy: How did the guards even get to Writer's Block?
I swear I sent them to the Amygdala.
Weren't they supposed to be sending a stress signal up?

Stash: Sir, this is how they did it:

[Stash shows Busy footage of the IGs flying through George's Mind]

Busy: They made their own storylines.

Stash: Sir, ever since Sanyu escaped from R&D in Episode 6
A lot of ideas have tried this, as a way of getting noticed.

George's Mind is overcrowded, sir.
Most ideas don't see any progress.
So instead of waiting for the Ambition Commission to give written
   permission . . .
They see Sanyu's way as a better process.

Busy: Mmm. Sanyu's way . . .

[Soundtrack: J Hus 'Must Be']

Busy: I'm coming back yeah.

[Busy gets up and starts to leave]

Stash: But sir we haven't finished—

Busy: You heard what I said, man.

SCENE 5: BACK TO GEORGE'S DREAM

**[Returning to the storyline of Scene 1, George continues to manage
the fallout of his explicit video with adult performer, Danielle (aka
Dani Daredevil). This story extends from Episode 11, 'Writer's
Block', which projects ten years into George's future as a social
entrepreneur. The Dani Daredevil scandal hits George at the height
of his success, sending shockwaves throughout his businesses and**

undermining his political ambitions. Scene 5 begins with George arriving at his office building surrounded by reporters. A meeting with his team reveals George's suspicions that someone within his company is leaking information]

Reporter 1: Is it true that you're in a relationship with Dani Daredevil?

Reporter 2: George, do you have any comment on the pictures that have emerged from your secretive meetup with Dani Daredevil?

George: No comment.

[George enters the building]

Receptionists: Good morning, Mr Mpanga.

George: Good morning, guys.

[George catches the lift, where a TV is playing a news report covering his scandal]

Sir Martyn Lewis: [From TV] *New details have emerged about the alleged relationship between spoken word artist, George The Poet, and adult performer, Dani Daredevil.*

Danielle: [From TV] *I respect George and Khadija. Whatever we had wasn't on their level.*

[Cut to George in a team meeting]

Team Member 1: G, everyone's talking. They're connecting your name with the porn thing.

Team Member 2: George, this is the last thing we need before the elections
Already it's affecting next quarter's projections.

Team Member 3: Our female support base has taken hits.
They place a lot of importance on your relationships.

Team Member 4: But support among young men continues to go through the roof.
In fact, that's been the case with most of the youth.

George: Alright, OK, listen. This is not the time for showing weakness.
Someone close to me is exposing secrets.
I did meet with Danielle, and as you all know I've got history with that girl.
But I made sure the restaurant only had people who could be traced back to this room. See, I had a feeling in my chest that someone would leak it to the press.
So, I have to assume one of you lot knows who leaked this.
[Return to reporters]

Reporter 3: George, are you concerned about the impact this will have on GSP activities?

Reporter 4: A poet and a porn-star front page news, George.
Sounds good doesn't it, mate?

Sir Martyn Lewis: With the Poet's businesses issuing woeful projections, the news also comes as a blow to George's Search Party in the upcoming local elections.

[Cut back to George's team meeting. They are all arguing]

Team Member 1: . . . I think you're bluffing. You ain't got nothing.

George: We'll see.

Team Member 2: George as much as you want to control the discussion,

This is on you. That video is disgusting.

George: Listen, as far as I'm concerned, everyone in this room's a
snake.
Whatever deal you made was a huge mistake.
We had an agreement. Everyone got to eat, and—

Team Member 3: Oh, look now he's gonna tell us how to be Black
properly.

[Members continue arguing among themselves]

George's friend: Bro, you got some powerful enemies.
Government, media, police.
Mandem that don't want you cleaning up the streets.
Not even gonna lie g. It could be anyone.

George's Critic: You see the thing about George Mpanga is a law
unto himself,
Unaccountable to anyone but himself and his
Small circle of friends, who seem to have made some new friends.
And for all his talk about the hood,
These frayed relationships leave him with – if you'll excuse the pun –
Loose ends. An unfinished, over-budget social housing project
And an election campaign in ruins.
I have no sympathy for George The Poet; this is all his own doing.

SCENE 6: DIJA'S OFFICE

**[In this dream, George is married to Dija (his girlfriend from Episode
10, 'A Bedtime Story'). The scandal weighs heavily on their marriage.
This scene finds Dija being interviewed about her husband's legal
troubles by police investigators at her workplace. Dija confidently
stands up for George in front of them, then privately becomes
consumed by anger towards him]**

Dija: [After an amicable conversation with the detectives]
Ladies, I'm sorry to disappoint.
But if you came for information about my husband's
Business dealings, you've missed the point.

At this firm our advisers offer support where Government can't
provide this.
Now, I've been compliant, I've been transparent,
And I've made my intentions apparent.
I'd like to clear the way for your investigation
To confirm what I already know: my husband is of upstanding
character.

And if he's not, then he shouldn't have married a barrister!

[Laughter]

Detective 1: Thank you for your time, Ms Simmons.

Dija: No, thank you.

Detective: Enjoy the rest of your day, Ms Simmons.

Dija: You too. Have a good day.

[Dija sits in silence and starts reflecting on her relationship. First, she recalls their wedding]

Dija: I, Khadija Jhené Simmons

George: Khadija Jhené Simmons . . . Will you marry me?
[Dija recalls asking George to be open with her about his past]

Dija: Babe, I have to ask . . . is there anything I should know?

George: Deej, you know everything, babe.

Dija: Yeah. But if there was . . . you would tell me, right?

George: Course.

[Dija recalls George's apology from Episode 11, 'Writer's Block']

George: I'm so sorry . . .

[Cut back to Dija's office. Her assistant knocks on her door]

Dija: Come in.

Dija's Assistant: Khadija, we've had a cancellation from Felicia.

Dija: Bye, Felicia.

Dija's Assistant: And you've got a note from Peter.
He said he was your sixth form teacher.

Dija: Oh.

[Dija's assistant picks up a bouquet from a nearby desk and carries it over to Dija's desk]

Dija's Assistant: Also, these arrived for you . . .

Dija: Oh wow. I used to love this colour. Put them on a windowsill, please.

Dija's Assistant: Khadija, all the windowsills are full . . . from the other flowers.

Dija: Oh. Er . . . could you pass them onto someone?

Dija's Assistant: I would, but Purple Hyacinths . . . such a specific meaning . . .

Dija: Such a specific meaning, you're right.
Put them in the bin.

[Soundtrack: Teyana Taylor 'No Manners']

Dija: The one with the brown lid.

Assistant: Maybe I'll just check if any local florists are interested first. It's just that they're so healthy—

Dija: Good thinking. Thanks, T.

SCENE 7: THE STRAIN

[The stress of the scandal takes its toll on George and Dija's marriage. Scene starts in the middle of Dija shouting at George]

Dija: Do we have to sit down and go through all your emails to find reminders and details about crazy things you've done with random females?

George: Babe I—

Dija: Don't. Touch me!

George: Khadija, this was before us!
It was just a moment on the tour bus.
How could I warn you about it if I didn't know she found a way to record us?

Dija: Of course, George has got a justification for everything George does.

George: What am I supposed to do, just leave you to assume the worst?

I'm tryna give you information—

Dija: Which you've only had the past ten years to do.
Cheers to you.
She's got kids, George. Argh.

[Montage of social media reactions to reports of tension in their
     high-profile marriage]

Vlogger 1: Oh my God you guys, Khadija is pissed over this video!
Apparently they were trying for a baby.
This must be driving her crazy!

[Dija addresses reporters outside their home]

Dija: As many of you know, my husband and I have
Had our marriage tested by recent events.
I see no need for pretence.
But this in no way affects my commitment to delivering affordable
     legal defence.
Still, beyond my profession, I would appreciate your respectful
     distance, in the broadest sense. Thank you.

SCENE 8: IDEAS GET DESPERATE

**[With the power struggle between Busy and the Insecurity Guards
in full swing, George's Mind has become an unpredictable place.
This tug-of-war between George's ambitions and his fears has left
many of his ideas feeling scared and confused. This scene opens
with two ideas, older and younger, reflecting on this harsh reality
during a Brainstorm]**

YG Idea: Yo my brudda, you got the time?

OG Idea: Coming up to seven still.

Younger Idea: Rah George's Mind don't ever chill.

OG Idea: Never will. Been on another level since he left the record deal.
What's a young idea like you doing out this time?

Younger Idea: I'm just tryna get out this mind.

OG Idea: Be careful. George's Mind is volatile.
Them Insecurity Guards are on the prowl.

Younger Idea: Yeah. They came to man's block. Talking about
Weak ideas claiming man's spot, but I didn't really
Know what they was on about.

OG Idea: Boy. This place has always been overcrowded. But
It's a real problem now.
What you up for this early?

Younger Idea: What? You call this early?
I'm tryna catch that worm, b.

OG Idea: Yeah, yeah, yeah, I hear that.
So, where's your ideas at?

Younger Idea: Right now, I'm focused on myself.
I'm too young to be bringing new ideas into the world.

OG Idea: Trust me, king. Best not to rush these things.

Younger Idea: What about you? Your ideas must be big now!

OG Idea: Nah, chill man's not *that* old.
I had ideas but now I'm off that road.
George forgot them . . .
Left man kind of short for options.

Younger Idea: What you saying? AC done you dirty.

OG Idea: I don't really think it's Ambition Commission's fault . . .
This attention deficit is a joke.
Anyway, it don't even matter, g.
I patterned a better strategy.
I track down good ideas that got forgotten.
Find ones they left behind and I adopt them.

Younger Idea: Swear down, you raise them yourself?

OG Idea: Nah. I shot them.

[Younger Idea looks unsure]

OG Idea: Don't look like that it's not as bad as it sounds.
You can sell ideas for the maddest amounts.
If G's not giving me no attention
Then I gotta get it through the street.
I'm not even greedy with it,
I just need enough attention to get me through the week.

Younger Idea: Yeah, but that's peak! That's kidnap!

OG Idea: Kidnap? Do you know how crazy life is for baby ideas?
They ain't like me and you – they can't even move.
Wait. You ain't seen one, have you?

Younger Idea: Come on, man there's bare young ideas on the block,
who you talking to?

OG Idea: Nah. Not young ideas. New ideas.
Like *this* . . .

[OG Idea opens his bag and reveals a dozen new-born ideas. They look like magical light bulbs]

Younger Idea: Yoooooo!

OG Idea: Yeah. See that one there?
Look how bright it's glowing.
I guarantee it's gonna help George write a poem.

Younger Idea: This is mad.

OG Idea: Blud, I find them all alone with nowhere to call a home.
I ain't got attention for all of them.
So I link them with whoever can afford to spend.

Younger Idea: Woah, woah, woah. So how much we talking then?

OG Idea: There's different factors, it all depends.
But between me and you . . .
I'm on my way to AC HQ.
I think Busy wants to buy all of them.

Younger Idea: What?! You're about to make a fortune then.

OG Idea: I mean like . . . if I get the green light, yeah.
That's fourteen right there.

Younger Idea: What you saying fourteen ideas right there?

OG Idea: Yeah man.

[OG Idea bends down to close his bag. Meanwhile Younger Idea gets ready to attack him]

OG Idea: I'm just showing you there's different ways to get your hustle on, likkle man.

350   [Younger Idea knocks OG Idea to the ground and robs him]

Younger Idea: If AC wants this bag, just tell them the price went up. It's Horsepower, bro.

[Soundtrack: Rose Royce 'Wishing on a Star']

SCENE 9: DIJA WANTS TO TALK

[Return to George and Dija's home. Dija finds George sitting silently in their living room]

Dija: We need to talk.

EPISODE 17: The Bag

Extra Info:

- 'The Bag' is a big metaphor about talent. Like talent, ideas have potential. But if they are never discovered, or are cut off too early, their potential goes unfulfilled. This episode shows how the genres of Jazz, R&B and Ska music began as simple ideas and grew into world-changing movements. In Chapter Three I explore these genres in more detail, but for this episode I wanted to illustrate the amount of value that came from some simple ideas. I want my listeners to see that potential in their own ideas, and in the ideas of the people around them.

- When I wrote this, I was also thinking about wealth and poverty. The episode features good ideas being destroyed by powerful insecurities. It reminds me of talented people who are held down by the pressures of their environment – I grew up with a lot of them. Those people are like good ideas cut off too early; they didn't get a chance to share their value with the world. Just like good ideas in an insecure mind, people living in poverty can be taken for granted. But just like average ideas in a confident mind, people living in privilege can go very far. I will always push for a world that sees the potential in everyone, regardless of their background.

Fun Facts:

- 'The Bag' has a few meanings: the bag of new ideas that were stolen at the end of the last episode, the 'bag of ideas' that I mention at the end of this episode, and the 'bag' as a slang term for payment. Secure the bag.

As Chapter 2 drew to a close I became more adventurous. It's like I was no longer scared of putting a listener off by getting too weird. Obviously, I never want anyone to feel left behind when I tell stories, but as I said earlier, I'm also like an athlete in training. I want to see how far I can push my abilities ... and I don't mind looking a little crazy in the process. So, Episode 17 was a special moment for all the good ideas who never got to shine earlier in the chapter. Again, the storyline was based on a real thought process I had; I wanted to explain the origins of R&B and Ska music, (for reasons that would become clearer in Chapter 3) but time was running out, and my insecurities were still waging war on my ambitions, so I had to stop worrying about making an episode that was easy to follow, and just throw my thoughts out there. Once again, I learned that perseverance paid off. Special thank you to our star player, Vidhu, whose talented friends brought life to some of the most creative scenes Benbrick and I have ever recorded.

SCENE 1: ANY OLD BAG

George: Do me a favour. Picture a bag. Ignore the voices, ignore the walls. Just hold that bag in your mind.

[Room starts to darken, room shakes, George waits nervously.]

George: We're getting there. Just a bit longer. Hold the bag in your mind.

George: [Breathing heavily] Thank you.

[Catches breath]

George: What you just did was important. You heard
What I articulated, and you participated.
Now I'm holding a bag designed by you, and
You can see it in your mind's eye, too.
Every time you listen back to this episode I
Want you to give me a different bag.
And next time give it a bit of swag, what do you call this? [Laughs]

This bag represents all the new ideas I'm
Bringing to Episode 17. These
Ideas come from everything I've ever seen.
So, let's just see what we've got . . .

[Pulls out a glowing idea]

George: Ooo look at that. The strongest ones shine bright
You see it's got a pretty little design, right?
That means the idea's patterned;
Ready for execution as soon as the time's right.

Some of these ideas will change someone's life
Some are outlandish, some of them are

Average Joes. But they all need attention
Otherwise they start feeling tension and
Switch into savage mode.

Now, I don't—

[Rabbit noises]

George: Wait. Don't tell me that's an—

Yup. Rabbit hole.

[Transition into Rabbit Hole]

George: Remember the last rabbit hole from Episode 13?
In the middle of the third scene? When I
Felt so scholarly 'cause we were discussing Sociology. I was
Quoting Pierre Bourdieu to make the
Point that context is everything. Then
Sandra mentioned something the other day
And it's been on my mind ever since.

Bourdieu had a lot of ideas, she re-
Minded me of one called *Habitus*. It's the
Link between our habitats, our
habits and our characters.
Your habitus is the reality in your
Head, based on the things you've witnessed
And in the case of a storyteller like my-
self that's what brings you business.

Anyone can do this.
Yourself included. So
Part of my plan for my community is to
Offer new storytelling methods
That create financial opportunity.

Opportunity based on utility, and I'm saying the
Highest form of utility is your
Ability to reach the youts in the street.
Storytelling for community development
Could be a huge industry.

Especially considering Karl Marx's theory of
Alienation, which explains a lot of my people's
Daily frustration.
Cos of the way we engage in the economy, we experience
crazy estrangement from our dreams.

Think about it . . .
You have to take whatever work you can get, and
That's what you do with your life. But
This might be the source of your problems
'Cause you don't control all of your options.

If commonly, your place in the economy
Makes you feel like basically a zombie,
Then generating financial opportunity from my
Story makes me the anomaly.

Now what if that economic model was
Available for the majority? What if your
Journey . . . and your philosophy . . .
Became your monopoly?

[Transition to room]

George: Remember – the social needs of a community should inform
its economic agenda.

Come. Bring a bag.

SCENE 2: IT'S A ROBBERY

[Soundtrack: The Notorious B.I.G. 'Playa Hater']

[Cut to Insecurity Guards (IGs) ambushing Ambition Commission (AC) ideas for control of Episode 17. The IGs demand to know where new ideas are being hidden. Their victims pretend not to know, until one of them gets shot. They raid other hideouts and find more ideas]

IG 1: Busy wasn't gonna put you on the
Podcast now you got a chance.

IG 2: You get to shoot your shot at last. Listen,
George's Mind is overcrowded, time is breezing
Past and Episode 17 is ours.

IG 1: Now. I don't know what promises he made you.

IG 2: Or what guarantees he gave you.

IG 1: But Busy is not here to save you.

IG 2: Horsepower. That's the only way to break through.

IG 1: We're giving you lot
five seconds to pick your best idea . . .

IG 2: Five, four, three, two, one.
You! Come.

[Jazz Idea trembles and steps up]

IG 2: Stop crying, man, I ain't even done nothing yet. What you got for me?

Jazz Idea: Throughout Chapter 2,

George has talked about the
Great power the Black artist has.
Busy ordered us to research Black music.
And he told me to start with Jazz.

IG 1: Bro, this idea ain't going nowhere!
Forget this yout.

IG 2: Hold on bro. This might be something we can execute.
Yo, let me get a preview.

SCENE 3: ALL THAT JAZZ

When I listen back to the last century
One thing becomes clear to me:
Black people are a lot more in sync than we
Sometimes appear to be.
Think about it. Over countless hours and
thousands of miles of migration, with no
government, or global news channel, we kept in
touch, through sounds and vibrations.

If telling your own story is the secret to survival
Music has been our lifeline.
This story is so much deeper than the latest
Drama – which, right now, is knife crime.

[Soundtrack: Sonny Rollins 'St Thomas']

In the 1950s and '60s about
Two hundred and fifty thousand people arrived in
Britain from the West Indies. Around the
Same time, African Americans were
channelling their passion and intelligence into a
new form. And the response was more than lukewarm;
Jazz had the factors and the elements that initially

made people trash it as backwards and irreverent,
Savage and malevolent. Then it broke the main-
Stream and became seen as glamorous and elegant.

But listen to that – it's way more amorous than decadent.
Listen to the sax and the swagger that it represents.

Listen to the beat,
Can't you feel the rhythm in your seat?

In the 1930s, a young family of US Virgin Island emigrants
Became Harlem residents. The
Baby of that family was called Theodore. At
Seven, he got a saxophone which he adored. His
Mum used to sing a song that made him relax; a
Song which, twenty years on, he played on the sax.

See, Jazz was from New Orleans, that's further south.
First it was only heard about through word of mouth.
Eventually it spread to the rest of the globe and
Every year from then it kept on evolving. For
Millions of voiceless African Americans,
Jazz was the greatest revolution. And
By the mid 1950s, Bebop was jazz's latest evolution.

This is the genre that literally put
Theodore's name down in history. He
Took simple lines, and improvised, and every
Improvisation had a different spice.
'St Thomas', by Theodore
'Sonny' Rollins, made him a legend. He
Changed the game in '56 and '57.
This guy cross-pollinated old Caribbean sounds with
African American and European styles—

[IGs interrupt]

IG 2: That's interesting still. Sonny what's his name . . .

IG 1: Yo lemme see that idea, g.

IG 2: So, what's the plan?

Jazz Idea: I was hoping George would be able to get some support, maybe funding-wise. I'm thinking a musical documentary. Maybe Island Records would be fitting . . . as they had a heritage of—

[IGs destroy the idea]

IG 1: GET THAT OUTTA HERE!

[IGs laugh]

IG 2: Get back to the drawing board!

IG 1: Come on man how much time wasting can George afford? Who's next? Come here. What you got for me blud?

R&B Idea: I was part of the research project at R&D looking at the origins of R&B.

IG 1: Swear down . . . Let's see what's popping bro.

SCENE 4: THE ORIGINS OF R&B

[Soundtrack; The Clovers 'Middle of the Night']

George: Doo Wop was early R&B,
and its connection to Jazz isn't hard to see.
It's just got that swing. Came from
young African Americans, I'm guessing it's a Black thing.

[George enters an American diner]

Waitress: Hey, how can I help ya?

George: Hi, do you lot do vegan hot dogs?

Waitress: Er, let me check.

George: Respect.
The harmony, the riddim and the vibe.
Right now, you're listening to The Clovers, 'Middle of the Night'
Yo, this ting was big in its own right.

Waitress: Really sorry, we don't do that I'm afraid.

George: Alright, B, don't worry about it.

Waitress: Alright, have a nice day.

[George leaves the diner and feels paranoid when he hears someone calling out across the street]

George: Course they ain't got vegan hot dogs – this is 1950s US of A.
And for obvious reasons, that's kinda awkward for me,
But Doo Wop's the music of the youth of today.

Fortunately, it's big in Jamaica.
Wanna go to Jamaica?
Let's go 1950s Jamaica!

[Cut to George aboard a ship to Jamaica]

George: Tom Wong was a hardware trader. He
Used to own a store with performing equipment.
Every so often he brought in a shipment of
Records, microphones, speakers and decks too.

He used to take them to parties and select tunes for
People to step to and flex to.

But listen to me, 1950s Kingston wasn't easy,
Things had gotten greasy. And these American
Songs were something that everyone could connect to.
Helped them to get through.

Remember what I said about Black people?
Thousands of miles of migration. No
Government, no news channel. We
Kept in touch through sounds and vibrations.

Imagine, Tom's sound system made everyone around listen.
From the hustler to the Rasta
He was the main instructor. And he
Caught the ear of a teenager named Prince Buster.

Through the sound system Buster was introduced to the
Song you're currently listening to. And
Swiftly over the '50s, the culture of the
Sound system grew. Tom was no longer the
Sole conqueror. There was a new breed.
Buster linked up with Coxsone and Duke Reid but the
R&B ting kinda slowed down.
So dem man dere made their own sound.

[IGs end the presentation]

IG 2: Alright I'ma be real yeah, see when you said R&B I was more
expecting a kind of Usher ting. New Edition. You know them ones there.

IG 1: Ay, let me see that idea quickly.

[IG drops the idea and breaks it]

IG 1: It's hot blud!

SCENE 5: DREAMS

George: See at this point in Chapter Two
I'm in the final stage of sleep.
And just like yours, my brain is deep.
All the information it's been trained to keep is
Retained in heaps.

And one of the things that happens at this stage of sleep is the
Brain starts forming connections, but not straight-
Forward connections. REM sleep prefers
Random, awkward connections that
Happen in all sorts of directions.

See, when awake, we tend to take a
Narrow view of what's possible. 'Cause
Human beings are super-logical. But
REM sleep removes this obstacle.

During REM sleep, logic doesn't work;
That's the precondition of a dream. This helps you
Glean intuition from the scenes you envision, yo this
Sleep thing isn't what it seems.

Now when you wake up, those connections can
become seen as *one dream*.
Think about it . . .

Nuff connections, *one* dream.

And even if you don't remember the detail,
The remnants can be felt. To
me this sounds like the theory of the invisible hand.

All these little connections . . .
One metaphysical plan.

Episode 17 . . . is not going how I planned.
I wanna kill my insecurities before they kill me.
But I doubt I can.
Got a bag of ideas.
Yet time's running out like damn.

Right now, my insecurities are
Running through this episode attacking my ideas
And I know exactly why this is;
They wanna amplify my fears, tell me that I
Can't make you understand my perspective.
Tryna undermine the potential between me
And every listener I connect with.
But they keep forgetting my secret weapon:
You . . .

SCENE 6: INSECURITIES KILL DREAMS

IG 1: Aight, who's next?

IG 2: You lot need to switch it up, though.
It's getting kinda boring.

Ska Idea: I've . . . I've got two ideas.

IG 1: Talk to me, my brudda . . .

Ska Idea: Well, George never finished Intern and Analyst's story from 'A Night to REMember' . . .

IG 1: True . . .

Ska Idea: His audience are clearly wondering what happened to them, so I was—

[IGs destroy another idea]

IG 1: Waffle!

IG 2: Sorry, bro, it's dead.

IG 1: Next. Next, next, next, come on . . .

IG 2: Fix your face, bro, it was a weak idea.

Ska Idea: I'm also part of a team that's been working hard
To help George explain the birth of Ska.

IG 1: Ska? What? Like *Lion King* 'Be Prepared'! That tune's greezy!

Ska Idea: Nah, nah.

IG 1: What?

Ska Idea: The music genre.

[IG 1 is embarrassed]

IG 1: OK . . .

[IG 1 starts laughing]

IG 1: Ay you better hope he stops laughing. Ediat.

SCENE 7: THE BIRTH OF SKA

George: Every piece of music is a journey. And that
Journey can be split into stages.
These stages are called bars.
And this is how music is written on pages.

Each bar has a number of beats.
These beats are steps that don't move.
The greatest music takes us through this journey in
Ways that are ever so smooth. Now the
Melody carries the whole tune, but the
Rhythm sets the whole groove. 'Cause the
Groove treats the beats like steppingstones. I
Can't wait to put this in a podcast episode.

Prince Buster had a stroke of genius about the
Steppingstones, so the legend goes. In-
Stead of setting the groove on the first stone, the
Groove stepped in on the second stone.
This is an approach people had never known.
Everybody's head was blown.
Ska was born . . . and it set the tone.

[Cut to George in Jamaica]

[Soundtrack: Theo Beckford & Friends 'Trench Town Ska']

George: This groove became the flavour of the nation.
Generation after generation, Jamaican innovation
kept on breaking limitations inspiring fakes and imitations.
All from some basic syncopation.

I need you to understand what this is.
Governments couldn't come up with this. If
Multinational companies funded research and
Creative incubation, they still couldn't have made this innovation.
You feel me?

See, the way I see it there's two ways revolution has always begun:
People raise their voices, or raise their guns.
This was a revolutionary time for the country
In more ways than one.

Edward Seaga: *It would have been nice to say independence caused people to want their own music, but the music preceded independence.*

[Soundtrack: The Skatalites 'Freedom Sounds']

This one's called 'Freedom Sounds'.
After centuries of getting beaten down by the
Spanish and the British – which we don't speak about –
Imagine how Jamaicans must've wanted to scream and shout,
Praying the playing field might finally even out.

You're listening to the Skatalites; about ten musicians who
Linked up to satisfy Jamaica's latest appetite.

These guys connected through the pioneers Prince
Buster, Duke Reid and Coxsone Dodd. Dem
Man dere were setting up studios across Kingston and they
Moulded the musicians into a proper squad.

In 1963 he set up a record label: the
Legendary Studio One. It was a
Message to the youth of a newly independent
Jamaica: you need no one.
We can make it happen right here.

And Studio One's the label everybody knew, so
Obviously, that's the one they're running to.
And among the new recruits was a younger group of youts. They
Came with a wave of kids from the countryside that
Ended up in the city, but not the comfy side;
Mandem. People that the government abandoned.
You know them ones when the so-called failures
Turn out to be the most hearty entertainers.
Coxsone was convinced they were special.
Robert, Winston and Neville were soon to be
Known as 'Bob Marley and the Wailers'.

[Soundtrack: The Wailers 'Simmer Down']

In summer '63 they recorded 'Simmer Down'
And they caught the talk from the ground in a sound.

Like I said, a lot of kids came from the
Country to the town and these young people were wild.
Out on the roads, out of control, rowdy and bold.

When I take in what he's saying, it makes my heart thump. He's
Telling guys to calm down before they get their ass slumped.
That's the story of my life; pleading for
Peace in the Ends hoping more people survive and I
See how they captured the energy with that Ska bump, by
Feb '64 the song took a chart jump.

The single went to number one; a little
Signal of the run to come.

Later that year, Millie Small's cover of
'My Boy Lollipop' sold 7 million copies.
Imagine how that changed the perception of music, which
Once was only ever really a hobby.

[Soundtrack: Millie Small 'My Boy Lollipop']

George: Millie bussing off of 'My Boy Lollipop' was
Like Stormzy going number one with 'Vossi Bop'.
Just some raw talent that shot their shot.
Coming from people who ain't got a lot. There's
International eyes on Jamaican youths now. So
What did they do? Create a new style.

[IGs stop and destroy this idea]

IG 1: Circle of life, bro.

IG 2: Hakuna matata, bro.
[Both laugh]

IG 1: Aight, next . . .

Rocksteady Idea: Man was working on Jamaican Rocksteady . . . but
Do what you're doing. Man's ready.

IG 2: This guy, you know . . .

IG 1: I like this one.

IG 2: He's got heart, innit!

IG 1: Blud. Man said 'Do what you're doing, man's ready'!

IG 2: Likkle soldier, alie?

IG 1: Play the ting for me.

George: The first thing Rocksteady did was slow down,
Meaning there was a lot more space to go 'round.
Kids from the Ska scene are getting kinda grown now;
They've grown out of the old style.

One of these kids was Jamaica's first child star
Delroy Wilson found his voice when he found Ska.
And as the boy aged,
Obviously, his voice changed.

[Soundtrack: Delroy Wilson 'Joe Liges']

You're listening to the sound of early Rocksteady. You
Notice how the third beat knocks heavy?
That was a new touch. And you
Notice how the horns ain't doing too much?

These were two of the newest developments from
Artists' experiments with the musical elements of
Ska and the Soul coming through from Americans.
Romance and heartbreak were the usual sentiments but
This one's a 1966 diss track and
Guess who the writer was pissed at . . .

Prince Buster! The one who invented Ska.
I don't even know how their problems went this far but
This song was written by a guy called Scratch. This
Wasn't the kind of scene where rivals clashed in a
Title match. So, it must have been personal.
Coxsone was the man Scratch and Buster were working for
Back in the '50s when they came up together
But success can change stuff forever.

Rocksteady lasts for a fifth of one decade
Eventually it becomes Reggae.
Over here that becomes Two-Tone, back ah yard,
Ragga, same time as Hip Hop, eventually
Ragga became Dancehall, which led to Jungle,
Gave birth to Garage, morphed into Grime. There's
Always gonna be new stories to tell,
Always gonna be more things that rhyme.

But my people been had a bag of ideas, others
keep reaching in and taking them, wasting them,
breaking them. Culturally appropriating them,
Following their own economic motivation and it's
gonna stay this way no matter what we say to them
until we write our own rules of engagement and es-
Stablish standard practice in how we trade with them.

[Bulb smashes]

By the way you know what last artist we played,

Jamaica's first child star?
Yeah, like a lot of his generation, he came over to the UK.
And shortly before his unfortunate passing in the early '90s
He had a son.
The boy went on to do music.

[Soundtrack: Krept and Konan ft. K-Trap & Headie One 'I Spy']

You might have heard of him . . . Konan.
One half of the legendary rap duo . . . Krept and Konan.

EPISODE 18: Concurrent Affairs

Extra Info:

- This episode was the perfect closing statement for Chapter Two. It incorporated the drama of previous episodes, while also speaking directly about history and politics. I'm always trying to find ways of making education more engaging because that's what I really needed when I was in school.
- I wanted to discuss my turning down the MBE, but I didn't want that to be the focus of the whole episode. An MBE is an honour given to someone by the British monarch, as a way of recognising that person's work. As I explain in the episode, this honour was deeply appreciated, but to have the words 'Member of the (order of the) British Empire' attached to my name for the rest of my life . . . seemed a bit off. I would have accepted it if it was called something different. Unfortunately, the British Empire wasn't a completely positive influence on Africa. And a lot of British people still don't know this, because this history hasn't been taught to them. As a public figure who feels strongly about the subject, I had a responsibility to tell our side of the story. If anyone else feels differently, that's OK.

Fun Facts:

- 'Concurrent Affairs' was actually the first name of this podcast. Back then, the plan was to mix journalism with a bit of drama, a lot like the Grenfell episode. I wanted to write about current affairs *and* love affairs, in order to achieve the Netflix Effect I mentioned earlier. But I decided on the title 'Have You Heard George's Podcast?' because it was more direct. Two years in, I finally felt it was time to use that original title for an episode.

Returning to the concept of Uganda and Britain as women in my life, I offered further insight into my feelings about both countries. In Uganda's case, I talked about regional tensions in East Africa, as well as the state of politics at home. With Britain, a nice conversation about the BBC (who were genuinely great to me and Benbrick)

turned sour when we started talking about British history. First she told me that I was getting too big for my boots, then I told her that I rejected an honour from the Queen, then she got offended and I left for Uganda. Concurrent Affairs. Special thank you to Anne, who voiced Britain to perfection. And much respect to Benbrick, because we got this whole episode done in two days.

SCENE 1: GEORGE AND UGANDA

[George is on the phone to Uganda, who is personified as a woman. This was first done on Episode 12, 'A Night to REMember'. When George and Uganda last 'spoke', they fell out over politics. This time, they are gentle with each other. George is more sensitive with Uganda as he realises politics is a triggering subject for her. Uganda responds better to George because she feels he genuinely cares. This episode was written shortly before George visited Uganda for his first ever Kampala show, in collaboration with entertainment company A Ka Dope. The opening scene is the reverse of Episode 12's opening scene]

George: Hello Uganda. You've been on my mind.
I'm coming next month but when I land, I'm still on my grind.

You know 20th December I've got my first Kampala
Show with A Ka Dope!
Yo that night I'm drinking pineapple!

[Uganda gets excited at the idea of George drinking her locally distilled gin, Waragi, in its newest flavour, Pineapple]

Uganda: 😆 Oyagala pynapo!?

George: Njagala pynapo!!!

[Both laugh]

George: I missed you.
But I want to be honest with you.
And I don't want that to be an issue . . .

It's been twenty years since we met
Where's all the time gone?

Uganda: Can you imagine?

George: I thought you were the most gorgeous thing I'd ever laid eyes on.
I was young, but I knew . . . I knew this obsession would be lifelong.
Uganda: You were so young, baambi.
How's Britain?

George: She's alright. Getting cold.
I'm sure you've seen there's an election coming.

Uganda: Are you running?

[George laughs]

Uganda: Oba you're still running from your destiny?

George: Yo if I became a politician now,
My mouth would definitely get the best of me.

Uganda: Yeah.
Politics is a touchy subject.

George: If I ask about your politics are you gonna get upset?

Uganda: You can ask.

George: How are you feeling?

Uganda: I feel strange.
I want peace . . . but I need real change.

George: You don't think you can have both?

Uganda: George . . . this is Africa.
We'll always end up back here.

In April they removed Bashir.
Opposition is boycotting local elections in Tanzania.
The ruling party is plotting against the president in Zambia.
This is our Africa.

[George pauses]

George: What's up with you and Rwanda?

Uganda: My sister . . . now, that one is a long story.

George: I saw they killed two Ugandans the other day. I'm sorry.

Uganda: They've even arrested two more since.

George: Don't you think Sevo should explain the situation?
If Ugandans are dying?
So far, I can't find much, other than him saying the Rwandans are
    spying.

Uganda: [Sighs] Like I said, George . . . long story.
At least starting from the troubles back in '94.
Good thing now no one has appetite for war.

George: Well, let's hope it doesn't conveniently escalate in
Time for the next election date.

Uganda: Election time is reflection time.

George: More like protection time.

Uganda: How is Brexit going?

George: Drop the first word out of that question and you have your
answer.

Uganda: [Laughs] Is Brexit going?

George: Uganda, who knows? Who knows?
Some people want in, some people want out,
Some of us can't remember what this was even about.
Some are selling dreams, some are selling their souls.
Right now, the Tories are doing well in the polls but there's
No telling with votes like this, anything goes.
No one knows who means what and who's pretending
Labour want a second referendum.
Lib Dems linked up with the Greens and Plaid Cymru
The road's long. The ride's bumpy.

Uganda: Eh!
You guys are struggling with this decision.
Should we be sending soldiers to the region?

[George laughs]

Uganda: Or maybe we give you an interim government,
Since you've failed to settle your argument in parliament?

George: I don't know why you're joking!
Your opposition is taking your president to the International
    Criminal Court.
And their petition is winning support.

Uganda: Those are just words.
You know these politicians are hustlers.
They have no plans. Just slogans.

Besigye has been complaining for so long
It's now just his job to sing the same old song.
To his core followers he can do no wrong.
Have you ever seen roller-skaters on the road?
Holding onto a matatu? Yeah, that's Besigye. He just needs to hold on.

George: [Laughs] You're so silly.

Uganda: Then your friend. Mr Bobi Wine.
Honourable Kyagulanyi.
Does he even have a fiscal plan?
Oba he expects to govern with his slogans?
Does he have influence in army?
How now do you govern with no guns?
No. It's just words.
In the end they're all hustlers.

[Silence]

George: Words.
Words become things.

Uganda: George, can I ask you something?

George: Mhm.

Uganda: Do you think we can ever be together?
And don't give me your poetry wolokoso –
Yes, or no?

George: Only if enough of you wants something new.

Uganda: I want peace.
I want to make it out of this decade in one piece.

[Soundtrack: Price Love 'You Can Fly']

SCENE 2 GEORGE AND BRITAIN

Britain: So, you're happy with how everything rolled out?

George: I mean . . . no doubt.
Not one part of me feels like we sold out.

Britain: Mmm I guess the BBC partnership really is working?
Looks like they've put some serious work in!

George: Britain, listen – they've been a dream.
I mean the BBC's an underrated machine.
I feel like everybody on my project played as a team and I
Still retained the space to say what I mean.
And they really picked the prime-time moments to
Slap my big face on the screen. I love it!
I love their support. I love their marketing budget.
They're taking my messages to the heart of the public.
And obviously, there's always controversy, and bureaucracy.
But as a project in democracy . . . for this
Whole thing to be funded by licence fee money . . .
It says a lot about you as a country.

Britain: Tell me more. About me as a country 😊

[George thinks]

George: Britain, I love you.
I don't even think you really know your worth.
Past hundred years, you've had a lot to adjust to.
Not long ago you used to roam the Earth controlling turf.
And even though you're not allowed to say it,
I get why you might want that to last.
But you know . . .
Life comes at you fast.

Britain: Ouch.

I guess I *have* had some soul-searching to do . . .
Have you ever tried to reimagine the old version of you?

Reimagine your changes, knowing there are so many more . . .
I don't even know anymore.
Am I really something to celebrate?
Am I every decision I ever made?

You know my favourite thing about your podcast?

George: What's that?

Britain: The Ambition Commission.
One of those episodes took me back to the Spanish Inquisition.

They used to seem unstoppable.

I look at them today and I just wonder how they lost it all.
George, they *ruled* the water.
But I'll never forget . . . 1588 . . . I caught up.

I don't mean to blow my own trumpet but
My naval force was outnumbered.
And a lot of people thought it would be the end of me.
That I'd be absorbed by, essentially . . .
A higher entity.
And lose track of my identity.
But that wasn't meant to be.

George: Must be nice.

Britain: Wait – that sounded wrong,
I didn't mean . . . look, I'm so sorry if—

George: You're sorry for what, Britain? Being honest.
You've always been ambitious.
That victory over Spain . . .
Set you up to literally own the game.
And now, all around the world they know your name.
But, you know, things change.
My grandad died in exile.

Did you know that?
When my dad was half the age I am now.
Funny how life pans out.

Britain: I'm sorry for your father's pain.

George: But you're not sorry for your *role* in it.
'Cause you and Busy share the same secret;
Ambition knows no limit.

Britain: You know, George, you probably think you're doing
  something clever
By not going into politics. But you're actually – tragically – wasting
  your talents.
And, I would say, running away from a challenge.

You have more strong opinions than New York has condominiums.
But you can't stand to be accountable to anyone.
And you can't help feeling like you're cleverer than everyone.

You buy time for yourself by appearing in entertainment,
But only for a limited period of engagement.
And that's just how you like it.
That way none of us can pin you down.
You have no responsibilities, your role in society is literally to think
  aloud.
You don't care about making England proud.
You don't care about *all* the issues you single out.
You know this fame thing is all swings and roundabouts.
So instead of accepting your role as a musician,
You hide behind truisms . . .
Ones you can sing and shout about.
Because if you didn't . . . who'd listen?

George: I turned down an MBE.

A friend asked me if I would accept it.
I just saw my parents' faces, and without thinking, I said yes.

Then I took a minute and reflected . . .
Reflected on my status.
And I felt a burning sensation in my chest.

Your forefathers grabbed my motherland, pinned her down . . .
And took turns.
They did that every day for a couple hundred years
And then left her . . . to treat her own burns.

Now all her children are born with a set of unique concerns.
And gaps in the information that we really need do to learn.
And not one of us knows why.

Why we got absorbed by, essentially, a quote-unquote 'higher entity'.
Why I have to fight for my identity.
George. People know me as this.
The name of some old colonialist.
And you're so conceited it doesn't even occur to you how lonely
    this is.
What they did was pure evil, and you can't see it 'cause that's your
    people.

Britain: I gave you everything.

George: There she is. That's the Britain that I know.
Wants you to feel like she's done you a favour by
Accommodating you. And tolerating you.
Just like my motherland did.
Which ended up with me not knowing any other language.
I'm utilising this citizenship to
Let this 'common-wealth' touch the streets.
But our human rights are privileges.
And our civil rights are luxuries.

Yeah, Brexit's tough.
But me and your pain ain't the same.
I'm not a Member of the British Empire.
I'm George Mpanga. And my name is my name.

[Soundtrack: Celine Dion 'Think Twice']

Britain: George . . . you of all people.

That was a mistake.

SCENE 3: GEORGE'S MBE STATEMENT

George: In Chapter 2 of my podcast, I claimed to have turned down an MBE, specifically in May 2019.

Although much of my podcast is fictional, this is a fact. I'd like to apologise to the friend who recommended me on my assurance that I'd accept. I didn't know I would feel this way.

I see myself as a student, admirer, and friend of Britain. However, the colonial trauma inflicted on the children of Africa, entrenched across our geopolitical and macroeconomic realities, prevents me from accepting the title 'Member of the British Empire'. The gesture is deeply appreciated; the wording is not. It will remain unacceptable to me until Britain takes institutional measures to redress the intergenerational disruption brought to millions as a result of her colonial exploits. I have no issue with other Black people who have embraced this title; I encourage variety of thought across our society *and* within my community. I encourage future generations to seek the relevant information in order to make an informed decision.

What do the words 'British Empire' mean to you?

I love this country, but I do so with transparency. I do so with a belief in the integrity of the British people. I will continue to give my life to the improvement of British society, but I will not be told how to feel about my history.

At this time, I'd like to express my deepest gratitude to Sandra Makumbi, Beatrice Nanteza, Vidhu Sharma and Claudia Amoah.

From the BBC I'd like to offer my warmest thanks to Dylan Haskins, Jason Phipps, Rhian Roberts, Jaja Muhammad, Anne Isger for her stunning performance as Britain, Tim Giles, Will, Ella, Elian, Jenny, the BBC Concert Orchestra, and anyone else at the BBC I haven't mentioned.

To my friends and family that have been patient with me through-out this process, I honour you.

Special thanks to Hatimax, and Artcoustic Sessions.

I'd like to thank all the press that have supported *Have You Heard George's Podcast?*

And last but not least, I'd like to thank the man that has walked me through this all; a friend, and a mentor, Benbrick.

CHAPTER THREE

Even though Chapter Two of *Have You Heard George's Podcast?* earned a Peabody Award, an NME Award and two gold ARIAs, Chapter Three needed a different approach. Anyone who says awards don't matter isn't telling the whole truth, because they do. They represent a value system. They teach future generations what mattered in the past, and to whom. So, since this podcast was always meant to be a conversation *with* society *about* society, all these awards told me that society heard me loud and clear – for which I am deeply grateful. Thank you to all the listeners who pushed this podcast to the heights it has reached. Without you guys, it would be hard to argue that I'm not crazy.

I can see how an artist might get overwhelmed by the success of their own instincts. Things that you did without thinking can look superhuman once enough people celebrate you, and that can make you self-conscious – like you can't afford to be less than great. It's natural to want to recreate whatever worked previously, but it's unnatural to actually do that. We can't rewind time; we have to move forward, and for me that meant empowering my audience. I always thought the best way to do this would be to give them a voice using my platform.

A Whole Digital Platform

But before I wrote a word of Chapter Three, the Coronavirus pandemic hit. This kept Benbrick and I away from the studio, and in that time, I sat at home listening to music that he'd send me for inspiration. Benbrick is resourceful like that – nothing can stop him from creating. Eventually, I wrote a poem outlining my vision of a digital platform that let audiences share their thoughts about the world by reacting to art. In my case, that art was *Have You Heard George's Podcast?* I wanted the audience's reaction to be respected as a social force. These lines show my thinking:

So if I'm gonna continue to write poetry – or articles, like I did for

Time magazine – I could make it so that every line has a theme that becomes a reference point like "I Have A Dream". And if this mobilises my network, there should be a platform that captures that; imagine an app doing the leg work of turning feedback into creative maps and stats.

I made a rough recording of the poem using my home studio setup, and sent it to a few trusted friends – Darshan, Anne and Benbrick. Over the next year, through countless Zoom calls, we grew the idea into a real-life digital platform called *Common Ground*. It created dialogue between me and my audience by inviting them to share their thoughts on each episode of Chapter Three, right after listening. Once we got feedback on all episodes, our plan was to turn it into a creative presentation that conveys the *Common Ground* community's thoughts in all sorts of fun ways. This was my first attempt at using my platform to give the audience a voice.

A Whole PhD

Around the same time, world-famous economist Mariana Mazzucato had invited me to do a research degree at her department in University College London (UCL) – *the Institute for Innovation and Public Purpose (IIPP)*. Mariana was introduced to me by our mutual friend, Tanya Moti, a sweet, sharp woman with a great mind for connecting people. When I first met Mariana, I was surprised at how quickly she took to my idea that Rap music could be used to organise community investment. Usually people respond to that with "Not everyone raps though", but Mariana understood my view of Rap as a storytelling system, developed from shared experiences (or, as Mariana would put it, "public value"). Another guiding light in my educational life has been my friend, Dr. Karen Edge, who once booked me to talk at the London Festival of Education. As a Reader in Educational Leadership at UCL, Karen agreed to supervise my degree with Mariana, helping me sharpen my concept of Black creativity as a learning system.

So, despite the success of Chapter Two, Chapter Three had to be different. It couldn't be a one-way delivery – art to consumer. It needed a feedback system to turn that delivery line into a loop, and unlock the potential of the artist/audience relationship. What if, one day, every artist created space in society for their fans to explore . . . whatever. An artist doesn't need a PhD to have something worth sharing, but ten years into my career, I was ready to have the kind of conversations governments couldn't ignore. The PhD was my way of learning how to improve my community's economic and educational life, at the level of Government.

A Whole Wedding

In the middle of the pandemic, I got down on one knee and asked my girlfriend, Sandra, to marry me. She said yes, and since then I've been amazed by how much happiness and inspiration our love has brought to others. We met as teenagers and quickly became each other's biggest fans. Over a decade later, Sandra helped me recruit new GTP team members and design better systems for the business. From there she grew into a Project Manager, then an Operations Director, and Events Producer.

EPISODE 19: Common Ground

Extra Info:

- Throughout Chapter 3, I returned to my original technique of using day-to-day life as podcast material. This is why Episode 19 starts with a conversation between me and my nephews. When Nicholas says his school friends know of me, it signifies how my profile is growing, but also shows the listener my life through the eyes of my loved ones. It echoes the first episode, which opens with 'My name's George the Poet, but right now I'm Uncle George.' I'm still encouraging my listeners to look deeply into their own experiences for inspiration.

- Across this chapter I also continue the balancing act of speaking to a multicultural audience. This is one of my first considerations when I shape a podcast chapter. Chapter Two started with a story about a famous African American, but Chapter Three opens with a look at tensions across Black Britain. I use later episodes to link this Black British story with the African American and Afro-Caribbean experience. As I've said before, it's unhealthy for Black people to look at ourselves only through Western education systems. We need to study our lives independently and identify patterns across the group.

- I used this episode to talk about an important theme that runs throughout Chapter Three: the market. My dream is for Black people to eventually control their own employment, because I'm tired of seeing wasted potential. Growing up, across my area I saw lower educational achievement lead to higher unemployment and crime. Children who went through this cycle often grew up to have children who did the same. But the root cause was poverty. Over time, I realised there was no single solution. Breaking the cycle would mean changing our whole way of life, which most people don't have the time, energy or support to do. In my view, the biggest restriction we have faced is our reliance on external employment that takes us away from the needs of our communities. This would change if we became super-organised. If we studied the markets in

HAVE YOU READ GEORGE'S PODCAST?

our lives and made long-term plans to create employment for our kids, things would get better. But this is literally my PhD; it's gonna take me a while to pull the whole picture together. Episode 19 was just an intro.

Fun Facts:

- The conversation between me and Marc in Scene 7 is based on a real phone call we had. One day he told me pretty much everything his character said in the scene, and after we talked it out, he agreed to re-enact it for the podcast. I will always appreciate bro's honesty. This is the same Marc who sat me down in 2018 and told me I'd been quiet for too long, prompting me to start 'HYHGP?'. The same one who had those wise words for me at the start of Episode 4, after my incident with the police. Love you, bro.

One thing I will always remember about writing Chapter 3 is the pressure I put on myself. Following the murder of George Floyd, Black Lives Matter protests caused the world to pay more attention to the challenges of the Black diaspora. I saw the glass as half-full: although I often find conversations about racial inequality frustrating and circular, in that moment, many people recommitted themselves to the kind of progress I had always dreamed of. And I wanted this chapter to be a part of that. So with Episode 19 I revisited the drama, and pointed to a golden opportunity: Black music. In previous chapters I hadn't been as direct in my focus on Blackness – it was just implied in the soundtrack and subject matter. But tragically, George Floyd gave us a chance to talk Black trauma, Black empowerment, Black creativity – all Black everything. In that respect, this episode sets the tone for the rest of Chapter 3. It was also a launchpad for *Common Ground*. Massive thanks to Anne, Darshan, Alex, Sigrid, Paul and Benbrick. These people worked like crazy to help me deliver *Common Ground* in time for the release of Episode 19.

Nicholas: ... I was saying that Year 3, Year 4, Year 5 and Year 6 know about you, and they were saying that I have a famous uncle.

[George laughs]

Nicholas: Because you're famous.

George: How did that make you feel?

Nicholas: Makes me feel proud.

George: That's a good word, I always feel proud about you lot, so it's nice to have the feeling back.

Malachi: What is this?

George: Where did they see me?

Malachi: You're creaming my hair.

Nicholas: Sorry?

George: Where did they see me?

Nicholas: They didn't see you but they knew about you.

Malachi: 'Cause you told them.

[George presses pause on his laptop]

SCENE 1: IN GEORGE'S OFFICE

[George sits quietly at his desk, distant noises from outside coming in through an open window]

George: People listen to this podcast for different reasons. I
Tried to get it ready for the Christmas season but I
Had to tweak some of my hopes and my dreams if you
Know what I mean 'cause . . . COVID-19.

In the past year we've all had to cope with struggles, so
I don't wanna bore you with my covid troubles.
I just wanna give you Chapter 3,
Along with a platform to feed back to me.
Plus this time I've got the BBC Concert Orchestra backing me, boy.
The first piece of music you'll hear, we recorded in lockdown but
   after that, everything you hear was recorded at Abbey Road
   Studios, you know like that.

Anyway, as I was saying: I wanna give you Chapter 3
Along with a platform to feed back to me.

SCENE 2: IN GEORGE'S CAR

[Cut to George entering his car and closing the door]

George: To get that done, I gotta sit in my car,
and refuse to leave until I've written a bar.
Once I've written something I'ma take it to Benbrick,
Record it, and find a way to make it eccentric.

'Cause if my podcast sounds normal, then I'm not
Giving you enough reason to listen. And I
Really need you to listen,
That's why I make it sound different.

SCENE 3: ON THE BLOCK

[George exits the car and stands outside an apartment block, where kids are playing]

George: So . . . welcome back. Give yourself a clap. You
Made the right decision by taking time to listen. This is
Why I said 'Let me not be a politician,
Let me write lyrics.' How many politicians get your
Undivided attention for twenty-five minutes?

Besides . . .

If you start listening to me at eight years old, and in
Ten years' time you're old enough to vote. That's
Ten years of listening to the poems that I wrote. In
Ten years I'ma reap the seeds that I've sown. It's
Politics man, I can't just leave that alone. I can
See the pattern. I can see what needs to happen. We
Need to move away from employment that
Doesn't solve our problems and makes us avoid them.

Put it like this: if what you do for your
Salary puts a strain on your sanity,
Or even just your fun and enjoyment . . .
Then, in an ideal world . . .
You should be able to find other employment.

I'm not talking about fantasy jobs where you just walk in and out. I'm
Talking *new* opportunities with no limitation.
You know, innovation.

SCENE 4: IN KAMPALA

[Cut to a field in Kampala, Uganda, where some kids are playing football]

George: Listen, no one can measure the hidden innovation
That's living in a nation.
Hidden because of timing and environment and
Just situations where citizens aren't given information.

No one can measure the hidden innovation
That's living in a nation.
Hidden because of timing and environment and
Situations where people ain't given information.

Every generation invents something.
And every invention meant nothing . . .
Until it meant something.

SCENE 5: INNOVATION IN BLACK MUSIC

[Cut to still images of the historical inventions mentioned in the following verse]

You think Alexander Graham Bell could have ever known
All the jobs he'd generated when he made the telephone?

Let me give a more recent example.
Twenty years ago Black Britain invented Garage.
Wiley got involved and he made it Grime.
His invention became my favourite genre but
When I got to Cambridge, I created mine.

My first innovation was poetry with a Rap style,
Which you'd recognise if you know of me from my background.
My second innovation was musical poetry;

Getting musicians and producers to flow with me.
But I'm an artist. I'm a free spirit.
I couldn't fit these lyrics into three minutes. Now
Picture me praying on that problem and God answering.
That's how I came to this podcasting thing.

Does it bother me when people copy me?
Not really. Take it. You don't need to ask.
Every decent innovation leads to imitation.
We're not the first, and we won't be the last.

The best demonstration is the next generation. I
Bet you any money they're gonna come up with something new
That leads to economic acceleration.

I've seen a lot of Black communities do this
And the vehicle among the young is usually music.
Black people have made popular new sounds from the
Early 1800s up to the 2000s.
And there's no sign of us losing this ability.
Music continues to improve our visibility.
Every Black society's been abused in recent history but
Music has supported us through this instability.

The richest artists in the world are Black.
One of them started off making sales of crack.
Which tells us that music's been a lifeline
In a system that's always held us back.

You know who I mean, right?
The only act with more number one albums than
Jay-Z is The Beatles.
And the whole foundation of their incredible sales is
Black music – they've said it themselves.

[John Lennon quote: Black music was my life and still is,' John Said.

'This whole change of style was started by Rock 'n' Roll, and Rock 'n' Roll is Black.']

George: Listen, I'm not as concerned with credit and sales as I
Am with seeing us develop ourselves. So
Given what we've given for the time it's been working, when
People take our Blackness and define it as 'urban',
Just so they can sell it without us taking credit
I find it disturbing.

And maybe I wouldn't *feel* it as much . . .
If we didn't *need* it as much.

Music is our golden ticket, and we're
Missing out on a lot if we don't admit it. We
Need change and if our position in the economy won't permit it, we
Need to use the opportunities inequality won't inhibit.

So I'm saying we can pull a lot of Black people out of perpetual
    poverty
By thinking of music as our intellectual property.

And on that cheerful note . . . welcome to Chapter Three of my
    podcast.

You ready? Let's go.

[Soundtrack: J Hus 'Repeat']

SCENE 6: GEORGE IN THE MARKETPLACE

[Montage of people introducing George The Poet. Scene opens with George managing his own stall in a busy indoor market. A customer approaches]

Customer: Excuse me. Hi . . . hey.

George: Oh, yes Miss, how can I help you?
Customer: I was just wondering what you're selling here.

George: Right . . .

Customer: I can't really tell.

George: OK so, basically, we sell poetry. Over here we've got music, a podcast, classic album, some timeless records. These are our social campaigns – we've done everything from diabetes to blood donation. And over here we have TV ads.

Customer: OK, so music campaigns, adverts, that kind of thing?

George: That's right.

Customer: But if I really wanted to understand more about you, what should I listen to?

George: Well, it depends what you're looking for. Do you wanna laugh? Wanna cry? Wanna learn something new?

Customer: [Laughing] I don't want to cry!

George: Alright, then I recommend the podcast.

Customer: I'm not really a podcast person.

George: Yeah, most people say that. Tell you what, put these on, have a listen to the reviews, and if you're interested, we can take it from there.

[Customer puts on headphones and hears positive reviews of *HYHGP*. She then removes the headphones]

Customer: Wow. People really seem to love your work.

George: You know. We try.

Customer: So what's an artist like you doing in the marketplace?

George: Boy . . . the market is how the art reaches the people. I mean, I've met you. You're gonna listen, right?

Customer: Mmm. Maybe. Anyway, I've got to go. Hope you have a good day.

George: Nice meeting you.

[Customer moves on, George gets back to work]

SCENE 7: PROS AND CONS OF THE MARKET

George: When you have a business that leaves
Customers with a sweet, unique aftertaste
Over time you're gonna craft a space that's
Just for you in the marketplace.

The thing about the market, it's 24/7.
People are buying but there's many more selling.
Imagine one corner with three different hustlers
All of them competing for customers.
One of them is rich already – they hit the belly –
The other two are trying to get paid 'cause they need it for
    sustenance.

We've all got to focus on whatever we want, but the
Market isn't kind to everyone.

And trust me, when the market isn't kind
It can be harsh like prison time.

The market doesn't care about human beings, or the
Difficult positions it puts you and me in 'cause
in a *real* market, there's no higher command
Than the laws of supply and demand.

People want what they want, and if
You can help them . . .
You've got a chance of doing well then.

I'm not a hundred percent in love with the market, but I
Recognise the need for money regardless.
All it takes is one pandemic to turn a creative mind into a struggling
    artist.
If life was fair the one hustling hardest
Would be the one to recover the fastest but
Life was never your bredrin.
And the market is 24/7.

[George's phone rings. He picks up]

George: One second.
Yo brudda.

Marc: Wagwan.

George: Everything good?

Marc: Calm. But you wouldn't know that 'cause you never phone back.

George: I know, I know, I know, akh.

Marc: I could be in jail for all you know. It's always
Me making the effort to call you, bro.

George: Brudda I know, trust me, it's just—

Marc: Know what? What do you think you know?
Cah I don't think you do, bro.
You see respect . . . it's not about words . . . it's how you act, my g.
No one's got your back like me.

The way I show my respect for you is protection.
I'm a protective yout.
But if months go by and I can't get a reply
That would take you a second to write . . .
It feels like you're shitting on my love for you, bro. And I
Know you don't mean it; I just want you to know.

You don't wanna be that famous guy from the
Hood that mandem don't chat to. But
G, if man can't follow your path, you
Know what I'm gonna go back to.

I rate what you've done with the poetry, and I
Know the world needs you . . . but so do we.

SCENE 8: HEAVY IS THE HEAD

[Soundtrack: Stormzy 'Crown']

Reporter 1: Young offenders locked in their cells almost all day, reckless violence and staff being attacked. A damning report into Feltham Young Offenders Prison.

Reporter 2: Shooting and death have been recorded in different parts of Uganda as angry protesters demand for the release of Robert Kyagulanyi.

Reporter 3: London, Manchester, Cardiff, Leicester and Sheffield saw the Black Lives Matter protests following the killing of George Floyd in the US city of Minneapolis.

John Boyega: We have always meant something! We have always succeeded, regardless! And now is the time! I ain't waiting!

David Lammy MP: The first British ships arrived in the Caribbean in 1623, and despite slavery, twenty five thousand Caribbeans served in the First World War and Second World War, alongside British troops.

Anthony Brown: We had people coming into our surgeries who are facing dismissal from their jobs, they've been here for forty years, never had any need for documents, but are being told by their employers they're going to be sacked!

David Lammy MP: It is inhumane and cruel for so many of that Windrush generation to have suffered so long in this condition and for the Secretary of State only to have made a statement today . . .

Florence Eshalomi MP: Does the home secretary recognise that there is structural inequality, discrimination and racism in our country?

Protester: The most important thing is what we do after . . . where this message goes and who can take something from this and do something impactful in their community.

SCENE 9: GEORGE APOLOGISES

[Return to George and Marc's phone call]

George: Bro, I apologise.
I know it's like I've been chasing them dollar signs
And I left you in the hood and now my thing's on the rise.

I don't think it's that, but I'm not arguing.
I just want to give you my perspective.

You know I see Black people like a worldwide collective.
Everywhere we go we've got Black people problems
Making us feel like we lack legal options.
Not just in the Ends; with the governments of Africa.
We've got so much conflict and we're struggling to patch it up.

Children need affection, youngers need direction
Workers need protections and free and fair elections, and the
More I study our people, bro, the more I
Realise how much time it's gonna take.
Over here we're trying to make it make sense.
Over there they're up against the violence of the state.

All of us agree we need to find another way
Some of us are mainly reliant on our faith,
None of us can say we have a political system that's
International, reliable and safe.

See, what that means is our survival is at stake, which
Makes me numb to how successful I'm becoming.
You look at me like I've won the rat race, but to
Me, bro, there's no finish line. I'm just running.

But you're right, I have been neglectful.
And that must feel a tad disrespectful.
True you're not the only one, the mandem wanna hear from me
I just been tryna pattern the next steps carefully.

Marc: I hear you g. Don't even apologise
We just feel a way because we're lonely and we're colonised
And we look to you for direction.
'Cause you're the homie. And you're qualified.

SCENE 10: GEORGE HAS AN IDEA

[Cut back to the block from Scene 3]

George: Everyone who's done well from a community like mine
Has had this conversation in some way, shape or form.
Asking themselves why where they're from, the
Way *they* performed ain't the norm.

Why couldn't everyone just focus on their passions? It's
Jarring when you start noticing the patterns.
Loads of things have happened. For a start,
Our history was broken into fragments.
But some of us became poets and adapted.
Nothing restored our soul the way that rap did.
Black music has always been a major earner . . .
But now we've got to take it further.

[Ambience of the block fades]

All I know is the kids make songs and the songs make jobs.
It really is that simple.
I'm not just talking any random jobs;
Ones that we've actually got a passion for.
Music is medicine that fixes you, and we've got
Medicine the whole world's addicted to.
And it comes naturally to us. Granted,
Not every artist is guaranteed to bus.
But every generation of Black artists
Makes a new sound that dominates the mass market.
I believe that's a talent we can trust and the
Full potential of it hasn't been discussed.

Black life is stuck in crisis after crisis.
And we can leave this nightmare.
If we make a long-term plan around this music
All the employment we need is right there.

Across the Chapter 3 scenes
I'm gonna show you what this actually means. And
You're gonna let me know if I'm making sense.
Your feedback is the main event.

SCENE 11: TRAIN OF THOUGHT

[Cut to George sitting in a train carriage]

See, my dream is for the audience to become a network.
Think about it: we've already done the leg work.
You've become my main support. You and
All these other passengers on my train of thought.

From Chapter 1 to
Chapter 2. Now I'm trying to hear back from
You for Chapter 3.
And I've come up with a way for you to chat to me.

It's called 'Common Ground': my brand-new online platform.
You should check it out; it's not long.
I made it for you. We're waiting for you. So check it out at
GTPCG.com

You might be wondering 'Why Common Ground?'
Well, imagine this podcast is a house
And every episode is a room. I
Didn't build this house to sit here alone, so
Anytime you visit me I'm over the moon.

The conversations we have when you come around . . .
That's us establishing Common Ground. If
You enjoy this podcast, give me your feedback. To
You it might be nothing, but trust me I need that.

GTPCG.com
Check it out. It's not long.

Now my train of thought can meet you at this platform so
Let me guide you through this journey. It's
Hard to predict where this experiment will take us 'cause
Right now, it's super early.

But all I know is . . .
Some of my biggest fans don't exist yet but
Overlooking them would be a total misstep.
When they arrive I wanna be there for them.
And I need you to help me prepare for them.

I don't know who, I don't know where and when but
One day they're gonna come across this work.
That's gonna bring them into my world and
I want their lives to change there and then.

Which is why I need my audience to become a network . . .
I wanna see how deep we can go.
I'm not a tech nerd, I'm not a comms expert, so I
Teamed up with three of the smartest people I know.

Darshan: Common Ground is like the afterparty to your podcast.

George: My bredrin Darshan, *he's* a design and tech nerd.
But he's also a social entrepreneur.

Darshan: This is a chance for that conversation to continue, where you listen to them, everyone listens to each other, ideas are exchanged, and from those exchanged ideas, magic can happen.

George: He understands a lot of humanitarian issues,
And he helps people and companies respond to them all.

Anne: Common Ground is not your average survey, guys.

George: Anne specialises in Strategy and Research.

Anne: We need to find out how different kinds of people can actually agree and come together to generate solutions, then feed all of that into data artistry to reward the listener's curiosity.

George: She's into Communications and Data Collection . . .
Meaning she's not just good at asking questions –
She's great at reflecting, and making connections.

Benbrick: Like, if we can get those first one hundred people interested in using this, we can grow to become a destination for people involved in your story, and give them a space to tell their story.

George: And you already know about Benbrick. The
Man helping me put this podcast together. Not
Only is he a world-class composer, producer and
Sound engineer . . . he's also kind of clever.

For almost a year we've been working on this platform
To allow me and my listeners to interact more.
So sign up – it's not long.
GTPCG.com

EPISODE 20: Young

Extra Info:

- This episode copied the format of Episode 9, 'Sabrina's Boy'; I analysed the life of a famous rapper to study the environment that shaped him. I think we should do this with rappers as much as possible, because the most successful tend to come from the harshest backgrounds. The sad reality is that they're not the only talented people from their area – the others just didn't make it. So, we need to get better at correcting the injustices that their life stories point to.

Fun Facts:

- The title is layered: 'Young' is a nickname Jay sometimes uses, (shortened from 'Young Hova the God MC'); 'young' also refers to the young Jay-Z that the episode focuses on, and 'young' is the last word of the episode, which Jay uses to describe most rappers, who he and I both argue, need more support.

When I left the music industry in 2015, I needed a reset. To figure out my next move, I thought about the basic ingredients of my career: storytelling and social responsibility. I started looking around for storytellers I admired, and as previously mentioned, Netflix and Disney helped me think big about the power of stories. But coming from an inner-city neighbourhood, with a lyrical ability I had picked up from that environment, I really took my lead from rap music. This was the storytelling that suited my accent, my interests and my perspective. By that point I had learned to treat rap like an archive of Black thought. I could listen to any rap song and find clues about the world around the rapper. But in my search for direction, I realised that some rappers gave me more clarity than others – none more than Jay-Z. I was drawn to Jay's ability to get what he wanted out of life, year after year, especially because he did it by telling his own story. To understand how I could do the same, I developed a habit of listening to all his albums, even when I didn't feel like it. During that period, I was reborn as an entrepreneur; Jay-Z's perspective helped me create new value as an independent artist, and I'm not the only one. Many of us aspire to overcome adversity, exceed expectations and create opportunities for others in the way he has done – so what's stopping us?

SCENE 1: GEORGE WRITING IN HIS ROOM

George: Look at me. Typing away.
Trying to see how many words I can write in a day. In
Two months I've got to write seventy thousand words.
I know it sounds absurd.
But I've got a head full of nouns and verbs . . . and
Music. Music helps me calm down the nerves.

[Soundtrack: Nines ft. Tiggs Da Author 'NIC']

George: So. Why am I writing a book? When
I could make more money from writing a hook . . .
When I've got a podcast that's doing well enough, and a
Woman to attend to since I fell in love.

[George's fiancée, Sandra enters George's writing room]

Sandra: Babe . . .

George: Yo.

Sandra: Don't forget you have a meeting in thirty minutes.

George: Alright, thank you very much, babe.

On one hand, I'm a artist at the top of his game, on the
Other I'm a philosopher with a lot to explain.

SCENE 2: UNCLE GEORGE

[Cut to George driving with his nephews chatting in the background]

George: I wanna teach people how to make money from their passion,
Using my career as a guiding light.

Some people can't do much with my advice. For
Others, my advice might suffice.

SCENE 3: GEORGE ON THE BLOCK

**[Cut to George walking through his old neighbourhood, music
blasting from the block]**

Plan A was to teach through music.

SCENE 4: GEORGE DOING HOUSEWORK

[Cut to George tidying up, TV on in the background]

George: Plan B was to do it through TV. I was
Working on both when I realised podcasting
was the best way for the audience to receive me.

SCENE 5: GEORGE WITH HIS COUSIN

[George's cousin reacts excitedly as they talk about the future]

George: That took about . . . seven years to figure out. I
Spent two of them seven years in a drought. I
Spent a lot of money on a lot of experiments and
This right here is what I offer as evidence.

SCENE 6: BACK IN GEORGE'S ROOM

George: I feel like I know why this podcast has become successful.
There's a formula to it, which I wanna share with
Everyone trying to write something special.

But it's impossible to tell you the formula without
Explaining certain things first. I'm talking about the
Business . . . and psychology of
working with words.

Now, I don't wanna waste your time,
As much as I don't wanna waste mine.
So, we need to make sure we understand each other,
And that's gonna take time.

For those who wanna learn more and wanna support me . . .
Best place to start is the following story.

SCENE 7: A MAN CALLED RAY

George: A man called Ray was stabbed to death, and
There was no criminal conviction. His
Brother, AJ swore to get revenge,
But he lost his way to a heroin addiction.

[Page turn]

George: For AJ, life before this
Revolved around a wife and four kids, but the
Tragedy broke him down for sure. And
Grief drove him out the door.

[A restless man leaves his family home]

George: For the youngest it was a hell of a burn . . .
Coming to terms with the fact Daddy would never return.
The kid ended up on the street
Trying to feed himself when there was nothing to eat.

When he was fifteen, his bredrin found a way. A
New opportunity several miles away.

[Cut to an open-air drug market in a run-down urban area]

George: Gone were the days of selling vials of yay;
Crack was moving 24/7 round the way. And
Yeah, Mummy raised him right. But they were hurting
and she was working day and night. The boy
Craved the comfort the dough provided. And
That craving made him open-minded.

[Page turn]

George: His ends was full of drug lords he didn't wanna work for.
So he didn't sell there 'cause it would start a turf war. The
Boy and his friend went further down the road,
Found an abode, stuck around and sold.

Do you remember any of your childhood goals?
You don't wanna hear mine. Mine were silly.
His was to sell crack until he reached a milli.

That said, since fifteen he was busy.
Everything changed, he forgot 'bout the rules.
Selling Class As now he dropped out of school.
Any time he left the house he bopped out with tools.
Pulled up in a new car and hopped out with jewels.

[A teenager hops out of a sports car]

George: Most in his age group were getting into beef
Fighting over real estate, flexing in the streets.

[Page turn]

George: He was in the trap house seven days a week but he
Moved down south and he never made a peep.

That's a lot of beef that he'd surely avoid. The more blocks needed
    work, the more he employed.
He was good at school, but he didn't see the point, people
Said 'It's such a shame about Gloria's boy.'

Just another trap-star trapping. The
Only thing he did as much as that was rapping, but
With a talent like his, something had to happen.

First it was a hobby. As and when, since he didn't
Work for anybody.
Then he got a reputation for rhyming well, but the
Only words he cared about were 'buy' and 'sell'.
As a teen he got used to dressing fly as hell, and he
Understood that nothing just happens by itself. He
Didn't want fans, he wanted clientele. For
This, he would risk a lot of time in jail.

SCENE 8: TYPICAL

[Return to George typing in his room]

George: Now where I grew up, the picture I've painted so far
Is typical. Breaking the cycle of fatherless boys becoming
Drug dealers . . . is difficult.

I've never seen a government do it and I've seen
neighbourhoods across the world struggling through it. But the
Few times I've seen people turn that experience into something
    positive,
They've done it with music.

[Page turn]

SCENE 9: A LIFELINE

George: Anyway, back to the kid.
When he wasn't dipping out the ends in his Volvo
He was making music with a friend called Rodolfo,
Usually in twos and threes with friends from his postcode.
Then he went back into ghost mode.

But one of those local guys got a record deal.
This brudda's name was Jonathan. The kid was
Back down south but Jonathan hadn't forgotten him
So as soon as he came home, Jonathan hollered him.

[Jonathan and the kid meet and enter an apartment]

George: The label would pay for Jonny to record abroad and he
Wanted to bring the kid. All aboard. This
Thing's about to take off, can you ignore the call?

The kid closed his eyes and he saw it all: he could
Give himself a chance to get out of the streets or
Keep on playing cat and mouse with police.
Deep down he knew he was living a lie.
So he decided to give it a try.

SCENE 10: NEW HORIZONS

[Cut to the kid boarding a plane]

George: You know what's so funny?
Even though this was Jonathan's opportunity,
The kid came with his own money.
For five years, he'd never slowed on his grind.
By now he was in control of his time.

SCENE 11: HARSH LESSONS

[Cut to the kid waiting outside an office while Jonathan argues with record label executives inside]

George: Couldn't say the same for Jonathan though. When the
Label made a decision, he wasn't involved.
They didn't care if his project was cold; they
Only cared about how many copies it sold.

[Jonathan storms out of the office]

George: The lesson was clear; respect wasn't there. But
That weren't the only thing the kid learned.

He studied the game like an intern. Reading it quietly like me in the
    library back in spring term.
Just kept working, and networking.

Eventually, when he came back to the Ends he found
Out feds arrested a batch of his friends for
What was to him an everyday thing. The
Sentences they received were devastating.

He couldn't see a future in record-making.
Jonathan just got dropped from his label. For the kid, the street
    option was stable.

So he dedicated himself to elevating his wealth.
And even though the same drug turning neighbourhoods to
War zones was generating this wealth,
He was ready to lie in the bed he made for himself.
Even when his own friend tried to kill him, he
Still found a way to get away from the shells.
Knowing he was under investigation as well, he
Kept escaping from Twelve with preparation and stealth.

SCENE 12: A COMMON DILEMMA

[Return to George typing and reflecting in his room]

George: Where I'm from this is a common dilemma.
People went through this a lot in my era.
If your options were making cash with your boys and making
Music for free, you'd make a rational choice.

I don't believe there's no other way.
Why is this so common for us? No one can say.
As a teen I was in a similar position
Crime was calling but I didn't wanna listen.
Mainly 'cause I lived with my younger siblings
And I knew the streets could be . . . unforgiving.

Plus, I was doing well in school, my grades were incredible.
I felt like I had what I needed to advance.
Young people *need* that sense of security.
Too many communities are leaving this to chance.

But there are still those unsung heroes
Who put in the time, and nurture the youth.
So come we get back to the story of the kid
And the struggle to take him from the kerb to the booth.

[Page turn]

SCENE 13: A GUY CALLED DAMON

George: All along, his old friend Rodolfo
Believed in the kid, even when he had no hope.
One day, Rodolfo met a guy called Damon.
Damon was building a name in entertainment.
Like the kid, Damon got his training from the street,
So, Rodolfo arranged for them to meet.

Damon turned out to be a useful connect.
Between him and the kid there was mutual respect.
All drug dealers need an exit plan,
Which by now the kid grew to accept. And
Even though their lifestyle was lavish and grand,
Damon had him a plan: to establish a brand.

SCENE 14: CRACK MUSIC

[A door opens, leading to a lounge in which an energetic audience awaits a live performance. George quietly walks over to the stage]

George: Selling drugs ain't a character trait.
It's no one's natural state.
So why is it a factor on so many estates?
People have to trade.
Work comes up, cash gets paid,
That's how a transaction's made.

[Soundtrack: Lonnie Liston Smith 'A Garden of Peace']

George: Some people make billions and tax evade,
Others sell crack cocaine and invest in their
Music until their tracks get played enough to attract some fame
And transition into legal ambition.

We hear a lot of music about crack cocaine but
Most of us can't explain how it attacks the brain.

To me crack looks like a different kind of smoke. It
Looks like a spirit that grips you by the throat
Jumps into your eyes and sits inside your soul.
I watched J***** dad lose control
Walking around with no shoes on road.

Auntie must have been heartbroken.
And I always thought . . .
What could make a man like him start smoking?

Now, what if you were young, and cash weren't attainable . . .
And crack was the only work available?
Could you stomach what it's doing to your people?
Would you call it opportunity or evil?

Damon made a choice, just like the kid.
That's why they teamed up like they did.
They came from the same place as entrepreneurs.
The look in their eyes said 'my money's gonna be longer than
    yours . . .'

They moved like celebrities with sponsors, awards, getting constant
    applause.
The business model was unconscionable but at
Seven figures they felt like they conquered it all.

So, like I said, Damon had him a plan; to establish a brand.
When he sensed opportunity, he grabbed it and ran.
And he saw it in this young, rich, arrogant man
With a talent for rap in a balancing act; trying to
Leave the streets before he's deceased but in
Need of a scheme to clean his pees.

Rap was the vehicle to tell their story so the
Plan was simple: sell their story.
Record one album, sell a hundred thousand,
Sign other artists, and try other markets.

Damon was convinced this guy was the hardest but
Labels weren't offering a record deal.
When he came around, they would act funny.
So he said 'Cool. Forget a deal.

Let's flip this crack money into rap money.'
Thank you.

[Audience applauds]

SCENE 15: A STAR IS BORN

[A montage of Jay-Z's accolades. Jay-Z walks through a door to the back of a New York apartment block]

[Soundtrack: Jay-Z 'Dead Presidents']

George: I just gave you the story of early Jay-Z.
As you can see, his journey's crazy.
At a young age, he started to rap. And
'Cause of that, he outsmarted the trap.

[Jay walks through another door and brings the audience back to George's room]

George: His first 25 years were like the
Opposite of his next 25 years.
Why him? Why's no one else *like* him?
I've got so many ideas.

I ain't gonna run through them all. It's fun food for
Thought but my theories are unprovable. Just
Know that as boys tryna battle irrelevance
Jay-Z was the closest thing we had to a president.

He always carried himself like a head of state,
Even when the industry treated him like a featherweight, he
Stuck to it, 'cause he believed he could sell a tape.
And lyrically, everything he said was great.

To this very day he's the one we're trying to emulate.
It's not just about the money that you generate;
It's about the character you demonstrate.

Jay-Z led the way in getting paid to tell it straight.
I don't know about you, but I can't think of a better fate.

So, let's go back to the start.
If you met this guy called Shawn as a young drug dealer,
How would you know he had a passion for art?
Whose job would it be to nurture the
Potential that he himself couldn't see?

SCENE 16: SHAWN'S POTENTIAL

[A quote from Jay-Z's mum, Gloria Carter]

Jay's Mum: *Shawn used to be in the kitchen, beating on the table and rapping into the wee hours of the morning. And then I bought him a boom box, and his sisters and brothers said that he would drive them nuts. But that was my way to keep him close to me and out of trouble.*

George: His mum saw it. Music had a hold on him. She
Used it to stay close to him and keep control of him.
Any parent can find it hard to keep control,
Let alone a working mum once the father leaves his role.
Yeah, AJ's departure took a toll.
And sometimes, only art can ease the soul.

[A quote from Jay-Z's song 'Blueprint']

Jay-Z: *Momma raised me/*
Pop, I miss you/
God help me forgive him I got some issues

[A quote from Ms Lowden, Jay's elementary school English teacher]

Ms Lowden: *... And my daughter said, 'Did you teach Jay-Z?' I said, 'Who's Jay-Z?'*
It was Shawn Carter! My little Shawn, he was a skinny little kid! He never smiled, that was when his father had left. I knew he was extremely bright, but he was quiet.

George: His teacher saw it. But Shawn decided the
Education system would never make a difference to
His needs, like getting paid, for instance.

Ms Lowden made Shawn feel special.
English became his favourite classes.
That little effort went a long way in
Shaping one of the world's greatest artists.

[A quote from Jay-Z's song 'Blueprint']

Jay-Z: *Kitchen table/*
That's where I honed my skills/
Jaz made me believe this shit was real ...

Narrative: *Jonathan, or Jaz-O, another promising rapper from the Marcy Projects, was four years older than Jay, and became an early mentor to him. Around this time, Jaz was struck by the immense potential and raw talent that young Shawn displayed.*

George: Jonathan saw it. Rapper to rapper, he
Saw that the kid had the competence for it.
He was nineteen, Shawn was fifteen.
Compliments had both their confidence soaring. But
Shawn didn't make time for constant recording. To
Him, earning from rap wasn't important.
He was in the streets 'cause he could make
Much more money from shotting than touring.

[A quote from Jay-Z's song 'Blueprint']

Jay-Z: *Labels turned me down, couldn't foresee/*
Clark sought me out, Dame believed . . .

George: Rodolfo, AKA DJ Clark Kent
Used to record little Shawn in his apartment. He
Says Shawn was even in a different class *then*.
Sixteen spitting 16s on a park bench.
But chasing money is a funny thing; there's
Never enough drinks for a thirst you can't quench.
Young Jay-Z needed a nudge.
And till it came, he didn't budge.

[An excerpt from a DJ Clark Kent interview]

Interviewer: *Why was Jay-Z not wanting to focus on rap at one point in time?*

DJ Clark Kent: *He was doing well. If you're doing well and you look at rappers and rappers aren't doing as well as you, you kinda look at them like, 'This is corny . . .'*

Interviewer: *Now, you actually introduced Dame Dash and Jay-Z?*

DJ Clark Kent: *Yes. Watching him with his artists made me tell him, 'You need to hear my boy . . .' So when I finally convince him to come to Brooklyn and he meets Jay he's like 'Wait a minute, he's just like me!'*

George: I don't know about you, but
Personally, I get anxious.
Thinking about the baby Jay-Zs in my community.
Could be rappers, might be gangsters.

Shawn was blessed with a mum like Gloria
How many others with a similar story are?

How many have a talented friend like Jaz-O?
How many young Jay Zs are seeing mad doe?
Dirty dollars making cold hard cents.
Do they have their own Clark Kents?

SCENE 17: HUSTLERS UNITE

[Return to George's writing room]

George: By the time Jay-Z met Damon Dash he was
Slyly addicted to making cash. And I
Mean addicted in all seriousness.
A lot of young hustlers experience this.
When it's not even a question of selling enough, and they're
Just so deeply enveloped in stuff that their
Family and friends ain't telling them nothing, 'cause they're
Addicts – for the adrenaline rush.
Especially the ones that have never been touched,
Believing they'll forever be levelling up.
Anyone in that position will tell you: the
World is never enough.

So, Damon believed, Rodolfo believed,
Jonathan believed, the locals believed,
Ms Lowden believed, Jay-Z's mum believed.
You know who didn't? The record companies.

They were like, 'How is this guy different from
Every other rapper that claims to run the streets?' They
Never saw Jay-Z becoming a somebody. So
Jay and Dame decided to self-fund the dream.
In comes Kareem –
Another street guy who lived comfortably.

Kareem was a member of Damon's crew
Investing is what he came to do, 'cause he

Made his loot the way Jay did too. Dame
Pitched him the vision of what they could do.
Kareem wasn't sure about Jay himself.
Not until the day he got a real display of the
Skills in Jay's vocal presence, when he
Battled a local legend . . . named Big L.

So, the three partners mapped out a route to success,
Broke it down and wrote it down.
Jay was the artist, Dame was the manager,
Kareem contributed an undisclosed amount. They
Made the opportunity some said they wouldn't get.
Roc-A-Fella Records was now in full effect.

[An excerpt from a Kareem 'Biggs' Burke interview]

Kareem: *There was always something in all of our lives that kind of changed, you know. Dame, when his mother died, Jay when his father left him as a kid and me being evicted when I was ten years old and living in a shelter for years. It was always that one thing in our lives that we had in common that we knew that we wanted to take over the world and do something that was ground-breaking.*

George: Damon had him a plan: to establish a brand
And diversify from fashion to producing films.
The first step was to drop Jay-Z's debut album,
So, they secured a distribution deal.
The details of the deal were a bit confusing still.
But we'll discuss that some other time.
Following a release their following would increase, but
Until the outcome was green, they were colour-blind.

SCENE 18: LESSONS LEARNED

[Return to George typing in his room]

I know Jay's narrative like the back of my hand
Mainly because I'm a passionate fan.
And when you're passionate about something
It's not hard learning from it.
Jay-Z gave me the blueprint to
Make my life story turn a profit.

I've studied him closely, by accident mostly,
Just through having his music on repeat, and
Watching him build a movement from the streets.

See, the success of any celebrity
Brings attention to the place that they're from.
Rappers store a lot of information in songs but
Listeners often opt out of taking it on.
Which is partly why Jay-Z's first album
Didn't get the greatest response.

But anyway. My point is this:

Shawn Carter's an extreme example of
Something that happens every day:
Children born into violent times
Finding a way out by writing rhymes. But
He was successful 'cause of financial freedom.
Freedom he got from a life of crime.
So, what do we do about the young Jay-Zs out
Here that ain't ready to leave the life behind?

If those kids are unsupported, they're gonna
Make the same choices younger Shawn did.
It's hard to prevent people turning to crime when
Good behaviour goes unrewarded.

But not all of these young people can be rappers
Let alone rappers on Jay-Z's level.
Most don't make it. But some of us do.
Like me. What made me special?

If I had to pick three things, I would say family support,
Hella rap and a whole lotta luck.
Know why that's sad? 'Cause it means there's still
No treasure map to the gold that I struck.

Black culture is big business, how the
Fuck does talent development still come down to luck?
Everywhere, young Black people are writing songs,
Full of potential, in need of the right response.
Every single year they shape the mainstream, in
Major ways and ways that *ain't* seen.
We need an investment model and I
Think we can take that straight from Jay-Z.

No he's not perfect. But he's the
Perfect picture of my hopes and my fears.
I hope for his level of growth with my peers.
I fear the popularity of dope boy ideas.
I hope to evolve how he managed to do, I
Fear the self-interest that mandem pursue.
I hope we face up to the challenging truth: that the
Streets can both empower and damage the youth.

[Soundtrack: Jay-Z 'My 1st Song']

SCENE 19: YOUNG

Jay-Z: *I never wanted to be a famous person. My intention was to tell my story and tell the truth.*

The realities of the situation are harsh, and they need to be told. We're the poets of our generation.

When most rap artists are popular, they're eighteen and nineteen years old, they're kids themselves. And they come from a rough neighbourhood. Self-esteem is low. We're all taught that we're less than and we're not equal to everyone else in the world.

And they're young.

EPISODE 21: Flying the Flag

Extra Info:

- I wrote this episode with lots on my mind. At the time, public figures were regularly being dragged online by angry people who focused intensely on something they had said or done, in order to discredit them. It was called 'cancel culture', and it made me think about the power of the media – especially the entertainment industry.

Fun Facts:

- I had some legendary special guests on this one. Zeze Millz did a great job as the voice of the General Public (of course) – she was so much fun to record. And Big Narstie, Alhan Gençay and Kae Kurd all did their thing too, helping me explain, like, 400 years of American history in about 3 minutes – much love and respect to you guys.

The main character of this episode is Business. But instead of telling a straightforward story about how Business shapes our world, I started by talking about Celebrity. Why? Because Celebrity is big Business. This episode comes after one about Jay-Z, who once said 'I'm not a business-man, I'm a business, man.' The entertainment industry is full of Black people who built successful businesses off the back of their own culture. And if you've made it this far into my work, you must know why that's important to me. As previously mentioned, my dream is for Black people to eventually control their own employment. For this to be possible across an entire generation, we need to identify sectors in which we have an advantage, and use those sectors to branch out – like Jay-Z did. But we also need to study how Business has affected humanity, good and bad. This is why I looked at American History. It's interesting how the business of colonisation made English settlers break away from their king, and then how the business of slavery gave the US an economic boost. Clearly, Business affects different people in different ways. It takes purpose, ethics and creativity for any business to uphold the values of a society. And as usual, I believe this can all be found in music.

SCENE 1: THEORY OF CHANGE

[George is sitting in his room, typing on his laptop]

George: Last episode was about Jay-Z. I
Used his life to break down my theory of change.
Which is all about Black music making serious change.

For me that's the most important point to make. I
Wanna share that message and avoid mistakes. So I
Used Jay-Z 'cause he's on the main stage.
His fame puts you and me on the same page.

See, pop culture is a group thing. And
When it comes to popular storytelling,
Jay-Z gave me the Blueprint.
On his last number one album he was forty-seven.

He had a
Lot of life experience before he was known. His
Music told *his* story alone. He could have
Died in the streets beefing with a rival, but
Telling his own story was his secret to survival.

Jay-Z's whole catalogue is like a
Treasure map starting in the Marcy Projects.
Casual listeners might not get this from his
Music, 'cause these bars need context. So if
You know his context and I know his context,
We can *connect* through his content.
These connections could lead to questions that
Help us find common ground when we need directions.

I mean . . . how did the three wise men find baby Jesus?
They followed a star.
Jay Z's not the three wise men, he's not baby Jesus,
Jay Z is the star.

If I can get my whole community to
See what I see in him . . . we
Might find investment opportunities that make our
Young people much more likely to win.

That's the *thing* when you get to be famous: you
Enter people's thoughts and get people to talk just by
Stepping through a door called 'celebrity status'.

SCENE 2: CELEBRITY STATUS

[George walks through a door that leads to a game show]

George: And that's why every public figure is
Locked in a certain relationship.
Some days it will make you feel good
Other days it makes you wanna—

[Another George bursts through another door. The audience laugh]

Other George: Break some shit!

SCENE 3: LOVE/HATE

[Cut to George relaxing at home]

George: Some days you'll be on Cloud 9 . . .

[The other George comes out of the toilet crying]

Other George: Other days you'll be lovesick.

[Audience laugh. The other George blows his nose]

George: Bro, you need more tissue?

[Return to game show]

George: And as every celebrity knows,
I'm talking about the general public.

Studio Audience: Ooooh!

George: Yeah, boo yourself!

SCENE 4: NEWS FLASH

[Cut to a parody news show. George is delivering his lines like a newsreader]

George: The thing about the general public is
She can just switch on you out of the blue. It's
Hard to resolve a disagreement with her
'Cause she'll always be louder than you.

[Cut to George inside a car, being booed and jeered at by an angry crowd]

And it doesn't take much to set her off, be-
Fore you know it she's shouting at you,
Clouding all your thoughts, demanding your remorse, and
If she doesn't get it she just talks and talks . . .

Bear in mind, she only knows you 'cause you built
Business that's commercially viable.
But if she doesn't feel you on a personal
Level, then you're personally liable.

But I'm sure she don't see it like this; there's
Two sides to every story. It's

Best if I give you an example of what
Happens when Jenny calls me.

SCENE 5: GEORGE AND THE GENERAL PUBLIC

[Phone rings, someone answers. George's voice comes through on the receiving end]

George: Hello?

[Soundtrack: Mahalia 'What You Did']

General Public: I know what you did. I know.

George: What?

General Public: And I wanna talk 'bout it. And I know you don't.

George: Jen, talk 'bout what?

General Public: I've been holding guard for so long, so long.
And I dunno where to start, I dunno where to start.

George: Jen, what did I do now?

[Montage of people's criticisms of George]

Critic 1: We've got to discuss this guy George The Poet . . .

Critic 2: I'm sick of seeing George the Poet on my screen . . .

Critic 3: George the Poet is a racist!

Critic 4: If you hate Britain that much, George, why don't you leave?!

Critic 5: George the Poet is a self-righteous hypocrite!

[Cut to George in a supermarket]

George: I was young when I got involved with the General Public,
And we've got a lot of love for each other. But I
See her other relationships and I think sometimes she
Kinda takes the piss. She
Looks for reasons to be distracted and offended but her
Energy is never really centred.

Then again, I'm not perfect. If she
Cancels me in the end, maybe I'll de-
serve it. But she
Cuts off so many people these days I
Just I just wonder if it's worth it.

[Cut to George conversing with a personified General Public, voiced
by Zeze Millz]

George: Jen, you're overreacting. I think you're
trying too hard to be socially tapped in.
You're moving a bit jumpy –
it's not every day witch-hunt b.

General Public: So now you're
gaslighting me after all I've done for you? George I'm *done* with
   you.

George: Jen, you can't just cancel everyone who
Doesn't see things your way. We've
Known each other for like ten years. You gonna
Write that off in one single day?

General Public: The George I knew had principles.
I'm not convinced of yours.

Nowadays you do business with
Anyone. George, it makes you look insecure.

George: Jen, I grew up around drug dealers
Doing drug dealer shit.
No one in the Ends wanted to be legit 'cause we
Had no leadership where we needed it.

General Public: Here we go . . .

George: But I didn't just abandon the mandem, or
write them off as evil kids. 'Cause if you
Wanna show people a pathway, you gotta
Start by meeting them halfway, Jen that takes patience.

General Public: This conversation can't continue until you apologise.

George: Jen, you need to learn how to compromise!

General Public: Did we compromise for George Floyd? 'Cause if
Not I don't see your point.

George: Nah, Jen you're on't do that. Don't act like I don't do my job.

General Public: When it suits you. But if you can't get some
Good press or a quick check you go really quiet.

George: When was I quiet?

General Public: Wiley.

George: *Wiley?* You needed me to comment on Wiley? Jen,
Why me? I've got stronger opinions on the
State of Lebanon. Or
maybe those issues ain't as relevant?

General Public: That's it! Change the subject 'cause you
Can't be bothered to engage the public.

George: Oh my God. Jen, you're done out here. Listen. All I'm saying
is, I don't owe it to you to explain everything I feel. Your
Problem is you confuse talking with action.

General Public: Like I said, the George I knew had principles. I'm not
convinced of yours.

[General Public hangs up]

SCENE 6: THE RISE OF MAHALIA

[George sits in his car]

George: That's my dynamic with the general public.
When we're on the same page I love it.
When we're not, all of a sudden I'm a
Talentless, race-baiting, Britain-hating, flipping pagan.

The thing is, she genuinely has multiple personalities.
And the tension that creates, only gets worse apparently.

[George switches on the engine, Mahalia's song resumes]

George: Oooooh.
Music makes me feel like nothing's wrong
One second I've got loads on my mind, next second I *love* this song.

It's called 'What You Did' by Mahalia and Ella Mai,
Setting the record straight with an ex that went astray
And it blows my mind how songwriters convert personal stress
Into commercial success.
Listen to the *words* that she says.

Mahalia: *You've become the reason I'm so down.*
Boy I won't excuse you, I don't wanna go down.

George: Mahalia's songs are unique, 'cause she
Writes about specific situations.
This time, it's the bitter disappointment that
Caused her to finish with a boyfriend.
It's about discovering your favourite person's fake, and
Coming to see them as your worst mistake. Most
Songs about disappointment are downbeat but this
One's bouncy, and it sounds sweet. Yet what they're
Saying is far from sweet. It's like 'Nah
g, you need to keep that apology far from me.
I do not forgive you, I want nothing with you. In
Fact if you really wanna bring my heart some peace
Get out my way while I let out my pain in an
R&B crossover masterpiece.'

[An excerpt from a Mahalia interview with SK Vibemaker]

SK: . . . you put your heart and soul on the line for everybody to hear your vulnerabilities.

Mahalia: Yeah!

SK: Was that easy?

Mahalia: No, it wasn't easy. And I had openly said that I wanted to be more vulnerable. 'Cause I felt like everybody's used to me talking about how I don't care and I'm over it, but I wanted people to feel that part of me that was like 'this . . . this actually hurts . . .'

George: It blows my mind how a songwriter
Converts personal stress into commercial success.
My community's got lots of stress.
I wonder how much of it can *we* convert into pop success.

I mean, what's 'success', right?

In Mahalia's case, her music's travelling at the craziest pace.
In 2019 she dropped her debut album, *Love and Compromise*
And it's safe to say she's on the rise.

From a business perspective, every successful
Song brings residual income. That's
Money that keeps coming in from a product,
Even though you only made the original thing once.
Bear in mind, she's in her early twenties. She's
Got her whole life ahead of her.
And already she's managed to cross over
To America.

[VO of an American TV presenter introducing Mahalia]

George: I keep coming back to America on this podcast 'cause
When it comes to entertainment those guys are rockstars.
They've got one of the biggest markets in the world.
And they've got a lot of artists living well.
You've got to admit, for a country with so much drama,
They do a good job of marketing themselves.

How did America become so attractive,
Capture our imagination and hold it captive?
Is this what the Founding Fathers had in mind? For
Answers, we gotta go back in time.

[Montage of American presidents, reversing in time]

SCENE 7: THE BIRTH OF THE UNITED STATES

[George has been transported to a cotton field in 1600s America]

George: To understand America's cultural dominance you
Gotta trace her wealth back to its ultimate origins.
We know she was built on the backs of slaves.
But, we're not discussing that today.

Back in 1607, King James the first of England
Commissioned shipping companies to
go to the American continent and set up British Colonies.

[Portrayal of King James by Big Narstie. King James addresses his men in a private meeting]

King James: Hear what I'm saying, yeah.
You man need to go over there, wrap that s*** up and come back with my pees, bro.

George: Now, the colonies were under the empire, and the
Empire was like a monopoly. Which meant
Everything the colonies produced was
The property of the monarchy.

SCENE 8: TENSIONS BETWEEN ENGLAND AND THE COLONIES

[Portrayal of a rebel by Alhan]

Rebel 1: F*** King James, bro! I'm putting in mad work, and giving him everything! It don't make no sense! F*** that guy! He's a p****!

George: Boom. Over the 1600s now, the thirteen colonies made good business.
But they didn't wanna be governed by Britain,
'Cause they were the ones that took the risk.

[Portrayal of the rebel cause gaining support, by Alhan and Kae Kurd]

Rebel 1: Hear what I'm saying, you lot are getting bumped.

Rebel 2: Where was he when man was in the trenches, moving bare slaves backs and forth?

Rebel 1: How you making money out here and you're just giving it to King James?

Rebel 2: Bruv, King James is an ediat!

Rebel 1: I say we just hold onto the land.

SCENE 9: THE FIGHT FOR INDEPENDENCE

George: They were the ones who came to a new land,
Killed off the locals and worked the slaves. To
Keep this going, they needed protection from
Anything that couldn't threaten commercial trade.

Protection from tax, tax to a government whose
Whole perspective was England-centred.
So by the 1770s the colonies were
Fighting a war to become independent.

[Portrayal of the war]

King James: Yeah! Light up dem b********! Ya know seh England ah run dis ting rudeboy.

Rebel 2: Why you running for, g? Come back your country!

Rebel 1: Don't run man!

George: In the end, they got what they fought for.
Made money selling cash crops and all sorts.

That was the purpose of slavery; you get
Millions of workers, but the labour's free.

[Portrayal of tortures]

George: The plan went well, but Britain gradually ran the world. Her
Rate of industrial development was great.
Put it like this though: if Britain was Lil Wayne in 2008
America was Drake.

SCENE 10: AMERICAN EXPANSION

[Soundtrack: Drake 'Lust for Life']

George: Pigeonholing her would be a hell of a mistake. Think
Lewis Hamilton when he started to realise he
Really knew how to drive.

[Archive of Lewis Hamilton's early success]

George: Think Facebook, 2005.

[2005 quote from Mark Zuckerberg]

George: By this point America's like the teen who
Fell out with her parents and flew the nest,
Made it independently mended that relationship
Eventually, then became a huge success.

[Page turn]

George: Oh, by the way, I'm gonna keep throwing out pop
References just to make sure you've understood.
Here's my favourite one, from *House of Cards*:
Think of America as Claire Underwood.

[Soundtrack: *House of Cards* Theme]

George: From a young age, she fell in love . . .
With her own ambition. She
Always believed she was destined for greatness and
Wouldn't let anyone else control that mission.
Commitment to getting what she wanted by any means
Necessary turned her into a cold tactician.

[Page turn]

SCENE 11: NEW OPPORTUNITIES AFTER WWII

George: So, America hatched a proper plan; by the
1800s, she'd snatched a lot of land.
And yeah, she had a lot of slaves working the soil
But she also had banks, trains and her own personal oil. The
Country was growing and money was flowing, but the
World Wars led to the world economy slowing.

Now, Europe is where most of the fighting happened.
America wasn't touched, so she style-and-patterned.
Most other countries' money was low, but America wanted to see
    her economy grow.
She couldn't depend on *them* to spend just then.
She'd have to grow wealth by her own self.
So she made it easy for more Americans to
Get into work and to buy goods.
That way she created producers and consumers
At a time when not a lot of them other guys could.

These 1950s policies were a mixture of socialism and capitalism.

The strength of our nation must continue to be used in the interest of all our people, rather than a privileged few.

George: Before the war, *Britain* was a leader of global capitalism. But by the end of the
'50s, as she entered the '60s, this
Former superpower was forced to make a massive decision.

The wind of change is blowing through this continent, and whether we like it or not, the growth of national consciousness is a political fact.

George: See after the war, Britain's position in the world wasn't half as secure.
Keeping the colonies was getting expensive, 'cause the
Colonies didn't wanna walk the same path as before.

Furthermore, after they served in war
People from the colonies wanted better for themselves.

When I went back to Jamaica it was shocking. My children would not grow up in a colony, so I came back on the SS Windrush.

George: To win the war, the Allies had hella foreign help.

The King was our King.

George: Now Britain had to think about her economic health.

The flag was our flag.

George: Colonialism was done.

How more British could we get?

George: The British Empire became the Commonwealth.

Queen Elizabeth II: *We need courage, so that we can show the world that we're not afraid of the future. We can take pride in the new Commonwealth we are building.*

George: At the same time, Russia and China
Almost fully turned their back on the system of Capitalism.
Asia started catching up, Africa didn't.
And the rest is history.

So, long story short, as a rich young country
The US became totally dominant.
Can you see why when you look across the media
American culture is globally prominent?

Yeah she stole the land and killed the witnesses but she's
Really good at building businesses.

SCENE 12: BACK TO MAHALIA

[Soundtrack: Mahalia 'What You Did (Acoustic)']

George: I say that to say this: given how influential
The USA is, it's a big
deal when something from outside –
Especially *our* side – ends up on
Their playlists.

[George enters a live music event, where Mahalia is performing]

George: If you want a music career, you better get used to the fear of
stagnation and failure, but
Right now that's not the case for Mahalia.

And I haven't even mentioned Ella Mai, the
Feature on this one, someone to celebrate.

[An excerpt from another Mahalia interview]

Mahalia: *I really wanna work with Ella Mai. I really like her. I feel like we connect.*

SCENE 13: THE RISE OF ELLA MAI

[Throwback to the opening scene of Episode 1 of *HYHGP*, with George and his nephews]

George: Around the time when I first developed this podcast
Ella Mai was climbing up the American pop charts.

[Cut to an Instagram clip of Ella Mai covering 2Pac 'Keep Ya Head Up']

George: This was a young woman from South London,
Singing on Instagram – not even pushing music or crowdfunding.

[Cut to an LA suburb]

George: Over in the States, there's a woman in LA who
Sees Ella Mai on her explore page. She
Shows her partner who's a record producer and
He thinks he can take her to a more mature stage.

And he didn't tell no lie. He's a
Well known guy. Goes by the name of DJ
Mustard.

[Soundtrack: Ella Mai 'Boo'd Up']

[An excerpt from a DJ Mustard interview]

DJ Mustard: *My girl found her on Instagram and sent it to me. She was like 'You should check her out', I was like whatever. Got in the car, I was on my way to studio and she sent it to me again like 'You really should, you know, check her out . . .'*

George: He's made a lot of hits, his brand is
Trusted. And even though he's all the way over there he
Saw her potential before many of us did. And in
Two short years, Ella just sussed it.

[An excerpt from Ella Mai's interview with Chuckie Lothian]

Ella Mai: *It's really insane what 'Boo'd Up' did. I see so many people saying, 'This is what you're gonna play ten years down the line'. To still be able to play the song and people go crazy, like every single time I do it. It's a crazy feeling.*

[A recording from the 2019 Grammy Awards]

Announcer 1: *For Best R&B song, a songwriters' award, the nominees are ... Larrance Dopson, Joelle James, Ella Mai and Dijon McFarlane for 'Boo'd Up'.*

'Boo'd Up''s a song the US market leaped on. It
Scooped up the gong for
Best R&B song.

Announcer 2: *... And the Grammy goes to ... 'Boo'd Up'!*

George: Ella Mai reached the status of the greats
All because she made it in the States.

[Another excerpt from Ella Mai's interview with Chuckie Lothian]

Ella Mai: *I don't necessarily think you have to live there and continuously work with American producers, like there's more than enough good producers here that can do it, but I think the English industry is very much pop-based.*

It's harder in England to remain true to what you really want to do, I think, when you're signed to a major label.

Looking at the industry in America now, I think it is showing the labels that there really is a need for this kind of music because everyone loves it, so why wouldn't you . . .

SCENE 14: FLYING THE FLAG

[Return to George in the marketplace from Episode 19. He is by his stall, reflecting, as members of the General Public show him support]

George: Black music taught me a lot about America. In
Fact, music taught me a lot about hella stuff.
Like the power of the market.
How many times have I seen a three-minute song generate
More energy than a movie longer than an hour and a half did?

All boils down—

Supporter 1: Poet!

George: Who's that? Yo!

Supporter 1: Yes, my brudda, love what you're doing. Real talk.

George: Respect, G.

Supporter 1: Hold it down bro!

George: Love, love!
It all boils down to the general public.
Maybe they like what you do, maybe they love it.
America's music industry was miles ahead when
Others were still getting out of bed.

Don't get me wrong – Britain's is also strong,
But Mahalia and Ella Mai make R&B

Britain doesn't always support those songs.
Maybe that's down to the general public
Maybe it's on the industry to have more faith in R&B
And spend more budget.

Ten years ago I was in the same dilemma. Before UK rap really came
    together I was
Studying it. Trying to make it as a rapper when
There was no money in it. Picture the
Younger me . . . trying to picture the older me,
Saying 'I don't wanna be pigeonholed' and switching to
Poetry.

Supporter 2: Hi Mr Poet!

George: Wa'am sister, you alright?
See, if Mahalia and Ella Mai can make it in the US,
Doing what they do best, and
Estelle, FKA Twigs, NAO, Jorja
Smith, Scribz Riley . . . who's next?

This podcast won a Peabody Award that
No non-American had gotten before.
In saying that, I'm not trying to brag; I'm
Highlighting the fact that we're flying the flag.

Wizkid did this with Afrobeats,
Ragga Dee did it for the Ugandan scene.
We all start off by doing what we love at a
Time when the money isn't guaranteed.

Put it like this: we take our skills and we
Find a way to make our skills pay our bills.
And if we get it right, more people can eat
We don't even need to compete.

R&B, Afrobeats, Rap, whatever . . .
As a generation, we adapt together. And
As a rule: *anything* that thrives in the streets
Has the potential to drive industries.

[Soundtrack: Nas ft. Lauryn Hill 'If I Ruled the World']

EPISODE 22: Mavado & Vybz

Extra Info:
- I aimed to write this episode in Chapter Two, but realised I needed to first explain the community I came from. So, I used Episodes 13 and 15 to describe the streets of North West London and the Jamaican influence all around us. That allowed me to start this one by diving straight in. The first line is 'Let me take you back to my teens', because I had already familiarised the audience with this era of my life.
- Because I ended this episode with Vybz Kartel's murder conviction, I didn't get to talk about one of the most fascinating aspects of the whole story: Kartel continued releasing music from prison, and has done so for over a decade now. Even crazier, he has consistently maintained his position as the most successful Dancehall artist of his era – all from a prison cell. He releases more music than his peers and even outsells all the newer, younger artists. It's unbelievable.

Fun Facts:
- This episode was born before the podcast. I wrote the first scene back in 2017 during my early experiments with audio storytelling. When the podcast took off, I always meant to return to the idea, so I'm glad the world has finally heard it.

Anyone who knew me as a teenager knew this episode was a long time coming. For about three years, our world was dominated by the voices of these two Jamaican Dancehall artists – Mavado and Vybz Kartel. Their music entered my life when I was about fifteen, and became the soundtrack to the streets. Having grown up in a very Jamaican part of London, I felt closer to this culture than I did to Uganda at that point. Also, as a young rapper, I was inspired by the volume and variety of music these guys made. But not everything that glitters is gold. They put a lot of energy into songs about death and destruction, and eventually that darkness consumed them. Speaking of consumption, I now find it fascinating that this dark subject matter plays the same role in the Black music market to this day – giving with one hand, and taking with the other. It turns our young men into stars, but also leads them to prison and death, over and over again. Are they all crazy? Or is there something else happening? This is a big question that I left alone for a while after touching on it in Episodes 1 and 5. For Chapter 3, I decided to take a few episodes to lay out some case studies and talk about gangsta culture on my own terms. Side note – this is one of our greatest episodes ever. Big up Benbrick for being willing to learn every day. And shout out to the community of Harlesden for putting me on!

George: Let me take you back to my teens.

SCENE 1: GEORGE IN THE BARBERSHOP

[Soundtrack: Mavado 'Last Night']

George: Imagine a North West 10 night-time drone shot.
Grocers . . . takeaways . . . phone shops.
We slowly zoom in to my main Harlesden spot:
The legendary . . . Cutz Barbershop.

[Young George (YG) entering the barbershop full of life. YG sings in the background while Older George (OG) narrates in the foreground. Eventually the older George asks the younger to be quiet]

George: That's me. Little fifteen-year-old G.
I remember being this age. I remember feeling this—
Wait, hold on. Yo, bro, chill!

YG: Oh, you're talking to me?

George: Yeah, you my guy I know you're loving the tune—

YG: I'm sorry.

George: I remember, but I'm talking to your future audience right now.

YG: My bad!

George: Yeah. So, I beg you just give us a little space, B . . .

YG: Let me just move this thing right here, sorry about the noise bro . . .

[YG drags a side table away from OG. OG goes back to addressing the audience]

George: This song came out when I was learning the difference between
Heart and bravado. This classic by the Jamaican artist Mavado
Hit the scene when I was fifteen. And I'm confident I've never seen it on the big screen.
'Cause between our world and the mainstream there was a slipstream.
Felt like we were living in a split screen.
But still, the mainstream was every kid's dream.

So, even though I never heard Mavado's music in a cinema
Mavado's music *was* the cinema.

You're looking at me like 'Cinema how?'
Just turn around and watch me sing my heart out . . .

[Narrative perspective returns to YG singing before the scene disappears]

SCENE 2: LAST NIGHT

[Cut to a small working-class neighbourhood in Kingston, Jamaica. It's late night, and almost everything is quiet]

George: It's called last night it's not about a candlelit dinner; it's about a shootout.

[Gunshots]

George: Mavado shot some guys from his neighbourhood or a distant community. And he's quite sure he murdered at least one of them.

[An empty shell from the shotgun blast bounces back into the original barbershop scene]

George: Now, for anyone from my background that's kind of uncomfortable to listen to, because it sounds like a self-snitching tune.
But I'm not giving information in the station,
I'm paraphrasing. How crazy is that?

[YG leaves the barbershop]

SCENE 3: THE WEREWOLF AND THE VAMPIRE

[Cut to a dark, eerie forest on a windy night. A wolf howls in the distance]

George: Mavado reminded me of a werewolf. Like a
Tortured soul who would howl at the moon,
Warning everybody to be careful. He
Poured his whole heart out on a tune.

But on the other side of the Dancehall underworld
There was someone else.
Tall and skinny, like Dracula. Looked
Like a vampire from Africa.
He had sharp little teeth and high cheekbones.
By this time, he was widely known.

See, Mavado sang like a fallen angel, but this
Other guy rapped like the actual devil.
He was so good, but he was so bad. And
No one was able to match his level.

In these early years of his career, he didn't
Do melody too heavily. But he could
Write bars. And he could write bars well.
His name was Vybz Kartel.

SCENE 4: INTRODUCING VYBZ KARTEL

[Soundtrack: Vybz Kartel 'Badda Dan Dem']

[An excerpt from Vybz Kartel's 2006 Chris Goldfinger interview for BBC 1xtra]

Chris Goldfinger: *Vybz Kartel ...*

Vybz Kartel: *Unique is the lyrics, unique is the name, unique is the style.*

Chris Goldfinger: *When it comes to girl lyrics ...*

Vybz Kartel: *That's me.*

Chris Goldfinger: *Alright. And when it comes to rudeboy lyrics ...*

Vybz Kartel: *That's me, too.*

Chris Goldfinger: *And you have the conscious lyrics when you're ready?*

Vybz Kartel: *Timely.*

George: At this time I was into the Grime scene
And one thing I loved was intricate rhyme schemes. So
Vybz Kartel blew my mind, he
Always made me wanna redo my rhymes. He was
Rough, he was smooth, he showed love to the youth.
Lyrically he had nothing to prove but he
Dropped more music than everyone else. He was his
Own cartel – didn't need anyone's help.

Vybz Kartel: *... cartel, which means a group of people come together limit and control both the prices and the competition. So, we're the cartel in the music cah we come fi control ...*

SCENE 5: HOW IT STARTED

[Soundtrack: Vybz Kartel & Mavado 'Sunrise']

George: He and Mavado started off as bredrins as well.
They shared a mentor, a legend himself:
Bounty Killer.
And when Vybz eventually fell out with Bounty,
Neither had any problem defending themselves
In a war of words. But Mavado was loyal to Bounty Killer, so he
stepped in to help. And in Kartel's mind,
This kid was getting kind of ahead of himself.

[Cut to back to the eerie forest]

George: From that point, one of the most epic
Feuds in Dancehall history kicked off. To
Me it was more engaging than
Anything happening in Grime *or* Hip Hop.

Across the underworld there was a big divide.
Every Dancehall fan picked a side.
Mavado the Werewolf or Vampire Vybz. You
Couldn't choose both, you had to stand either side.

Vado was 'Gully', Kartel was 'Gaza'.
Think it's just music? You wouldn't believe the drama between
Cassava Piece's David Brooks and Portmore's Adidja Palmer.

[An excerpt from a 2009 TVJ news report]

Newsreader: *The Government is defending its decision to intervene in the Dancehall rivalry between deejays Mavado and Vybz Kartel, whose open contempt for each other has divided their fans in what is known as the 'Gaza/Gully' conflict. Jamaica House says it was a matter of responsibility to intervene in the conflict, which has such wide-reaching tentacles.*

George: Bounty Killer had his own recent drama
People said his rival, Beenie Man, tief'd his partner.
For years they'd been having lyrical war, but that
Animosity never took physical form.

Now, for the first time, people's attention shifted:
Mavado and Kartel. Both of them were gifted;
Vado sounding like a spiritual gangster, and
Vybz Kartel, the prince of lyrical banter.

But this music was driven by visceral anger.
Bullets were flying, people were dying. The Jamaican
Government stepped in, said enough of this death ting.
Called a press conference where the two of them
Embraced each other as bredrins.

SCENE 6: A SHAKY TRUCE

[A clip taken from the TVJ news report]

Mavado: Me and Vybz, we're not really enemies, you know what I mean, it's just about music. People take it to a different level.

Vybz Kartel: Yeah man, we're agreeing with what Mavado said a while ago and as a matter of fact, we have plans to do another collaboration. We are coming back with—

[Both start laughing, the clip ends]

George: But the truce didn't last; soon they were back at it.
For both of them, clashing had become a bad habit.

Kartel dissed Mavado's slain father
DJs in the Gully were banned from playing Gaza.
Ironically, this made the game larger.

Artistically, it made me train harder.
Every other week there were two new songs and a
Worldwide debate – who came harder?

Finally, they took it to the stage . . . at a
Legendary annual event called Sting.
This was a monumental thing.
The crowd at Sting would crown the king.

So, in front of thousands of fans and critics, they
Jumped around and shouted their gangsta lyrics.
Then out of nowhere, Mavado leaves the stage.
No one knows why but he seems enraged.
To this day it remains a mystery.
Vybz Kartel wasted no time claiming victory.

SCENE 7: GANGSTA BEHAVIOUR

[Cut to George reflecting in his writing room]

George: That was thirteen years ago.
I've thought about it most days since then . . .
How my late teens were dominated by these
Gangsta, genius Jamaican men.
How their beef made its way to the Ends
To the extent that I'd debate it with friends.
How they got ratings for saying insane things. And
How the Jamaican government cracked down on
Violent music after their legendary
Face-off at the 2008 Sting. And
How . . . in my opinion,
Dancehall hasn't been the same since.

The clash exposed a big problem that we had:
A lot of kids just wanted to be bad.

Mavado used to scream 'Gangsta for Life' even
Though he lost a lot of friends, thanks to the life. And
Vybz Kartel loved to play the villain.
From *singing* about killing, he made a killing.

Why were they so obsessed with this way of living?
With all this Gangsta behaviour?
Let's go back to Jamaica.

SCENE 8: POLITICAL VIOLENCE IN JAMAICA

[Soundtrack: Damian Marley 'Welcome to Jamrock']

[Cut to George on a speedboat patrolling the Jamaican coastline]

George: Allegedly, Jamaica's been a distribution
point for South American drugs since the '70s,
Moving coke to North America from Medellin,
Causing more carnage than most countries have ever seen.

Furthermore, by the late '70s,
Jamaica's prime minister Michael Manley was very
Friendly with some of America's main enemies.
He was especially friendly with the Cubans
To the US he was potentially a nuisance.

[Archive of Michael Manley talking about Cuba]

Michael Manley: *We have that friendship with Cuba as part of a world alliance, of Third World nations that are fighting for justice for poor people in the world.*

George: America wanted him out, so they did something about it.
The CIA smuggled in hundreds of thousands worth of
Rocket launchers, grenades, and guns to the towns of

Kingston, fuelling political violence, a
Difficult time for this beautiful little island.

And that's the Jamaica Mavado and Vybz Kartel were born into.
That's the generation they were talking to.

Both of them were born on election years,
Kartel in '76, when insurrection fears
Led the government to declare a state of emergency,
'Cause of all the hatred and murder scenes.

Vado was born in 1980, when Edward Seaga replaced Michael
    Manley as Prime
Minister.
The picture was quite sinister:
800 killed. And the promise of tomorrow remained unfulfilled.

[A clip from the BBC documentary *Blood and Fire: Jamaica's
Political History*]

Commentator: *America breathed a sigh of relief as Edward Seaga
put the ghost of socialism to rest.*

George: You're listening to 'Welcome to Jamrock' by Damian Marley,
This is the song that made me a yardie.
He gave his voice to the silent majority
Living with political violence and poverty.

[An excerpt from Damian Marley's interview with Seani B for BBC 1xtra]

Damian Marley: *Well, you don't have to be ghetto to be human. And
being human you should care about people.*

George: It was 1978 when Damian was born.
Just another baby in the storm.
He was Bob Marley's youngest son, and

This would be reflected in the way he would perform. In his lifetime, violence in Jamaica was the norm.

CHAPTER THREE | 22: MAVADO & VYBZ

In fact, Bob was attacked in Kingston
Shortly before he met Damian's mum, Cindy.
People say Bob got shot for tryna bring peace
After that he left the West Indies.

[A clip from Bob Marley's interview with Gil Noble for WABC-TV]

Gil Noble: *You never saw the gunman?*

Bob Marley: *At that time, no.*

Gil Noble: *But you know who did it.*

Bob Marley: *Yeah, mi know them.*

George: They say he got shot for playing both sides in the
Middle of a bitter campaign. For his
Son to be painting the same picture of Jamaica like
Thirty years later . . . really is a damn shame.
Listen to the man's pain . . .

SCENE 9: GANGSTA SOCIETY

[Return to George in his writing room]

George: Mavado, Vybz Kartel and Damian Marley inspired me.
They made me want fans that admire me.
But what I didn't know when I was younger was the
Background of that gangsta society.

This music emerged from the wreckage.
Every verse was aggressive, but the words had a message.

There's no such thing as a perfect perspective, but
Other forms of storytelling weren't as effective.

Damian Marley's perspective was Rastafari.
Which is why he's one of the few artists I trust, I can't lie.

He always found a way of promoting peace and unity,
Projecting strength and speaking beautifully.
Like his dad. Maybe his uplifting
Message reflected the life he had.

But what about Mavado and Vybz?
The life they wrote about is hard to describe.
Both of them embraced the darkness with pride and
Drew people into the Gully/Gaza divide.

They sent out a message, and the market replied.
We loved it. All that thug shit.
All that bad boy energy made club hits.

Mavado and Vybz were not Marley kids.
They made their money from shows and party gigs, like
Most Dancehall artists at the time.
And anyway, record sales had started to decline.

When they clashed the response was crazy
Before long Mavado had a song with Jay-Z.
And Vybz? Come on man, you know the vibes.
What does a cartel do, by definition? Control the price.

[A clip from a Vybz Kartel interview]

Interviewer: *On some level wasn't that good for business? I mean everybody else was shoved out of the picture and people were focusing exclusively on Vybz Kartel and Mavado.*

Vybz Kartel: *Not on 'some' level, on all levels it was good, know what I mean? That is how Mavado and I saw it. It's all about commercial, all about capitalist, all about making the money.*

George: After the government ended the clash,
Fans were invested, spending the cash.
Vybz started growing as an entrepreneur, he had
Protégés, alcohol, condoms and more.

They both released as many songs as before, and
Both agreed that they were no longer in
war.

Both of them had gained recognition, and
This recognition changed their position.

SCENE 10: A NEW DIRECTION

[Soundtrack: Trippple Bounce Riddim]

George: Mavado and Kartel
Pretty much controlled the mood on the ground, but
Visa problems stopped them from moving around.
Without shows it would be hard to get paid, so the
Violence in the music started to fade.

[Soundtrack: Mavado 'Hope and Pray']

George: Mavado sang about better living and money
This is how he shaped his definition of 'gully'.
More happiness, less clashing and hollering. He
Grew his female fanbase and international following.
To be fair, Mavado sang about a lotta things
And, you know, he could *proper* sing.

Meanwhile, Kartel changed too. But in
Many ways he was still the same yout.

He toned down the violence . . . ish.
Wanted to fly, but he was denied this wish.
Still, he was the master of coordinating energy.
His music started incorporating melody.

[Soundtrack: Vybz Kartel 'Mr Officer']

George: And despite government pressure
Vybz Kartel stayed as rugged as ever.
Fans worldwide were loving the bredda. He was like a supervillain
    with a paper and pencil.
Sometimes he released two different songs – in
One go – on the same instrumental.
Like this:

[Soundtrack: Vybz Kartel 'Bicycle']

[An excerpt taken from Vybz Kartel's 2010 interview with Robbo Ranx]

Vybz Kartel: *Dancehall is going through a happy phase, you know you ah go always have time inna di music when clashing ah go gwan because you can't get rid of that, know what I mean?*

SCENE 11: PUSHBACK

[Previous soundtrack is stopped like a cassette tape. Return to George in his writing room]

George: Vado and Vybz released so many songs, but
Love from the fans wasn't the only response.
Yeah, they were two of Dancehall's largest artists but
Not everybody was their target market.

As Dancehall became more violent and sexual,
A lot of Jamaicans felt misrepresented.
The sound grew globally, got a lot of criticism
Locally and this never ended.

[Excerpts from the BBC World Service documentary *Jamaica: Does Music Shape Society?* Featuring former Commissioner of Police Carl Williams and campaigner Aza Auset]

Carl Williams: *I am confident that there is a link between ... Dancehall music and violent crime.*

Aza Auset: *The reason why it is so promoted in Jamaica is because it is a way to keep Black people in a very low state of mind with very low ambition.*

George: For years, people put up with Dancehall culture, but this New generation was far more vulgar.

Critics said Dancehall was full of self-destructive
Messages and silly behaviours.
Resentment slowly spread beyond the island
Over to Jamaica's Caribbean neighbours.

Narrative: *Trinidad and Tobago, St Vincent, Barbados, the Grenadines and the Bahamas have all banned controversial Dancehall artiste Mavado for his pro-gun and anti-gay lyrics.*

A state-owned radio station in Guyana has banned Vybz Kartel from the airwaves, saying his music brings 'nothing positive' to the industry.

George: As a matter of fact, campaigners tried to clean up Dancehall with the Reggae Compassionate Act.
Activists applied a lot of pressure but Mavado and Vybz said 'There's no way I'm signing whatsoever.'

The artists complained about freedom of speech, and
Critics said 'No you're supposed to know the limits.
Freedom of speech doesn't mean you can breach people's
Safety with gun talk and homophobic lyrics.'

And this is the problem with markets.
Any society run only by profits is heartless.
The Market doesn't care about human beings, or the
Difficult positions it puts you and me in.
'Cause in a market society there's no higher command
Than the laws of supply and demand.

So how do you regulate a popular artist who's
Topping the charts with socially irresponsible art?
Who never claimed to be right or wrong from the start.
Whose only way out of poverty was to
Write raw songs from the heart.

In Feb '09, Jamaica's Broadcasting Commission
Gave in to public outcry. They
Banned TV and radio stations from
Playing songs with certain subjects outright.

SCENE 12: STILL GANGSTA

[Soundtrack: Day Rave Riddim]

George: Still, this is a story about gangsters.

Both Mavado and Vybz Kartel had
Hundreds of lyrics about killing police.
There's no record of them actually doing it,
But this mentality was big in the streets.

Remember what I said about the '70s? How
Jamaica became a drug hotspot . . . allegedly.

Yeah. That changed things entirely.
Paved the way for Kingpins in Jamaican society.

They were linked to hella politicians. Which is why nuff of them have
never gone to prison.

So in 2009 when the US implied the
Jamaican government was kind of responsible
For protecting shottas and hiding them from the law,
The writing was on the wall.

Next year Jamaica agreed to extradite the
Highest one of them all: Christopher 'Dudus' Coke.
He put up a fight – and nothing small.
State of emergency – the violence was like a war.

Dudus was a well-loved community figure, and the
Whole situation was a national embarrassment.
So fresh resentment added extra tension between the
Law and the mandem in the garrison.

[Soundtrack: Mavado 'Nuh Bleach Wid Cream']

[Return to George in his writing room]

George: The year after that, an off-duty cop
Killed Mavado's friend outside a club
Mavado got an assault charge while the killer got no charge.
And even though he was used to this kind of stuff, he was
Stressing. He wanted to leave Jamaica.
Felt like his time was up.

Meanwhile, Vybz Kartel . . .
Vybz Kartel.

SCENE 13: VYBZ GETS CONVICTED

George: Like Mavado he ended up in a predicament;
The government was sick of him.
There was only one way this was bound to go.
Police kept shutting down his shows. He couldn't
Travel, so he commercialised his influence and
Used his popularity to shove it down their throats.

Then one day, something strange happened.

On September 30th, 2011
Vybz was arrested for marijuana possession.
Three days later he was charged for a burner
And for taking part in a murder.

They said back in July he helped to plan the
Shooting of a man called Barrington 'Bossie' Burton.
But 'cause of a lack of witnesses and evidence,
The jury couldn't know for certain.

During trial he was charged for a second murder, this
time of an affiliate – Clive 'Lizard' Williams.
Kartel and his co-defendants
Denied involvement and maintained their innocence.

He beat the first case.
But he lost the second.
According to the prosecution, Lizard was beaten to
Death at Kartel's home 'cause he lost some weapons.

When Vybz was first charged with murder,
He was thirty-five years old you know.
And when he was finally sentenced
He got thirty-five years, no parole.

'Cause of discrepancies in the case people claim he fell
Victim to a system that held a personal grudge.
Maybe. Or maybe he was just a vampire,
Who couldn't control his thirst for blood.

SCENE 14: MAVADO GETS A BREAK

George: But what about Mavado?

[Soundtrack: Mavado 'Unchanging Love']

George: Mavado finally got a break from Jamaica. While
Vybz only saw his kids on prison visits
Vado moved his family to Miami and
Thankfully secured US citizenship.

He expanded his brand internationally, working with
Rappers like Chip and Nicki Minaj.
When he eventually he signed to DJ Khaled,
His US fanbase would quickly enlarge.

But home is where the heart is
And even though he was making his paper,
Vado was a Dancehall artist.
And he couldn't stay away from Jamaica.

Can't blame him.
In the little time I spent there recording songs,
I saw Jamaica as a magical place.
But for Mavado, that's where it all went wrong.

SCENE 15: SON OF A GANGSTA

George: Ten years after the Kartel beef, when
Vado had long since chosen the path of peace
His fifteen-year-old son got into
Drama in their hometown, Cassava Piece.

It started with an argument between his son,
Dantay, and a local twenty-three-year-old called Lorenzo.
Vado allegedly punched up Lorenzo.
After that he should have left the ends though.

Instead, he hung around after backing his son.
And Lorenzo came back with a gun. He
Shot up Mavado's car and Vado drove away.
At least that's what the locals say.

Allegedly, Mavado's fifteen-year-old
son, Dantay, couldn't let it be.
According to Lorenzo's dad, a few nights
Later, Dantay and two other guys
Broke into Lorenzo's house, beat him up,
Stabbed him up and shot him in the head a couple times.

He said they tried to remove the head of his son and
Gave up halfway 'cause the machete was blunt. He
Said one of them asked Dantay if they should do the
Dad too, but Dantay said he was done.

The kid was arrested not long after, and
Held on remand for many, many months.
Finally, he was found guilty of murder on
January 28th, 2021.

It's like Mavado predicted it
Every time he said it on a verse.

'Gangsta . . . for life'.
I guess the son of the werewolf inherited the curse.

[Wolf howl]

Mavado: It's just about music. People take it to a different level.

Vybz Kartel: It's all about commercial, all about capitalist, all about making the money.

EPISODE 23: Back to UG

Extra Info:

- This episode builds on my long-running practice of using day-to-day life for podcast material. As I've said before, this practice stems from the idea that every experience matters. No aspect of your life is uninteresting. For me, the wedding-planning process that Sandra and I embarked on in 2021 was a rich source of inspiration for the podcast. It made me think about our shared Ugandan heritage as well as a possible future in the country. To be honest, the thought of writing about this was kind of intimidating, because it's deeply personal and full of sensitive questions about my relationship with Uganda. But writing this episode helped me, as well as others in the diaspora with similar feelings, as well as those back home who connect with my work.

Fun Facts:

- Halfway into recording this episode, Uganda went into lockdown, making our plans for a Ugandan wedding impossible. At that point I knew I'd have to write a follow-up episode to touch on this, which became Episode 27, 'True Love'.

They always say 'marry your best friend' ... and they're right. As I explain in this episode, Sandra and I weren't *looking* for love, we just found it by being good to each other for years. This friendship saw me through so many stages – from being a Grime MC, to an A-level student, to a Cambridge undergrad who left the negativity of the music and the Ends behind. Sandra was there, making me laugh every day. Fast forward to 2020, I proposed, she said yes, and then we had an idea: let's get married in Uganda. That decision came from our mutual love of our ancestral home, which I've expressed throughout this book and the podcast. Uganda has always been a place of fun, family and freedom for me, and for Sandra it was no different. In fact, throughout my twenties I was flirting with the idea of completely relocating there (which was the source of my arguments with Uganda in Chapter 2). But in reality, the same Uganda we have been enjoying all these years has failed to bring prosperity to most of her people, and has yet to produce a strong, trustworthy political system. As a soon-to-be-married man, whose livelihood depends on freedom of speech, I have to face this reality. Uganda is no longer about holidays and parties; the country is at a crossroads. However, Uganda is similar to most African countries in that her potential lies in her young, creative, entrepreneurial population. I just pray that the progress of the continent's music scene over the past ten years is a sign of things to come.

Sandra: Earlier on, I couldn't stop laughing at the fact that we pulled up to a supermarket and they said to Rodrick, 'Are you armed?' And Rodrick was like 'Nah.' And they were like 'OK you can go.' [Sandra and Rodrick laugh]

First of all, how sexist! What if I'm armed? You didn't ask me if I'm armed, number one. Number two, if he's armed, is he's gonna say he's armed? I don't think so. So literally I'm ... [Sandra sighs] They're just fake. They're just fake.

[Soundtrack: Bebe Cool 'Wire Wire']

SCENE 1: GEORGE TELLS UGANDA THE GOOD NEWS

[George is on the phone to a personified version of his home country, Uganda (first introduced in Episode 12, 'A Night to REMember'). Having proposed to his girlfriend, Sandra, in London during the pandemic, George now reveals their plan to wed in Uganda. Sandra is also a British Ugandan, so this is a homecoming for both of them]

George: Hello, Uganda. How are you?

Uganda: I'm fine, George, how are you?

George: I'm OK ...

Uganda: Mhm, and how is Sandra?

George: Sandra's good, we were talking about you earlier, actually.

Uganda: Good things, I hope?

George: All good things, come on.

Uganda: OK, how's wedding planning? Are you planning Kukyaala?

George: Yup, all of that.

Uganda: What's the plan with Kwanjula?

George: Kwanjula is underway ... you know her family handle that. But yo, Uganda ...

Uganda: Yes please?

George: We wanna do the white wedding with you too.

Uganda: Eh! Are you sure?

George: Of course! Why not?

Uganda: But, George, there's so much planning to do! You have to pick a venue, you have to pick a church, you have to find a wedding planner, you need a Ugandan wedding planner. George, I'm serious by the way, people miss the food dates ...

[George laughs happily at Uganda's enthusiasm]

Uganda: But what happened? I was so sure you were going to have your wedding in UK. What happened?

George: Uganda, it's like I always told you, man. You mean a lot to me, you mean a lot to Sandra, and it's our culture that brought us together, so it's only right that we ... we come home to bless our union moving forward, you know what I mean?

Uganda: Oh, Georgie! You're too cute ...

[Message notification from George's phone. It's another voice note from Sandra]

Sandra: Roderick was like 'We're going to pick someone at the airport' and he was like 'Do you have any documents? Any documents to show you're going?' I was like 'Ssebo, I don't have any documents.' I said 'Here's a picture of her on the plane earlier today. She's my sister, we're here to plan my wedding.' He said 'Ah you go. You go, you go.' I was like . . . what? [Sandra laughs]

[George laughs while recording his reply]

George: Babe, that's our Uganda! That's your country! And you love it really . . .

SCENE 2: GEORGE IN LOVE

[Scene opens with George in his writing room, where he spent most of lockdown. This is where much of *HYHGP* Chapter Three was written]

George: I remember when my feelings changed towards my best
    friend.
These new feelings put me under so much pressure,
I had to express them.

I was like 'Sandra . . . I think I love ya.'

[*EastEnders* music]

George: She actually doubted at first.
But I showed her my heart, and actions speak louder than words.
Now she's proudly my fiancée,
And I'm proud to be hers.

I actually remember falling for Sandra . . .
Realising I wanted to call her my partner.
It was December 2019.
You were there! Remember the Chapter Two finale, when I'm on the
    phone to Uganda, and I say this:

[Flashback to Episode 18, 'Concurrent Affairs']

George: I'm coming next month, but when I land, I'm still on my grind.

Uganda: Mmm.

George: You know, 20th December I've got my first Kampala show.

Uganda: Mhm . . .

George: . . . with A Ka Dope . . .

Uganda: So exciting.

[Return to George's writing room]

George: Yeah, Sandra produced that Uganda event. My first ever Kampala show.
It was such a success, big up A Ka Dope.
By that point we'd never even held hands
One year later I proposed.

Don't get me wrong though, it's been a long road.

Let's take a trip down memory lane . . .

SCENE 3: GEORGE AND SANDRA'S ORIGIN STORY

[Soundtrack: Flukes 'Wifey Riddim']

[Flashback to the day George met Sandra, thirteen years prior]

George: Sandra and I were close friends for twelve years,
And that's a friendship I held dear.

If she ever had something to say, she never felt scared,
You know them girls there.

I literally met her because I'm Ugandan.
Her cousin was one of the mandem.
First, I didn't realise this. Outside his name was Crisis,
And he didn't live too far from my bits.

Almost fifteen summers ago . . .
I can't remember if I got my brothers to roll . . .
But me, Crisis and our friend called James
Went to a Ugandan sports day.
As soon as we got to the venue we ran into
Sandra in a random hallway.

[Reconstruction of Younger Sandra (YS) meeting Younger George (YG)]

YS: Are you Ugandan?

YG: Yeah, I'm Ugandan, still.

YS: Ohhh . . .

George: Now, anyone who knows she and I
Knows we got a certain vibe.
The road we've been on since is a long one,
A two-person drive.

Instantly we just clicked.
Our humour was identical, you'd
Think we were reading a script.

[Page turn]

SCENE 4: GEORGE THE MC

[Soundtrack: Fergie 'Glamorous']

George: At that time, I was finding my voice,
Starting to rhyme with my boys.
'Cause of her brothers, Sandra could appreciate bars.
Not all girls cared about music like that,
But she seemed to rate ours.

I didn't just rap to street instrumentals;
I used commercial beats.
And a song that I wrote to 'Glamorous' (by
Fergie) called 'School of Hard Knocks' . . .
That became my first release.

[Flashback to sixteen-year-old George (YG) rapping at home]

George: Like I said, back in my mid-teens,
I was a rapper, with big dreams.
I wanted to be famous, wanted currency and
Status, but didn't want my projects to be brainless.

Most of my friends rapped about violence
But I had a different method.
I focused on being a person my siblings
And spitting an uplifting message.

[YG gets phone call from fourteen-year-old Sandra (YS)]

YG: Hello?

YS: [In a faux Ugandan accent] Hello my darling!

YG: [In a faux Ugandan accent] Hello madam . . .

George: Sandra just hit fourteen
But she saw the potential of my little dream.
She pushed my music, always wanted to listen.
It's like she knew my vision would come to fruition.

[YG performs new verse to YS]

George: Sandra liked when I rapped with no music
Which she was the first and only person to say.
To be fair, I only did it with her when I was
Spitting a verse written earlier in the day.

[YG completes the verse and YS gives her feedback]

George: But it wasn't easy.
Nothing at the time was easy.
When I wasn't making crossover songs
I was making Grime. And Grime was greezy.

[Page turn]

SCENE 5: GRIME WAVE

[Soundtrack: Griminal on Tim Westwood]

George: Grime was the sound of the roads, at a time when the
Violence was out of control.
Pride was getting more and more expensive; you
Needed something to walk the ends with. And the only form of
    protection in
Our price range was a knife. If you
Didn't wanna make that investment . . . you
Might just pay with your life.

This music *literally* became a way to survive.
For people who didn't think they could make it in life
This was motivation for staying alive.

[Page turn]

[Soundtrack: Dot Rotten on Westwood]

George: Dot Rotten was a perfect example.
He was a genius with his verses and samples.
Another frustrated teen
Just like us, chasing dreams. His
Mum kicked him out, his area was mad,
So, he spent his time rapping and producing.
We all did it for the love of the culture.
Looking back, we were establishing a blueprint.

I wanted to rap, nothing more nothing less.
When I learned about a Ugandan called Double S my
Mind was blown, his voice was so clear,
It motivated me more to find my own.

[Soundtrack: Double S on Westwood]

Double S was a problem –
Another legend from Tottenham.
Can you hear the discipline?
Just listening taught me things that I've never forgotten.
His rhymes weren't overcomplicated
But his flow was concentrated.

[Return to George's writing room]

George: Double S used to run with a bredrin,
Another Tottenham kid who was also becoming a legend.
One of them Jamaican youts who was feeling himself.

This guy made Grime more appealing to girls.
Sandra loved him. By the time he was sixteen
He was known over half of London.
A natural born performer –
Radio or stage show, he never found it hard to function.
This guy came with bags of charisma,
Never talked badness just bragged to the listener.
Never said he did stuff, never said he flipped skunk but . . .
Chipmunk was Chipmunk.

[Soundtrack: Chipmunk on Westwood]

George: My favourite MCs were older than me, but
Age-wise these guys were closer to me.
When no one was asking our generation how we felt,
Grime was there for us emotionally.

But after a while, every MC sounded
Like an angry teen running his mouth.
All of that was about to change though
'Cause of a new sound coming from South.

[Soundtrack: Giggs 'Saw']

George: Giggs' emotional road man perspective . . .
Did not carry no romantic message.

See, the thing about Grime . . . Grime was fast, and
By my late teens enough time had passed for
Listeners to crave more space for reflection
That's where Giggs brought a change of direction.

This was grown man stuff. It was so gangsta.
His controlled anger. His heavy spirit . . .
Best believe, me and Sandra knew every lyric.

[YS and YG sing along to 'Saw' word for word]

SCENE 6: CRIME WAVE

[A clip from the Journeyman Pictures documentary *Who is to Blame for London's Increasingly Violent Gangs?*]

Commentator: *... being in the wrong place at the wrong time can have fatal consequences. Last year twenty-seven youngsters became casualties in this bloody struggle. Mayor Ken Livingstone has guaranteed more than a million pounds for youth projects, but that money is taking a long time to filter through.*

George: The year before I turned eighteen, my city had its
Highest ever number of murdered teens.
When I listened to the music all I heard was greez but the
Violence hurt the streets; it wasn't accidental.
And even though this music saved people's lives,
I started to feel like it squandered that potential.
After a while, I started moving on from rap in general.

Just before my nineteenth birthday, I was
Chilling at Sandra's with her and her mum.
When I got a call from my parents, my mum was
Crying, so I felt nervous at once.

[Flashback]

YS: Are you OK?

George: My Dad said I got into Cambridge.
I ran outside, I nearly slipped on the ice.
I'm thinking 'As a rapper I might not make it
But at least I not trapped in the bits with my guys.'

I was gonna *make* something of myself.
Imagine all the youngers I could help.
I thought all they needed to see was someone from their world
Showing them what they could accomplish for themselves.

Sandra was slyly worried this was now 'goodbye'.
Like I would just forget her. How could I?
She was one of my best friends.
Which my teenage ego wouldn't let me confess then.

[Page turn]

SCENE 7: GEORGE GOES TO UGANDA

George: My mum suggested that I take some time to
Unwind before the Cambridge grind.
So, I spent half a year in Uganda
And it changed my life.

[Soundtrack: Obsessions 'Jangu']

George: I studied my people, how they survive, and the
Things about myself I'd never noticed . . .
It was a spiritual journey, man. I
Talked about it in Episode 6.

[An excerpt from *HYHGP* Episode 6]

George: *I was in Kampala on my own for the first time too,*
Close your eyes, imagine a birds-eye view.

[Cut to lively Kampala streets]

George: While I was out there, I thought about the Ends,
The lifestyle claiming all my childhood friends.
I wished I could fly the whole hood to Uganda,
Just walk around with them, absorb the powers dem.

Don't get me wrong – in Ugandan society
There's all sorts of malcontent.

There's greed, corruption, people starving,
But even the orphans in the streets were laughing.

I can't explain it.
Fifty years before, the country never even existed.
The British forced all these kingdoms together, and a
Whole lot of people resisted.

By 2010, Uganda was popping.
When I came back people thought man had a problem.
I was down in the dumps. Cah I caught feelings for the
Country after living there for how many months.

Sandra thought I was being melodramatic,
Acting like a recovering heroin addict.
I'd daydream about Uganda and drift away.
She loved it too, but in a different way.

As a kid, you visit with parents.
But as a teenager it's a different experience.
The more I tried to explain this to Sandra, the
More she got tired of entertaining my drama.
Until we went together the following year,
She thought I was just over-excited.
But then Sandra lived her best life, and
Came back with the same emotions that I did.

SCENE 8: THE DIASPORA REDISCOVERS THE MOTHERLAND

[Soundtrack: Madtraxx 'Skamaress']

[Cut to the Kampala party scene. YG and YS are in the club with their cousins and friends]

John Masembe: *Welcome to Kampala! In this city, every night is a club night! Pate ebeera pate!*

George: Looking back, we were part of a trend.
Ugandans were so accommodating, for most of our
Holidays we just wanted to party with them,
And be with our cousins, uncles, aunties and friends.
Mentally for me, it was far from the ends.
It was mad seeing Black people laughing again.

Across the entire diaspora,
More of us were becoming inspired by Africa.
The continent was a symbol of optimism
Africans held all the top positions.

Aggie Turwomwe: *George, you really need to come and work in Uganda. Do you know how much work you can do here? Hey . . .*

George: And even though we were lucky to live in rich countries
The Motherland showed us what was missing.

The people, the sun, the cultural healing,
The food, the vibe – it was the ultimate freedom.
For the first time in my life, I wasn't 'Black'.
I think I got attached mainly 'cause of that.

[Soundtrack: Bobi Wine ft. Juliana Kanyomozi 'Maama Mbiire']

George: During this time, African music was making rapid
improvements.
Probably 'cause of music production *and* distribution becoming
more digital,
And more Africans having computers.

Not to mention a young mass of consumers
Creating new superstars and massive producers.
According to this Wikipedia page, in the
2010s, nineteen was Africa's median age.

Uganda's music scene was soon seeing a change, there was
More demand on the international stage.
All Africans are part of the same story, but
Music put us on the same actual page.

[Soundtrack ends abruptly. Transition into ominous ambience]

George: And that's how one of Uganda's most popular singers, Bobi
    Wine
Ended up in a position to become a politician.

SCENE 9: THE CRACKS START TO SHOW

George: I usually spend my birthdays in Uganda
But not in 2021.
This year I didn't even get a birthday message from
Anyone back home. Anyone.

It wasn't a case of just *out of sight, out of mind* . . .
If anything, I wish it was that.
Nah. The government cut off the internet for about
Five days before bringing it back.

I'm gonna tell you something about Uganda
Which you might already know . . .
The older she gets, the
More her insecurities show.

She was born into trauma and tears.
She saw a lot of violence during her formative years.
Then she met a man called Museveni.
He told her everything she needed to hear.
He told her she deserved freedom from fear.
Told her he was prepared to stand for her freedom.
And Uganda believed him.
With good reason.

He fought. And he won.
Yet despite all that he's done
Thirty-five years later, Uganda's still poor and dysfunctional.
Meanwhile, Museveni and everyone around him
Look awfully comfortable.

Comfort is a funny thing.
It's not just a money thing.
It's different for everyone; for me and my friends,
Comfort was the thought of leaving the Ends.

In Uganda, comfort varies.
Gunfire for sixty months is scary.
Scarier than what just went on in November.
But most Ugandans are too young to remember.

[An excerpt from 'Why Museveni Went to War' by New Vision TV]

Narrator: *The government conducted a genocide, killing every-body who did not flee the country fast enough to Sudan and Congo.*

George: Yet they're too old to be told they're too young.
That day is done. This is a new one.
Museveni came with the promise of democracy . . .
Did he produce one?

Not according to Bobi Wine.
When he became a politician,
Democracy was not what he'd find.

Bobi headed up the opposition.
The government didn't really want the competition.
For three years now, the singer's been beaten and imprisoned,
Like a lot of other politicians.

This year I didn't get a birthday message from my
Fam or my fans on the Ugandan side, 'cause the
Government shut down the internet during an
Election, and the country's hands were tied.

[A clip taken from the Channel 4 video 'Uganda blocks internet after elections']

Presenter: ... *but the Ugandan government is obviously very anxious about these elections. Why cut the internet?*

George: When I was nineteen, I fell for Uganda 'cause I was
Sick of the inner-city gangster vibe, but on
January 14th, 2021
Uganda's gangster side was amplified.

[Another clip from the Channel 4 video 'Uganda blocks internet after elections']

Presenter: *Do you think that Bobi Wine can really win this election?*

Voter: *Erm . . . if it's free and fair, yes, he can.*

George: People cried about a rigged election,
Kidnappings and media misdirection.
Museveni insisted he was protecting Uganda from
Foreign agents planning an insurrection.

[A clip taken from the Channel 4 video 'Uganda election: President Museveni says opposition are agents of foreign interests']

President Museveni: Bobi Wine in particular is an agent of foreign interests.

George: All of this leaves me with the question . . .
Given the limits on freedom of expression,

And given that social critique is my profession . . .

Who would I become . . . if I moved to Uganda?

I'd have to adapt. That's just a fact.
'Cause the reality is, Africa's trapped.
Old dictators, young populations.
What happens next is not a fun conversation.

Yet fun is what brings us back to the continent.
Africa's sun gives us African confidence.

SCENE 10: HARD TRUTHS

[Return to George in his writing room]

George: I told you about Sandra's cousin we call 'Crisis'.
Yeah, made the move.
He was born and raised in London, he's younger than me,
But UG is where he always wanted to be.

I had the same dream throughout my twenties but my
Twenties ended in 2020. And in the
Last few days of that crazy year,
I asked Sandra to marry me.
If all goes well, after the wedding we'll be
Thinking about starting a family.

Now, in asking Sandra to marry me, I'm
Making her mother and her father a guarantee.
I'm saying their baby's safe with me.
Saying I'll protect her, faithfully.

That means I better know what I'm doing. I
Need to consider her in every goal I'm pursuing.

We both have a great relationship with UG.
A relationship I don't wanna ruin.

But the older Uganda grows, the more her insecurities show,
As we already know.
The situation's heating up. The press get beaten up for speaking up.

A straightforward pathway does not exist.
Only novices expect this from politics.
But most of us young Africans outside the continent
Tend to focus on the positives.

See, on January 14th, 2021
I hit thirty.
I released a film, called *Black Yellow Red*
Reflecting on this journey.

I based it on parts of Episode 6 and
Episode 7, and added some more.
I tried to explain in under fifteen minutes
Why Ugandan politics is mad insecure.

I presented different perspectives.
I didn't want Ugandans feeling misrepresented or disrespected.
And I felt relieved 'cause it was well-received on
Both sides of the political divide.
To any young people tryna follow my pattern,
Take time . . . 'cause it was difficult to write.

SCENE 11: GOD'S PLAN

[Soundtrack: Afrigo Band 'Mundeke']

George: But none of this is one man's problem to solve.
At the end of the day, God's in control.

And He's *been* in control since back in my mid-teens
When I was a rapper with big dreams.
Back when I didn't have a pound to spend,
It was God's plan that led me out the Ends.

God's plan brought me to my wife-to-be, and
Showed me that Uganda had the life for me.
I believe God's got a plan for Africa,
A day that I pray I'll be alive to see.

For now, though, I've got a wedding to pay for.
I'm marrying the woman I was made for, I'm grateful.

Sandra and George – that's the movie.
And this is Act 2: Back to UG.

[A recording of Sandra and George running through wedding planning itinerary]

Sandra: *So, finalise the menu and flowers, check on wedding invitations, select and order the cake, send guest list to the host of the bridal shower, purchase wedding shoes . . . blah blah blah.*

But when we go back to Uganda, I think that's when we'll get to do that.

EPISODE 24: The Sixties

Extra Info:

- I wrote this episode to begin explaining where Gangsta culture came from. To get the full picture, listen to Episode 26, 'Vibrations'.

Fun Facts:

- 'A Change is Gonna Come' is one of my favourite songs of all time. I'm grateful that I got to open a podcast episode with it.

Three decades of my life had passed before I realised that Black people were owed a revolution. Not revenge, just a moment to reset, and find our own rhythm in an economic system that never allowed us to reclaim what it took from us. Having grown up in an era where the most influential Black people in Western media were athletes and entertainers, I started searching history for the last time the Black diaspora was represented primarily by people who actually wanted to lead. Research led me to the 1960s. As I explained in Episode 9, the Black celebrity templates of today were basically invented in the '70s, but before then, the most famous Black people were, from what I can tell, civil rights leaders, socially conscious singers, and African politicians. So I started studying Black people in the '60s, and I made some more interesting discoveries. During this decade, African Americans and Africans on the continent were going through similar things: they were both trying to renegotiate their relationship with the West. I also discovered that violence usually ended their efforts. When I mentioned this to my mum, who is like a history expert, she said it had never occurred to her. In fact, most people I've mentioned it to have rarely made the connection between the failures of the civil rights movement and African independence in the 1960s. The lost revolution. This was the decade in which Malcolm X toured Africa, earning support from state leaders to take a case against America to the United Nations. The same decade in which young, good-looking, well-spoken activists like Patrice Lumumba and Huey Newton restored Black pride, not with their bodies, or with their money, but with their character, and their ideas. It's kind of suspicious to me that all that potential disappeared in one generation. In the decades that followed, dictatorship took over much of Africa, the Black family declined in America, and Black icons had less and less to say about creating a new way of life. There was definitely something about the '60s. Shout out to Nikissi Serumaga. And a special thank you to my grandfather, the late Andrew Frederick Mpanga.

SCENE 1: A TURNING POINT

George: There's something about the '60s.

[Soundtrack: Sam Cooke 'A Change is Gonna Come']

George: Freedom was in the air.
Africa was finally gonna get to spread her wings.
But the dream and the reality . . .
Two separate things.

This was the Civil Rights era.
The American Dream was still the American wish.
Change was promised, but the reality?
Different kettle of fish.

Both Africans and African Americans
Found themselves suddenly reacting to developments
That changed the world in a short space of time.
Establishing new precedents, new establishments, new
   presidents.

The process was messy. A lot of blood was spilt.
A lot of sisters hurt; a lot of brothers killed.
What would you have done? Would you offer up your skills?
Or avoid the struggle, and bottle up your guilt?

['A Change is Gonna Come' refrain]

. . . That damn hook . . .
You're listening to 'Change is Gonna Come' by Sam Cooke.
Beautiful song, but the backstory's crazy, though.
This next verse got banned from radio . . .

Sam Cooke: *I go to the movie/*
And I go downtown/

And somebody keeps telling me/
'Don't hang around'...

George: Can you imagine?

[George stops the music]

SCENE 2: REFLECTING IN THE WRITING ROOM

[George is sitting at his desk, where he spent most of lockdown trying to write Chapter Three]

George: At the start of the '60s,
New Black leaders offered people new ideas,
Friendship and guidance.
But by the end of the decade, a lot of these
New movements would descend into violence.

If it wasn't African Americans assassinating Malcolm,
It was the Congolese executing Lumumba.
Or COINTELPRO, or some military coup.
Or just heroes falling from grace, like Nkrumah.

You see, Black people never had no overall system of getting things
    done;
They were starting from scratch.
Most figureheads who were part of this batch of
New leaders found it kinda hard to adapt.

Dreams of an integrated market were scrapped.
After Malcolm X, Martin got capped.
And the next generation started to act more
Militant, sometimes even targeting Blacks.

I'm saying: Africans were never a unified group, they
Formulated kingdoms, tribes and clans.

And in the 1880s, European powers
Devised a plan to divide the land.

So the only thing a lot of Africans had in common was
Exploitation at the hands of foreigners.
Other than their colour they were different from each other

Just 'cause two people are from the same race
Doesn't mean they're coming from the same place.

They had different problems, they had different needs.
Different myths, beliefs, different histories.
It was deep. Some of them had twisted beefs and they
Had to swiftly fix these issues in the '60s.

How were these Africans gonna pull it together?
Democracy? Is that what they'd seen from European authorities
In all those years they spent as colonies?

How did Black America plan to behave?
A generation raised by the grandkids of slaves.
With nothing to show for sacrifices their ancestors made.

It took the West a long time to come together.
And in the space of a decade, Africa's children
Had to make that happen . . . under pressure.

Just 'cause two people are from the same race
Doesn't mean they're coming from the same place.

But violence? Violence is a language everyone understands.
Not words and elections . . . guns in hands.
Africa flirted with capitalism and socialism,
But her leaders were overwhelmed by a broken system.
And the scary thing is, sixty years later, that
Fundamental dysfunction is still so persistent.

My father's father found out the hard way.
By the end of his life, I'm sure he remembered
Ugandan Independence as a dark day.

SCENE 3: GEORGE'S GRANDFATHER

[Throwback to 1920s Uganda]

George: Andrew Frederick Mpanga was born
thirty-seven years before this thing we call Uganda.
He started off as a village boy, and became
One of the biggest lawyers in the Kingdom of Buganda.

He was driven by the love of this Kingdom.
In the '40s and '50s, he studied in England – in
York and Oxford, where he got a great education.
Then he came back to shape legislation,
'Cause everything was changing.
Europeans were leaving Africa. Could become a messy situation.
Unless there were arrangements like protection from enslavement.
And laying out the law to avoid this playing out in war
Would involve some stressful conversations.

The Buganda Kingdom had a special kind of status.
Unlike a lot of guys they never got colonised.
They stayed independent and enjoyed privileges with the British
Causing major resentment.

We're talking about a civilisation that could trace their
Monarchy back over thirty generations.
And they had strategic advantages that made the
British come seeking a partnership.

But the Baganda were no angels . . .
They were driven by competition.
In the 1890s when Britain wanted to invade the neighbours,
They ended up trading favours.

The nearby tribe of Bunyoro lost three
Quarters of its people in the violence that followed.
Britain and Buganda agreed they would split the land,
So, they saw their relationship expand.

Could it have been different if someone just warned them?
'Cause that right there would come back to haunt them.

SCENE 4: THE BIRTH OF UGANDA

George: Britain expanded her control of the region,
And named the whole operation after Buganda.
They colonised more neighbours, Buganda kept that special status,
And this was the start of Uganda.

My grandad was born in the third decade of this experiment.
I used to wonder how his life would've been without colonial rule,
But it's irrelevant.

The Kingdom of Buganda had complex political structures,
Which Britain used to organise the locals.
And that influence ran deep;
Religious, economic, political, social.

For Buganda and Britain, it worked well enough.
The colonisers explored the land and fell in love.
They started selling stuff like cotton and coffee and
Buganda was getting a cut.
But little did she know, Britain was setting her up.

See, the 1900 Uganda Agreement guaranteed
Buganda her own land in the region.
Buganda was happy to be homies with Britain, but
Independence was her only condition.

And in 1953 Britain changed her mind, because . . . colonialism.

Instead of Buganda staying a separate nation,
Britain wanted her to join an East African federation.
And when Buganda 'Nah, you can't dismantle the ting'
Britain cancelled her King. Sent him to England.

[A recording of Kabaka Muteesa II (KM)]

KM: *Well, it's very difficult indeed. I am, of course, on public assist-ance. And that is complicated enough.*

This was Kabaka Muteesa II.
Britain pressured the Baganda to
Find another king, but that's not
Something they were prepared to do.

Two years later, Kabaka came home after negotiations.
But by this point the British Empire
Carried a lot of negative associations.
And even though they kept a hand in local trade,
In 1962, Uganda broke away.

So, at thirty-seven years old, my grandad
Found himself Attorney General of an
Old kingdom in a new country surrounded by
Other kingdoms turning federal.

In fact, they were all thirty-six/thirty-seven; my
Grandad, Kabaka, the new Prime Minister.
They were young, and their journey was so epic
You'd think it was a movie by New Line Cinema.
But the peace didn't last.
The Prime Minister, Dr Milton Obote
Wasn't a fan of Buganda privilege.
He planned to reimagine the land in his image.

Now, remember what happened in the 1890s – that
First Buganda deal done with Britain . . .
When they ran up on Bunyoro and took their land.
Yeah, that decision was still unforgiven.

The beef never ended.
So Obote decided to resurrect it with a referendum.
Buganda didn't want it.
The people of Bunyoro were on it.
And of course, they won it.
Buganda lost the territories fair and square, to be
Fair they were never really theirs to share.
And that was in 1964. In less than two years, this
New constitution saw a lot of wear and tear.

But it really kicked off in 1966 . . .
It was all downhill from there.

SCENE 5: THE 1966 CRISIS

**[The following is based on a true discovery George made while writing
Chapter Three. In a creative conversation with Nikissi Serumaga, the
Ugandan filmmaker showed George a recording of her grandfather,
Robert Serumaga (Sr.), interviewing his grandfather, Andrew
Frederick (A. F.) Mpanga. The recording was made for the BBC in
1966, during the midst of Uganda's constitutional crisis. George's
paternal uncle David Mpanga discovered the recording years later
and made it available online]**

Nikissi: *Hey George. Your Uncle David found this incredible recording of my grandfather. He's interviewing yours for the BBC. It's
around the 1966 crisis.*

Robert Serumaga: *Recently, dramatic developments in Uganda's
constitutional structure have caused some worry in certain quarters in Uganda and outside Uganda.*

George: *Yo Nikissi that's mad. My Jajja died when my dad was a boy. I've never even heard his voice before.*

Robert Serumaga: *In the studio now, I have Mr Fred Mpanga, the Attorney General of Buganda, who is representing the Buganda Government here in London at the moment. Mr Mpanga, do you think that Buganda have any means of defending their stand?*

A. F. Mpanga: *I think they have. In Buganda, the whole population, which is about 2.5 million, they are all behind the Lukiko (Parliament of Buganda). They stand by the 1962 Constitution, which was made by the people with their own consent.*

George: [To Nikissi] *Yo, this is making me kinda emotional.*

Robert Serumaga: *Mr Obote defends himself by saying the Kabaka of Buganda did invite foreign troops to come and invade the country and says that he had to suspend the constitution, do you agree with this?*

A. F. Mpanga: *I do not. All that the Kabaka did was consult with the British High Commissioner there whether the British Government would come and assist Uganda maintain its constitution.*

Nikissi: [To George] *It's like the King reached out to Britain for help, because the Prime Minister was trying to take over, but Britain left him hanging.*

A. F. Mpanga: *In February there were mysterious troop movements. The commander ordered the troops back to barracks. Two days after, Dr Obote said he knew about these troop movements long time before, but he never informed anybody.*

Robert Serumaga: *Are you, in fact, suggesting that, rather than the Kabaka being the person who is trying to stage a coup d'état, it was the Prime Minister, Dr Obote, who's trying to do this?*

A. F. Mpanga: *People have been saying that.*

George: [To Nikissi] *The way they talk is so dignified and calm. But this situation must have been tearing them apart inside.*

Robert Serumaga: *Now, do you think this is a situation which might develop in some kind of civil war?*

A. F. Mpanga: *The thing is, you see, Buganda are not armed, and Dr. Obote has got arms and men . . . we don't know what's going to happen.*

Nikissi: [To George] *Man, that part when your grandad says, 'We don't know what's going to happen,' It really gets me. It's literally sixty years later, and we still don't know.*

George: [To Nikissi] *Mmm. Sixty years later, Ugandans still turn to the international community for help.*

Robert Serumaga: *The Kabaka has asked for United Nations inter-vention according to* The Times *here in London last week. What is the next move going to be, you think?*

A. F. Mpanga: *One doesn't know. What you want to do now is to awaken a world conscience as to what's going on in Uganda. You've got Dr Obote introducing his own constitution and you've got Buganda sticking to the 1962 Constitution, thereby having two constitutions in one nation, and you can't have that.*

SCENE 6: VIOLENT PATTERNS

George: Hundreds of years of Buganda history . . .
Decades of colonial alliance . . .
But when it all came down to it,
Uganda's future was decided only with violence.

When you study Black people in the '60s, you
Realise this violence was part of a pattern.
No matter where they were,
Whenever they tried to build a new way of life
Someone started attacking.

But think about it, though:
Most Black people in the '60s
Lived in societies they were forced to be in.
Ones that didn't have an organic course to freedom.
Societies forged by Europeans.

And the Europeans were way more united in their
Aims than the Africans were.
And sixty years later,
Compare the White world to the Black world,
You still see this pattern at work.

SCENE 7: THE COMPLEXION COMPLEX

[Return to George in his writing room]

George: You might be thinking
'What's all this 'White world/Black world' stuff?'
Well, think of it like this:
When a group of people have a dark or fair complexion,
That doesn't necessarily mark a shared direction,
But racial divisions shaped how we're living.
And for most people that's part of their perception.

Now, this complexion complexity is what the
Nation of Islam helped Malcolm X to see.

[An excerpt from Malcolm X's 1963 interview at Berkeley]

Malcolm X: *In the past fifteen years, dark nations have emerged in Africa ... prior to ten years ago, most negros associated Africa with a savage, jungle-like place. In their mind's eye they could see the image of someone running around with a spear ... After the war, when the United Nations was set up in New York City, Black people began to look at men like Tom Mboya, they began to see men like Nkrumah, they began to look at Lumumba, they began to see men like Nasser, they began to see Balewa and Azikiwe, who could exchange intellectually with Whites on an international level in a political form and hold their own. This made the Black people in this country realise that what the Honourable Elijah Muhammad had been teaching all the time actually had substance. And they began to identify themselves with the Black world and the Black struggle more closely than they identified themselves with this so-called White world.*

SCENE 8: MORE VIOLENT PATTERNS

George: After six years in a prison cell, where he
Got the name 'Satan' 'cause his life had been a living hell.
After serving in the Nation of Islam and
Leaving behind the parts of it that ain't in the Koran
After years of arguing that people with darker skin would
Never find freedom by pleading and bargaining,
After making all these powerful, popular friends, after
All that, Malcolm X got shot in the Ends.

Now think about this carefully: the next year –
'66 – the Black Panther Party was formed.
Young Black people, carrying guns in broad
Daylight – this was hardly the norm.

[A recording of Huey P. Newton, co-founder of the Black Panther Party for Self-Defense]

Huey Newton: *We use the black panther as our symbol because ... he'll back up first, but if the aggressor continues, then he'll strike out.*

George: They weren't a faith group like the Nation of Islam but they
Loved their people and wouldn't let racists bring them
Harm. And they shared the view of the Nation that there's
No freedom if the liberation isn't armed.

[Another recording of Huey Newton]

Huey Newton: *... the Constitution guarantees the citizen a right to bear arms on public property.*

George: Thenceforth, the Panthers became known as a
Community defence force.

[A clip of Black Panther Party member Ericka Huggins]

Ericka Huggins: *... every city, small or large, wanted a chapter of the Black Panther Party.*

Newsreader 1: *FBI director, J. Edgar Hoover, today asserted that the Black Panthers represent the greatest internal threat to the nation.*

[Gunshot sound effect]

Newsreader 2: *... very sad news for all of our fellow citizens and people who love peace all over the world ...*

George: Just as their movement started to pop,
In 1968, Martin was shot.

Newsreader 2: *... Martin Luther King was shot and was killed tonight in Memphis ...*

[Soundtrack: The Last Poets 'Black Soldier']

George: Put that all together, and you can see how this
Period was basically the start of Hip Hop.

Young Black people started to speak openly . . .
Through street poetry.
For the Black struggle they were war reporting.
Black pride became more and more important.
They made their own politicised space where they criticised
Racism in politics and law enforcement.

Many politicians didn't wanna give Black people increased freedoms
Exactly for these reasons.
These new voices weren't no Baptist choir.
Sounded like they were praying for a Black Messiah.

[Recording of senior Black Panther Party figure, Fred Hampton]

Fred Hampton: . . . *with the last words on my lips: that I am a revolutionary! And you're gonna have to keep on saying that!*

George: At twenty-one years old, Fred Hampton
Led the Black Panthers in Illinois.
At the same time, he was deputy-leader of the
National Party, and he didn't disappoint.
He took on a do-or-die mission to bring street
Gangs together under a unified vision.
The FBI snuck into his apartment building,
Sprayed bullets all over the yard and killed him.

When Fred Hampton died, so did his
Plan for gangs of the future.
If you wanna learn more, watch *Judas and the Black Messiah*,
Starring Uganda's Daniel Kaluuya.

Needless to say, the gangs never unified.
Black leadership was looking like suicide.

But even though Fred was murdered, in a way,
A vision like his was emerging in LA.

SCENE 9: THE GANGSTERS BECOME THE LEADERS

[Soundtrack: David McCallum 'The Edge']

George: For many teens in the Black suburb of Compton,
Gang life was more than a form of defiance.
It was about protection from all of the violence.
In '69 some of them formed an alliance.

They called themselves the 'Crips'
And unlike the Panthers,
They *embraced* their own political captivity.
Panthers were known to stand for their own.
Crips, they were known for criminal activity.

The gang's appeal captured the streets
Over time their numbers matched the police.
But even though their presence was vast and strong,
The unity didn't last for long.
The Crips broke up into different sets.
Divisions were driven by murder and disrespect.
Getting involved was risky.
A war broke out between the 8 Trey Gangsters and the Rollin' 60s.

I grew up in London's Black inner city and it was similar . . .
A little too similar.
What's the chances of all these Black communities
Genuinely choosing this path?

All our young Black gang members
Are living proof of what was done to their ancestors.

We saw gang violence from childhood.
And the crazy thing is – no matter where we were in the world –
We made it sound good.

SCENE 10: THE MUSIC TELLS THE STORY

[Soundtrack: 2Pac ft. Snoop Dogg '2 of Amerikaz Most Wanted']

George: 2Pac was raised by a Black Panther
Snoop Dogg grew up as a Crip.
This is what makes Gangsta Rap gangsta.
From the anguish and the anger
Comes the language – it's an anchor.

They were both born in 1971, when the
Panthers and the Crips were close to their prime.
You can hear the culture in most of their rhymes.
But when it came to black liberation,
That generation gave with one hand and took with the other.
They looked a bit rougher. And they taught the world
Never to judge a book by its cover.

They were America's first generation of Black leaders to
Actively disrespect their kind.
They soaked up the negativity of their environment and
Chose to openly reflect their times.

[An excerpt from a 2Pac interview for BET]

2Pac: . . . *and if I didn't talk about the violence, everybody would act
like the violence wasn't there. We as rappers brought that violence
that we seen on the street, we put it in our records . . .*

George: The self-destructive nature of Gangsta Rap
Is tied to the assassination of the Black man.
And *I'm* saying that as a rap fan.

What other profession has as many millionaires that go to jail?
The number's depressing.

See, when we record in the booth, we're
Supporting the youth by reporting the truth.
And Tupac Shakur was the proof.

SCENE 11: THE REAL BLACK HISTORY

[Back in George's writing room]

George: Black history is so much more than
Slavery and civil rights. It's the
Lived experience of every single African
Every single day and every single night.

It makes no sense to expect white countries to
Teach our kids this stuff; they never will.
It's our job to give these kids the information they
Need to negotiate a better deal.

By the time a Black child turns thirteen they should
Know their history like the back of their hand.
That's the only way they stand a chance of
Breaking the cycle, and having a plan.

Life don't come with a manual. But at
Least you can use Black music as a handbook.
Telling your own story is the secret to survival.
Look at Sam Cooke.

[Soundtrack: Sam Cooke 'A Change is Gonna Come']

George: It was 1963 when he wrote this one.
You can tell by the way each note was sung that he was

Singing for his people's freedom. He was rich and
Famous, but he couldn't buy equal treatment.

As one of the first soul singers with a nationwide fanbase,
Sam sometimes felt alone in the White man's space.
His clean-cut image could go out the window if he
Dared to speak the truth to the White man's face.

But he did. And it did.
Not long after recording this song,
Sam Cooke, the damn-near perfect artist, was
Killed under suspicious circumstances.
But the world remembers his work, regardless
Same way, I honour my grandfather's struggle.
Seems like Black life was never far from trouble . . .

But there's something about the '60s.

EPISODE 25: Who Hurt R&B?

Extra Info:

- My first body of work as a spoken word artist was inspired by R&B. This was my EP, 'The Chicken and the Egg', which told the story of a dysfunctional relationship becoming a problematic family. The EP was well-received, but I didn't continue in that lane, because I felt bad. Our communities have struggled with family drama for decades now – I didn't want to make art that just perpetuated this story without offering something new. This is why, even though R&B is my favourite music to write to, I fell back and focused on educational content, like this podcast. Still, I wanted to understand why it was so common for us young writers to talk about traumatic relationships, and this episode is my conclusion.

Fun Facts:

- This episode contains my favourite soundtrack out of all the episodes. Sometimes I just listen to it for the songs.

My favourite R&B music of today . . . is really sad. It sounds beautiful, as R&B always has, but a lot of it is about the inability to trust, the need for physical satisfaction from someone who is undeserving, or just the fear of being alone forever. When I was born, R&B was the bestselling Black music genre in the world. Rap was growing fast, though, and by the end of the decade it outsold R&B. Then things got interesting. By the mid-2000s, rap had become less aggressive and more melodic. Then by the end of *that* decade, Drake. From the 2010s onwards, the line between Rap and R&B has become increasingly blurred, with the most successful rapper in the world also doubling up as an R&B singer. This reflects the transformation of both genres. Drake popularised introspection and vulnerability in rap, but even when Chicago's drill scene rejuvenated rap's gangsta spirit, melody was here to stay. Now, these rappers can't stop singing. Meanwhile, after being relegated to the sidelines by rap's commercial dominance, and ridiculed for its softness by a generation petrified of social media humiliation, R&B seems to have adapted to the times. Even sonically, nowadays it uses the same drums and bass as rap. Both female and male R&B singers regularly express the same prideful disdain for their sexual partners as rappers. The dynamics in their relationships sound exploitative, defensive and untrusting. I find it really hard not to link this to the fifty-year decline of the Black family. Marriage, divorce, babies out of wedlock – all the statistics reflect the harsh realities told in the music. So where did it all start? Who hurt R&B?

SCENE 1: WHERE'S THE LOVE?

[Soundtrack: Ginuwine 'Differences']

George: When Sandra and I got engaged,
We noticed something strange.
There wasn't much new R&B to listen to 'cause
We were loved up, but people were singing a different tune.

See, back in the day, R&B music was
All about being in love.
But something's happened in the past fifteen years, it's
Like everyone's seen enough.

[Soundtrack: Jhené Aiko 'P*$$Y Fairy (OTW)']

George: Now when I'm looking for Cheesy R&B,
The closest thing to it is Sleazy R&B

Otherwise, it's Sunken Place R&B, or
My-situationship-did-me-greezy R&B.

[Soundtrack: Kaash Paige 'Love Songs']

George: Imagine my position. I just wanna relax with
Bae, cah I just put a ring on her finger, so
now I'm tryna fling on a singer who's got some
We're-getting-married kinda tracks to play.
But none of our favourite R&B acts today have
Anything like that to say.

[Soundtrack: George The Poet 'Baby Father']

George: It's not a criticism. Just an observation.
My first EP was no different. I was
Heavily involved in the conversation.

Now, even though R&B is Black,
Maybe this one isn't just a Black issue.
Maybe the whole world's going through the same thing and
I just hear it in the music I'm attracted to.
'Cause I definitely hear it in Rap. It's
Hard to tell if it's the cause or effect, but
Rap makes relationships in our generation
Sound kinda mad when you pause and reflect.

[Soundtrack: Cardi B ft. Megan Thee Stallion 'WAP'; Megan Thee
Stallion 'Cash Shit'; Rick Ross ft. Kanye West & Big Sean 'Sanctified';
Drake 'Chicago Freestyle']

George: Most rappers – both male and female –
Sell sex – wholesale and retail.
But no love, no responsibility.
Just hoes and sponsors, living free.

They talk about the opposite sex like they're objects,
The irony is both sides are slyly obsessed.
They target the opposite sex on most projects, just
Listen to them with no context, it's so complex.

[Soundtrack: Chris Brown ft. Lil Wayne & Tyga 'Loyal']

George: The men all seem to want the same woman:
And guess what . . . that's yours.
The women only want money and sex, but if they
had to pick one they'd say 'Money, of course!'

They both swear they don't need each other, but
Everyone brags about being a greedy lover.
No one even expects the men to be faithful and
People make the women look less than mentally stable
So, their public breakups tend to be painful.

And when everyone's hurt and no one's even regretful, the
Music gets more and more openly disrespectful.
That's why everyone's n***** and b******
At this point it's cultural, it's not even an insult at all.

So, what happened? Who hurt R&B?
And what's it gonna take to repair this state of affairs?
You know me, I'm just gonna go back in time and take it from there.

SCENE 2: THE CANDI STATON STORY

George: In 1974, Canzetta married James.
From previous relationships she carried pain.
But she and James clicked through their work in music.
And before long, she later said, James turned abusive.

Canzetta told a colleague she feared for her life. She
Wanted out but didn't know where she could hide.
As her colleague, David, listened and contemplated, he
Started to write a song about Canzetta's dilemma.
When she heard the song he'd been working on,
Canzetta knew it would change things forever and ever.

David gave it to her to record and she
Sang from the heart; it struck a personal chord,
It was a self-empowering, angry statement
Released under her stage name: Candi Staton.

[Soundtrack: Candi Staton 'Young Hearts Run Free']

George: Listen to the lyrics . . .

Candi Staton: *What's the sense in sharing, this one and only life? /*
Ending up, just another lost and lonely wife? /
You'll count up the years, and they will be filled with tears! /

George: Did you hear what she said? That's dread.

Candi Staton: *Love only breaks up, to start over again/*
You'll get the baby, but you won't have your man/
While he is busy loving every woman that he can . . /

George: Mad.

Candi Staton: *Say I'm gonna leave a hundred times a day/*
It's easier said than done/
When you just can't break away! /
Ooh, young hearts run free/
Never be hung up, hung up like my man and me . . . /

George: This song wasn't about lovebirds and sweethearts
But it went straight to the top of the R&B Charts.

Narrative: *'Young Hearts Run Free' by Candi Staton was another*
monumental women's empowerment anthem born from the 1970s
disco movement, popular in the urban club scenes of New York and
Philadelphia

Candi Staton: *Oh, young hearts, to yourself be true/*
Don't be no fool when love really don't love you! /

SCENE 3: THE DISCO LIBERATION

[Cut to George in an American diner, with 'Young Hearts Run Free' playing from a nearby speaker]

George: Candi was stuck in an abusive relationship,
But what set her free was the music she made from it.
This enabled her to free herself from James, and the
Song's success suggests people felt the same.
For a long time, R&B had dealt with pain, but

Not always in a way that put women in the driver's seat
Especially not to this kind of beat.

Candi Staton: *Self-preservation is what's really going on today . . .*

George: Self-preservation, you know.

[An excerpt from Candi Staton's interview with Paul Morley for Guardian Music]

Candi Staton: *It was written because I was going through a difficult period at that time. I had hooked up with someone that I should never have looked at twice . . . he threatened my children, he threatened me . . . I was trying to get away from him, and I would tell David about it . . . David kept saying 'Well, you'll find a way.' Little did I know he was writing the lyrics to 'Young Hearts Run Free' . . . the first time I heard the music I knew we had a hit record. I knew it.*

Positive music for women really didn't come into effect until the mid 70s, you know when Disco started to emerge. Before then, we were stuck with the 'If you leave me, I'll die' – give me a break!

Paul Morley: *Is it because of the male writer, writing in a way for a powerless woman?*

Candi Staton: *Yeah, you know you had males on the microphones, playing your records during those days . . . you didn't have too many female DJs. And so, when we started talking about them, it was nothing much for them to say, except take it.*

I mean, these are message songs, wrapped up in nice dance music.

['Young Hearts Run Free' refrain]

Candi Staton: *I have to picture abuse. If I'm singing a sad song, I have to picture myself being in that room with him and he's being very mean to me. And then the emotion comes.*

SCENE 4: PATTERNS OF TRAUMA

George: Candi Staton used this music to
Speak out, and she wasn't the only one.
Black women were battling against what was happening to them –
Fathers left behind lonely mums.

Listen back to Episode 20; this was when
Jay-Z's father started to disappear, too.
Where to? The family wouldn't know for months.

In fact, this was happening to all my favourite rappers then;
2Pac, Biggie, Snoop Dogg, 50.
The only exception was Nas. And his father's
Presence is something you could detect in his bars.

Now, it's sad to say, but many societies
Have a long history of spousal abuse.
Yet what was new in African American society was this
Generation of men walking out on the youts.

Disturbing as it is, it's now nothing new.
At the time it almost came out of the blue.

In the West it looks like a Black man dysfunction but
Historically, that's not how Africans functioned.
It's like these Black men were all . . . reacting to something.

[Clips taken from Jay-Z's interview with Sway for MTV, and the Scandinavian talk show *Skavlan*]

Jay-Z: *As a kid, you know, you look at your father, that's like your superhero . . . 'nobody could beat my pops' . . . so to have that person that I looked up to most in the world removed out of your life is like a traumatic experience. Like, no one could ever match that pain. I've always been guarded; I've always built a shield around myself because I never want to ever experience that pain.*

[An excerpt from 2Pac's interview with Ed Gordon for BET]

Ed Gordon: *Do you look back and say 'Damn . . . I missed something big'?*

2Pac: *Every day. I um . . . I know for a fact that . . . had I had a father – and I hate saying this 'cause White people love hearing Black people talk about this, but had I had a father, had I had some of these opportunities, I'd have been able to help my mother more, she wouldn't have went the road she went, I could have been a better son . . . It was the absence of my father – I'm dealing with him being 'Daddy' not being there, my mother's dealing with him being 'My man' not being there . . . so many problems in our community that affect everything. So, by me not having that, I ain't never wanna hear nothing about no kind of relationships between a Black man and a Black woman, I knew they didn't work. 'Cause as far as I knew, my daddy was the coolest dude out there, and my momma was a Panther, so if they didn't work, it don't work!*

[An excerpt taken from 50 Cent's interview with Larry King for Ora TV]

Larry King: *What about your dad?*

50 Cent: *I never knew my father. You know, I never actually met him . . .*
You know, some people have that thing where they actually want that parent that they haven't had in their lives for a long time.

Larry King: *You don't?*

50 Cent: *Nah, I have no interest in it. You know, the mistakes that I made earlier on, Larry, he could have been there to help me not make those mistakes.*

Larry King: *Damn right.*

George: This generation of African Americans
Found ways to bridge the gaps in their development.
One of them grew up to be the actual president.

[A clip of Barack Obama discussing the importance of strong families, taken from CNN footage]

Barack Obama: ... *You know, don't get me wrong, as the son of a single mom, who gave everything she had to raise me, with the help of my grandparents I turned out OK. But ... we've got single moms out here, they're heroic, what they're doing. And we are so proud of them. But at the same time ... I wish I'd had a father who was around and involved ... loving, supportive parents ... that's the single most important thing.*

[Reflecting on the rappers' trauma]

George: It's like these Black men were all ... reacting to something.

2Pac: *Had I had a father, I'd have been able to help my mother more.*

Jay-Z: *I've always been guarded.*

50 Cent: *I never knew my father.*

SCENE 5: MUSIC REFLECTS CHANGE

[A clip from Lauryn Hill's BET Rap City interview]

Lauryn Hill: *I've always been surrounded by love, so I've never had any empty spaces as far as like, attention, you know what I'm saying, and love. And it wasn't until later that I started to meet people who didn't grow up with the same security and the same sense of love and affection that I grew up with, and I saw how it affected them. It really made me think about how blessed I was to be born into the family that I was born into.*

[Soundtrack: Lauryn Hill 'Doo Wop (That Thing)']

George: Lauryn Hill was born in 1975,
The year Candi Staton released 'Young Hearts Run Free'
And at the age of twenty-three, it's
Like she gave the world an updated sequel,
Telling the story of her sexually free, but
Deeply frustrated people.

By 1998, things had gone from bad to
worse for Black American love.
No matter how hard the Black family fought for a
Stable foundation, it's like it was never enough.

Changes in the job market, a decline in
Real earnings since the '60s, crack,
Higher incarceration, lower education,
All the little tricks around voter registration –
Economically slowed a generation
Making marriage feel much more like a burden than a show of
　　dedication

To the older generation, these new lifestyle
Changes were downright outrageous. Before the
'70s yeah, if you had a baby with someone
Everyone expected you to marry the person –
Whether or not you felt happy or certain.
Whether or not the relationship was actually working.

But this was based on the compliance of women, and
Women took an increasingly defiant position.

[Soundtrack: Whitney Houston 'It's Not Right but It's Okay']

George: Towards the end of the twentieth century,
Feminism went beyond the academic prism,
Into music and television.

Feminists argued that women were taken for granted,
And demanded the world place more importance on their lives.
This liberated spouses forced to compromise and
By the end of the decade, divorce was on the rise.

Narrative: *In 1970, 64% of adult African Americans were married. This rate was cut in half by 2004.*

While marriage rates have dropped for African Americans, the birth rate has not. Thus, the number of single-parent homes has risen dramatically for Black women.

Now, don't get me wrong.
I'm not trying to say that all this divorce was caused by feminism alone.
Nah. To me, it's just a reflection of the
Different directions in which men and women have grown.

Across the Black world, there were other factors that
Made marriage seem increasingly unattractive.
And if I had to pick the main one, my guess is
Probably the long-term effects of poverty.

SCENE 6: THE EFFECTS OF POVERTY ON THE AFRICAN AMERICAN FAMILY

George: Throughout his career, the Black American
Economist, Walter E. Williams, acknowledged this.
He argued that higher labour costs
Forced Black families to take a loss.
And it's not like his opinion would change when the
Government raised the minimum wage. Nah, he found that
Instead of forcing businesses to make expensive payoffs,
Higher wages led to layoffs,
Leaving working people with slashed salaries.
And apparently the hardest hit were Black families.

Another big problem was welfare, plus millions
Not having the option of healthcare.
Many saw these Black people drowning at the bottom,
And reacted by looking down on them and scoffing,
As if they had forgotten how the country had gotten itself
there, like these problems had origins elsewhere.

Welfare support became a way of life for
Many Americans fighting to stay alive.
In bigger cities, poor Black communities were
Placed in federal public housing; sometimes
More than several hundred thousand.
Often in conditions that were harsh and unpleasant. And
　　imagine . . .
The government offered less support to these families
If the father was present.

So, young Black men, raised with no dad
Couldn't get work, started to go mad.
As welfare support became a way of life, the
Drug game became a way to thrive.

By the '8Os when Black America was hit with the
Crack epidemic, the effect was epic.

In 1980, 140,000 Black men were locked up.
Once crack hit, that figure shot up.

[A clip from 'The Race Against Crack' by the Glide Memorial Church
Conference]

Presenter: *Today our prisons are jammed with crack users, our
courts backlogged with their cases. Families have been shattered,
lives lost and a whole new generation is growing up in crack's
shadow.*

George: In twenty short years the numbers had risen; there were 800,000 brothers in prison.
Coming home to estranged families,
Living under the thumb of the system.

A lot of boys grew up too stubborn to listen and
Going to jail would almost become a tradition.
Female-headed households became the norm and
Many men didn't know any other condition.

And out of this troubling vision
A new culture emerged.
A culture of boys who turned to the streets
And became ultra-submerged.

SCENE 7: MUSIC REFLECTS CHANGE AGAIN

[Soundtrack: Dr Dre & Snoop Doggy Dogg 'Bitches Ain't Shit']

George: These new kids wanted to be pimps,
Rather than what we refer to currently as 'simps'
They came across angered and tough.
And their language was *rough*.

This culture of disrespect towards women from
Men with ironically female support systems was
Heavily rewarded by the market, and
Gangsta Rap gets the thanks for that.

To be fair, it was first made popular by
Blaxploitation movies of the '70s.
Kids in the communities these movies came from
Grew to be drug-dealer-groupies and celebrities.

Young men and women with absent fathers
Adapted by acting heartless.

This generation – Candi Staton's kids – had
Lost a lot of respect for Black relationships.

This culture of misogyny is probably the
Biggest failure of manhood in the slums.
It's sad to see how standard it's become, but
By the '90s the damage had been done.

Black men were celebrating denigrating Black women.
Grandparents found the younger generation baffling, but
This wasn't a Black self-generated accident;
Systemic oppression would accelerate this happening.

How long would Black women take this disrespect from
Black men before they'd demonstrate it back to them?
African American males more likely than
Anyone else to end up dead or in jail.
Not representing anyone except for themselves . . .
Definitely not thinking about protecting the girls.

But yo, these women were more than capable of defending
    themselves.
Through music they got their two cents in as well.

SCENE 8: R&B FIGHTS BACK

[Soundtrack: Destiny's Child 'Bills, Bills, Bills']

George: By the '90s, Black American women were
Sick of men who leant on their girls but
Never put money towards the rent or their bail,
Like the cost of living wasn't already expensive as hell.
So, they used music to vent to the world.

['Bills, Bills, Bills' pre-chorus]

George: At this time, Rap music portrayed women being put down,
But R&B portrayed women putting their foot down.

['Bills, Bills, Bills' chorus]

George: And these songs weren't just about financial strain they were
Calling men out for their lies and their games.

[Soundtrack: Sunshine Anderson 'Heard It All Before']

George: But one song will stick in my mind forever as the one that
defined this era.

[Soundtrack: TLC 'No Scrubs']
George: See, for many women, being approached by irresponsible men
Had become a constant event.
And this song was for them.

['No Scrubs' pre-chorus and chorus]

George: With seven weeks on top of the Billboard 200,
'No Scrubs' was an instant national treasure.
But when you listen closely, you can hear a
Generation of men under real financial pressure.

['No Scrubs' breakdown]

George: Yeah, it was R&B. But it wasn't no
Love song; it was a song about showing no love.
'No Scrubs' got played in most clubs.
And what made it work was fire inside of it.
Black women sick of it. Tired of it.
Sick and tired of hiding it.
Sick of riding with a guy that's full of pride and shit
Ain't providing shit, and
Wonders why you treat him like a kid.

SCENE 9: WHO HURT R&B?

[George in the marketplace]

George: The story of who hurt R&B is so long
There's no way I'm covering it all today.
We just got through twenty-five years
In like twenty-five minutes and there's
Still so much more to say.

Like how Hip Hop overtook R&B, and
Made singers wanna be more hard than sweet.
And how Rap started using melodies.
I mean, by this point R&B can't compete.

But apart from the sound, the
Change in music really starts on the ground.
The breakup of Black love created generations
That found it safer to act tough.

I can't help looking at the racial element, and
Thinking about our history, 'cause it ain't irrelevant.

In the UK, 59% of Black Caribbean and 44% of Black African
children grow up in single parent families, compared to 22% of
the population overall.

And we're supposed to believe this is all a coincidence?
Like Black women are just crazy and Black men are just lazy?
Are you kidding?

The question isn't 'Who hurt R&B?'
The question is 'Who didn't?'

[Soundtrack: Jazmine Sullivan 'Pick Up Your Feelings']

EPISODE 26: Vibrations

Extra Info:

- This was meant to be Episode 25. I wanted it to follow directly from 'The Sixties', but since this one dealt with the '80s, and 'Who Hurt R&B?' dealt with the '70s, I chose to organise the episodes according to the timeline. What I've ended up with is a sandwich: Episode 24, 'The Sixties', about the sabotage of Black leadership giving way to gang culture; Episode 25, 'Who Hurt R&B?' about the sabotage of Black families leading to unhealthy dynamics between men and women; then Episode 26, 'Vibrations', about how poverty, guns and drugs imposed on Black communities gave birth to Gangsta culture. The main theme linking all these episodes, as ever, is music. Music held the story together.

- Another theme linking these episodes is the role of the market – specifically, the music industry. So much Black trauma has been broadcast by the industry that some people believe it serves a wider plot to undermine the whole race. I don't know about that, but I do know that Black people have come up with trauma-free genres of music that still became popular around the world (just look at Afrobeats in 2021). So, I used this episode to argue that Black people have a deep-rooted African gift of responding to their environment through music. Mix that with the Gangsta conditioning of the '80s and you get two highly addictive, highly problematic genres.

Fun Facts:

- I started writing this episode before the 'Mavado & Vybz' one, but I thought the listener might get more from it after a deep dive into Dancehall culture. As I said towards the end of the episode, both Mavado and Vybz were proteges of Bounty Killer. For me, this speaks volumes.
- The episode was originally called 'Bad Boys'.

Episode 22 was about the story of Mavado and Vybz Kartel: from the music's impact on me as a teenager, to the artists' influence on their country, to the Faustian nature of street culture. A little later, Episode 24 looked at the sabotage of Black leadership in the 1960s – another trauma that the Black world never fully recovered from. I hope that my listeners can see the link between these episodes. As I said in 'Mavado & Vybz', the two artists were born in 1980 and '76 respectively – the most violent election years in Jamaica's history. Here is where we tie it all together. In Episode 26, 'Vibrations', I continue to argue that none of this is a coincidence. Even though Black populations across the world have formed different cultures, they share a history of violent injustices, perpetrated by Western powers. Injustices like the CIA bringing guns into Jamaica throughout the '70s, and training ghetto youths to kill their (Black) political opponents. Injustices like that same CIA facilitating the distribution of crack cocaine throughout Black America in the '80s, as a form of payment to anti-communist rebels in Nicaragua. Injustices like the FBI's illegal Counter Intelligence Program (COINTELPRO) of the 1950s and '60s infiltrating Black empowerment movements, coercing members to frame, sabotage and murder their peers – or just doing it themselves. Injustices like the Jamaican government supporting America in crushing the cultivation of cannabis by poor Jamaican farmers, only for America to slowly legalise the herb at its own convenience, after locking up hundreds of thousands of African Americans for the same plant. Injustices like Britain undermining the King of Buganda, then refusing to help when Ugandan independence went up in flames. Like Belgium orchestrating the murder of the Congolese hero, Patrice Lumumba. Like France, one of the richest nations in the world, turning Haiti into one of the poorest in the world by forcing it to pay the equivalent of $21 billion in 'reparations' (for abolishing slavery) over 122 years – and refusing to pay compensation to Haiti as recently as 2015 – *after* the earthquake. Black History Month did not teach me this. Black music did. Mavado and Vybz Kartel didn't come from nowhere; they were created by a system bigger than them. This system hides in plain sight, but Black music exposes it. The reason it's still so hard to see is because the countries behind the abuse don't teach it in their schools, and the ones that survived the abuse are still too poor to control the international agenda. Most of them have been putting out fires since they 'won' independence. But there's another reason that's even more clever and more subtle than all of this. It's the fact that, in Western media, Black icons are no longer 'traditional' thought leaders – they look too good, they sound too cool; they must be sex symbols. And sex symbols can only be sex symbols. Still, even when we can't put it into words, the story exists in our bodies, and we pass it on through our beats, our rhythms, our vibrations.

SCENE 1: WHERE ARE THE LEADERS?

[This episode continues to explore questions of Black leadership and Gangsta culture introduced in Episode 22, 'Mavado & Vybz' and Episode 24, 'The Sixties'. In this opening scene, George is having a good time with his friends when his mind wanders back to these questions]

George: Even when I'm just chilling with the mandem
I've got the same thoughts on my mind.

Just 'cause two people are from the same race,
Doesn't mean they're coming from the same place.
Hence the political divisions that keep
Putting Black leaders in difficult positions.

In this country, when a Black yout gets stabbed,
The instant reaction is 'Where are the leaders?'
But there really ain't no 'leaders' like that,
In the Ends, it's only parents and teachers.

For some of these kids there's no other authority
They ain't tryna hear about no government policy.
They're coming from poverty. Parents left their country
Probably 'cause the 'leaders' weren't running it properly.

'Where are the leaders?' Nah. The real
Question is *who's taking care of the street kids?*
Mummy's at work, he's out there with the dealers . . .
Couple enemies are tryna tear him to pieces.

See, most of these young Black gang members are
Living proof of what was taken from their ancestors.
That's why they take pride in war;
They're *dying* for something worth fighting for.

And this society has no moral authority to
Give these youths a sense of purpose.
So, they get what they can.
They rep for the gang.
And blow fast money on an expensive purchase.

Sixteen years of Black History Month in school
Never explained any of this.
Music held the story together.
Music will tell the story forever.

SCENE 2: MUSIC HOLDS THE STORY TOGETHER

George: Over thousands of miles of migration,
Black people stayed in sync through sounds and vibrations.
And if you want a great example, just look at
American Rap and Jamaican Dancehall.

In the 1960s, R&B music by young African Americans
Came just before Jamaican Ska music started rapidly developing.
Consumers were wowed – I'm talking about two different sounds.
Cousins, in the form of musical styles.
Two different groups of Nubian youths who made their own
Genre, which went on to grow stronger.

[An excerpt from Sam Cooke's interview with Dick Clark on *American Bandstand*]

Sam Cooke: *Well, if you observe what's going on and try to figure out how people are thinking . . . I think you can always write something that people will understand.*

George: Slowly, the same thing happened to both genres.
They started to grow conscious.
Within a decade, Ska became Reggae.

Reggae was influenced by Rastafari and the
Rasta ting was no-nonsense.

[A clip from Akala's documentary *Roots Reggae and Rebellion* for
the BBC. Voice of Prof. Carolyn Cooper]

Prof. Carolyn Cooper: *Rastafari became a manifestation of the
spirit of resistance. So it is that whole history of enslavement,
oppression, exploitation of labour.*

George: Now, R&B was fighting with the same old monsters:
With the frustration of political suffocation –
Best demonstrated in Panthers – plus the
Breakdown of the family, and the influx of drugs
Came the next generation of gangsters.

[A clip taken from the BBC documentary *Soul Deep: The Story of
Black Popular Music*]

Commentator 1: *The ability of Black people to express their true
selves, with all their warts and all their Saturday night ecstasy and
all their Sunday morning spirituality and down-home facts about
what life is like and what love is like and what heartbreak is like . . .
came through more and more.*

George: It isn't hard to see what this did to R&B.
Over the '70s more singers start to speak.
Black trauma develops a dark mystique.
Meanwhile Jamaicans in Jamaica start to leave.

They were seeing violence like you can't believe
And it was linked to politicians usually,
Mainly in impoverished communities.

[A clip from Don Letts' BBC documentary *Blood and Fire –
Jamaica's Political History*]

Don Letts: *The gangs of Tivoli and Trench Town helped themselves to the imported weaponry. Rival politics had become sectarian, with daily battles between PNP and JLP supporters. Shootouts left hundreds dead, and others caught in the crossfire.*

Michael Manley: *The cabinet has accordingly advised the Governor General to act and proclaim a state of public emergency.*

George: Some of those Jamaican emigrants chose
North West London as their place of residence.
A lot of them chose New York City to settle in
And their kids became Americans.

SCENE 3: FORCED SOCIETIES

[Return to George in his writing room]

George: I said it before.
Most Black people in the '60s and '70s
Lived in societies they were forced to be in.
Ones that didn't have an organic course to freedom,
Societies designed by Americans and Europeans.

You can hear it in the music!
How crazy is that?
Music is the way we react.

SCENE 4: THE MUSICAL REACTION

[Soundtrack: Bob Marley 'Get Up Stand Up']

[Cut to a Jamaican neighbourhood in 1970s New York]

George: Think about it: Jamaican music in the '60s was driven by

Neighbourhood events with big speaker systems.
And the '70s Jamaican New York community
Used those big speakers as a source of unity.

Local African Americans copied this practice and
Adapted it for their events.

[Cut to an African American house party of the same era]

[Soundtrack: The Sugar Hill Gang 'Rapper's Delight']

George: The cultures interacted like they were friends sharing schoolwork.
A new thing was pioneered by DJ Kool Herc.

So, the person controlling the music was the DJ, and
People were uplifted by the tunes that he'd play.
DJ had a hype man with a mic in his right hand,
This guy was called the MC. His vibe was
Cool and friendly. And of course, he spoke in rhyme.
Obviously, MCs evolved over time.

SCENE 5: THE CRACK EPIDEMIC

George: Now, as I mentioned on this podcast, Episode 9,
A lot happened in the 1980s.
Black America saw a new drug coming in,
Courtesy of Ronald Reagan's government. And the
mainstream made these guys seem crazy. So
Who told the story of the crack epidemic?
Rap gets the credit.

Rap gets the credit cah . . . somehow it just
Captured America. And then it just
Took over the whole world. Who would have thought a
Community project would go so well?

[A clip taken from the ABC News 20/20 Hip Hop special report of 1981]

Commentator 2: *It's not a Black music phenomenon. We've had records that have been number one in countries throughout the world where there is no Black folks.*

Commentator 3: *It's always been a part of what's been happening. There's not much, you have to understand, this comes from a culture where you don't have much to begin with.*

SCENE 6: AMERICAN/JAMAICAN PARALLELS

[Return to George's writing room]

George: By the time Hip Hop reached me,
I was learning things my teachers couldn't teach me.
See, there was a lot of anger around the Ends,
And I saw it all in my childhood friends.

The maddest thing is, I never saw my community
Anywhere in British media.
So Hip Hop was coming like a magic mirror, like . . .
Like finding a page about yourself on Wikipedia.

The blocks were familiar, problems were similar.
But my community was mainly Jamaican.
And like African Americans, everything their ancestors had
Been through was insanely frustrating.

By the 1980s, back in Jamaica,
Kingston was ravaged by savage behaviour.
That's when gun-clapping and drug trafficking came up
And surprise, surprise . . . the songs happened to change up.

SCENE 7: THE BIRTH OF DANCEHALL

[Soundtrack: Billy Boyo 'One Spliff a Day']

George: After the Rasta consciousness of Reggae,
This next evolution was less *revolution*;
More *individualism*.
You can hear it in the production . . .
It's all in the minimalism.

[Cut to a 1980s Kingston dance hall]

George: The local dance hall for the poorest Jamaicans
Was where they released all their frustrations.
Crime and poverty got worse in the '80s and the
Politicians responsible weren't gonna make peace.

Everyone in the ghetto had to fight to eat, but
In the dance hall they were back in the driver's seat.

It's similar to Hip Hop: someone provides the beat,
Someone from the beat-provider's team rides the beat.
Different sides compete in a friendly rivalry. And the
Crowd get loud whenever the vibe is sweet. This
Happened across the island several nights a week.
For a minute, you could forget that your life was bleak.

[Soundtrack: King Jammy 'Sleng Teng Riddim']

George: This music became the soundtrack of life in the ghetto
And the streets embraced it right from the get-go.
It documented the era of dons and tugs
And the constant inflow of guns and drugs.
Artists started to speak like they were part of the street life and
This was long before Instagram.
So, they painted pictures with action-packed lyrics and

No one captured that spirit like Ninjaman.

[Soundtrack: Ninjaman 'Murder Dem']

George: Ninjaman became known for gun lyrics and
He clearly had loads of fun with it.
He always made these noises, put on crazy voices and
Live on stage he destroyed it.
But Ninjaman was just the start.
Gunman art was gonna blow up;
Ninjaman was just the spark.

SCENE 8: RAP AND DANCEHALL ARE COUSINS

George: The story's identical to Hip Hop in the States, you know:
Young Africans ripped off by the status quo.
That's why I say that over thousands of miles of migration,
Black people stayed in sync through sounds and vibrations.

It's a great example:
American Rap and Jamaican Dancehall.
They're cousins. And the family resemblance is crazy.
Imagine them when they were babies.

Born within weeks of each other.
Hitting the streets as a younger.
Bitterness, grievance and hunger: that's the
Taste of Ghetto Nutrition.
Somehow that Ghetto Nutrition gave
Both these ghetto youts vision.

Both of them spoke in a rhythm – it just came
Naturally when they were joking and riffing.
Compared to their olders their process was different;
Open promotion of smoking not sniffing. And

Also their criminal involvement was different;
Cokeheads were sniffing the coke *they* were shifting.

Two cousins, growing up in the '80s.
No longer a couple of babies.
One in New York, the other in Kingston –
Former colonies whose grandmother was England.

One was the child of those Jamaican emigrants who
Chose the US as their place of residence.
Remember what I said about them . . .
How their kids became Americans?
Yeah, the other was the child of Jamaicans who stayed,
Both ancestors came to those nations as slaves.

So, when Dancehall started turning gangsta, full of
Hungry young artists, burning ganja . . .
It's no surprise that Hip Hop started changing.
'Cause they were cousins, going through the same thing.

In all of us, the past survives.
You can literally study history through these artists' lives.

[Excerpt from Sam Cooke's interview with Dick Clark on *American Bandstand*]

Sam Cooke: *Well, if you observe what's going on and try to figure out how people are thinking . . . I think you can always write something that people will understand.*

George: Even though the Brits and the Americans severed
Links between African slaves and their heritage,
The descendants of those slaves used their African instincts
To musically establish an imprint.
And the music enabled them to confront institutional
Racism and react to it in sync.
[Clip from Akala's documentary *Roots Reggae and Rebellion* for the

Prof. Carolyn Cooper: ... *It is that whole history of enslavement, oppression, exploitation of labour.*

George: See, when Dancehall started representing the gunman
Hip Hop did the same, and this was unplanned.
But it's because their reactions have *been* linked.
That musical reaction is an African instinct.

That's the good news. Now let's get to the ... other news.

SCENE 9: STREET JUSTICE

George: The stresses on the Western Black community
Led to a long-term lack of unity.

White people trusted their justice systems, but
Black people saw a lot of unjust decisions.
So, without authorities on which they could depend,
Black people handled justice through their neighbours and friends.
And when you look across the Black inner city of London ...
This explains the state of the Ends.

In African American street music,
The only thing bigger than the cult of the dollar is this
Culture of honour. And via the music market
That mentality became the ultimate product.

Same in Jamaica. When conflict is handled
Neighbour-to-neighbour and kids in the street make
Money when they sing what they see,
Conflict brings entertainment and paper.

Now the demand for Black men beefing in music is

Running out no time soon. They're thinking
'I can't stop the conflict in the streets, but I can
Use that energy to promote my tune.'

Yet with all the hood's stress and financial pressure,
Watching a street yout become a national treasure can
Genuinely make any young Black woman,
Any young Black man feel better.

It happens to me. I'm thirty years old, and it
Still makes me happy to see these rappers succeed.

But since they come from beef and conflict,
In some ways they all read from one script.
And I'd be lying if I said I don't believe that
Some kids follow their lead into dumb shit.
Let's take the story of
Two boys who grew up to have a huge voice.

SCENE 10: CHRIS & RODNEY

[Cut to George entertaining his nephews]

George: Chris' birthday was 21st May
First baby of two Jamaicans in Brooklyn.
Three weeks later, back in Jamaica, a
New-born baby named Rodney arrived.
Growing up in Kingston, Rodney got shot when he was
Fourteen. Thank God he survived.

'Cause just like Chris, he was the chosen one.
From a young age they were both exposed to guns.
At twelve years old, Chris started selling drugs.
They both discovered a certain art and fell in love.
Rodney was performing in dance halls getting love.

At the same time, Chris started stepping up.
They were gun-toting teens with unspoken dreams,
Gaining respect in their local scenes.

[Cut to Chris skipping class]

George: Chris dropped out of school at seventeen, selling
Coke coming via Jamaica from Medellin.

[Chris exits school into New York street ambience]

[Soundtrack: Eric B & Rakim 'Paid in Full']

George: New York hustlers had funds and rides.

[Cut to a street in Kingston]

[Soundtrack: Supercat 'Boops']

George: Kingston bad man just had guns and pride.

[Cut to George in a small, rickety plane]

George: There weren't many pilots or sailors in Brooklyn
But somehow the drugs kept flooding in.
Same thing in the ghettos of Kingston.
But somehow the guns kept coming in.

[Return to George in his writing room]

George: This new generation would document it all,
But they didn't wanna sing; they did another thing.
For Chris, it was called 'rapping'.
For Rodney, it was called 'chatting'.
Different countries, very similar pattern.
How does this happen?

[Return to the streets of New York during the New Jack era of the late '80s/early '90s]

[Soundtrack: Ice-T 'New Jack Hustler (Nino's Theme)']

George: Crime in New York was on a constant rise and
Chris got locked up, to no one's surprise.
Hip Hop was turning into Gangsta Rap and it
Got a wider audience thanks to that.

[Soundtrack: Mad Cobra 'Bad Boy Talk']

George: Now, Jamaican society never quite succeeded
In containing its violent streak.

[Return to the streets of Kingston, the soundtrack emitting from a sound system]

George: Rodney expressed this with gunman art.
Bold, cold but still fun and smart.
His lines were bleak, and his mind was street.
In a room full of artists tryna ride the beat, he always
Got a reaction when it was time to speak.
And in 1993, he signed to VP
And recorded a vinyl – finally.

[Soundtrack: Bounty Killer 'Coppershot']

SCENE 11: RODNEY = BOUNTY KILLER

[A clip taken from Bounty Killer's 1994 classic feature with Jamaica TVJ ER host Anthony Miller]

542

Anthony Miller: *Fashionable clothes, jewellery and of course, a cellular phone. All the trappings of success that separate deejay star Bounty*

Killer from the scores of struggling entertainers all over Kingston.

[A clip taken from Bounty Killer's 'Odyssey' interview with Yendi Phillipps]

Bounty Killer: *Coppershot's a rudeboy anthem and . . . it was really an experience I made that song from. And then that song end up come buss mi.*

George: Rodney Price – aka Bounty Killer – came from
Dancehall, but he wasn't a dancing artist.
The kid was a lyricist with the wickedest images
Big in the streets because his bars hit hardest.

And he was from a new generation of Ragga fans
All of them were influenced by Ninjaman and Shabba Ranks.

[Another clip taken from Bounty Killer's 'Untold Story' interview with Yendi Phillipps]

Bounty Killer: *Ninjaman pon the high-pitch 'mi look, mi seh', Shabba Rankin' with the deep tone 'I'm not going to a circus' – so . . . Shabba Rankin and Ninjaman were my two favourite deejays at the time.*

Rodney shot to fame, quicker than you would expect
Gunman art was now in full effect.

[Another clip taken from Bounty Killer's 1994 classic feature with Jamaica TVJ ER host Anthony Miller]

Bounty Killer: *I have nuff friends who take to the gun. Most youts turn to the crime and violence.*

George: He talked about violence 'cause that's what he'd seen.
Remember, little Rodney got shot at fourteen.

[A clip taken from the BBC documentary *Reggae: The Story of Jamaican Music* Part 3: As Raw as Ever]

Bounty Killer: *I was angry 'cause I got shot accidentally, innocently, I didn't even know who shot me. The system shot me. The streets shot me.*

George: Coming up, Bounty Killer was a *sufferer*
So, he styled himself as the poor people's governor.

[Another clip taken from Bounty Killer's 1994 classic feature with Jamaica TVJ ER host Anthony Miller]

Bounty Killer: *Yeah, it's me. That's why I always deejay about down in the ghetto. I'm not suffering, but I know they are suffering.*

George: He became the blueprint of what was to come,
Banging out hits like shots from a gun.
Journalism in the form of high-class lyricism,
Very controversial, but he bypassed criticism,
Claiming his lyrics were only social commentary.
You know, the sociology of local poverty.
Insisting he wasn't wrong for stating the facts.
Personally, I think it's more complicated than that.

But that's another story. For now, let's just
Say Bounty Killer was hugely influential.
And by the mid '90s it wasn't just the ghettos of
Kingston who'd see his potential.

SCENE 12: CHRIS = THE NOTORIOUS B.I.G

[Return to George's writing room]

George: Meanwhile, back in Brooklyn

Chris came home from jail.
Now he was a dad, trying to feed and clothe his girl
So, he made a demo to promote himself.

Chris knew he had talent.
But he didn't know what to do with it yet.
Luckily, the demo he recorded
Caught the ear of a certain music exec.

His name was Sean. Not Brooklyn Sean.
Nah. *Harlem Sean.*
And when Harlem Sean met Brooklyn Chris . . .
A star was born.

[Soundtrack: The Notorious B.I.G. 'Juicy']

[A clip from a 1994 interview]

Biggie: *Who is The Notorious B.I.G.? It's a n**** that's been stressed out all his motherfucking life. Single parent never home, got intro-duced to the drugs, got paid off the drugs, fucked up off the drugs, now I got a record deal.*

George: Christopher Wallace – aka The Notorious B.I.G. –
Was the other Jamaican.
A lyricist who won the love of the nation.
Everyone agreed his stuff was amazing.

His music made it to the top of the playlist, which
Only West Coast rappers had gotten away with.
Chris, or should I say, Biggie, came like a reminder:
New York was nothing to play with.

He became the new East Coast template
Soon to be immortalised by a fatal friendship. But
That's another story. For now, let's just
Say B.I.G was hugely influential.

He taught millions how to use their voices
And how to use these instrumentals.

[Another clip from the 1994 interview]

Biggie: *What I had to overcome? I don't know, poverty, police . . . I'm just a n**** from the hood that got a little rap skills, man.*

George: Just like Bounty Killer, Biggie was raw. He
Kicked in the door, making mad noise.
Matter of fact their whole generation: they weren't into
No serenading – they were bad boys.

[Soundtrack: Craig Mack 'Flava in Ya Ear' (Remix)]

SCENE 13: PARALLELS BETWEEN BIGGIE & BOUNTY

[Soundtrack: Bounty Killer 'Disrespect']

[Return to George in the marketplace]

George: Alright, alright.
So, what can we learn from the lives of Biggie and Bounty Killer?
Well, like I said, just 'cause two people are from the same race
Doesn't mean they're coming from the same place,
But racial divisions shaped how we're living
From the US to Jamaica to Britain.

Bounty Killer was born three weeks after The Notorious B.I.G.
First of all, look at their names: 'Killer'
'Notorious' . . . do you see what I see?

They represent a turning point in Black life when
Black guys found it safer to act like the bad guy.
But this didn't happen at random. You gotta

Match their lyrics with their lives to understand them.

They grew up in the ghettos of the US and JA,
Where their ancestors were forced to live. By the
Time they were born their areas were full of
Guns and drugs and unsupported kids.

Now, the rest of the world seemed comfortable with this
Until these unsupported kids found a voice. The
Market loved it but many harshly judged it,
Believing that street life was purely down to choice.

[Cut to George with his nephews. They are a reminder of the innocence of youth]

George: Bounty was *fourteen* when someone shot him.
Biggie was twelve when *he* started shotting.
The whole thing is bigger than them;
It's a situation that was given to them.

So is it a coincidence then, that
Biggie was dead before he turned twenty-five off the
Back of a conflict that started in the Ends?
Or was this the path given to them?

On Episode 22 I talked about the feud between
Mavado and Vybz Kartel. Is it a coincidence that
Both of them were Bounty Killer's protégés
And now none of them talk? I can't tell.

All I know is the stresses on the Western Black community have
Led to a long-term lack of unity.
And without authorities on which they could depend,
Black people handled justice via neighbours and friends.
And within their communities, which are clearly frustrated,
Conflict resolution deteriorated.

So instead of asking 'Where are the leaders?'
The real question is 'Who's taking care of the street kids?'

SCENE 14: IT'S ALL RELATED

[This final scene returns to George's original setting in the opening scene (daydreaming among friends) implying that this whole episode has been one long daydream]

George: Remember: with the
Frustration of political suffocation –
Best demonstrated in Panthers – plus the
Breakdown of the family, and the influx of drugs came the
Next generation of gangsters.

But these gangsters used their African instincts
To musically establish an imprint. And the
Music enabled them to challenge institutional
Racism and react to it in sync. *Think.*

When Dancehall started representing the gunman
Hip Hop did the same, and this was unplanned.
It's because their reactions have *been* linked. That
Musical reaction is an African instinct.

[Soundtrack: The Notorious B.I.G. ft. Bob Marley 'Hold Ya Head']

George: See, over thousands of miles of migration,
Black people stayed in sync through sounds and vibrations.

[Earlier quotes return]

Biggie: *Single parent never home, got introduced to the drugs, got paid off the drugs, fucked up off the drugs, now I got a record deal.*

Bounty Killer: *I have nuff friends who take to the gun. Most youts turn to the crime and violence.*

Don Letts: *The gangs of Tivoli and Trench Town helped themselves to the imported weaponry. Shootouts left hundreds dead, and others caught in the crossfire.*

EPISODE 27: True Love

Extra Info:
- This episode gave me a chance to explain to our followers in Uganda why we weren't doing a wedding there anymore. Between announcing our plans to marry in Uganda on Episode 23 and recording Episode 27, the country went into lockdown, leaving us in limbo. We decided to go for a UK wedding and celebrate in Uganda as soon as we had the chance.
- Shortly after the episode was released, Uganda started coming out of lockdown. This gave us a small window of time to plan a Ugandan celebration for December, and we took it!

Fun Facts:
- Sandra had no idea I was working on this episode. She actually heard it for the first time when we were on our honeymoon.

I haven't always been a romantic guy. Romance wasn't on my radar, I didn't need it, I didn't care. But going from friendship to relationship to marriage with Sandra has changed me. As I explained on Episode 23, 'Back to UG', we grew together over twelve years before becoming an item. That's a big change for anyone, but in that change, I discovered the importance of romance. It's what allowed us to transition from how we were before into what we are now. Romance is literally just being thoughtful, and it means something different to everyone. The whole point of romance is to show consideration for your special person, in a language they can receive it in. Between my wife and I, time pressures have been a big challenge – especially as I was completing this podcast while she was putting our wedding together. So, I thought it would be nice to dedicate an episode to her. Writing this one was like trying to paint the wind; it's hard to depict something that can only be felt. I'm not on social media every day, so I use this podcast to share my highest truth. Publicly, I talk to my listeners about music, Black life and big ideas, but privately, I think about my wife all the time. And even though I could do a whole podcast on her, I just want to invite my audience in for a second to spread the love. As mentioned on Episode 25, 'Who Hurt R&B?', there are enough negative portrayals of relationships out here. It's only right that we tell our story, too. It's an extra bonus that so many young Ugandans have been inspired by our journey, as they always let us know. Thank you, guys. Be good to each other!

SCENE 1: LOVE WINS

[Soundtrack: Wizkid ft. Tay Iwar & Projexx 'True Love']

George: Ay, you see Sandra, yeah?
I'm gonna marry that girl.
I was so excited just before I proposed,
I must have told Meghan and Harry as well.

[An excerpt from Meghan and Harry's *Archewell* podcast]

Meghan: *That's amazing.*

Harry: *That's great.*

Meghan: *And George and Sandra, congratulations.*

Harry: *Congratulations, guys. George, hopefully it was a yes. If it wasn't, then this is kinda awkward, so . . .*

Meghan: [Laughing] *We're gonna go with it was a yes. Of course, it was a yes.*

Harry: *It was a yes. In which case, congratulations.*

George: I used to think I would never be bothered
To show the kind of care that a woman wanted from a man.
But Sandra never fronted on a man,
So I matured, and put something on her hand, you understand?

Kenny: *I'm Kenny Mpanga, and I've known George for twenty-one and a half years. When he's around Sandra, I see a lot of joy. I've never seen any other person outside the family make him as happy as Sandra.*

Nathan: *My name is Nathan Fox. I've known G for almost twenty*

years now. What I've always noticed and always loved is the level of care that they show for each other.

Meghan: *No matter what life throws at you guys, trust us when we say, love wins.*

Harry: *Love always wins.*

Meghan: So true.

SCENE 2: ASK THE BROS

[Cut to clips of George's brothers talking about his relationship with Sandra]

Freddie: *I've known George for thirty years, since I was two years old in 1991. That's when my little brother, George, came into my life. They bring out the best in each other.*

Barney: *What I remember about George and Sandra is just, like, them laughing about stupid things that no one else is laughing about. They won't even explain the joke to you, they're already laughing in among their bubble. I just remember seeing that.*

Damini: *George and Sandra have always been very, very, very close, right? They always had, like, a strong connection. I'm looking forward to them, quote unquote, 'empire building', like. George is a visionary, Sandra is a doer.*

Benny B: *When George is around Sandra, it's usually accompanied by lots of laughter and lots of prosecco.*

Suuna: *One of the biggest blessings is to marry your friend, let alone your best friend. It's a beautiful thing to see, man.*

CHAPTER THREE | 27: TRUE LOVE

James: *George is the most amazing person I've ever met. You know, he's a guy who changed my life, literally. I personally watched them grow up as best friends. Sandra was always his biggest supporter. She was always that woman by his side, always screaming the loudest, supporting him as a person and as a friend. I knew that one day, deep down, they'd actually get together.*

Mikes: *Him and Sandra go way back. If there's anyone who's fitting for the role, it's Sandy.*

Marc: *George has a lot of integrity, and he brings joy wherever he goes. I do put a lot of the growth down to Sandra.*

Nathan: *In two weeks' time, we'll have another toast, but for now, this one's for George and Sandra.*

[All]: *To George and Sandra!*

Mikes: *This is one hundred percent what life is for.*

SCENE 3: UGANDA'S BLESSING

[Phone ringing. A personified Uganda answers, surrounded by cheering and excitement]

George: Hello? Ay, ay, Uganda? Ay, Uganda, congratulations! Yo! Uganda can you hear me?

Uganda: One second. One second, George. Hello, George, how are you?

George: [Laughing] How am I? Uganda, how are you? We just watched Joshua Cheptegei take gold at the Olympics after his silver the other day.

Uganda: I know! I know!

George: And Peruth Chemutai.

Uganda: [Inaudible].

George: Aye, Uganda, I can't hear you. Can you hear ...? Uganda? Hello?

Uganda: I said, we are celebrating this side.

George: Mm.

Uganda: You know we've just come out of lockdown, so people really needed something to be happy about, eh?

George: Yeah, I can imagine. It must have been mad for you lot, yeah?

Uganda: Yeah. It's not been easy.

George: You know – nah, go on.

Uganda: Eh? No, I was just saying, it's been tough, you know?

George: Mm-hmm, mm, mm.

Uganda: Eh.

George: Yeah, how are you holding up?

Uganda: Yeah, for us, we are there, just surviving. You have this Delta variant that has taken so many lives.

George: Mm, it's sad, man.

Uganda: Yes. So many lives.

George: How's the vaccine rollout?

Uganda: Yeah, the vaccine could have slowed things down a bit, I guess, but you know, they failed to reach people and . . . the rest just fell to rich people. For us, we are at the back of the line, as ever.

George: Yeah. It's not right, man. I'm sorry.

Uganda: Hmm. But forget about that. How is wedding planning coming along?

George: Ay, to be honest, Sandra has done such an amazing job of pulling it all together.

Uganda: Oh, bless her.

George: You know, obviously . . . you know, we were looking forward to celebrating with you, but when you went into lockdown, we had to change plans. And if it wasn't for Sandra's spreadsheets and her attention to detail, I really don't know how we would have pulled off this wedding in two months.

Uganda: Ha! George, let me tell you something, OK? Sandra was sent to you from God. As in, you were made for her, she was made for you . . .

George: Facts. Facts.
And you know, Uganda, we really wanted to have our wedding with you. I hope you don't think that because of the—

Uganda: Ah, ah, ah, ah, ah! You don't need to explain, George. You tried your best. Sandra came and visited, but Covid has disorganised us so much.

George: True. It's true.

556

Uganda: Suppliers can't supply. People can't move. We still have those restrictions of twenty guests per wedding. Can you imagine?

George: Yeah, it's crazy, 'cause I remember you saying a couple of years ago that . . . how did you say it? You said . . . I'm gonna get an African bride and take her back to this side but, you get me, I just didn't want you to think it's like that.

Uganda: George, seriously, you were born from that side. Your wife was born from that side. Yes, Uganda loves you both and we believe you love us too, but we need you to be happy, and if you can find happiness wherever you are, then we're happy for you. Better you're that side, telling your truth, supporting your woman than over here just . . . Eh? You're just here. Now, why are you here? No plan, no platform, no point. Just sitting in these bafunda, telling people what you had in UK! [laughing]

George: [Laughing] Ah, Uganda.

Uganda: Seriously, it's OK.

George: Thank you for understanding.

SCENE 4: CHANGE OF PLANS

George: So, we had to switch up at the last minute,
Couldn't waste time, we had to be fast with it.
Uganda's Covid situation was bad, so we changed plans,
And the change-up was mad.

[Soundtrack: Sara Tavares 'Balancê']

George: We pulled this wedding together in two months,
Which is something I intend only ever to do once.
And when I say, 'we',
I really mean my lady.

It's amazing what can happen when you give someone a chance
To do what comes naturally to them.

Fifteen years ago, as a rapper and a student,
I was establishing a blueprint.

Sandra was blessed with different strengths,
She was super-organised, and she put on sick events.
She used to plan her birthday party for most the year,
Now logistics and production is her whole career.

You know why that works for me?
'Cause I'm useless at all of that stuff, personally.
But Sandra wouldn't be happy doing my job,
So, our strengths balance out perfectly.

Just imagine the benefits:
As stressful as planning a wedding is,
'Cause of her passion for production and logistics,
Sandra's been indirectly prepping ahead of this.

And I think her talent has rubbed off on me,
I'm learning how to organise stuff properly.
She made me step up my game for date night,
And now I've got tricks at my own disposal.

I learned how to plan surprises,
And built my way up to pulling off a whole proposal.

SCENE 5: THE PROPOSAL

[Soundtrack: Benbrick 'Sandra's Hand']

George: One cold December evening,
George wanted to pop the question on the hotel terrace,
But he thought Sandra might prefer the central heating.

He'd been through mad back and forth just to get there

Since the Rona decided to end their freedom.
But luckily, he pulled it together
With the help of Petra, Birungi, and Jessle all the way from Sweden.

Sandra knew George like the back of her hand,
But right now, she struggled to look back at her man, 'cause what?
How had this distracted African man patterned a plan this lavish?
Simple. He was driven by the vision of having her hand in marriage.

George approached Sandra's parents months before,
If he didn't, then she would have been uncomfortable.
So, they held it down even when their baby girl was down,
'Cause they trusted George to be responsible.

See, he wanted to take care of Sandra, she deserved it.
Since day one, she'd been perfect.
When they met, they were schoolkids.
Automatically, George supported everything Sandra did,
And Sandra supported everything George did.

Every time they spoke, they would laugh until they cried,
And to this day, it's hard to kill their vibe.
Then one night, twelve years into their friendship,
George felt emotions inside him swelling up,
And that was the night he fell in love.

To anyone who knew him, this would sound absurd,
But the only opinion he cared about was hers.
By this point, they knew each other so well,
In every look, they shared a thousand words.

Sandra was sceptical at first,
But fortunately, her perspective was reversed
Once George put in the effort and the work.

It's like their days brightened when they became an item.

In lockdown, you'd think they were stuck on the Cayman Islands.
George bought the ring in September
And planned this moment for months while remaining silent.

Then finally, he got down on one knee,
Relieved that he hadn't forgotten his verse,
Pulled out a small, grey box,
Opened it up and said the following words:
Sandra Diana Makumbi . . .

[Cut to original footage of Sandra's reaction]

Sandra: [*Screaming*] *Baby!*

George: Will you marry me?

Sandra: *Yes!*

[Laughter]

SCENE 6: FOUNDATIONS

[George and Sandra are having a virtual meeting with a photographer ahead of their wedding]

[Soundtrack: Chozen Blood & Winnie Nwagi 'Yitayo']

George: You know what's mad?
At thirty years old, I'm discovering emotions I didn't know I had.
I got endless attention for Sandra.
More than I thought I could spend on a partner.

I'm so blessed with her mum,
And I'm friends with her father,
And for some reason, I get to be the man she's perfect for.

That's how you know God's work is pure.

[Cut to Sandra handling wedding logistics in the car over the phone while George drives]

[Soundtrack: Vinka ft. Kent & Flosso 'Overdose']

Sandra: *You know those flowers, yeah? Are they easy to move? Like, if I wanted to move them from the . . .*

George: It's the same story that you've heard before.
When we first met, yeah, we weren't mature.
But, you know, in life . . .
Some changes are just irreversible.

It's like one day I looked up and
Sandra and I had the deepest bond.
The fact she'd been in my life for so long
Makes me always wonder what other blessings I'm sleeping on.

I love her smile,
I love her dark complexion,
But it's more than attraction,
And it's past affection.

We're from the same culture,
That's part of our connection,
And culture holds value,
Like an art collection.

[Cut to banter between George's friends in his home. The narrative perspective leaves them behind and travels to the kitchen, where Sandra is cooking Ugandan food]

[Soundtrack: Orezi & Sheebah 'Sweet Sensation']

George: Oi, I walk into the kitchen and she's cooking the same food
My mum, my sisters and my aunties do.
And she's always listening to Ugandan music,
It feels like I'm at a Ugandan party, too.

But Sandra's more than a pretty face and a good cook,
She manages man's business. It's a good look.

SCENE 7: TEAMWORK MAKES THE DREAM WORK

[Cut to GTP's July 2021 'Common Ground' show at the Barbican]

George: *Thank you to my GTP team: Vidhu, Shanique, Luke, Birungi, and, you know, my team is headed up by my wife-to-be, Sandra. Thank you very much to Sandra . . .*

[Applause]

George: *No, no, yeah, yeah, yeah, yeah, yeah, all of that.*

[Return to George's writing room]

George: I bring the strategy,
She brings the structure,
And it's been smooth sailing
Since we bucked up.

I'm not gonna pretend I could foresee this path,
It started a few years ago when I needed staff.
She ran me a flawless recruitment drive and, hence,
She now runs operations and produces my events.

We have a small team she coordinates, and they're all amazing.
See me, my vision is forward gazing.

But Sandra, Vidhu and Birungi, they watch my back.
You know like that . . .

[Vidhu performing an original poem, 'My Name is Vidhu']

Vidhu: *My ancestors are headmistresses and lawyers; I live to talk of their reign. Never will my voice quiver when asked about my name. My name is Vidhu, it means moon shining high up in the sky. My name is Vidhu. If you're going to say it, just make sure you pronounce it right.*

[Return to George's writing room]

George: Vidhu, she's my content manager,
Patterning my content calendar.
When I'm in podcast mode with all the writing,
Who do you think's doing all the organising?

I don't know how she finds the time,
She's a poet too,
But she's just that kind of person
That makes no excuse.

She's solution-driven,
She does what she's supposed to do.
Ready to show and prove,
Even when I'm slow to move.

[George on a call with Birungi]

Birungi: *As you know, I'm co-editor of my uni's online magazine. You did a poem, 'There are no choices without chances' . . .*

George: *Yeah.*

Birungi: *Basically, I just wanted to have that YouTube link, just 'cause it is very, like, social . . . Like, everything you said . . .*

CHAPTER THREE | 27: TRUE LOVE

George: Birungi's my assistant.

Sandra designed a system where she controls the emails and the
     diary,

Which is perfect, 'cause she can hold details like a library.

I got a team of talent people that inspire me.

It's the sense of family for me.

Our team works 'cause our personalities agree.

We make joint decisions in allocated timeslots,

And everybody's strong point is someone else's blind spot.

And this whole system came from the mind of my life partner,

My future wife, Sandra.

SCENE 8: VALUE YOUR NETWORK

[Cut to George as a teenage rapper]

George: When I met Sandra as a teenage rapper,

I didn't know we'd someday work together.

I was trying to pass my exams, make music and money.

It was long, but it was worth the pressure.

Every verse, every word was personal treasure.

Me and myself having a heart-to-heart reflection.

We were MCs,

It was part of the culture,

And culture holds value like an art collection.

But you see, Sandra was my best friend,

Vidhu came directly from my fanbase,

Birungi, she's Sandra's cousin.

Her brother, Crisis, was my right-hand man when we were
     teenagers,

Just, you know, spitting bars and hustling.

[Return to George's writing room]

George: See, when you've got a good idea,
And you're prepared to do the leg work,
You're going to find so much value in your network.

[A voice note left on Common Ground by Amara Agili-Odion]

Amara Agili-Odion: *When I came to the Barbican with my mum, I saw this Black lady with really long braids, wearing all black and sandals. You know, with a Gucci belt, and immediately I knew that this must be George's wife. There must have been something about her, her aura, her presence that just . . . It just consolidated it for me. I knew that he had gotten engaged, but I hadn't been on social media to see any of the images or anything like that. I'd only read about it. But there was something about her aura. I was just constantly looking that I'm sure this is the woman. Her presence, I don't know, it just reflected that. Or, better yet, I'm just gifted. Which people often do tell me.*

SCENE 9: TRUE LOVE

[Soundtrack: Mac Ayres 'Jumping Off the Moon']

George: I know I sound like a man who's self-satisfied,
Now that he's gotten his dream girl as his bride.
But the aim of this episode is not to gloat,
The aim is to offer hope.

Marriage is currently something
Our inner-city culture does not promote,
And personally, before I got with Sandra,
I hadn't really given it much thought.

To be honest,
I didn't trust myself to give someone else

Consistent commitment and support.
You know men take longer than women to mature.

But now that I know true love,
I can't keep it a secret.
I know too many people that need it.

[George and Sandra joking around]

George: I'm talking love.
Like the love of the culture
That made a man called Fred Semugera
Organise the annual Ugandan get-together
Where fourteen years ago me and Sandra met each other
And formed a friendship stronger than any other.

I'm talking love.
Like Sandra's love for spreadsheets,
Which enabled her to deliver a wedding in under ten weeks.

Or my love for poetry,
Which has allowed my friends and my audience to grow with me.
Or the love that I have for my community,
Which leads to art, which creates employment opportunities.

There's so much you can do with all the love in your life,
But it starts with loving your life.

[George and Sandra joking]

Sandra: *I'm gon' be OK, 'cause I'm getting married.*

George: *You'll be aight. You gon' be straight.*

Sandra: *I'm gon' be aight. I've got some sharp pains right now in my chest, but guess what? God is good all the time, and all the time, God is good.*

EPISODE 28: Songs Make Jobs

Extra Info:
- This is my first full recap episode. I wanted to try this technique because I usually dump a lot of ideas into the podcast without giving my listeners space to reflect.
- Working on my PhD with Mariana Mazzucato's *Institute for Public Purpose and Innovation* helped sharpen my ideas while writing this chapter.

Fun Facts:
- 'HYHGP?' was heavily influenced by the TV show *The Wire*, which is why the first scene of 'Songs Make Jobs' takes its name from an episode in the show's first season. *The Wire* made me want to start conversations.

This one takes its title from a line in the first episode of Chapter Three, 'Common Ground'. 'Songs make jobs' is the best way I can summarise the arguments of the podcast. It's a statement that has stood the test of time and proven true for Black people in different parts of the world. I just want to *do* something with this truth. And I believe the best thing we can do is bet on the ability of our young people to continue making world-changing music. We can do this by investing in the people and spaces that help to nurture local talent – investing as a community. By definition, this investment will allow the community to retain a stake in the success of that talent. Why wait for external people to do it? Of course, I'm oversimplifying the model (and downplaying the need for cash), but for now I just want people to grasp the idea.

The entertainment industry offers us a launchpad for a bigger plan. Countries like Botswana, Singapore, Rwanda, and Norway have all been able to create stability for their people by forming a plan that plays to their strengths and sticking to it. I think the evidence presented across this chapter suggests Black people as a whole should start thinking in the same way. Granted, just because two people are from the same race, doesn't mean they're coming from the same place . . . but racial divisions have shaped how we're living. With the most powerful Black leaders killed, compromised, and bought off, we – the collective children of Africa – find ourselves in need of protection, and I believe that strength lies in our shared culture. We didn't need governments to create the music that has supported us for so long. We didn't need anyone to teach us how to be innovative and influential – our youth have done it on their own, over and over again. However, if we don't take full responsibility for these young people, they will be lured into the traps laid out by a world that has an appetite for their self-destruction.

SCENE 1: ALL THE PIECES MATTER

[An excerpt from George's interview with Zeze Millz]

Zeze Millz: *What do you think needs to be done for the relationship to be better between young Black men or Black men and the police?*

George: *If we can all get to the point where we can generate enough jobs around us to control the activities of our young people in the areas that we're from, then the police relationship will improve.*

Zeze Millz: *I've never looked at it like that.*

George: *It's doable, man.*

Zeze Millz: *Yeah. Do you know what, and I think that we're starting to even, like, madeyouthink, I don't know if you realise—*

George: *Big up madeyouthink.*

Zeze Millz: *Yeah, I don't know if you see that now he, like, posts jobs . . .*

[Soundtrack: Mahalia Jackson 'Summertime/Sometimes I Feel Like a Motherless Child']

[An excerpt from George's conversation with his PhD supervisor, Mariana Mazzucato, who is reacting to the first few episodes of Chapter Three]

Mariana Mazzucato: *. . . and you also kept using, maybe some of the words – I'll tell you what I wrote down, 'cause I was writing down stuff that was making me think . . . when you say 'kids make songs and songs make jobs', hahahaha, how cool is that? But the question is how to make songs make jobs?*

That's why I think what you and I are speaking is the same language. We're both interested in change, but systemic change as opposed to just cute little stories on the side that people can talk about. What does it actually mean in terms of preparing the economy...

Zeze Millz: *Do you ever feel like us as Black people, we play the victim too much? Do you feel as if we're never gonna necessarily progress as people if we constantly keep saying...*

[George starts laughing]

Zeze Millz: *Why are you laughing?*

George: *When America and Jamaica cooperated to allow the sale of guns and drugs in the streets of Kingston in order to fund a political war that was supposed to suppress the rise of left-wing politics in Jamaica...*

Zeze Millz: *Right...*

George: *At the same time as the American government allowed crack cocaine to be sold all throughout African America ... at the same time as my community was largely allocated particular housing ... as happened in Chicago, as happened in LA, as happened in Kingston, as happened in ... everywhere else across the Black world... one of the consequences of all this was for Black men to be less psychologically, financially and emotionally supported in leading their communities...*

If we ain't got the academic space to say that and there's no GCSE that's ever gonna let me get to the bottom of that story, then I'm gonna have to sit here and act like the mandem are just crazy for no reason, when that doesn't happen on the continent. On the continent there's a culture of readiness to marry...

SCENE 2: THE MODEL

[George is in his writing room, typing on his laptop]

George: In 1871, a group of formerly enslaved African Americans went on a singing tour to raise funds for their young college, Fisk University.

The tour raised $40,000 for the Tennessee school – which is over $800,000 in today's money – and in the process, it introduced the Northern hemisphere to the so-called Negro Spiritual.

In the one hundred and fifty years since, this story has repeated itself over and over again.

[An excerpt from Sam Cooke's interview with Dick Clark on *American Bandstand*]

Sam Cooke: *I think the secret is really observation. Well, if you observe what's going on, try to figure out how people are thinking ... I think you can always write something that people will understand ...*

George: These spirituals – which were basically observations about the Black experience – they captured the hearts and minds of people who didn't even see enslaved African Americans as equals. And they laid the foundation of future innovation for future generations.

This template is still intact today. Young Black people have empowered their communities through music against all odds, generation after generation ...

[A clip taken from the ABC News 20/20 Hip Hop special report of 1981]

Commentator: *It's always been a part of what's been happening. There's not much, you have to understand, this comes from a culture where you don't have much to begin with.*

George: Black artists keep emerging from poverty and becoming successful using African storytelling techniques.

However, despite the success of their music, the social and economic pressures that shape the Black experience have gone unresolved.

[A clip from the BBC News documentary *London's Bleeding*]

Commentator 2: *It's pointless, 'cause we're just killing each other, it's Black on Black, we're just killing each other and it's pointless . . .*

Narrative: *In 1970, 64% of adult African Americans were married. This rate was cut in half by 2004.*

George: Black life is still battling for stability. Why can't this stability come from music?

SCENE 3: GEORGE'S PHD

[In George's writing room]

George: So, what do you think? You just heard the opening passage of my PhD proposal.

A PhD is a university degree based on your own research. So, imagine, you've got to bring a new idea to the subject.

So why am I doing a PhD? Obviously, this podcast contains some very original ideas, and they all need support to reach their full potential, you feel me? Half of that support is provided by you. Obviously, with this chapter, we gave you Common Ground. That's my online platform that allows us to discuss the topics in each episode. By hitting up GTPCG.com, you're enriching the space that we made with this podcast. Like these guys:

Kasana: *I'm listening to another person who understands the idea of the wealth behind their culture and er the wealth behind the authenticity of community and personal stories.*

Jade: *There's no doubt that there is power in Black music. I'm really excited to listen to how George is gonna lay out the realities of that.*

George: The other half of this work is policy influence, and I'm not there yet. There's no point talking about the power and the value of Black culture without an investment plan. That's why I've gone back to school at the Institute for Innovation and Public Purpose, supervised by the founder of the institute, Mariana Mazzucato, and Dr Karen Edge, my mentor in all things education.

See, when I throw out ideas like 'Black music can create economic stability for Black people' . . . I mean it.

SCENE 4: GEORGE'S VISION

[Soundtrack: Dave ft. Stormzy 'Clash']

[An excerpt from George's interview with Zeze Millz]

George: Around all of these superstars are jobs that make the superstar viable. We can plan more jobs around the fact that we're not gonna run out of talent.

[Cut to George and his brothers rapping along to 'Clash', highlighting the significance of music in their lives. Cut to George backstage at a live performance of 'Clash']

George: Every artist needs a lawyer, an accountant, a graphic designer, a photographer, a videographer, a sound engineer, live musicians, stage production crew, a marketing team, a PR team. Listen, some artists need fitness instructors, stylists, security, translators, financial advisers . . .

Why can't more of these jobs come from the same community as the artist? Why can't we make a plan to invest in the eight-year-olds of today, so that by the time they leave school in ten years they've got the training, the work experience and the qualifications to become the lawyers, accountants, graphic designers, photographers, videographers . . .

[Return to live performance of 'Clash']

George: . . . the translators and the financial advisors for the stars of *tomorrow* – their own friends.

Oh, you don't think these kids know anyone who's gonna be a successful artist? Then you need to go back and listen to this chapter properly.

SCENE 5: REFLECTING ON CHAPTER THREE

George: I was about to write a whole new verse where I was gonna break down my theory for, like, the ninety-second time . . . then I realised, I've said it already.

If you have any doubts that our young people can become superstars from the inner-city situation they find themselves in . . . can I remind you what I said on the Jay-Z episode?

SCENE 6: LESSONS FROM JAY-Z

[Throwback to Episode 20, 'Young']

George: Shawn Carter is an extreme example
Of something that happens every day:
Children born into violent times.
Finding a way out by writing rhymes.

Everywhere, young Black people are writing songs,
Full of potential, in need of the right response.
Every single year they shape the mainstream,
In major ways and ways that ain't seen.

[Throwback ends. Cut to George outside the block, kids playing nearby]

George: Love that episode, man. Oh, you still don't believe that our kids can become stars? Might I remind you what I said on Episode 21, 'Flying the Flag'?

SCENE 7: LESSONS FROM BRITISH ARTISTS

[Throwback to Episode 21, 'Flying the Flag']

George: See, if Mahalia and Ella Mai can make it in the US
Doing what they do best, and
Estelle, FKA Twigs, NAO, Jorja
Smith, Scribz Riley . . . who's next?

This podcast won a Peabody Award that
No non-American had gotten before.
In saying that, I'm not trying to brag; I'm
Highlighting the fact that we're flying the flag.

[Throwback ends. Return to George outside the block]

George: Listen man, our young people can do anything they put
their minds to,
Especially when it comes to music – they will surprise you.

Remember in Episode 23, 'Back to the UG', when I talked about
Grime giving us an outlet for our frustrations?

SCENE 8: LESSONS FROM GRIME

[Throwback to Episode 23, 'Back to the UG']

George: Dot Rotten was a perfect example.
He was a genius with verses and samples,
Another frustrated teen.
Just like us, chasing dreams.
His mum kicked him out, his area was mad, so, he spent his time
rapping and producing.
We all did it for the love of the culture.
Looking back, we were establishing a blueprint.

[Throwback ends. Return to George outside the block]

George: So, the evidence presented in Chapter Three of this
podcast indicates that young Black people can turn a difficult situation around by making music, and they have done so across the
world.

Remember later on in Episode 23, when I talk about the rise of
African music from the 2010s onwards?

SCENE 9: LESSONS FROM AFRICAN MUSIC

[Throwback to Episode 23, 'Back to the UG']

George: During this time, African music was making rapid improvements.
Probably 'cause of music production and distribution becoming more digital,
And more Africans having computers.

Not to mention a young mass of consumers
Creating new superstars and massive producers.

And that's how one of Uganda's most popular singers, Bobi Wine
Ended up in a position to become a politician.

[Throwback ends. Return to George outside the block]

George: Yeah, the rise of African music from the 2010s onwards indicates that there is a global opportunity. If these young people can get the music market popping in situations where they don't always have fundamental rights, like freedom of speech, what else can they do?

Let's look back at the American and the Jamaican context that I provided in Episode 26, 'Vibrations'.

SCENE 10: LESSONS FROM JAMAICAN AND AFRICAN AMERICAN MUSIC

[Throwback to Episode 26, 'Vibrations']

George: Even though the Brits and the Americans severed
Links between African slaves and their heritage,
The descendants of those slaves used their African instincts
To musically establish an imprint.

And the music enabled them to confront institutional
Racism and react to it in sync.

[A clip from Akala's documentary *Roots Reggae and Rebellion* for
the BBC. Voice of Prof. Carolyn Cooper]

Prof. Carolyn Cooper: *It is that whole history of enslavement,
oppression, exploitation of labour.*

George: See, when Dancehall started representing
the gunman
Hip Hop did the same, and this was unplanned.
But it's because their reactions have *been* linked.
That musical reaction is an African instinct.

That's the good news. Now let's get the . . . other news.

The stresses on the Western Black community
Led to a long-term lack of unity.

White people trusted their justice systems, but
Black people saw a lot of unjust decisions.
So, without authorities on which they could depend,
Black people handled justice through their neighbours and friends.
And when you Look across the Black inner city of London . . .
This explains the state of the ends.

In African American street music,
The only thing bigger than the cult of the dollar is this
Culture of honour. And via the music market
That mentality became the ultimate product.

Same in Jamaica. When conflict is handled
Neighbour-to-neighbour and kids in the street make
Money when they sing what they see,
Conflict brings entertainment and paper.

[Throwback ends. Return to George outside the block]

George: So, not only are these young people being creative about very difficult situations, not only are they building markets from scratch – markets that are driven by the skills they pick up in their home environment. On top of all of this, these young people are holding up a mirror to society and giving us a side of the story that we can't find anywhere else.

As I've tried to explain throughout this chapter, that insight has given me a richer understanding of the Black community at home and worldwide, which the education system couldn't give me ... and which I *needed*.

SCENE 11: LESSONS ABOUT WORLD HISTORY FROM BLACK MUSIC

[Throwback to Episode 26, 'Vibrations']

George: With the frustration of political suffocation –
Best demonstrated in Panthers –
Plus the breakdown of the family, and the influx of drugs came the
Next generation of gangsters.

But these gangsters used their African instincts
To musically establish an imprint. And the
Music enabled them to challenge institutional
Racism and react to it in sync.

[Throwback ends. Return to George outside the block]

George: But this isn't about me convincing you that I'm really smart. Nah, this is about Black music creating an economic safety net for more Black people. So, what have we learned?
Number one, we've learned that Black music provides a unique education, as I tried to show in Episode 22, 'Mavado & Vybz'.

SCENE 12: BLACK MUSIC AS AN EDUCATOR

[Throwback to Episode 22, 'Mavado & Vybz']

George: You're listening to 'Welcome to Jamrock' by Damian Marley,
This is the song that made me a yardie.
He gave his voice to the silent majority
Living with political violence and poverty.

[An excerpt from Damian Marley's interview with Seani B for BBC 1xtra]

Damian Marley: *Well, you don't have to be ghetto to be human. And being human you should care about people.*

George: It was 1978 when Damian was born.
Just another baby in the storm.
He was Bob Marley's youngest son, and
This would be reflected in the way he would perform. In his lifetime, violence in Jamaica was the norm.

In fact, Bob was attacked in Kingston
Shortly before he met Damian's mum, Cindy.
People say Bob got shot for tryna bring peace
After that he left the West Indies.

[A clip from Bob Marley's interview with Gil Noble for WABC-TV]

Gil Noble: *You never saw the gunman?*

Bob Marley: *At that time, no.*

Gil Noble: *But you know who did it.*

Bob Marley: *Yeah, mi know them.*

George: They say he got shot for playing both sides in the
Middle of a bitter campaign. For his
Son to be painting the same picture of Jamaica like
Thirty years later . . . really is a damn shame.
Listen to the man's pain . . .

[Throwback ends. Return to George outside the block]

George: Aight, so number one, Black music provides a unique educa-tion. Number two, Black music is an ethnography. It is a study of a culture from the perspective of the people in it. I made this point on Episode 25, 'Who Hurt R&B?'

SCENE 13: BLACK MUSIC AS AN ETHNOGRAPHY

[Throwback to Episode 25, 'Who Hurt R&B?']

George: The story of who hurt R&B is so long
I ain't covering it all today.
We just got through twenty-five years
In like twenty-five minutes and there's
Still so much more to say.

Like how Hip Hop overtook R&B, and
Made singers wanna be more hard than sweet . . .

But apart from the sound, the
Change in music really starts on the ground.
The breakup of Black love created generations
That found it safer to act tough.

I can't help looking at the racial element, and
Thinking about our history, 'cause it ain't irrelevant.

In the UK, 59% of Black Caribbean and 44% of Black African

children grow up in single parent families, compared to 22% of the population overall.

[Throwback ends. Return to George outside the block]

George: So, number one, we've learned that Black music is educational. Number two, we've learned that it's like an ethnography. It's a study of a culture from the perspective of the people in it. And number three, we have learned that Black music is a successful commodity. It's a safe bet. It's a sure thing.

Remember what I said in Episode 19 about the power of having your own space in the market?

SCENE 14: BLACK MUSIC AS A COMMODITY

[Throwback to Episode 19, 'Common Ground']

George: When you have a business that leaves
Customers with a sweet, unique aftertaste,
Over time you're gonna craft a space that's
Just for you in the marketplace.

[Throwback ends. Cut to George in his writing room]

George: Black music has been delivering that sweetness for a long time now. And given that track record, it has established its own place in the market – for us, by us.

SCENE 15: THE WAY FORWARD

[Soundtrack: Solange Knowles 'FUBU']

George: But there's a slight problem. The distribution of Black music relies on an industry that is not designed to solve Black issues. An industry that will support Black men in tearing each other down and disrespecting Black women.

But it's hard to blame the industry, 'cause in a market society there's no higher command than the laws of supply and demand. And as long as there is a demand for this messaging in Black music, the industry will do what industries do.

Still, it's 2021, guys – a hundred and fifty years since the Fisk Jubilee singers made their first recording. And guess what? We need this music just as much today as they did back then. And we need it for different reasons from the music industry. We don't just need this music for profit, we need it for progress 'cause telling your own story is . . . yeah, you know the rest.

[Soundtrack: Benbrick 'Falling Tide']

George: That said, telling our own story is only the start.
We need to know what to do with it.
There's value in everyone's story.
If anything, our music has proven it.
In every generation, Black music creates a
Few hundred superstars but at the same time
It leaves a lot more talented hungry youth to starve.
It's not just producers and artists;
Every Black life contributes to this market.

So, since our music keeps billions of people in a state of enjoyment,
Shouldn't it create more stable employment?
Not just superstars . . . jobs in the community.
There should be a funding pot for the community to reinvest some
    of the money generated from
Energy that these artists got from the community – including me.

The jobs we need already exist but they're

Unpaid, so they're taken for granted.
The people and the spaces that develop these kids
Go a long way in shaping an artist.
These people and spaces need funding to take
Raw talent from the neighbourhood all the way to the market.
No one's gonna bring that dream to life on our behalf
But we should chase it regardless.

See, if more Black communities had more jobs
That supported young Black talent, this would instil solidarity,
This would give the children some clarity
And this could help to build up the family.

[An excerpt from George's conversation with his PhD supervisor, Mariana Mazzucato]

Mariana Mazzucato: . . . so I feel like how we're trying to reframe, unpick, reshape is very much in tune with what you're thinking about, but we have a lot to learn from both your own methodology – 'cause with you we've talked about, you know, your podcast not as a separate thing that's gonna take you away from the PhD, but that's like the fieldwork, right, that's the lab, the living public lab. So, it's gonna help us rethink our own narrow ways of thinking about what is research, what is fieldwork, but also the kind of audiences you're reaching and the stories you're telling and the analysis you're apply-ing, it will teach us a lot.

And my dream, and I think this is what's gonna happen, is that you're gonna influence a lot of scholars. There'll be, you know, baby George PhDs just like you talked about the baby Jay-Zs, you know, the baby Georges hahaha . . . following in your footsteps in a line of research and the methodology that you're laying out.

George: This episode was written by myself, George The Poet, and produced by myself and Benbrick.

ACKNOWLEDGMENTS

Firstly, I'd like to thank my producer and friend, Benbrick (btw his name's one word not "Ben . . . brick"). This guy is a rare talent and a pure soul. He listens to me talk about anything for any length of time and always finds something valuable to add. His contributions to this podcast could fill another book – music production, original composition, sound innovation – the things I've seen him do make him the most underrated musician in the country, in my opinion.

Secondly, thanks to my wife, Sandra. We've been best friends for half our lives and a professional team for years now. Sandra's honesty, intelligence, intuition and jokes have enriched every area of my life. Without her, I don't know how I would deliver this work to the world. Thank you, baby!

To my family, I give thanks for your patience, support and understanding while I chase these ideas for years on end. Special thanks to Kenny for taking in the podcast on the deepest level. Also, special thanks to Prince and Kali for inspiring me every time we speak.

My endless thanks and appreciation goes to my team, which over the years has included Beatrice Nanteza, Vidhu Sharma, Birungi Nakiwala, Claudia Amoah, Kojo Oteng and my guy, Nabil Al-Kinani. You guys supported me in the earliest stages of this, and I'm forever grateful. Special acknowledgment for Mikey J, who helped me incubate these ideas before putting them into action.

I'd like to thank Dylan Haskins and Jason Phipps from BBC Sounds for approaching us so early in our journey, and truly valuing this podcast. In fact, thanks to everyone at the BBC who has listened to, shared, marketed, and broadcast *HYHGP*.

Charlie Brotherstone, my book agent, gets my unending gratitude for giving me the space to figure out what I want to write, and helping me take it to market. My process isn't straightforward but having an agent as thoughtful and open-minded as Charlie makes everything easier. Thanks bro. Thanks also to everyone at Hodder & Stoughton – specifically Bryony and Cameron. I'm grateful for what we've been able to do in just a couple of years.

My Common Ground team hold a special place in my heart for their unrelenting commitment to realising a shared vision. We wanted to try something undefinable, and we did it. Common Ground is still in its early stages, but what we have learned on this journey so far will stay with me for the rest of my life. So, many, many thanks to Darshan Sanghrajka, Anne Whitehead and Benbrick.

HYHGP was elevated by the thoughts of our guests, who provided a real human insight and comic relief across all the topics we explored. For this reason, my deepest thanks go to: Dun D, my mum, the community of Harlesden, Jade Alleyne, Freddie Mpanga, Michael Mpanga, Sophia Thakur, YenDeezy, Jamelia, Marcelline Menyie, Guala, Scyph, Elham Saudi and Lawyers for Justice in Libya, Anne Kansiime, Julie Adenuga, TrueMendous, Jamala Osman, Sir Martin Lewis, J Man, GK, Diggy, Stephen Boateng, Natalie, Zizi, Vidhu Sharma, Cristale, Young Talented Individuals, Lola, Damini, Matthew Walker, Barney Artist, Mandi, Anne Isger, Petch, Henry Stone, Ty Logan, Arnold Jorge, Hussein Manawer, Andrew Bell, Tyra Mai, Tasneim Zyada, Kenny Mpanga, CJ Obi, Jawad Ifraz, Chris Bernard, Kenny Imafidon, Aaron Daniels, Lams, Marc 5, *JET* magazine, AKA Dope, CNN, Podbible, NTV Uganda, David Lammy, Windrush Campaigner Anthony Brown, Florence Eshalomi, Jane Wing, Remel London, Mo Gilligan, Krishnan Guru-Murthy, Robert Bruce, John Boyega, Evan Rogers, Jade Alleyne, Anne Isger, Tom Kelly, Adam Miller, Ms Lowden, Torrie Maas, DJ Clark Kent, DJ Vlad, Kareem Burke, Andrew Marr, Evan Rogers, ZeZe Mills, Big Narstie, Alhan Gençay, Kae Kurd, SK Vibemaker, Lewis Hamilton, Bloodworks Live Studio, Chuckie Lothian, Jamaica TVJ, Georgette, Aneeka, BBC

World Service, Former Commissioner of Police Carl Williams, Aza Auset, John Masembe, Aggie Turwomwe, the late Kabaka Mutesa II, the late Andrew Frederick Mpanga, the late Robert Serumaga, the late Malcolm X, the late Huey Newton, Candi Staton, Paul Morley, the late Tupac Shakur, 50 Cent, Jay-Z, Larry King, Lauryn Hill, James Lewis, Suuna Mugaga, Meghan & Harry, Amara Agili-Odion and Mariana Mazzucato.

Of course, this podcast wouldn't work without the amazing music that runs throughout it, so I'd like to give a massive thanks to every single artist we featured: Dun D, Ambush, Jorja Smith, Klashekoff, More Fire Crew, So Solid, Chika Dole, Abi Ocia, Mucky, Ghetts, Maleek Berry, Guala, Bonnie Beretta, 1011, Radio & Weasel, Coco Finger, Rabadaba, Isaac Blackman, Bobi Wine, Mega, KwayOrClinch, Maverick Sabre, Bobby Womack, Grandmaster Flash and the Furious Five, 50 Cent, Ari Lennox, IAMDDB, Skepta, J Hus, The Weeknd, Headie One, SL, A Pass, Price Love, Shalamar, Mark Kavuma, Patrin, Big Zeeks, Gappy Ranks, Bernie Man, Busy Signal, The Diplomats, Roll Deep, Vybz Kartel, Teyana Taylor, Rose Royce, The Notorious BIG, Sonny Rollins, The Clovers, Theophilus Beckford, The Skatalites, The Wailers, Millie Small, Delroy Wilson, Krept & Konan, K Trap, Celine Dion, Koffee, Marc 5, Stormzy, Nines, Tiggs Da Author, Lonnie Liston Smith, Jay-Z, Mahalia, Ella Mai, Ray Charles, Drake, Lil Wayne, Jeff Beal, Nas, Lauryn Hill, Mavado, Vybz Kartel, Damian Marley, Stephen McGregor, Bebe Cool, Flukes, Fergie, Dot Rotten, Double S, Chip, Giggs, Obsessions, Madtraxx, Bobi Wine, Juliana Kanyomozi, Afrigo Band, Sam Cooke, The Last Poets, David McCallum, 2Pac, Snoop Dogg, Ginuwine, Jhene Aiko, Kaash Paige, Cardi B, Meg Thee Stallion, Rick Ross, Big Sean, Drake, Giveon, Chris Brown, Candi Staton, Lauryn Hill, Whitney Houston, Dr. Dre, Daz Dillinger, Destiny's Child, Sunshine Anderson, TLC, Jazmine Sullivan, Bob Marley, The Sugarhill Gang, Billy Boyo, Ninja Man, Eric B. & Rakim, Super Cat, Ice-T, Mad Cobra, Bounty Killer, Craig Mack, WizKid, Sara Tavares, Chosen Blood & Winnie Nwagi, Vinka, Kent & Flosso, Orezi & Sheebah, Mac Ayres, Mahalia Jackson, Dave and Solange.

Special thanks go to the BBC Concert Orchestra and Abbey Road Studios! Recording with these guys has lifted the standard of our work – it's been a complete honour. Thank you all for loving this podcast.

And finally, my sincerest appreciation goes out to every single listener. The artists, poets, musicians, students, teachers, parents, support workers, inmates and everyone around them – thank you all for opening your mind to my words. For every article and interview that went out (especially to Amanda Sawyer, Rebecca Mead, Ciaran Thapar, and Tara Joshi) I'm grateful. For every panel that awarded or even nominated our podcast for anything – thank you. I didn't know where this journey would take me, but I'm glad it brought us together.